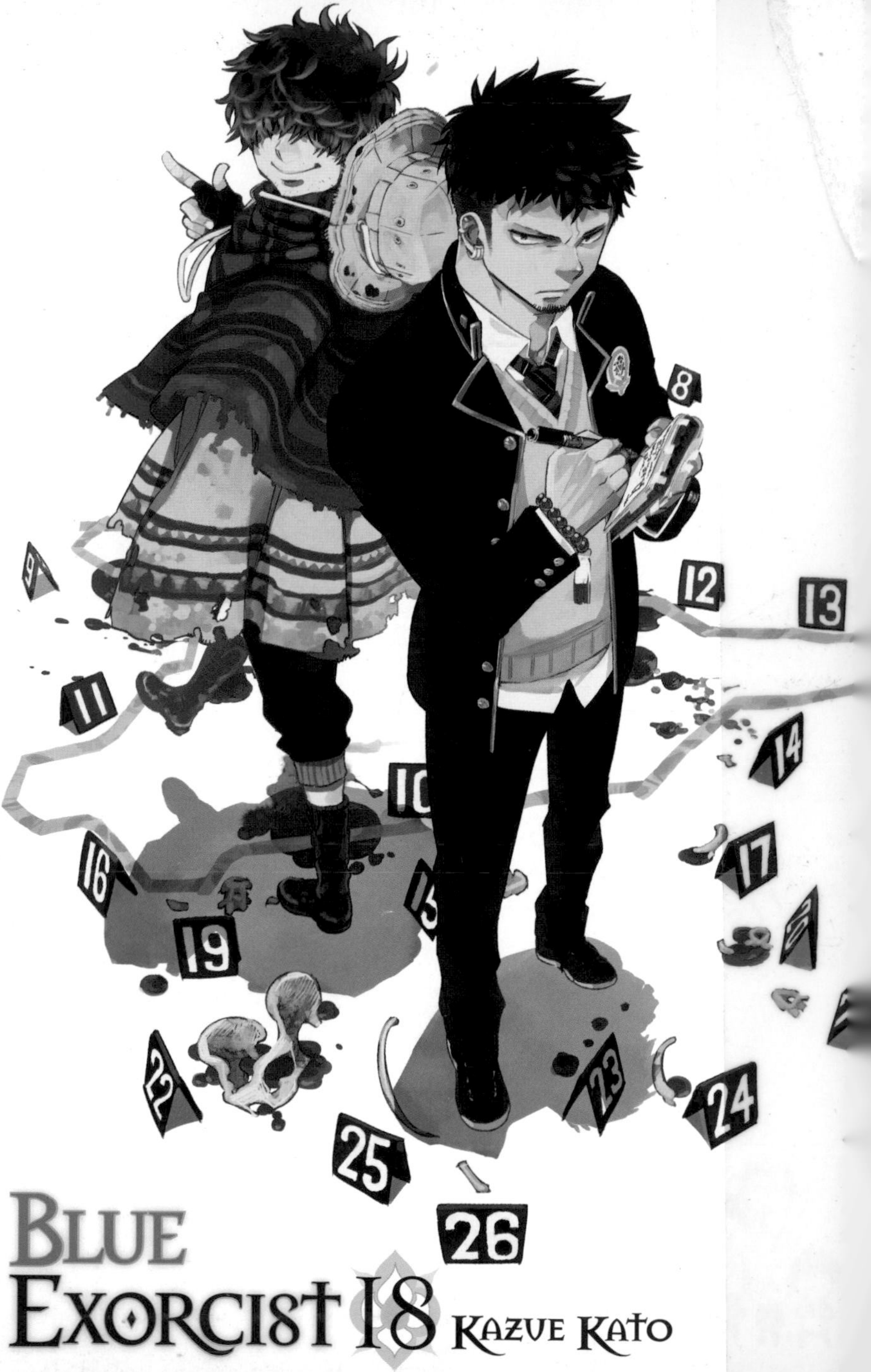

BLUE EXORCIST 18

KAZUE KATO

BLUE EXORCIST

Contents 18

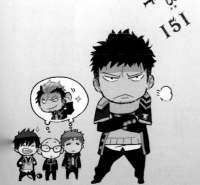

CAST OF CHARACTERS

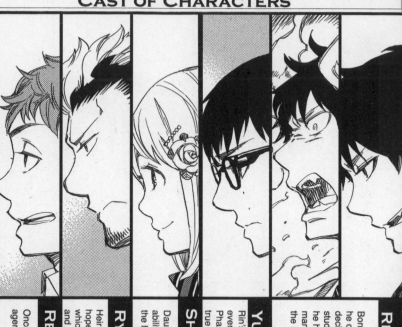

RIN OKUMURA

Born of a human mother and Satan, the God of Demons, Rin Okumura has powers he can barely control. After Satan kills Father Fujimoto, Rin's foster father, Rin decides to become an Exorcist so he can someday defeat Satan. Now a first-year student at True Cross Academy and an Exwire at the Exorcism Cram School, he hopes to someday become a Knight. When he draws the Koma Sword, he manifests his infernal power in the form of blue flames. He succeeded in defeating the Impure King and affirmed his determination to live with his flame.

YUKIO OKUMURA

Rin's brother. Hoping to become a doctor, he's a genius who is the youngest student ever to become an instructor at the Exorcism Cram School. An instructor in Demon Pharmaceuticals, he possesses the titles of Doctor and Dragoon. Todo told him that his true nature is that of a demon.

SHIEMI MORIYAMA

Daughter of the owner of Futsumaya, an Exorcist supply shop. She possesses the ability to become a Tamer and can summon a baby Greenman named Nee. She passed the high school entrance exam, so now she is a classmate of Rin and the others.

RYUJI SUGURO

Heir to the venerable Buddhist sect known as Myodha in Kyoto. He is an Exwire who hopes to become an Exorcist someday so he can reestablish his family's temple, which fell on hard times after the Blue Night. He wants to achieve the titles of Dragoon and Aria.

RENZO SHIMA

Once a pupil of Suguro's father and now Suguro's friend. Currently, he is a double agent providing information to both the Illuminati and the Knights of the True Cross.

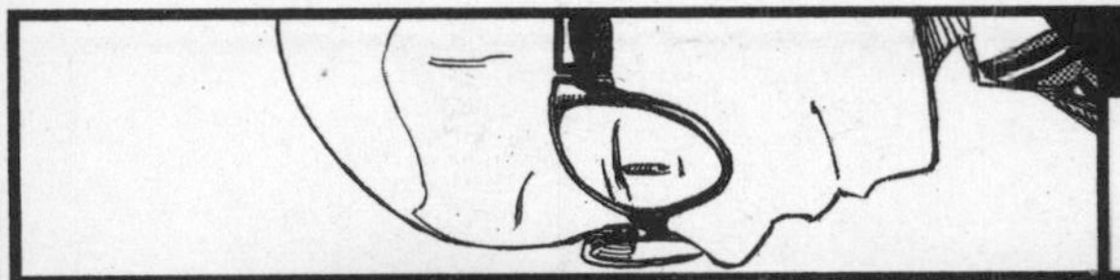

Miwa Konekomaru

He was once a pupil of Suguro's father and is now Suguro's friend. He's an Exwire who hopes to become an Exorcist someday. He is small in size and has a quiet and composed personality.

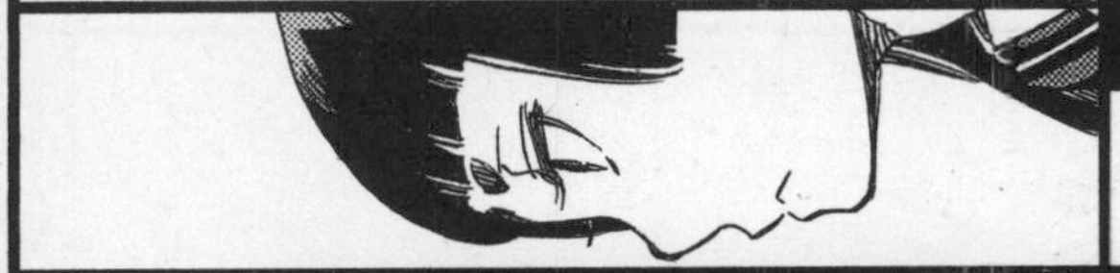

Izumo Kamiki

An Exwire with the blood of shrine maidens. She has the ability to become a Tamer and can summon two white foxes. The Illuminati has taken her captive, but with help from Rin and the others, she escaped and settled her grudge against the insane professor Gedoin.

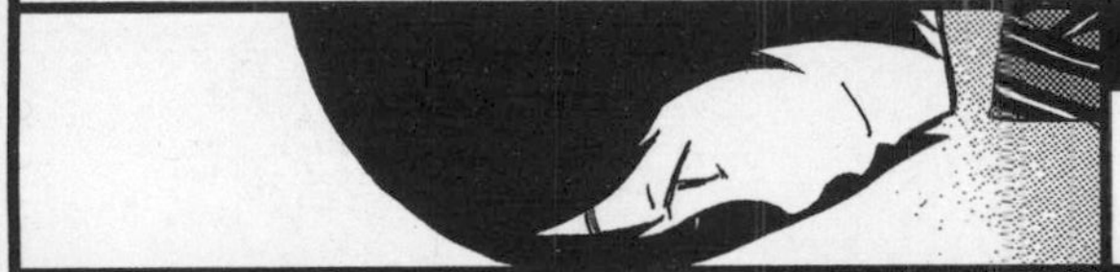

Noriko Paku

An old friend of Kamiki. The two girls joined the Exorcism Cram School together, but Paku dropped out when she couldn't keep up. Now she takes classes in the general curriculum at True Cross Academy Private High School.

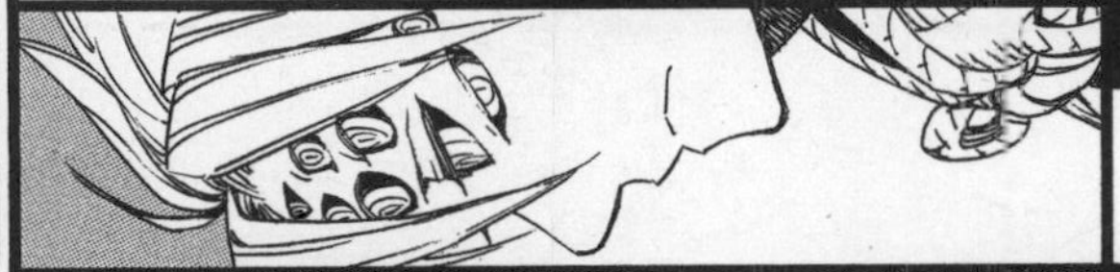

Hachiro

Hachirotaro Okami, the Dragon God. He is a super high-level Hydra demon who possesses strong divine power and the ability to regenerate, making him nearly immortal. He and Shura's ancestor entered a contract whereby he would provide a Fang sword in return for its bearer's death at the age of 30.

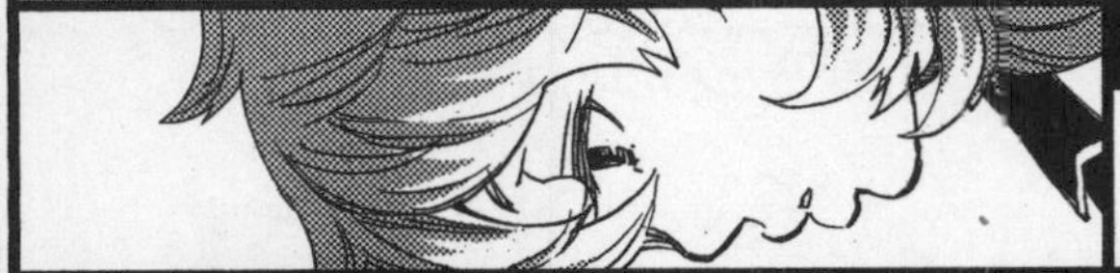

Shura Kirigakure

An upper-rank special investigator dispatched by Vatican Headquarters to True Cross Academy. She's a Senior Exorcist First Class who holds the titles of Knight, Tamer, Doctor and Aria. She used to be Father Fujimoto's pupil.

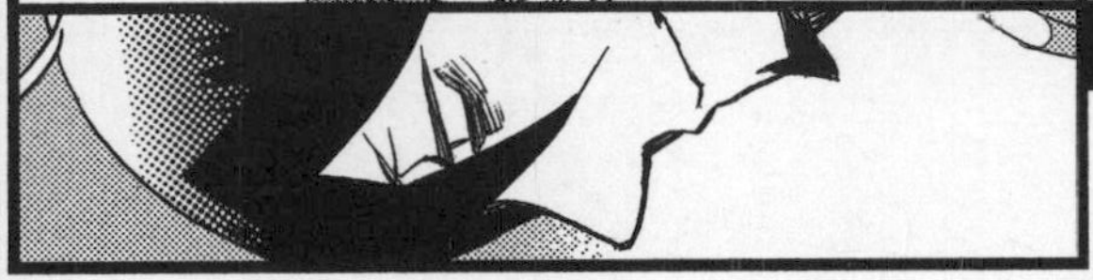

Mephisto Pheles

President of True Cross Academy and head of the Exorcism Cram School. He was Father Fujimoto's friend, and now he is Rin and Yukio's guardian. The number two power in Gehenna and known as Samael, King of Time.

BLUE EXORCIST

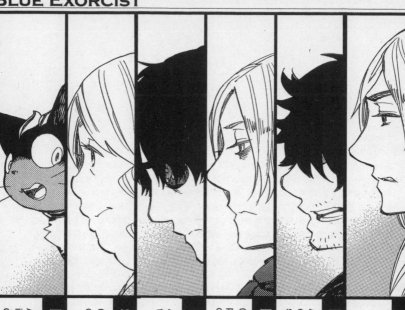

ARTHUR A. ANGEL

A Senior Exorcist First Class and the current Paladin. He wields the demon sword Caliban and is certain that Rin, as the bearer of Satan's blood, should be destroyed.

LEWIN LIGHT

As Arch Knight, he is Arthur's right-hand man as well as number two in the Order. An expert in Arias and summoning, he goes by the nickname "Lightning." He is currently stationed at the Japan Branch to investigate the Illuminati.

LUCIFER

Commander-in-chief of the Illuminati. Known as the King of Light, he is the highest power in Gehenna. He plans to resurrect Satan and merge Assiah and Gehenna into one.

IGOR NEUHAUS

A Senior Exorcist First Class who holds the titles of Tamer, Doctor and Aria. After he tried to kill Rin, the Order suspended him.

SHIEMI'S MOTHER

Owner of Futsumaya. She tends a garden left by her mother and watches over her daughter Shiemi, who has begun attending the Exorcism Cram School.

KURO

A Cat Sidhe who was once Shiro's familiar. After Shiro's death, he began turning back into a demon. Rin saved him, and now the two are practically inseparable. His favorite drink is the catnip wine Shiro used to make.

● THE STORY SO FAR ●

UNKNOWN TO RIN OKUMURA, BOTH HUMAN AND DEMON BLOOD RUNS IN HIS VEINS. IN AN ARGUMENT WITH HIS FOSTER FATHER, FATHER FUJIMOTO, RIN LEARNS THAT SATAN IS HIS TRUE FATHER. SATAN SUDDENLY APPEARS AND TRIES TO DRAG RIN DOWN TO GEHENNA BECAUSE RIN HAS INHERITED HIS POWER. FATHER FUJIMOTO FIGHTS TO DEFEND RIN, BUT DIES IN THE PROCESS. RIN DECIDES TO BECOME AN EXORCIST SO HE CAN SOMEDAY DEFEAT SATAN AND BEGINS STUDYING AT THE EXORCISM CRAM SCHOOL UNDER THE INSTRUCTION OF HIS TWIN BROTHER YUKIO, WHO IS ALREADY AN EXORCIST.

RIN AND THE OTHERS SUCCEED IN DEFEATING THE IMPURE KING, AWAKENED BY THE FORMER EXORCIST, TODO. MEANWHILE, YUKIO FIGHTS TODO, AND AS THE BATTLE RAGES, HE SENSES THE SAME FLAME IN HIS OWN EYES AS HIS BROTHER. AFRAID, HE KEEPS IT A SECRET.

LATER, MYSTERIOUS EVENTS BEGIN OCCURRING AROUND THE GLOBE. A SECRET SOCIETY KNOWN AS THE ILLUMINATI IS BEHIND THESE INCIDENTS, AND SHIMA IS THEIR SPY. ON MEPHISTO'S ORDERS, HE INFILTRATED THE ILLUMINATI TO WORK AS A DOUBLE AGENT AND WAS SUPPLYING INFORMATION TO BOTH SIDES.

MEPHISTO INFORMS RIN AND YUKIO THAT SHURA HAS DISAPPEARED AND ORDERS THEM TO FIND HER. THEY FIND SHURA NEAR LAKE TOWADA IN AOMORI PREFECTURE BUT ARE SHOCKED TO LEARN THAT SHE WILL SOON DIE DUE TO A CONTRACT HER ANCESTOR ENTERED INTO WITH THE DEMON HACHIROTARO OKAMI. TO DISSOLVE THE CONTRACT, THEY CONFRONT HACHIROTARO AND FORCE HIS RETREAT. HOWEVER, HACHIRO TRIES TO DRAG SHURA TO SLEEP WITH HIM AT THE BOTTOM OF THE LAKE. RIN LAUNCHES AN ATTACK THAT HE LEARNED FROM SHURA, BUT CAN HIS FLAME REACH ALL THE WAY DOWN TO HACHIRO?!

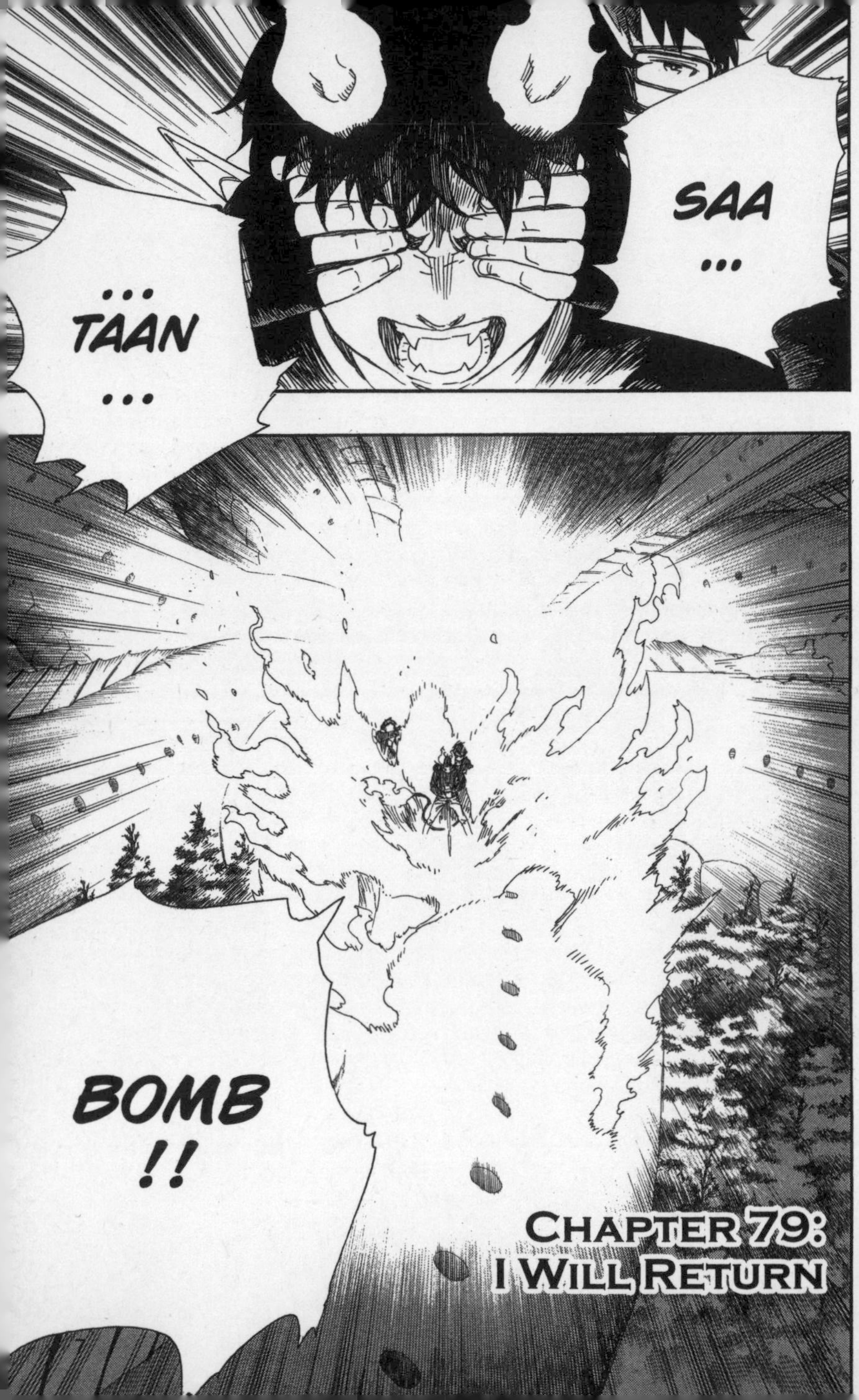
SAA ...
... TAAN ...
BOMB !!
Chapter 79:
I Will Return

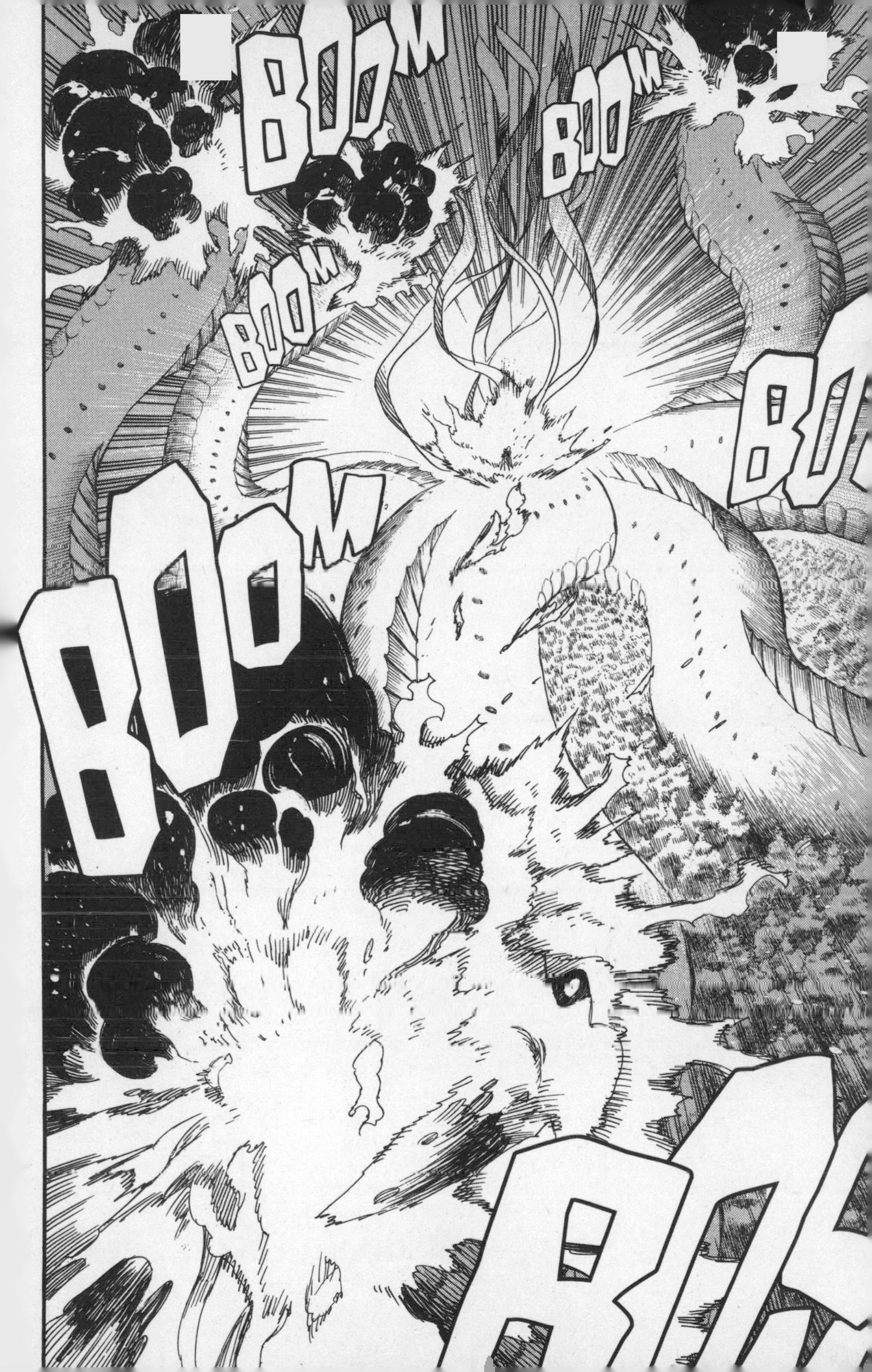
BOOM
BOOM
BOOM
BOOM

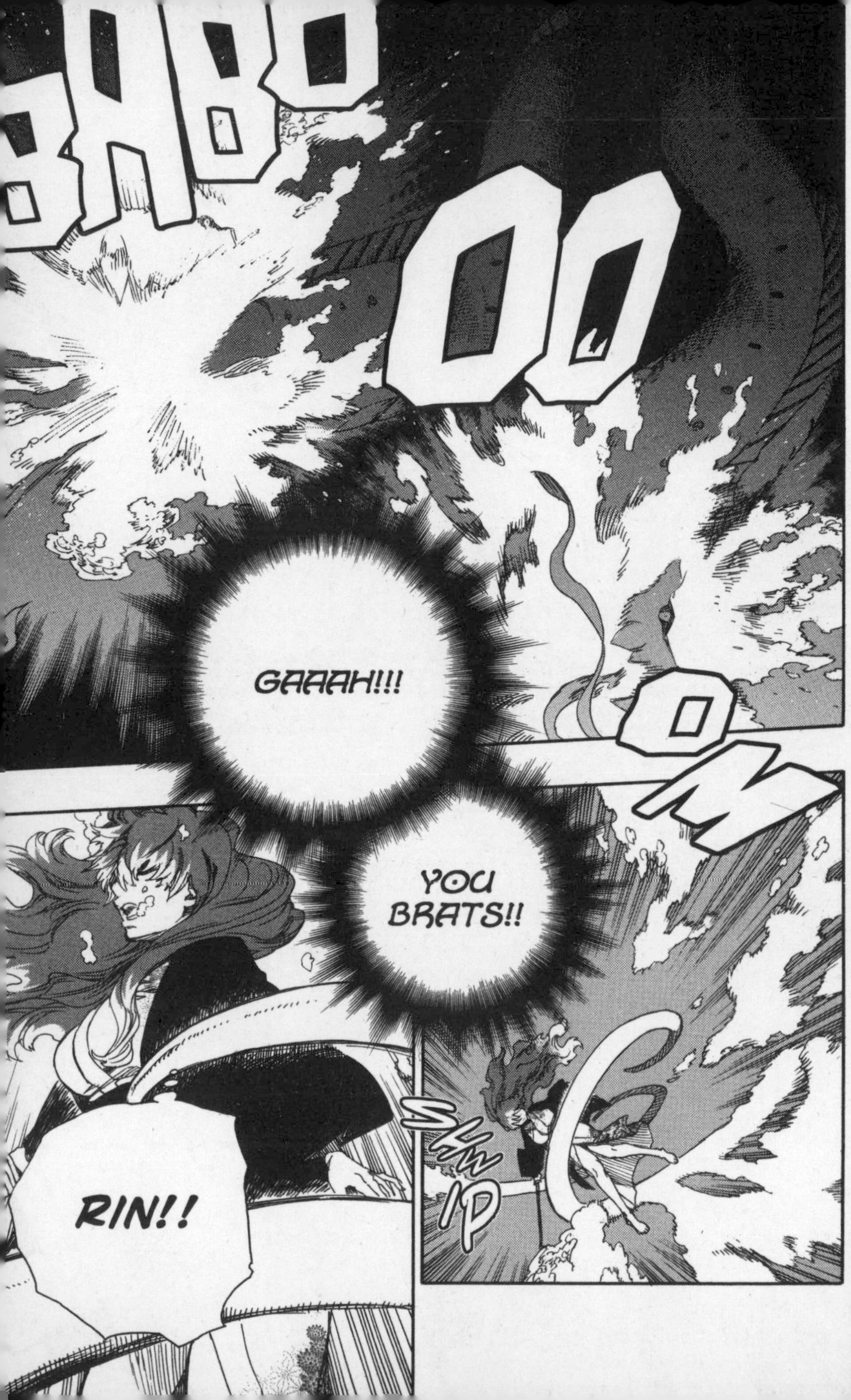
BABOOOOM
GAAAH!!!
YOU BRATS!!
SHWIP
RIN!!

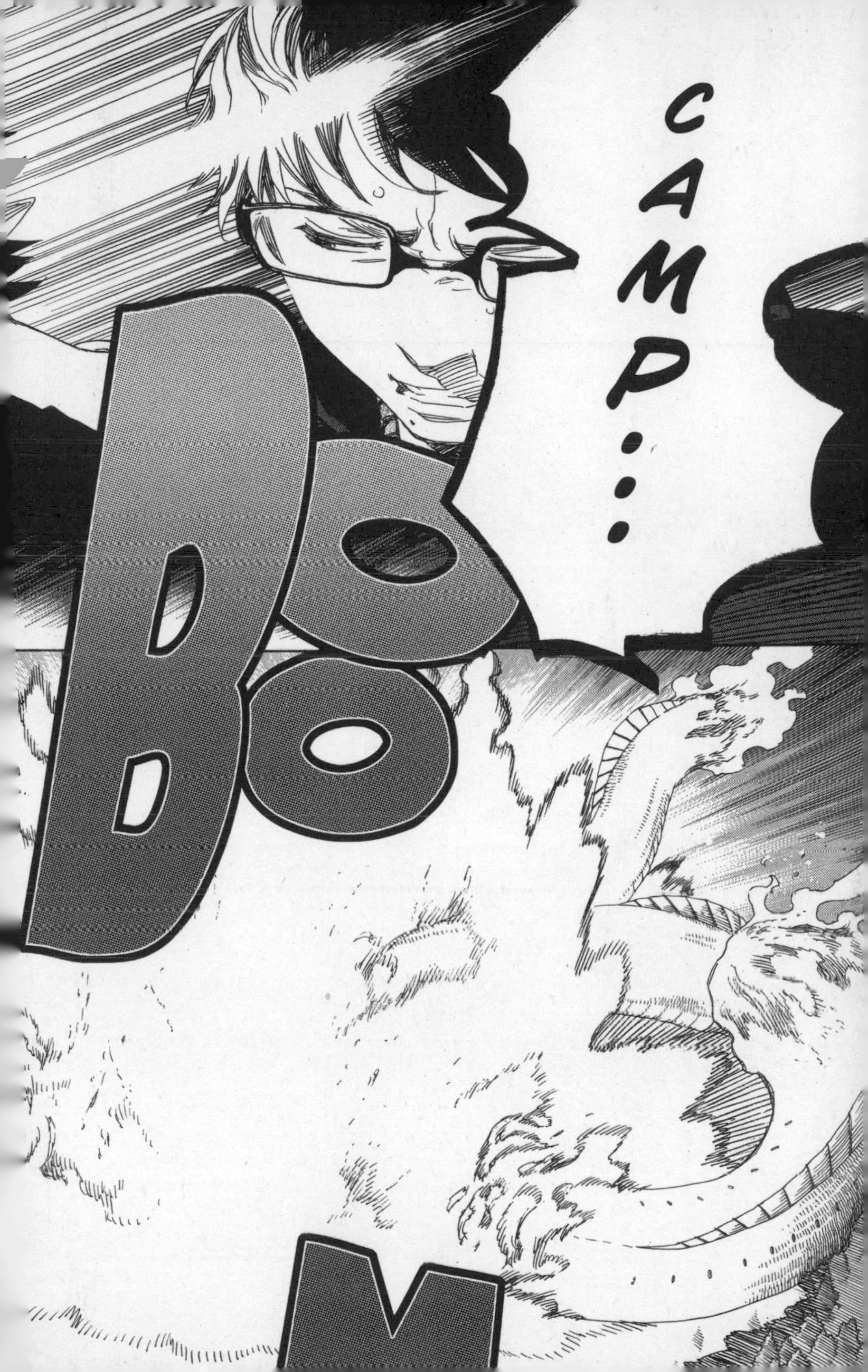
CAMP...
DOOM

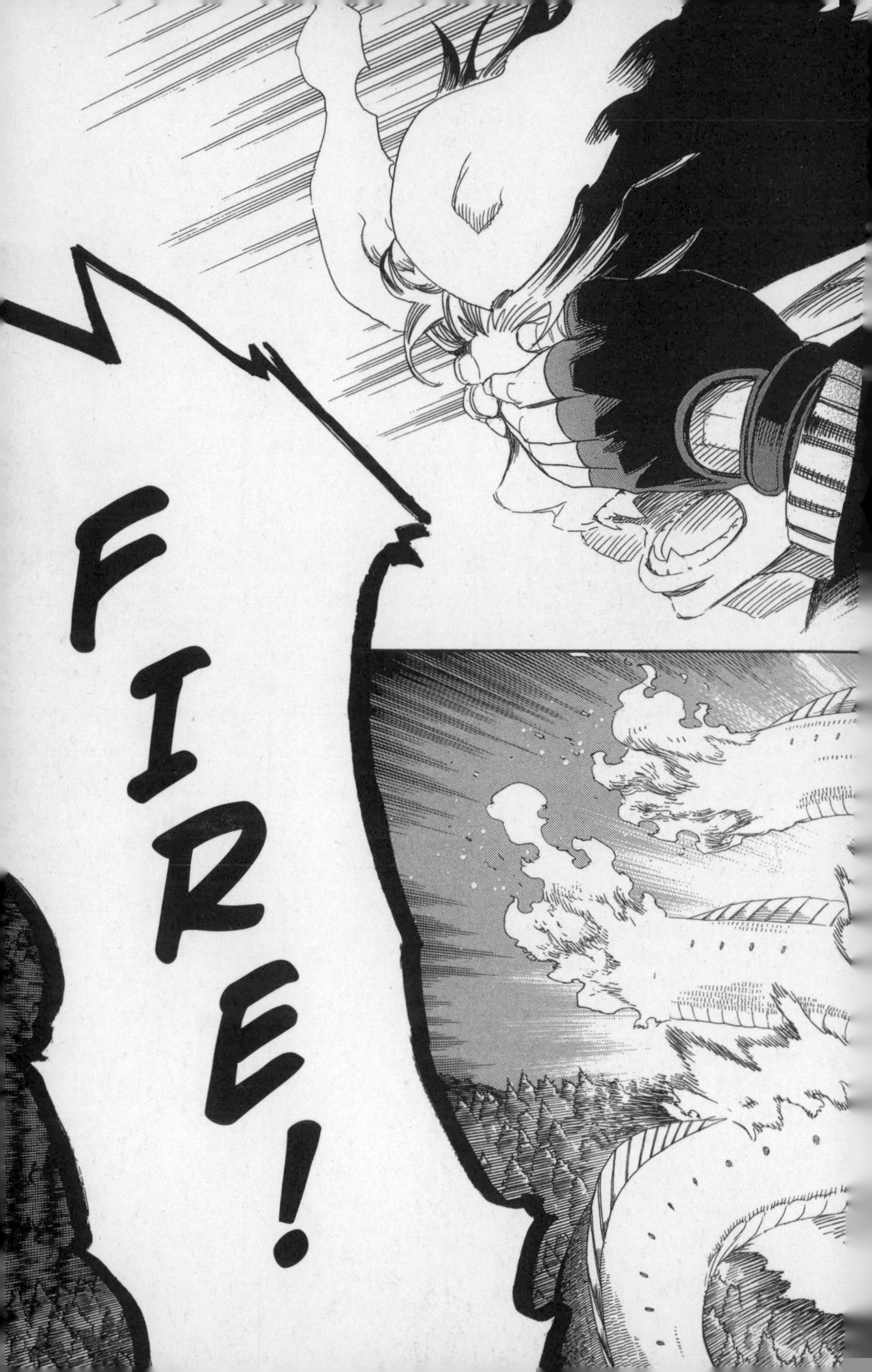
FIRE!

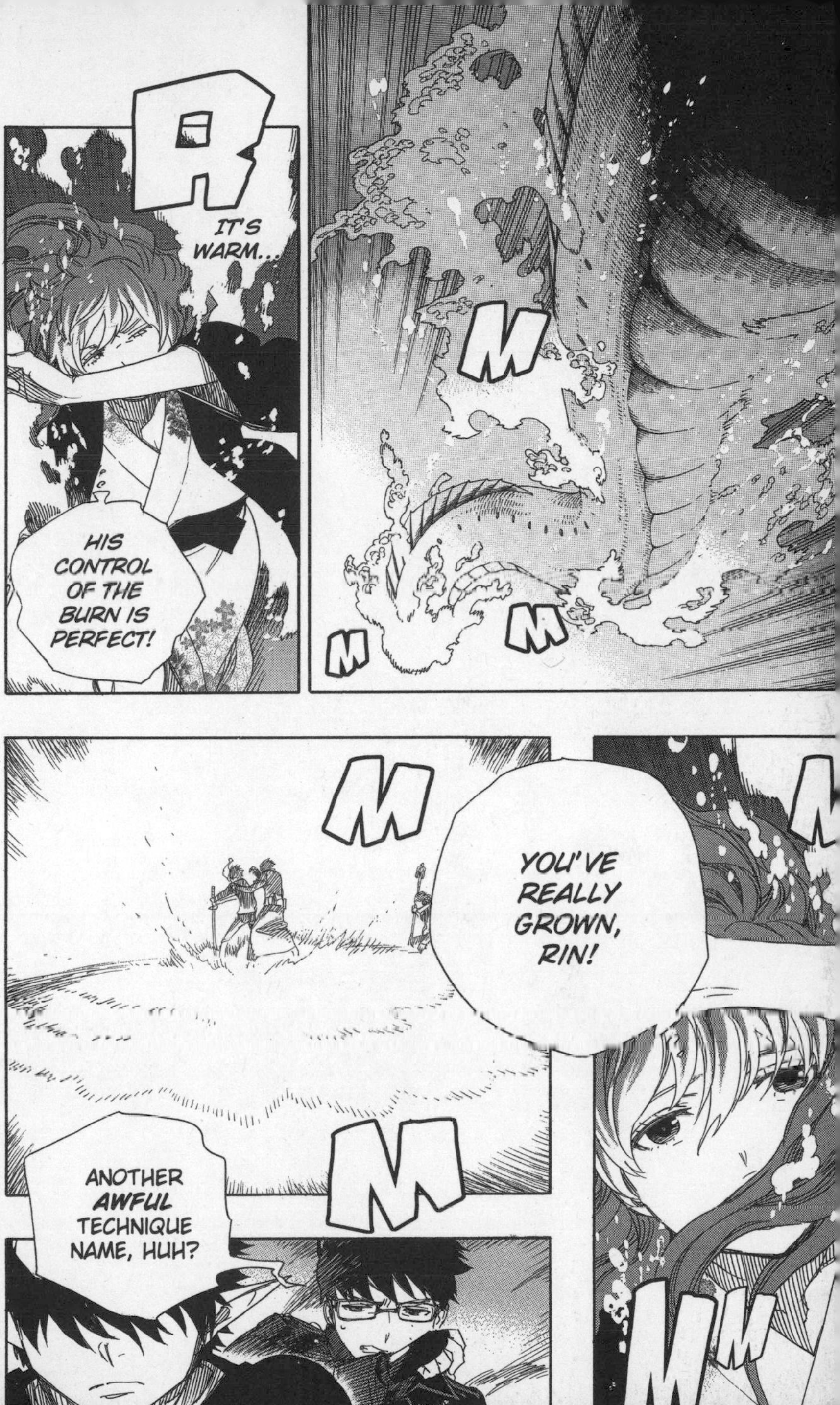
M
M
M
R
IT'S WARM...
HIS CONTROL OF THE BURN IS PERFECT!
YOU'VE REALLY GROWN, RIN!
M
M
MM
ANOTHER **AWFUL** TECHNIQUE NAME, HUH?

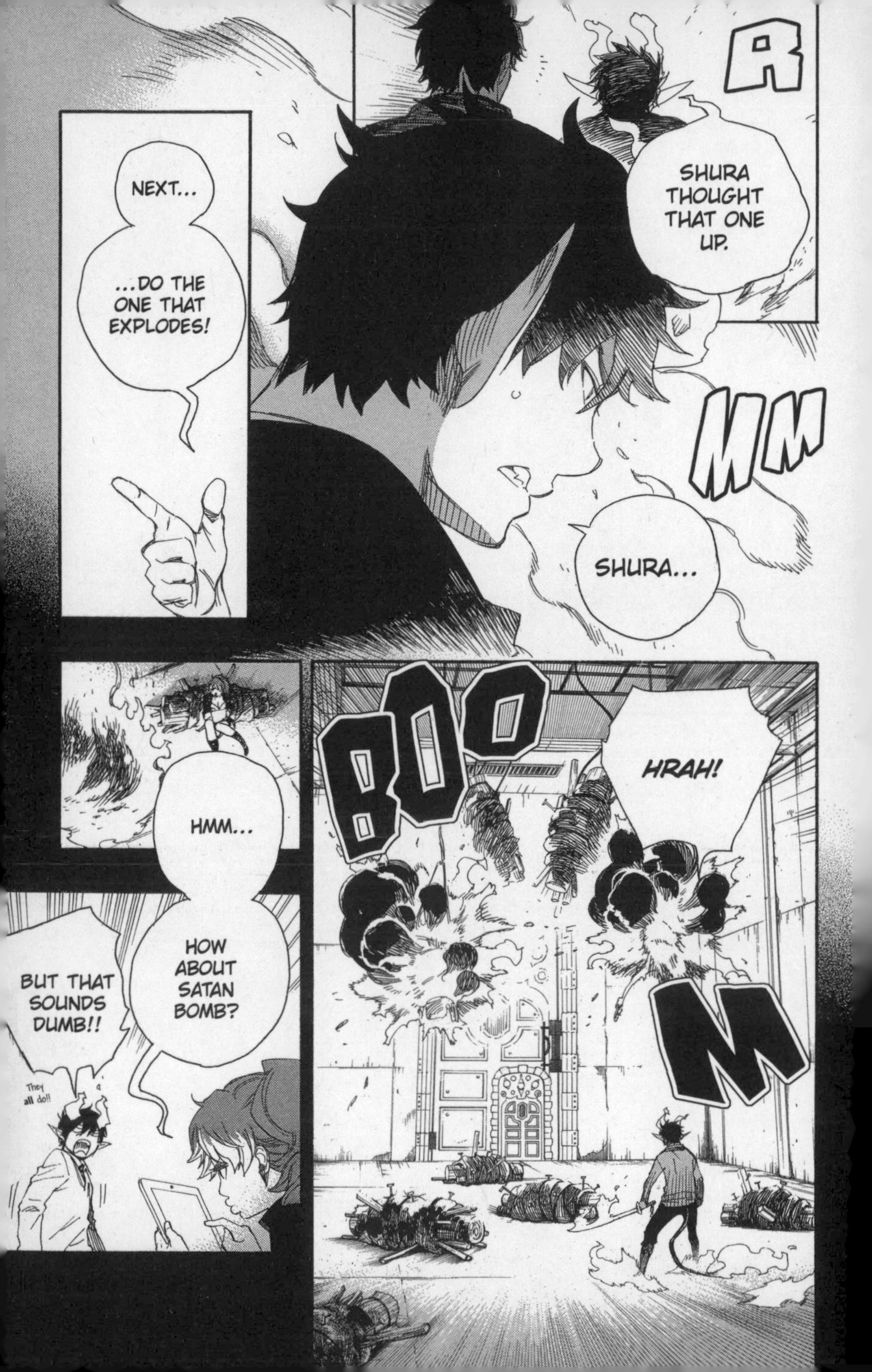
R
SHURA THOUGHT THAT ONE UP.
MM
SHURA...
NEXT...
...DO THE ONE THAT EXPLODES!
BOOO
HRAH!
M
HMM...
HOW ABOUT SATAN BOMB?
BUT THAT SOUNDS DUMB!!
They all do!!

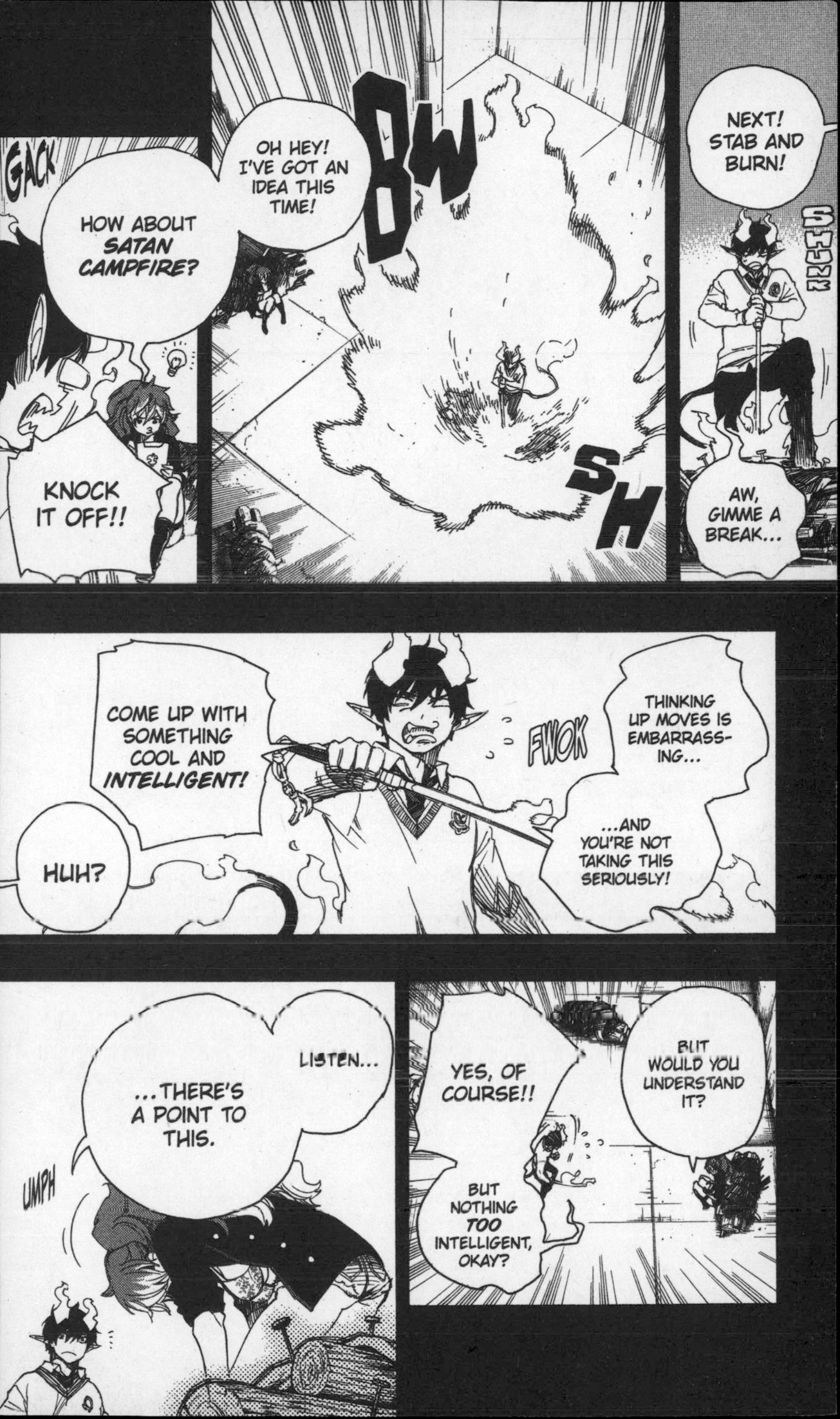
NEXT! STAB AND BURN!
SHUNK
AW, GIMME A BREAK...
BW
SH
OH HEY! I'VE GOT AN IDEA THIS TIME!
GACK
HOW ABOUT *SATAN CAMPFIRE?*
KNOCK IT OFF!!
THINKING UP MOVES IS EMBARRASS-ING...
FWOK
...AND YOU'RE NOT TAKING THIS SERIOUSLY!
COME UP WITH SOMETHING COOL AND *INTELLIGENT!*
HUH?
BUT WOULD YOU UNDERSTAND IT?
YES, OF COURSE!!
BUT NOTHING *TOO* INTELLIGENT, OKAY?
LISTEN...
...THERE'S A POINT TO THIS.
UMPH

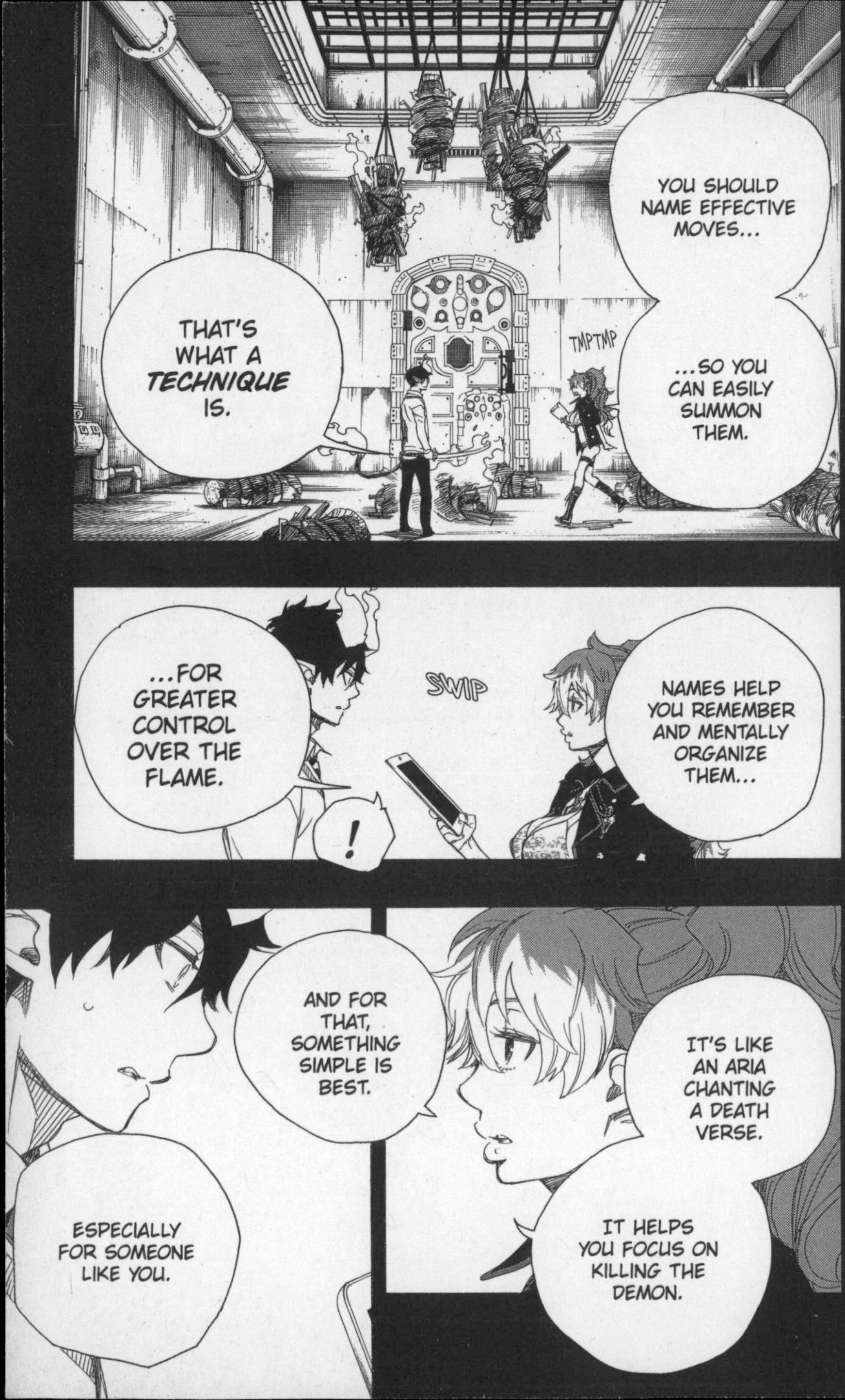
YOU SHOULD NAME EFFECTIVE MOVES...
...SO YOU CAN EASILY SUMMON THEM.
TMPTMP
THAT'S WHAT A *TECHNIQUE* IS.
NAMES HELP YOU REMEMBER AND MENTALLY ORGANIZE THEM...
SWIP
...FOR GREATER CONTROL OVER THE FLAME.
!
IT'S LIKE AN ARIA CHANTING A DEATH VERSE.
IT HELPS YOU FOCUS ON KILLING THE DEMON.
AND FOR THAT, SOMETHING SIMPLE IS BEST.
ESPECIALLY FOR SOMEONE LIKE YOU.

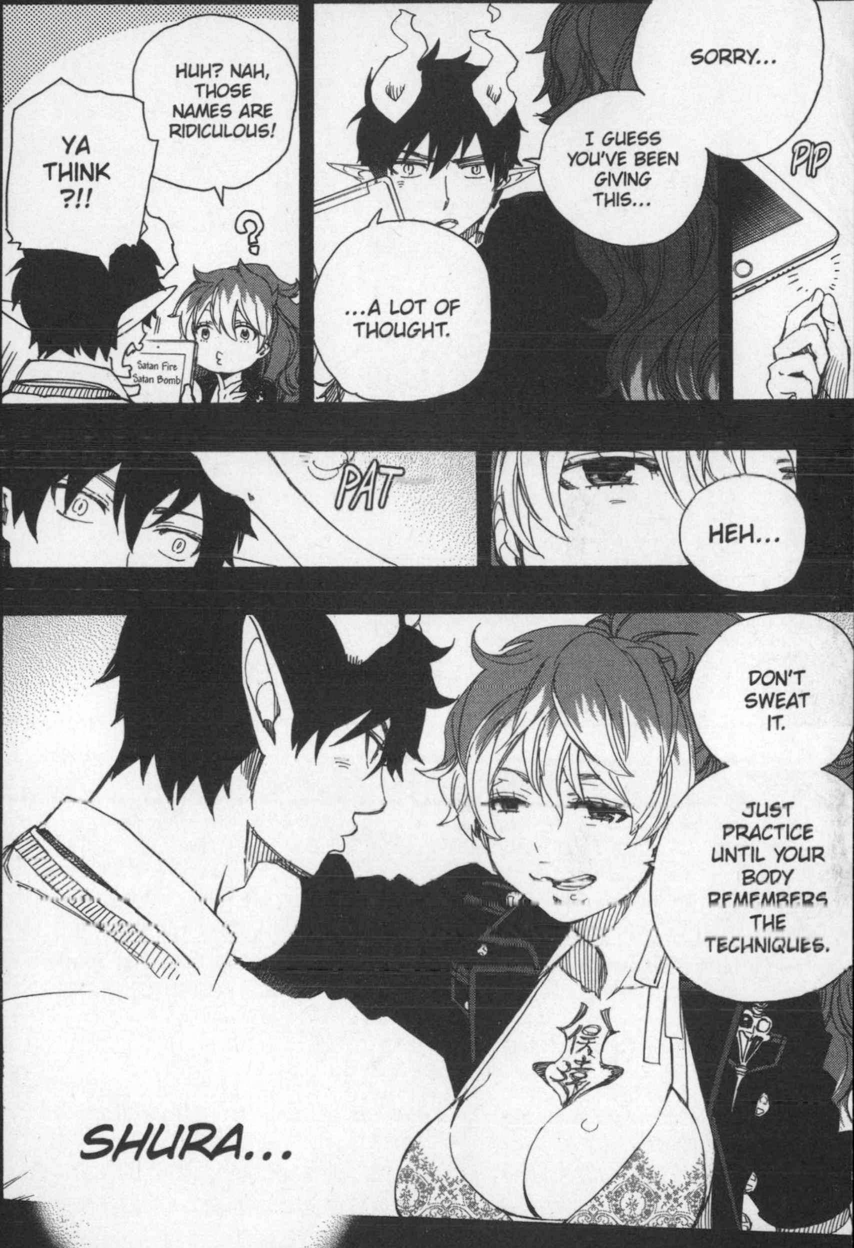
SORRY...
I GUESS YOU'VE BEEN GIVING THIS...
PIP
...A LOT OF THOUGHT.
HUH? NAH, THOSE NAMES ARE RIDICULOUS!
YA THINK ?!!
?
Satan Fire
Satan Bomb
HEH...
PAT
DON'T SWEAT IT.
JUST PRACTICE UNTIL YOUR BODY REMEMBERS THE TECHNIQUES.
SHURA...

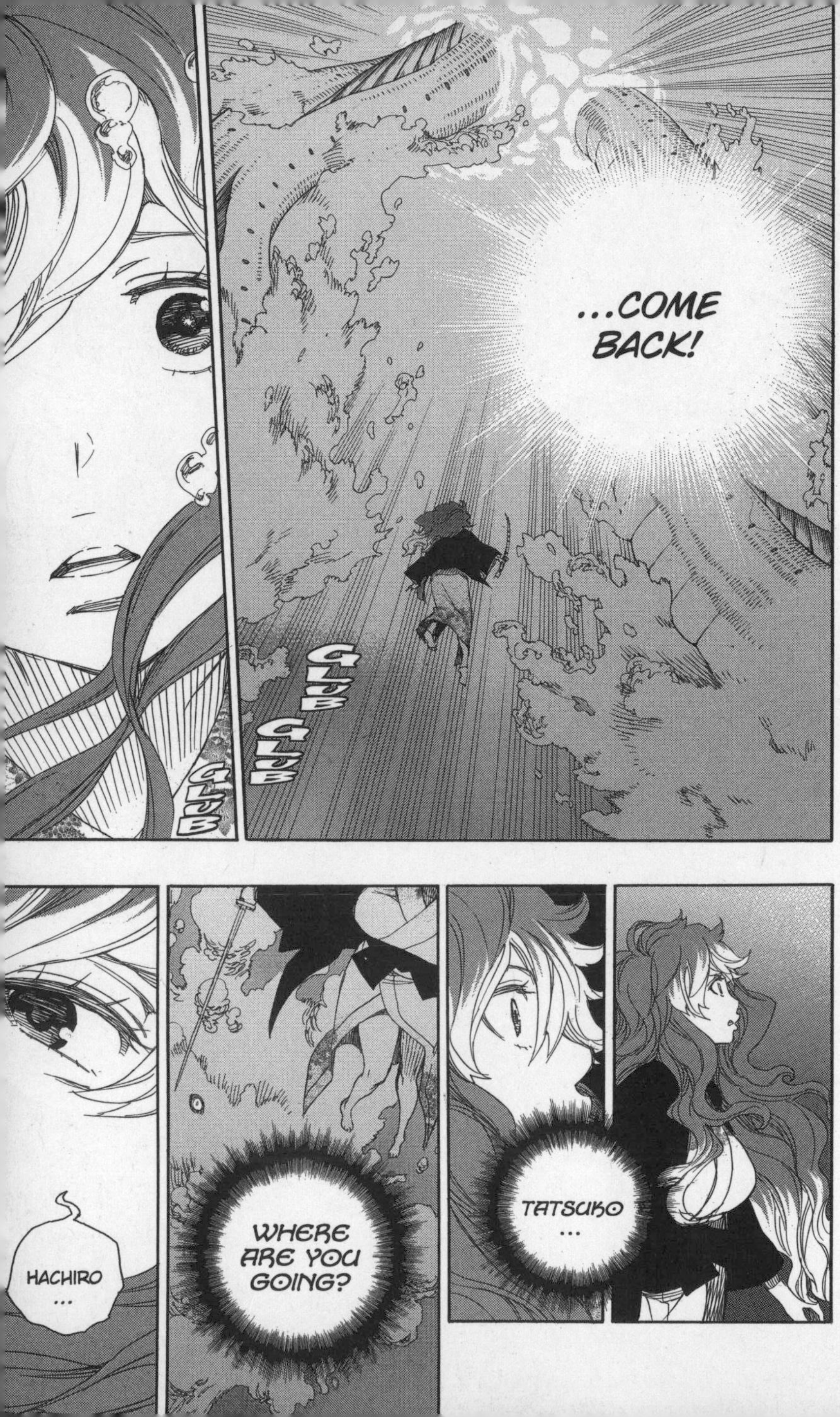
...COME BACK!
GLUB GLUB GLUB
TATSUKO ...
WHERE ARE YOU GOING?
HACHIRO ...

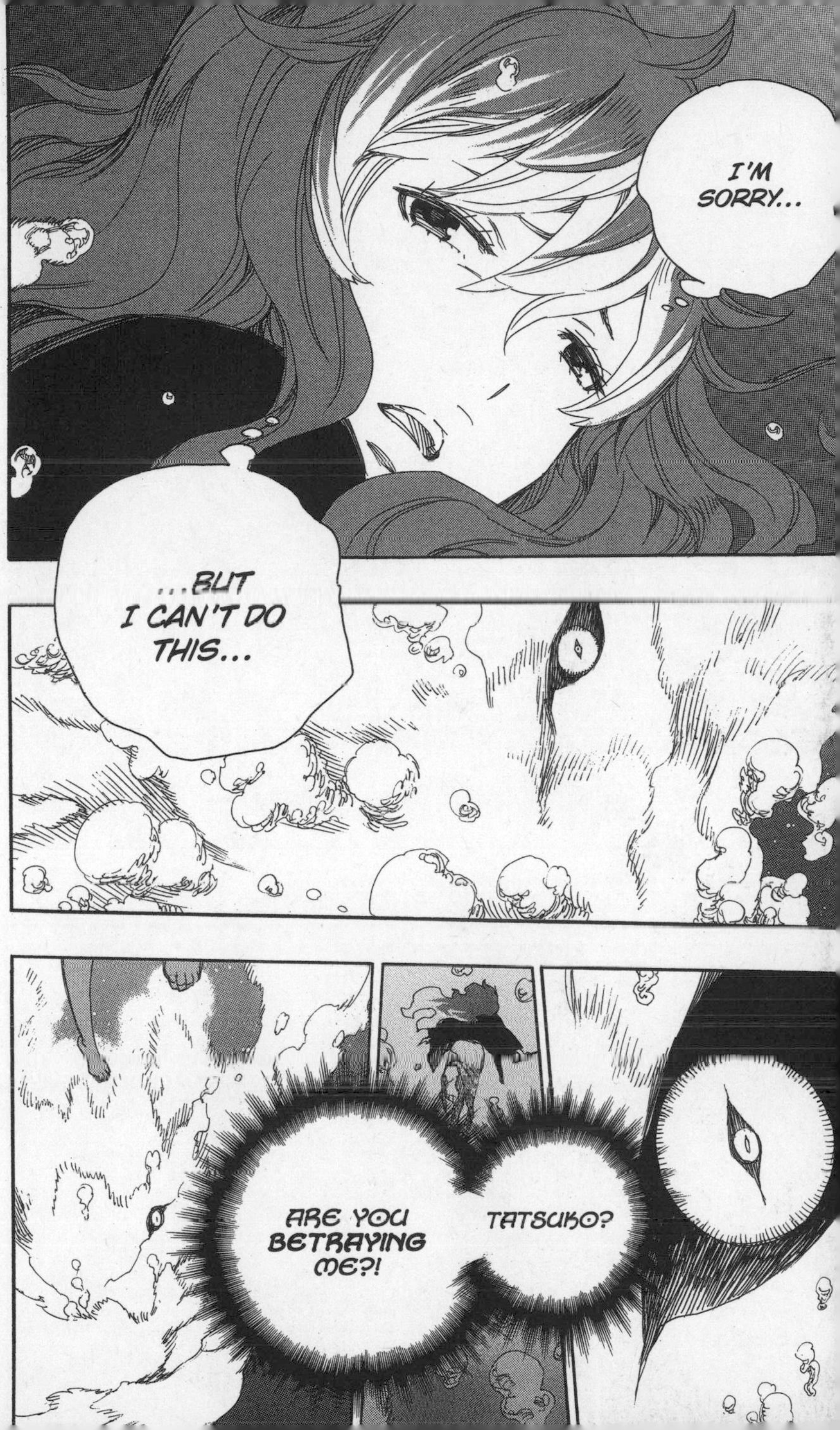
I'M SORRY...
...BUT I CAN'T DO THIS...
TATSUKO?
ARE YOU BETRAYING ME?!

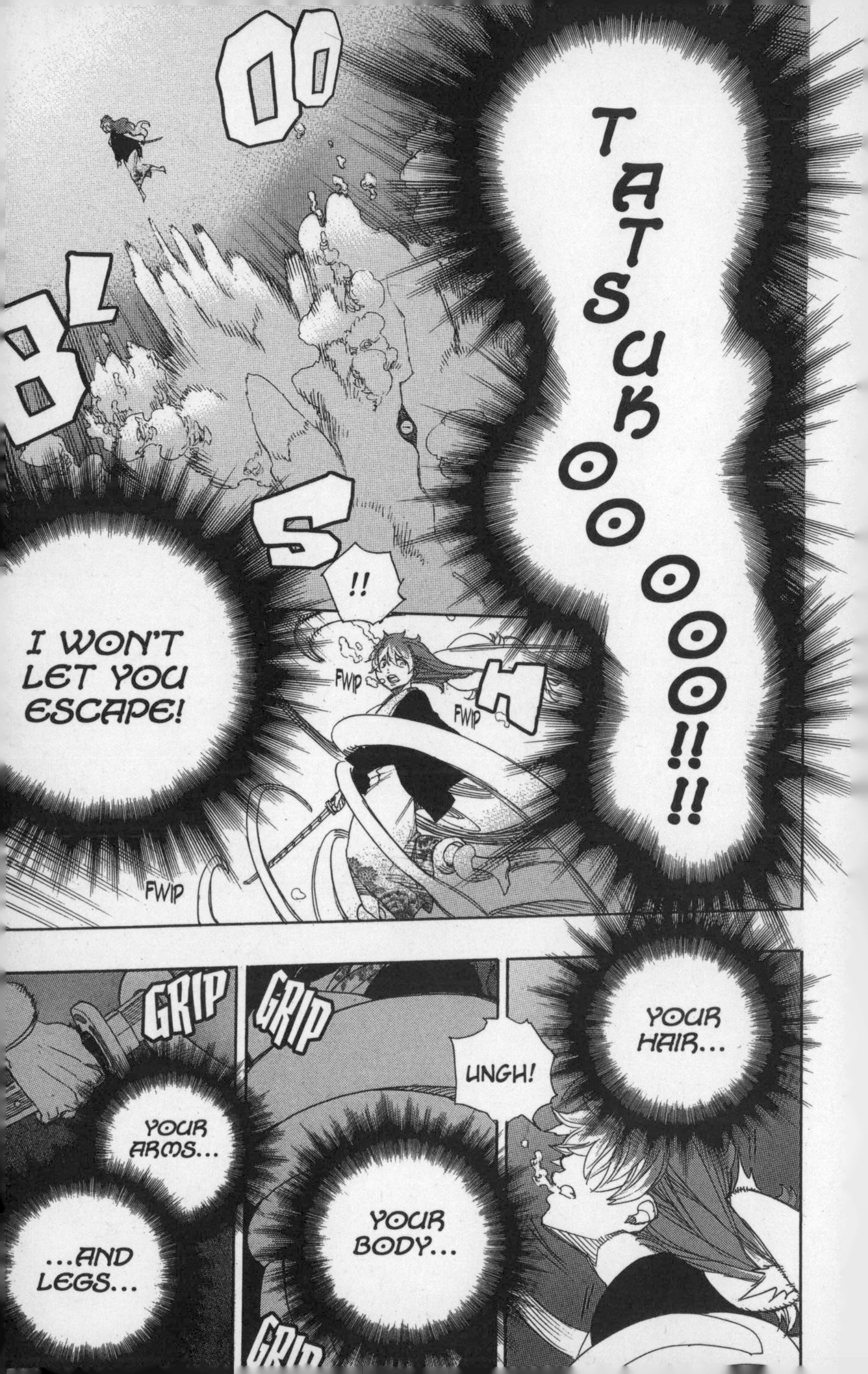
TATSUKOOOOO!!!!
BLOOSH
!!
FWIP
FWIP
I WON'T LET YOU ESCAPE!
FWIP
YOUR HAIR...
UNGH!
GRIP
YOUR BODY...
GRIP
YOUR ARMS...
...AND LEGS...

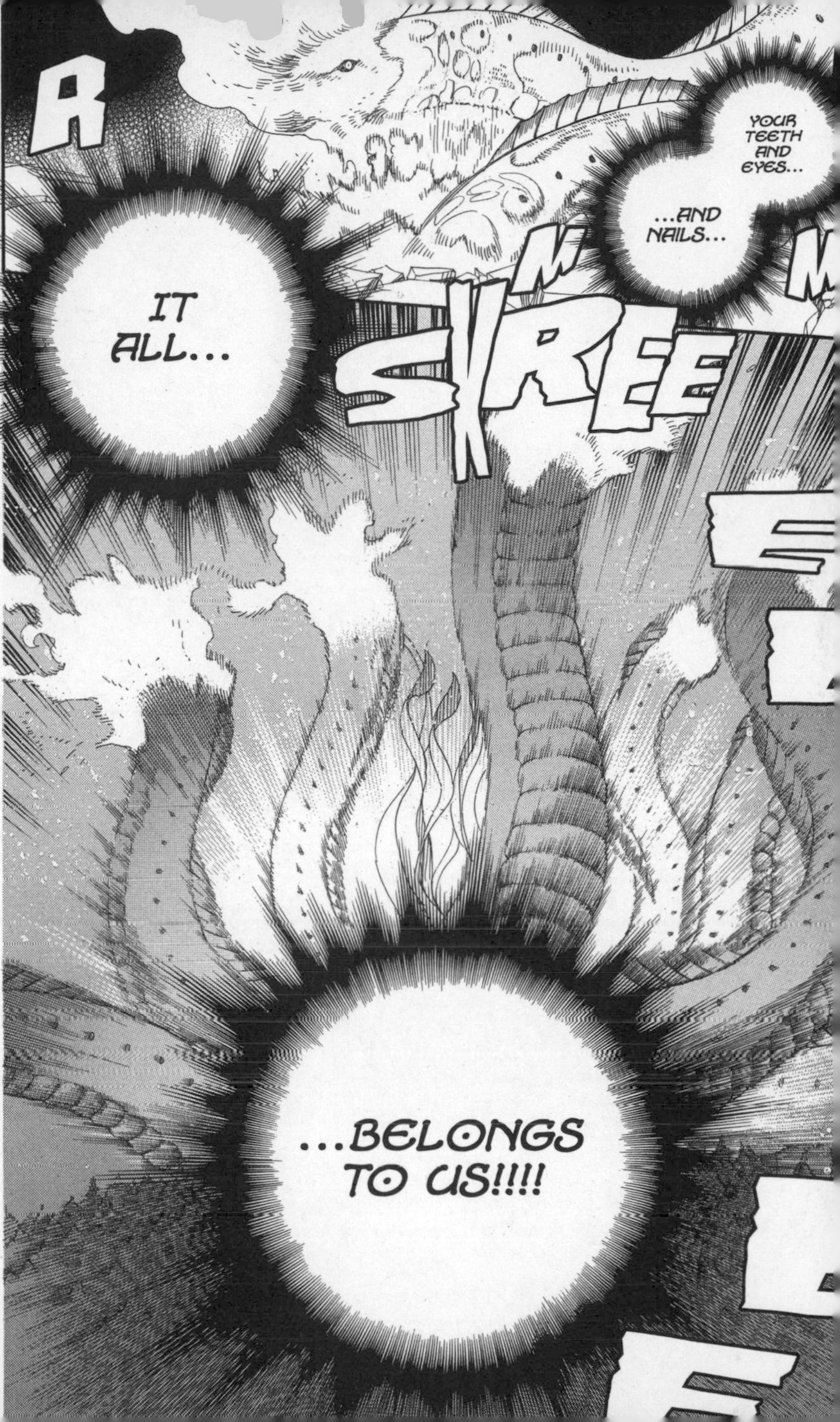
YOUR TEETH AND EYES...
...AND NAILS...
SKREE
IT ALL...
...BELONGS TO US!!!!

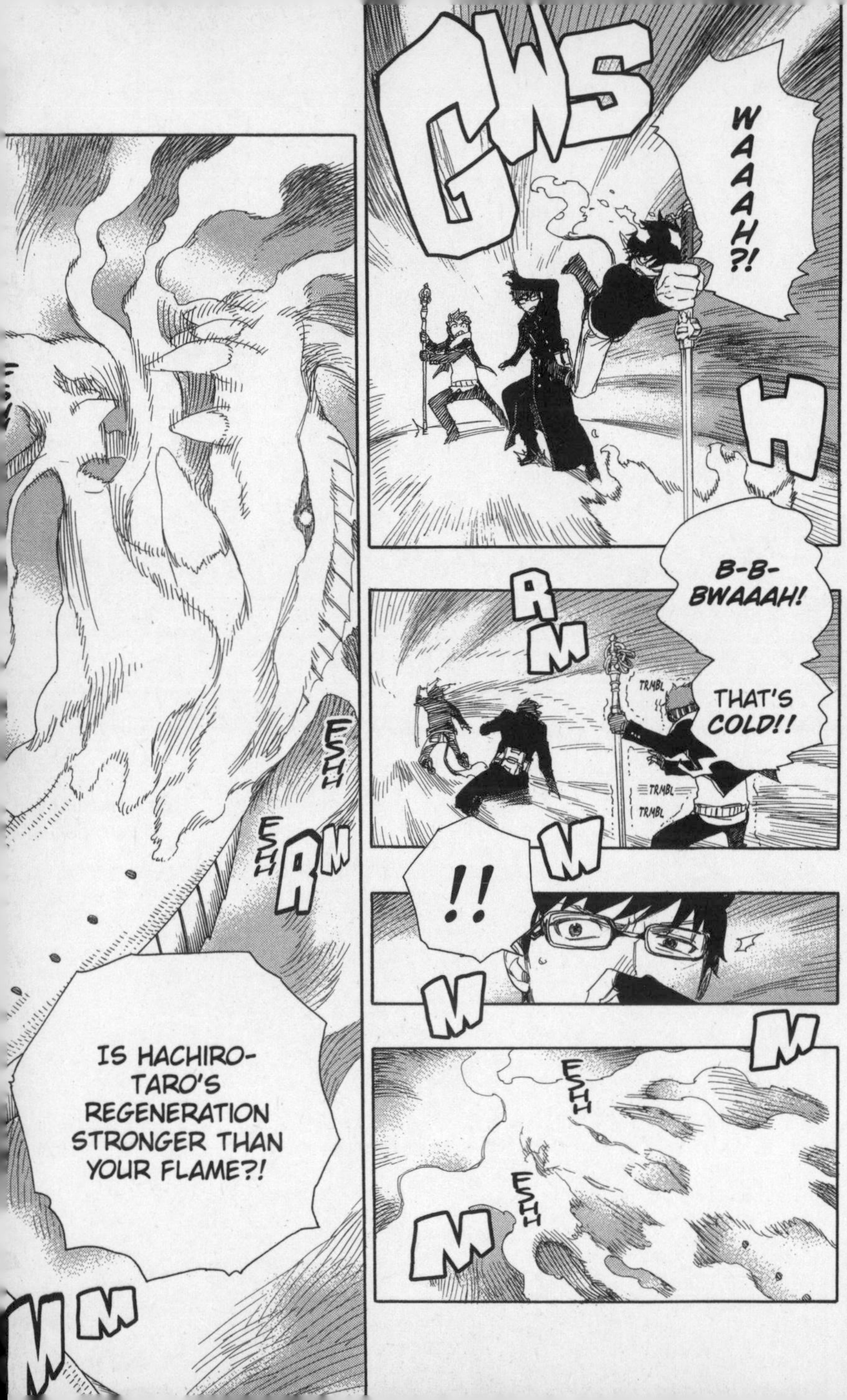
GWS
WAAAAH?!
H
B-B-BWAAAH!
THAT'S COLD!!
RM
TRMBL
TRMBL
TRMBL
!!
M
M
M
ESHH
ESHH
M
ESHH
ESHH
RM
IS HACHIRO-TARO'S REGENERATION STRONGER THAN YOUR FLAME?!
MM

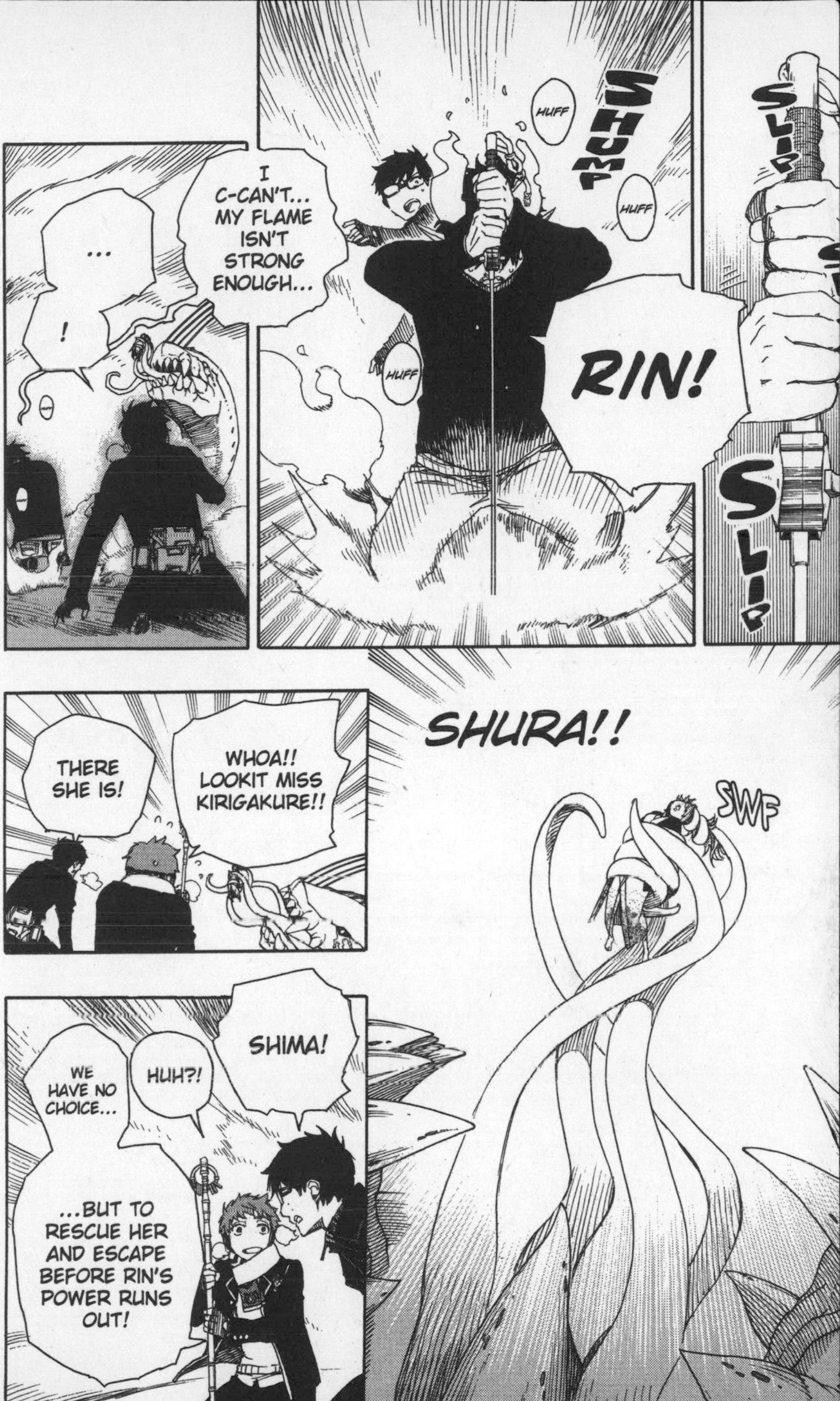
SLIP
SLIP
SHUMP
HUFF
HUFF
RIN!
I C-CAN'T... MY FLAME ISN'T STRONG ENOUGH...
HUFF
...
!
SHURA!!
SWF
WHOA!! LOOKIT MISS KIRIGAKURE!!
THERE SHE IS!
SHIMA!
HUH?!
WE HAVE NO CHOICE...
...BUT TO RESCUE HER AND ESCAPE BEFORE RIN'S POWER RUNS OUT!

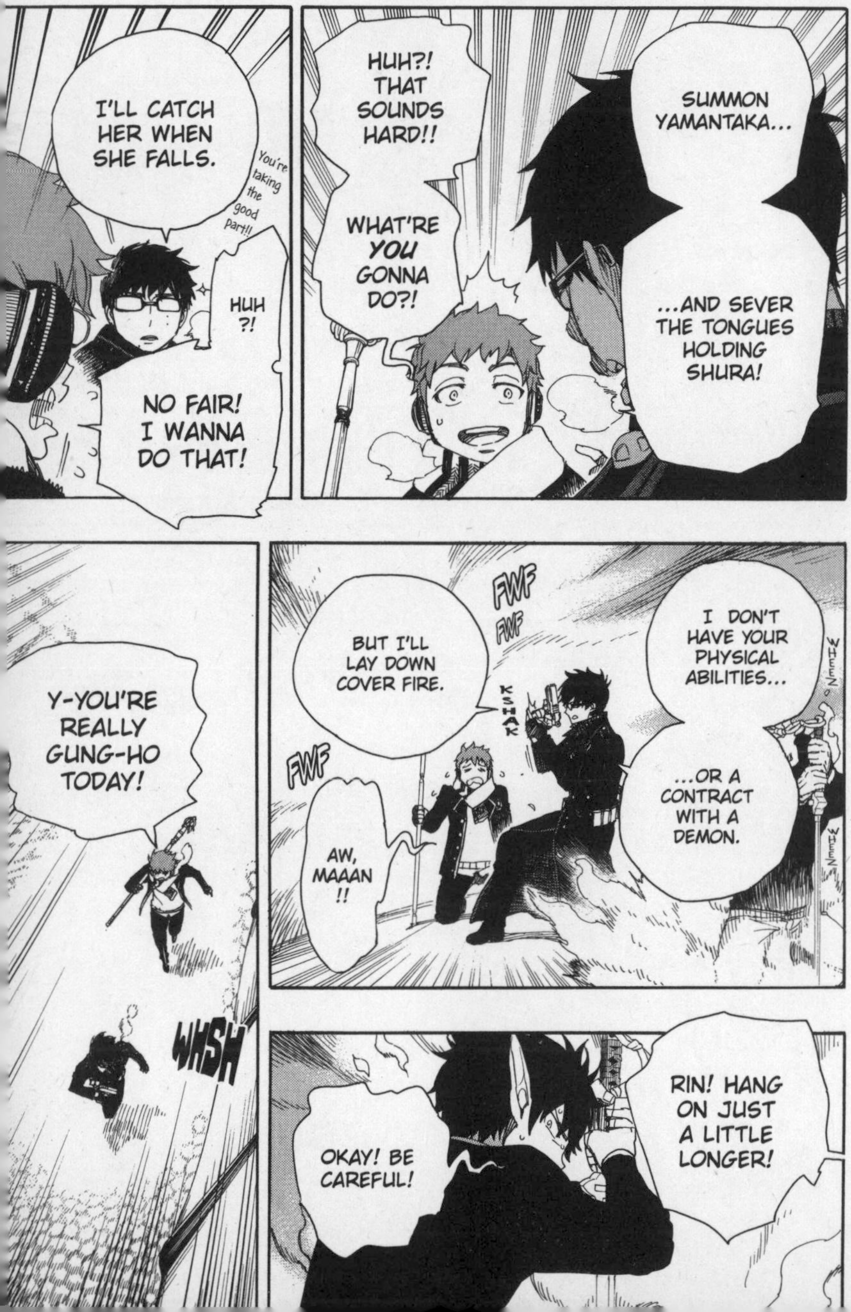
SUMMON YAMANTAKA...
...AND SEVER THE TONGUES HOLDING SHURA!
HUH?! THAT SOUNDS HARD!!
WHAT'RE YOU GONNA DO?!
I'LL CATCH HER WHEN SHE FALLS.
You're taking the good part!!
HUH?!
NO FAIR! I WANNA DO THAT!
I DON'T HAVE YOUR PHYSICAL ABILITIES...
WHEEZ
WHEEZ
...OR A CONTRACT WITH A DEMON.
FWF
FWF
BUT I'LL LAY DOWN COVER FIRE.
KSHAK
FWF
AW, MAAAN!!
RIN! HANG ON JUST A LITTLE LONGER!
OKAY! BE CAREFUL!
Y-YOU'RE REALLY GUNG-HO TODAY!
WHSH

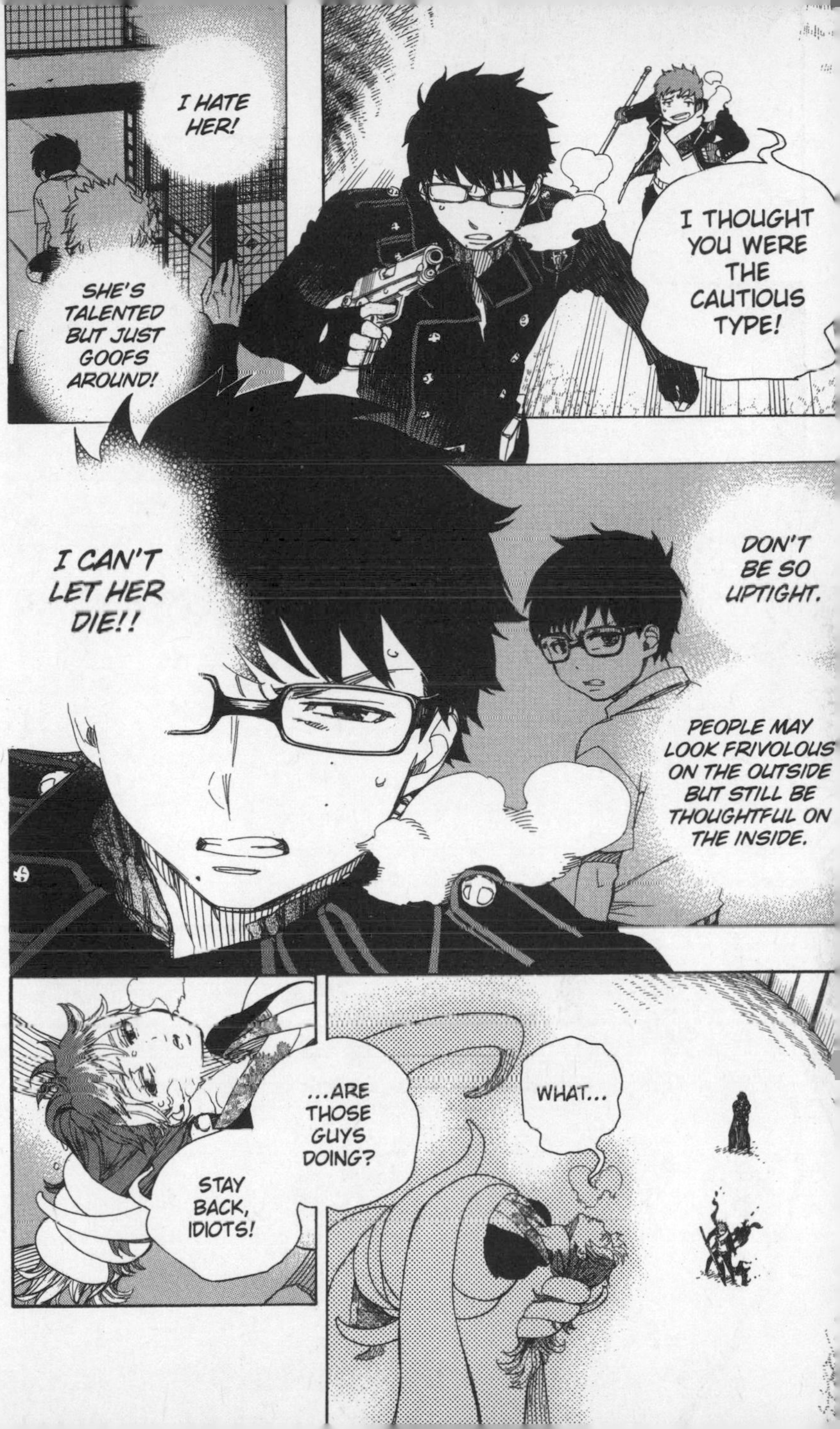
I THOUGHT YOU WERE THE CAUTIOUS TYPE!
I HATE HER!
SHE'S TALENTED BUT JUST GOOFS AROUND!
DON'T BE SO UPTIGHT.
PEOPLE MAY LOOK FRIVOLOUS ON THE OUTSIDE BUT STILL BE THOUGHTFUL ON THE INSIDE.
I CAN'T LET HER DIE!!
WHAT...
...ARE THOSE GUYS DOING?
STAY BACK, IDIOTS!

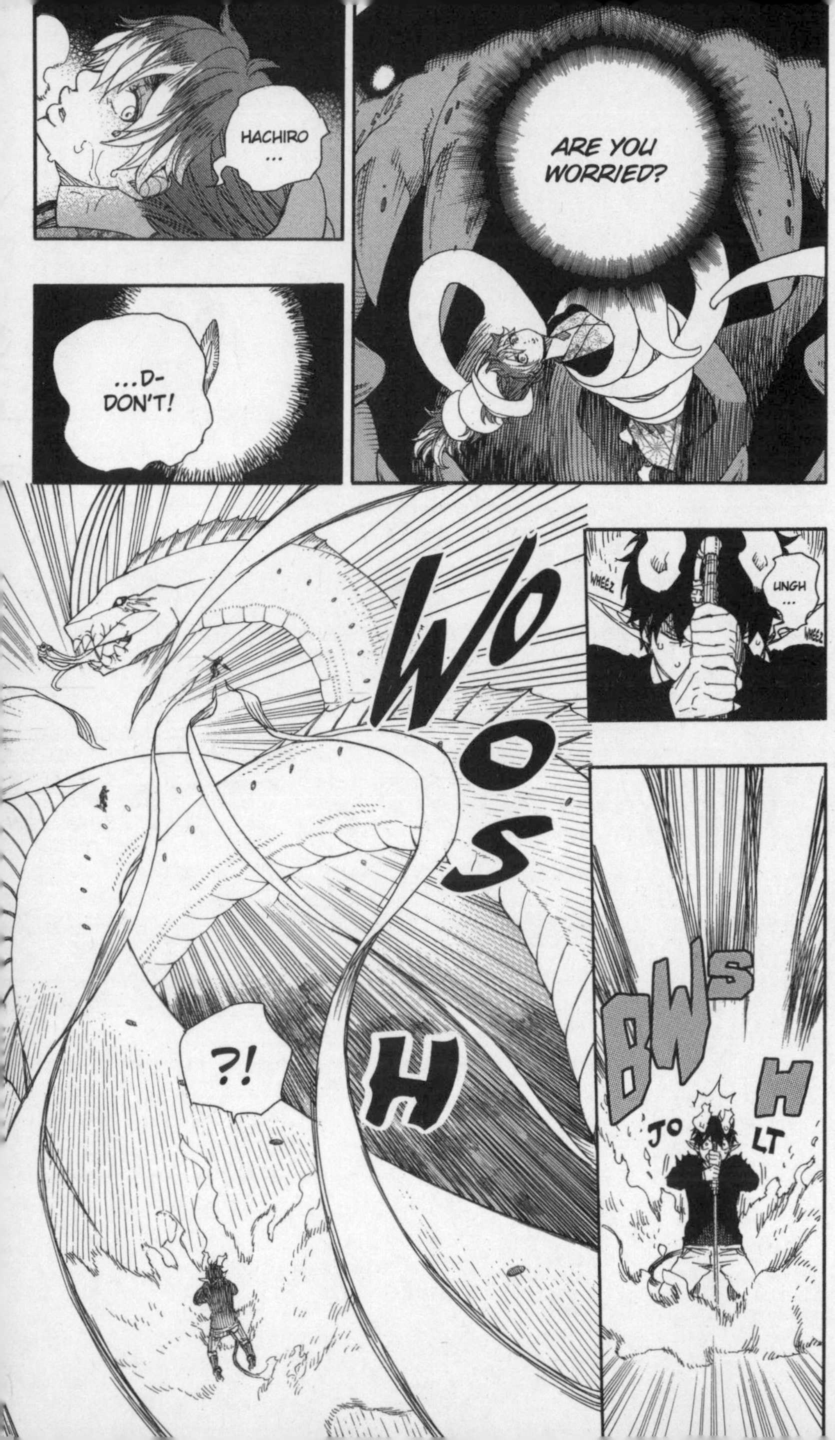
ARE YOU WORRIED?
HACHIRO ...
...D- DON'T!
WHEEZ
UNGH ...
WHEEZ
BWSH
JOLT
WOOSH
?!

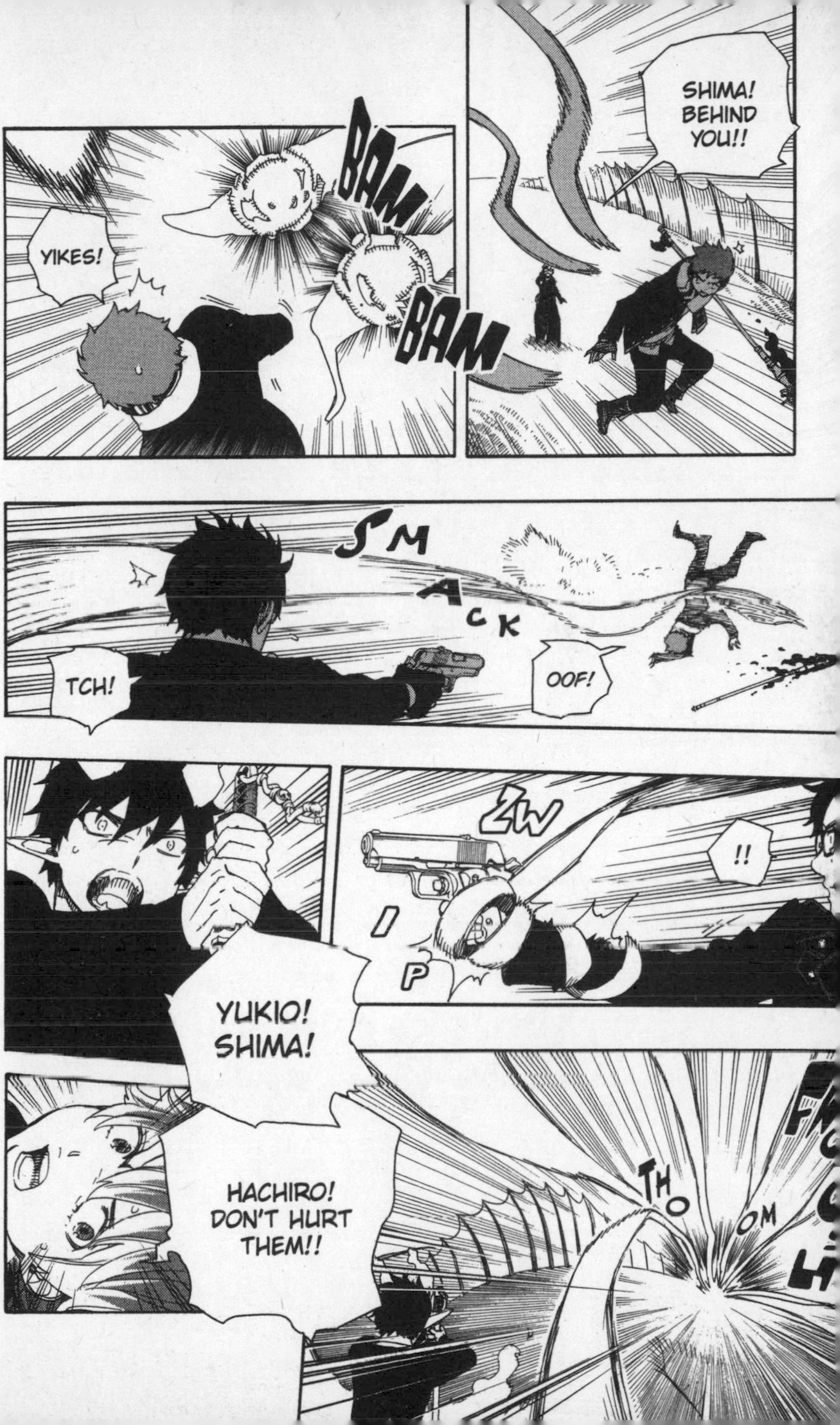
SHIMA! BEHIND YOU!!
BAM
BAM
YIKES!
SMACK
OOF!
TCH!
ZWIP
!!
YUKIO! SHIMA!
THOOM
HACHIRO! DON'T HURT THEM!!

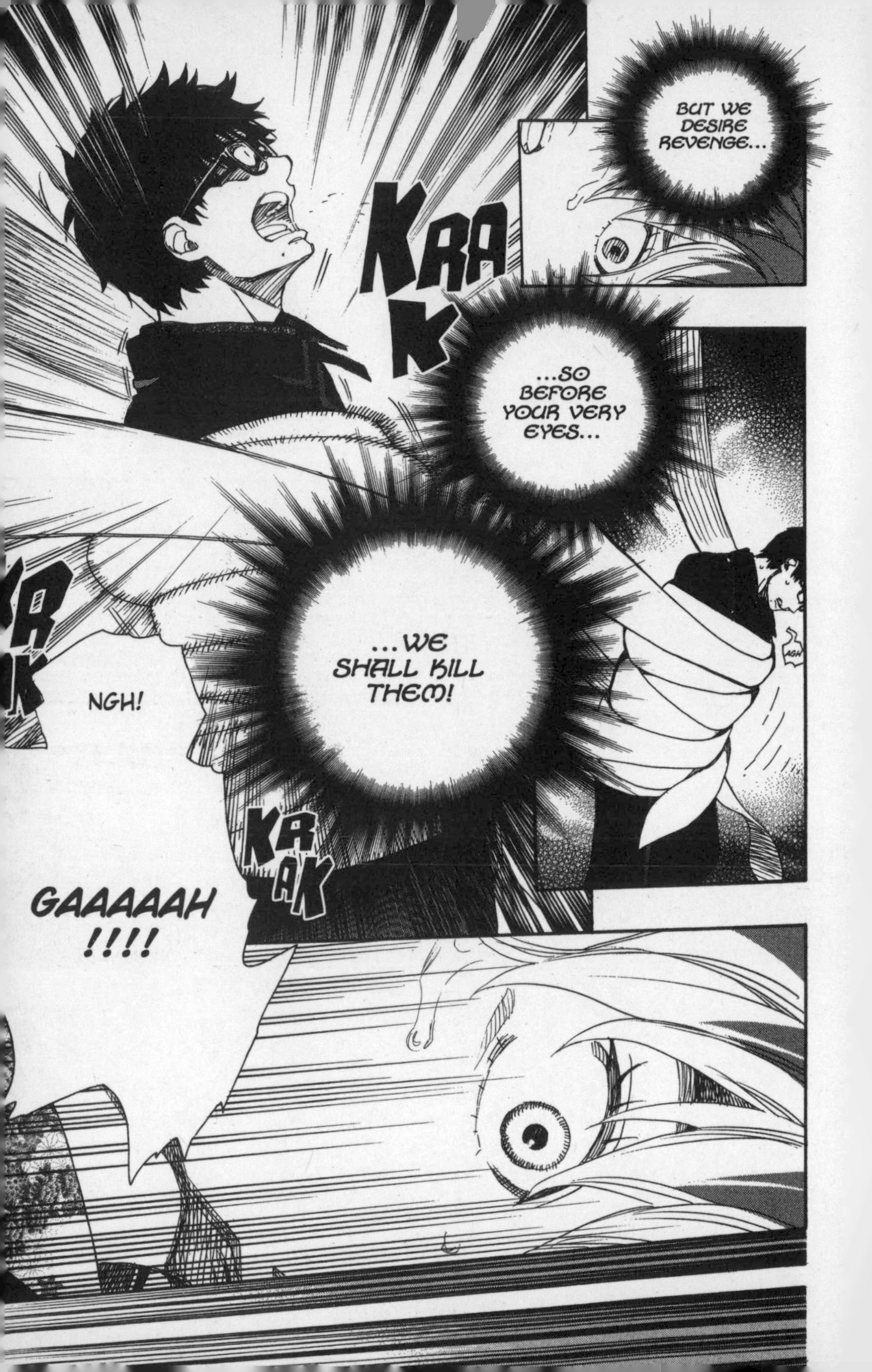
BUT WE DESIRE REVENGE...
...SO BEFORE YOUR VERY EYES...
...WE SHALL KILL THEM!
AGH
KRAK
KRAK
NGH!
KRAK
GAAAAAH!!!!

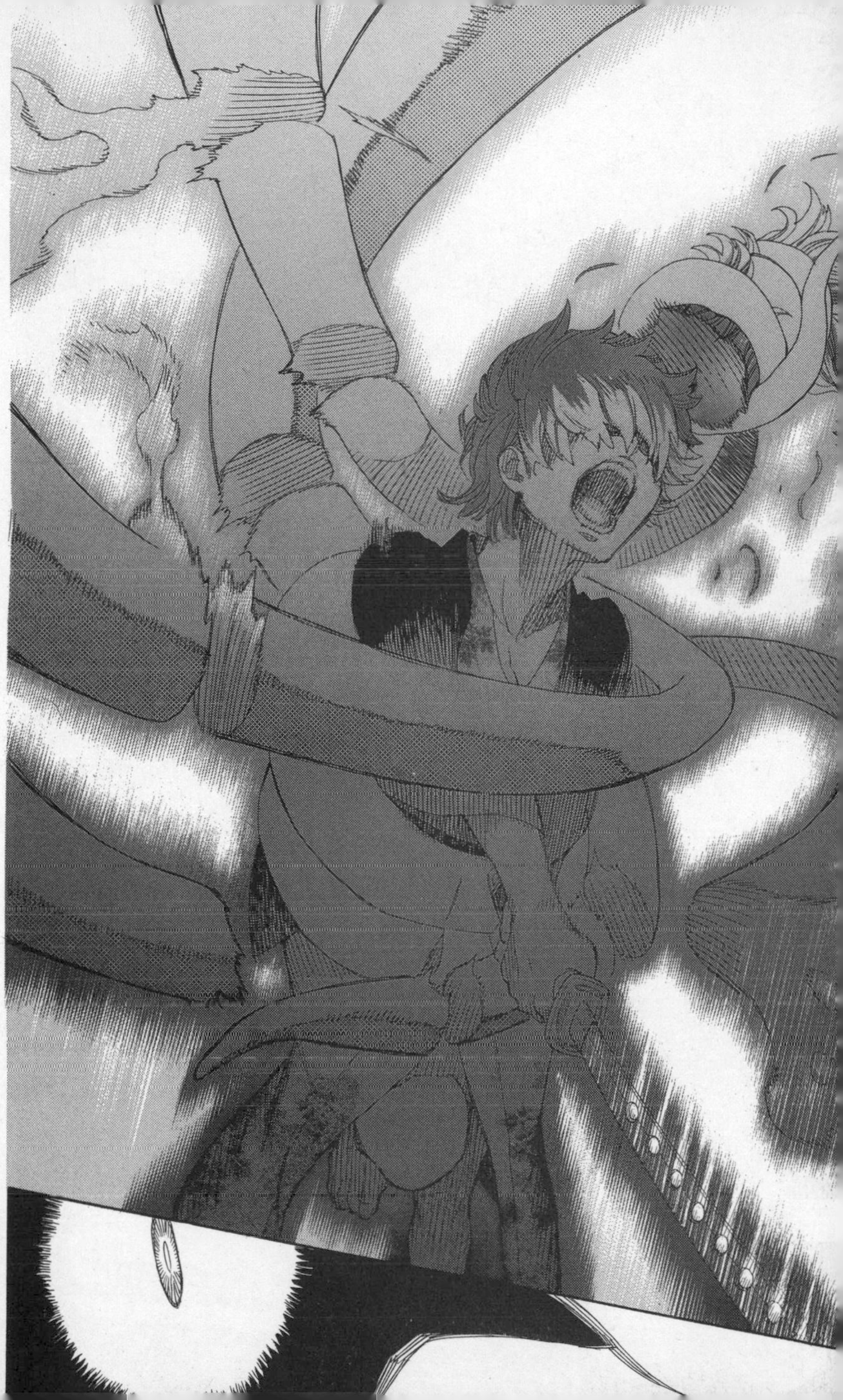

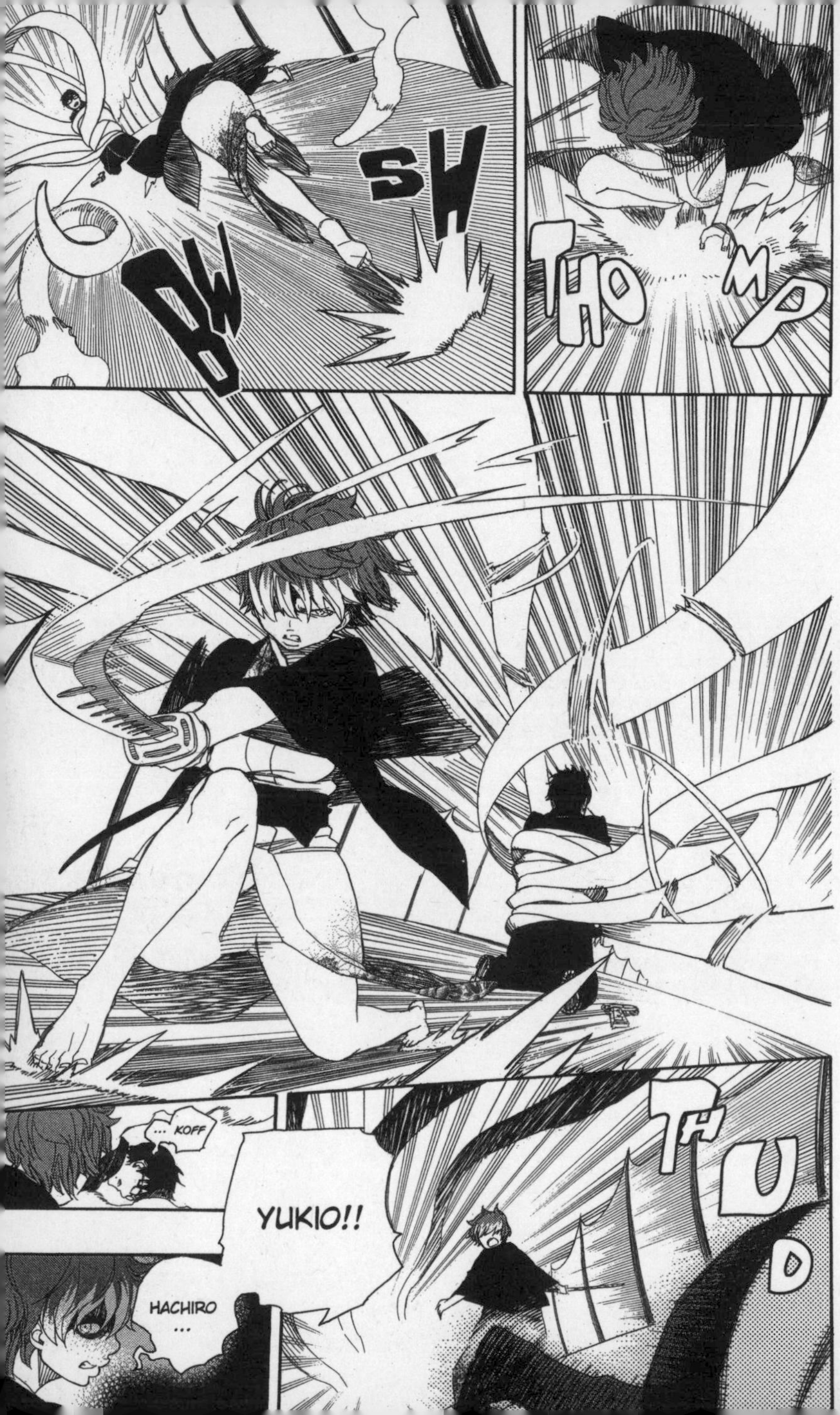
THOMP
BWSH
THUD
YUKIO!!
... KOFF
HACHIRO ...

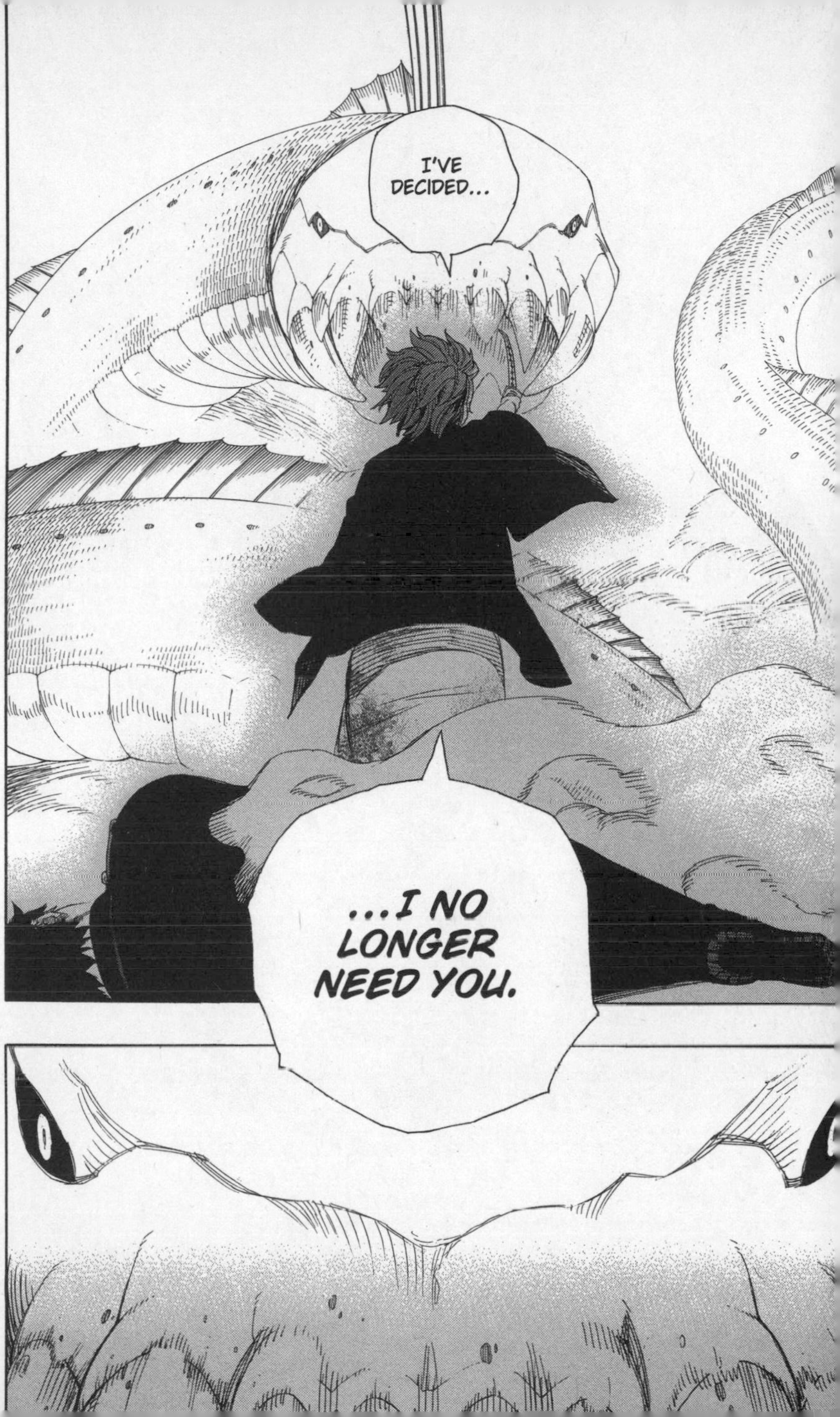
I'VE DECIDED...
...I NO LONGER NEED YOU.

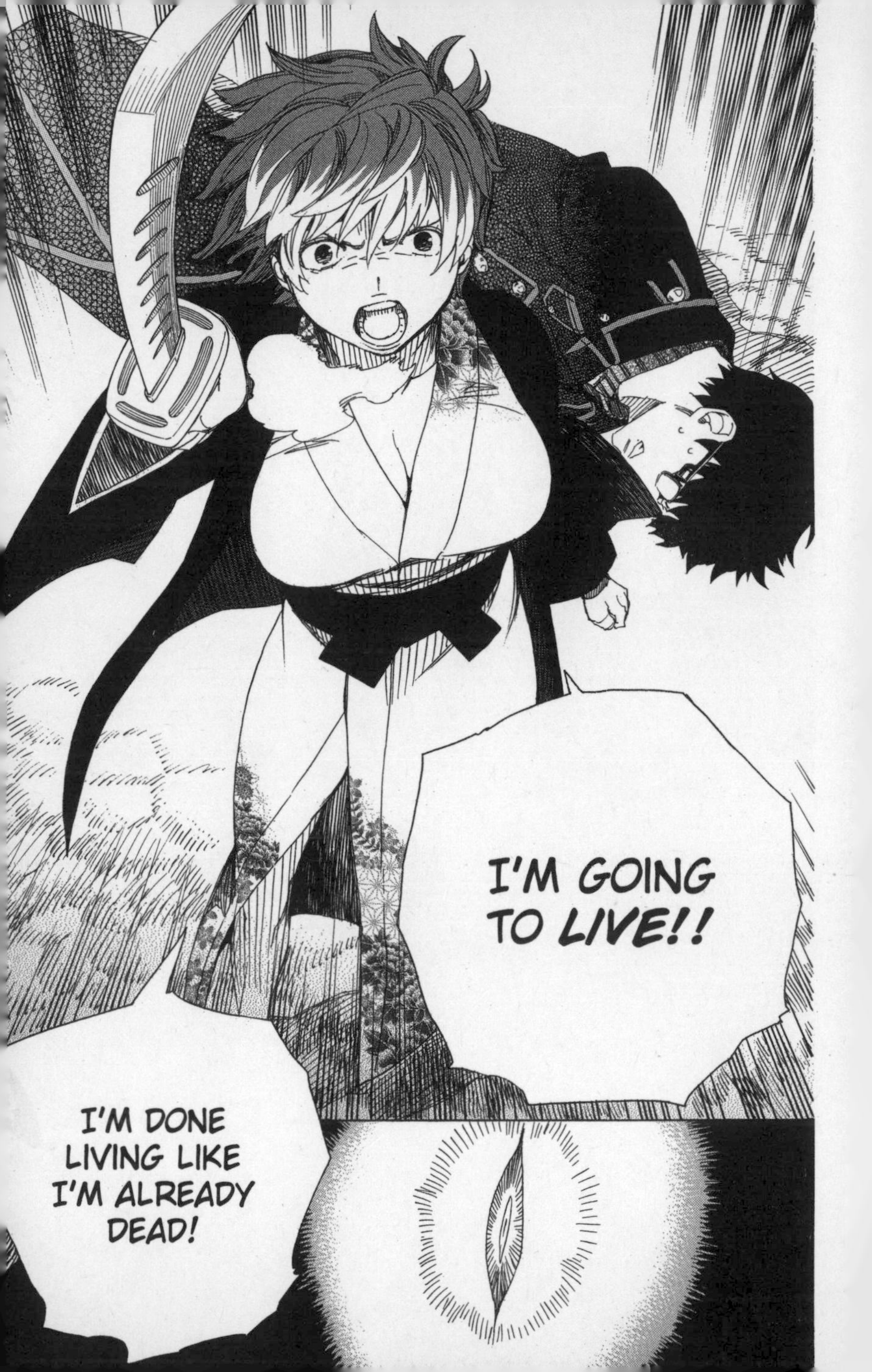
I'M GOING TO LIVE!!
I'M DONE LIVING LIKE I'M ALREADY DEAD!

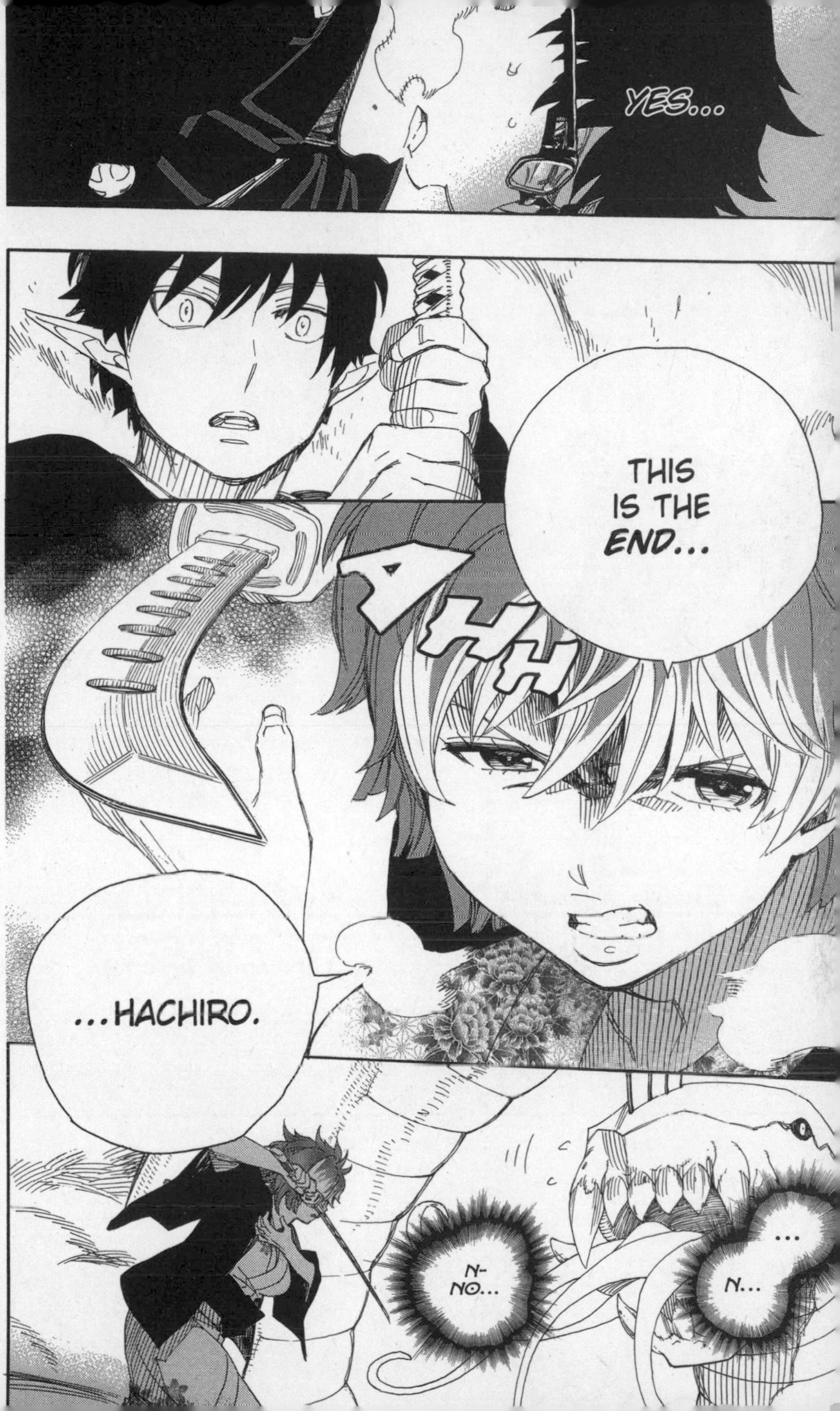
YES...
THIS IS THE END...
AHH
...HACHIRO.
... N...
N- NO...

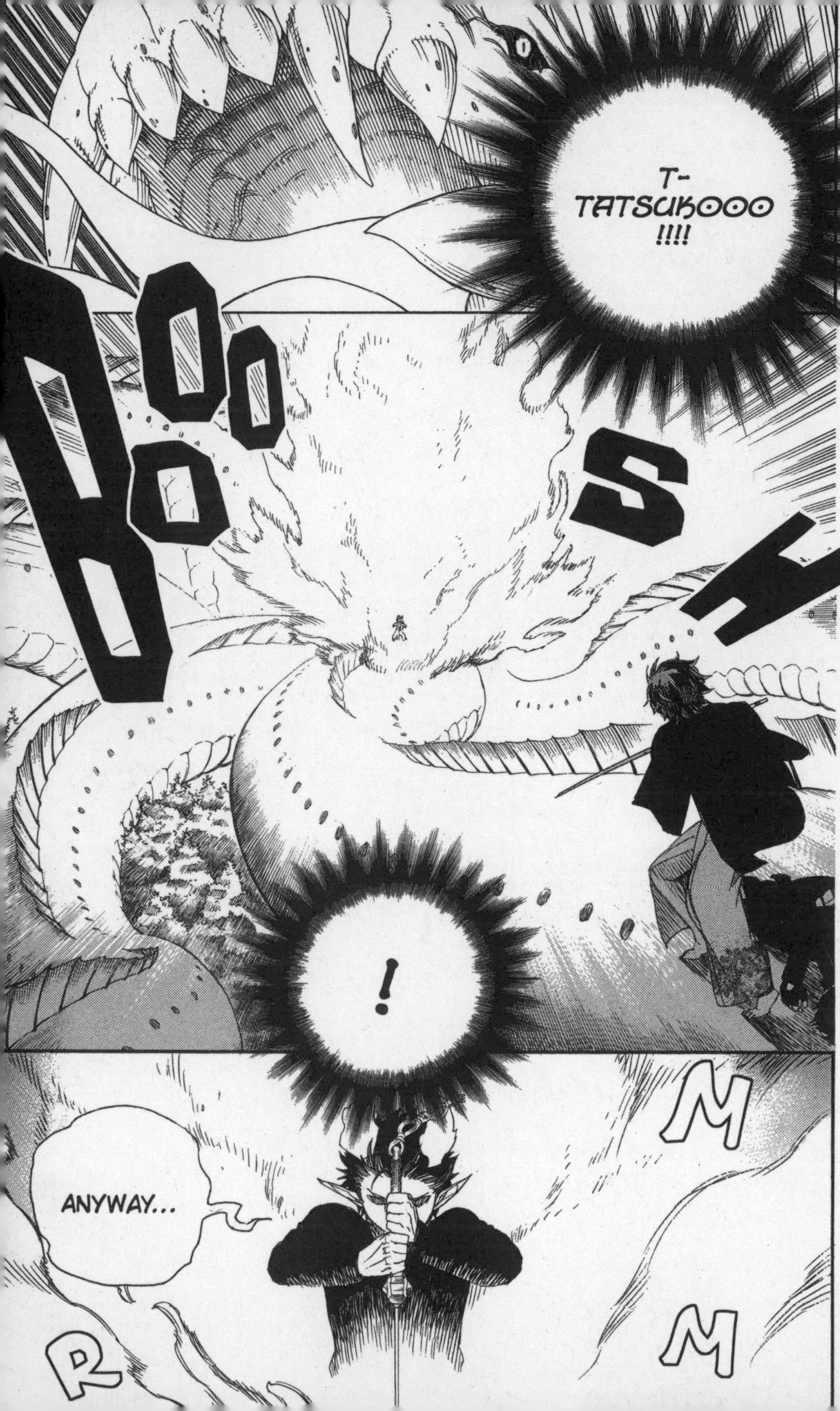
T-TATSUKOOO!!!!
BOOOOSH
!
MMM
ANYWAY...
R

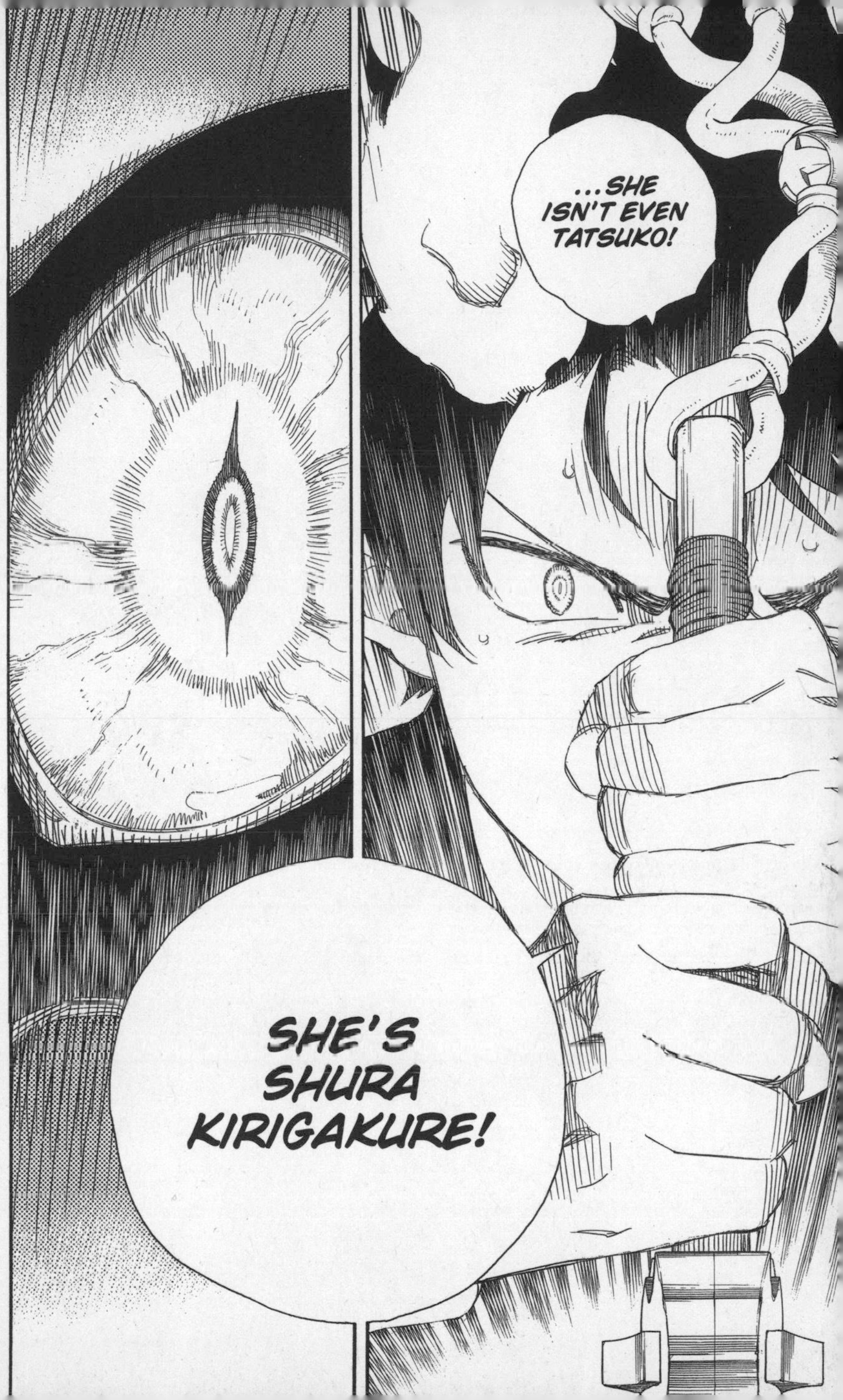
...SHE ISN'T EVEN TATSUKO!
SHE'S SHURA KIRIGAKURE!

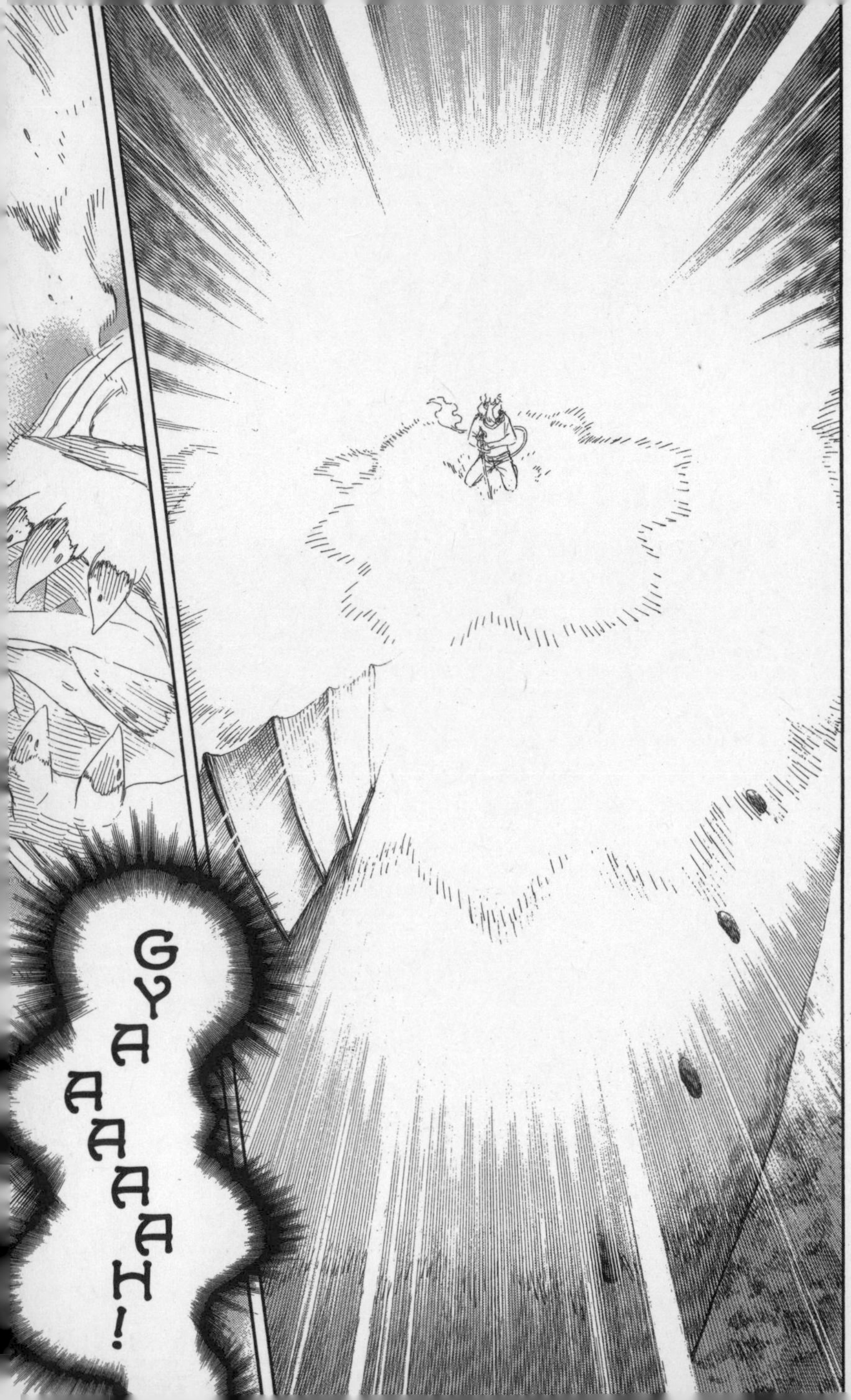
GYAAAAAH!

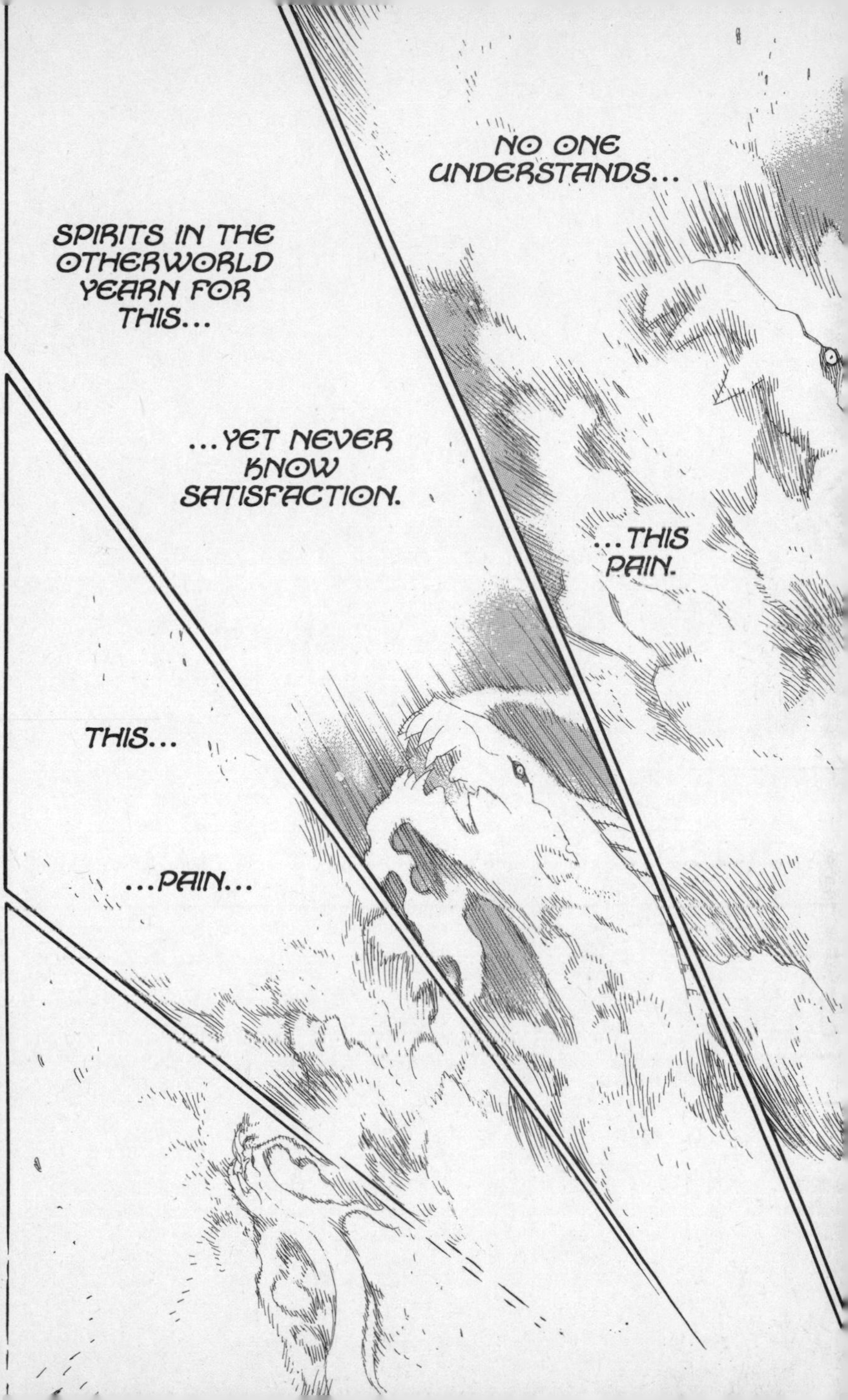
NO ONE UNDERSTANDS...
...THIS PAIN.
SPIRITS IN THE OTHERWORLD YEARN FOR THIS...
...YET NEVER KNOW SATISFACTION.
THIS...
...PAIN...

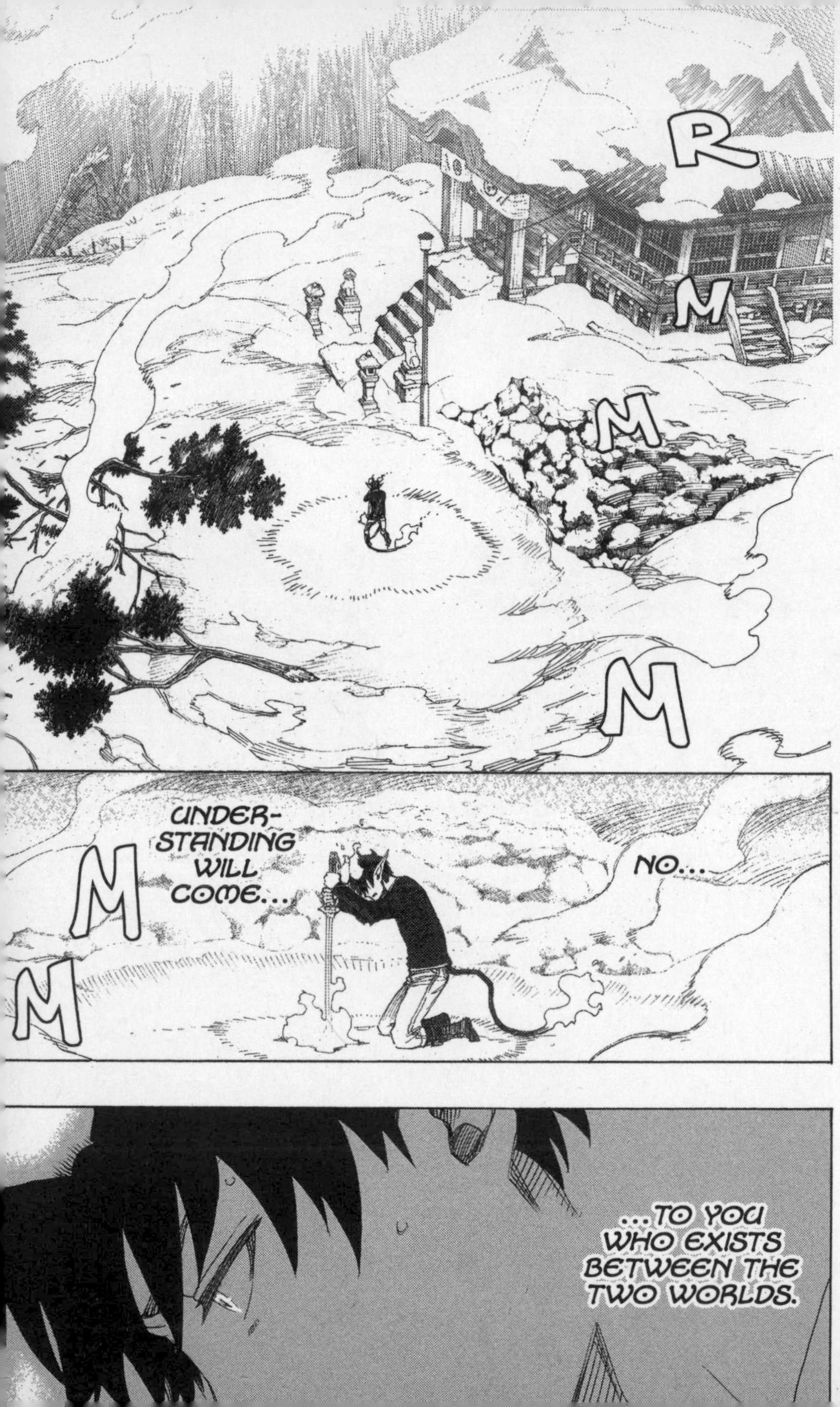

R
M
M
M
NO...
UNDER-STANDING WILL COME...
M
M
...TO YOU WHO EXISTS BETWEEN THE TWO WORLDS.

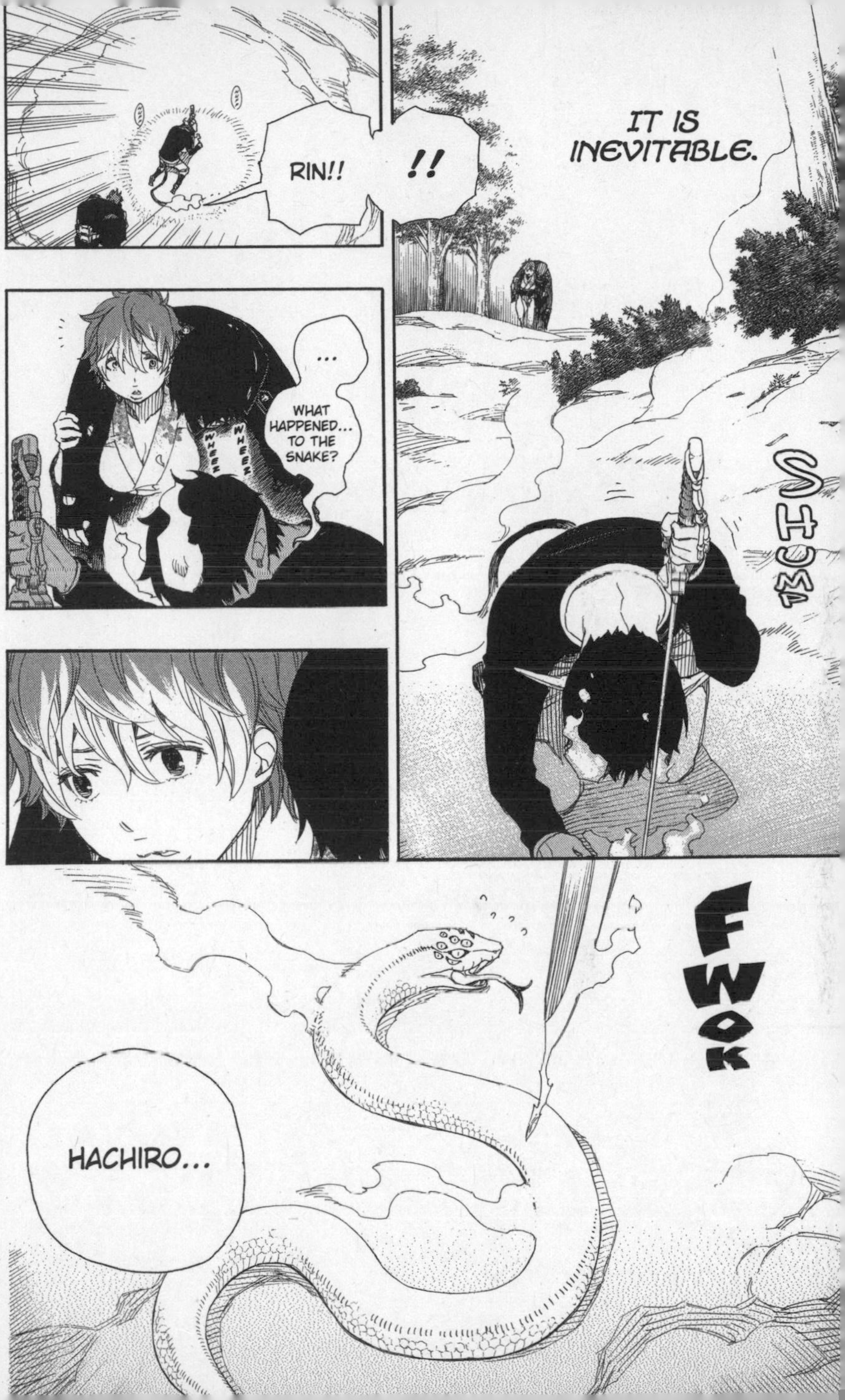
IT IS INEVITABLE.
SHUMP
!!
RIN!!
...
WHAT HAPPENED... TO THE SNAKE?
WHEEZ
WHEEZ
FWOK
HACHIRO...

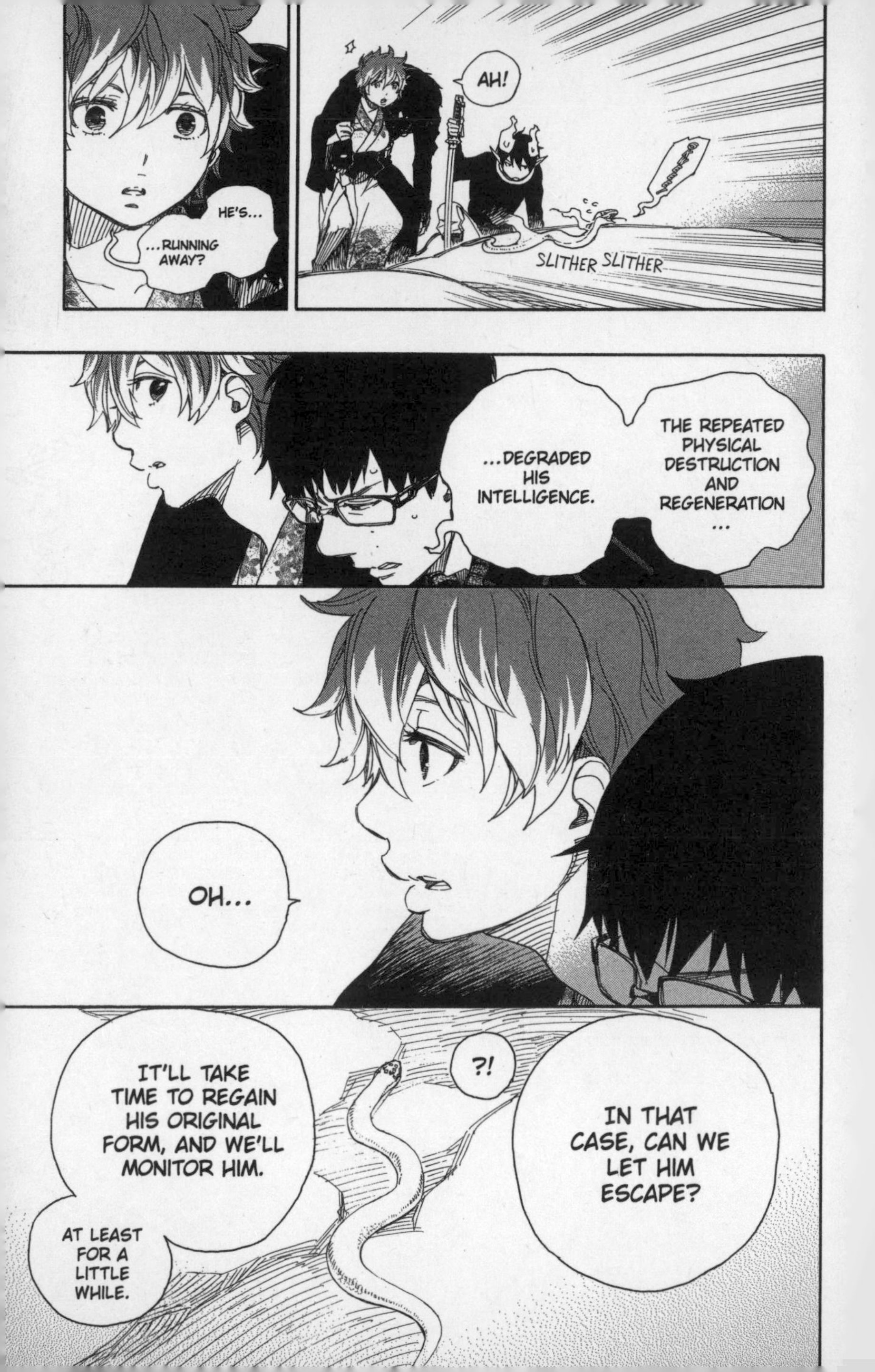
AH!
SLITHER SLITHER
HE'S...
...RUNNING AWAY?
THE REPEATED PHYSICAL DESTRUCTION AND REGENERATION ...
...DEGRADED HIS INTELLIGENCE.
OH...
IN THAT CASE, CAN WE LET HIM ESCAPE?
?!
IT'LL TAKE TIME TO REGAIN HIS ORIGINAL FORM, AND WE'LL MONITOR HIM.
AT LEAST FOR A LITTLE WHILE.

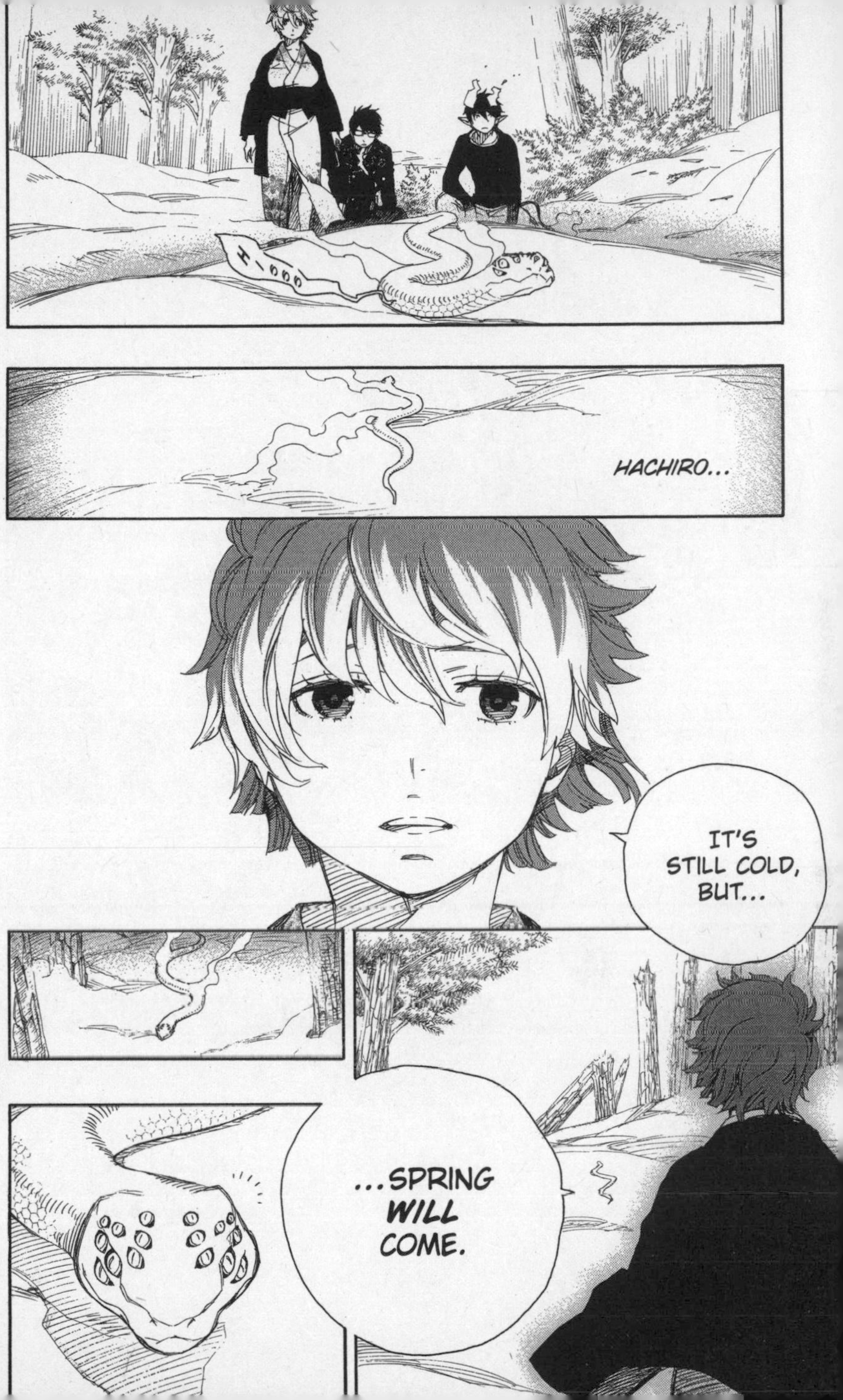
H-sss
HACHIRO...
IT'S STILL COLD, BUT...
...SPRING *WILL* COME.

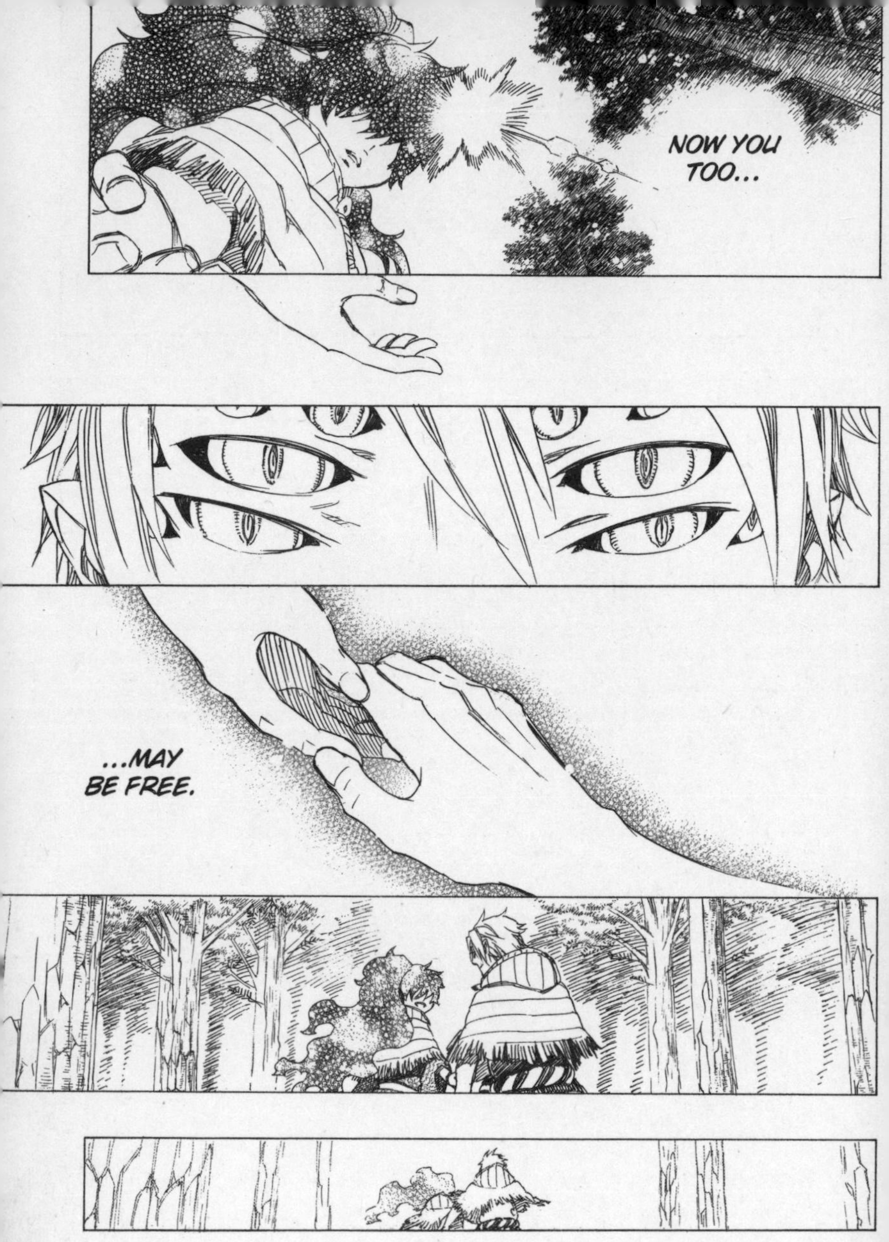
NOW YOU TOO...
...MAY BE FREE.

Blue Exorcist Chapter 79: I Will Return

FWOMP
I'm shtill awive.
SHIVER
SHIVER

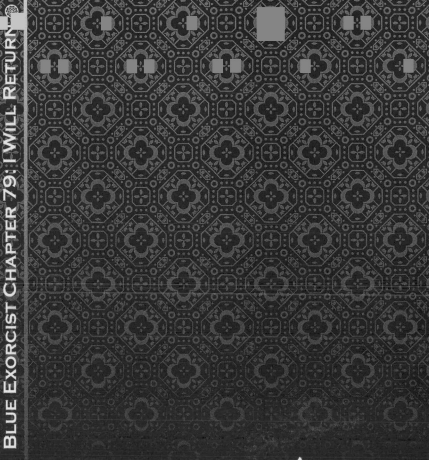

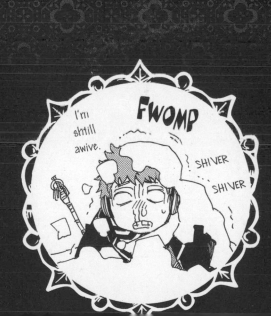

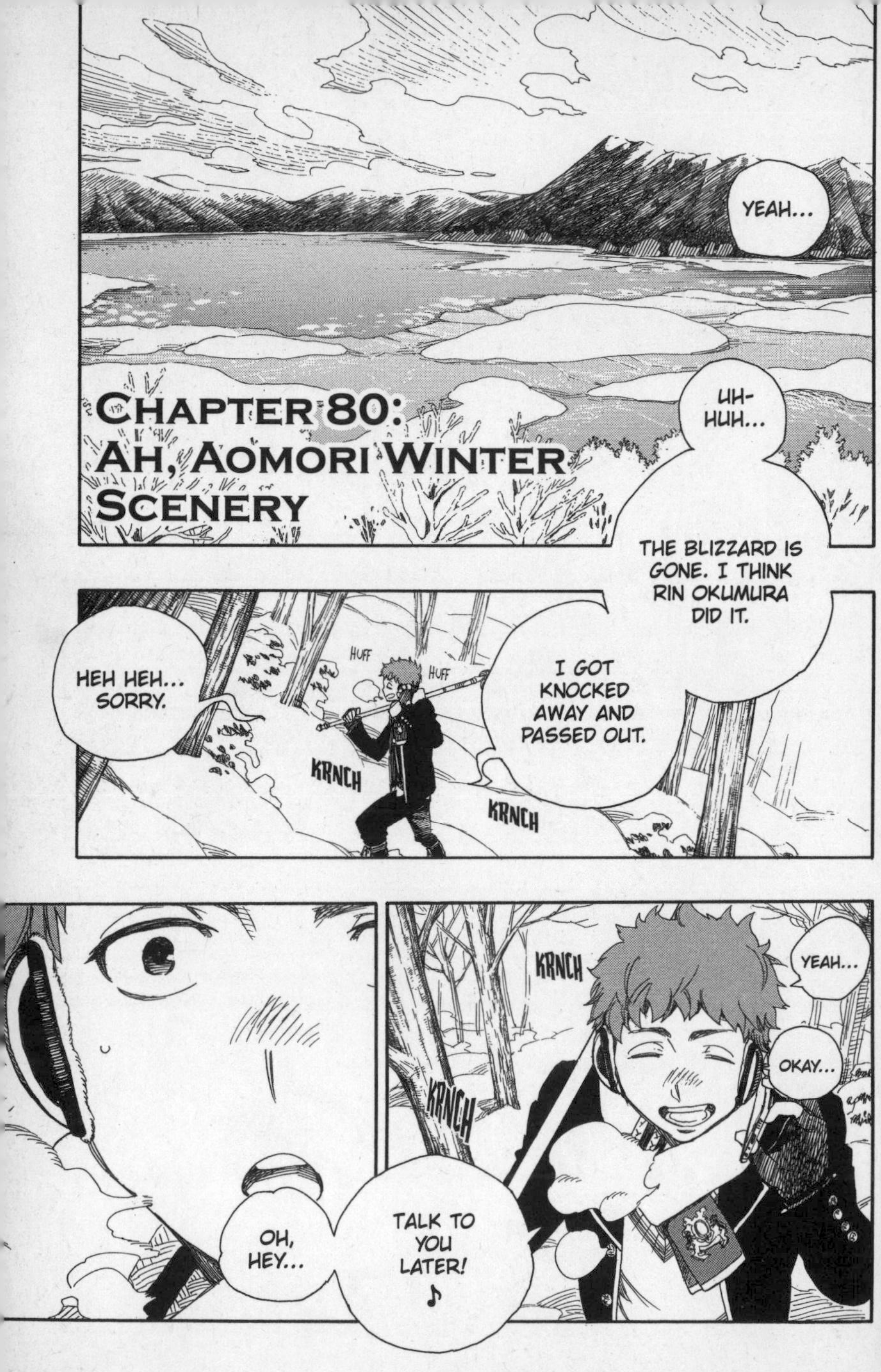
YEAH...
UH-HUH...
CHAPTER 80: AH, AOMORI WINTER SCENERY
THE BLIZZARD IS GONE. I THINK RIN OKUMURA DID IT.
I GOT KNOCKED AWAY AND PASSED OUT.
HUFF
HUFF
KRNCH
KRNCH
HEH HEH... SORRY.
YEAH...
KRNCH
OKAY...
KRNCH
TALK TO YOU LATER! ♪
OH, HEY...

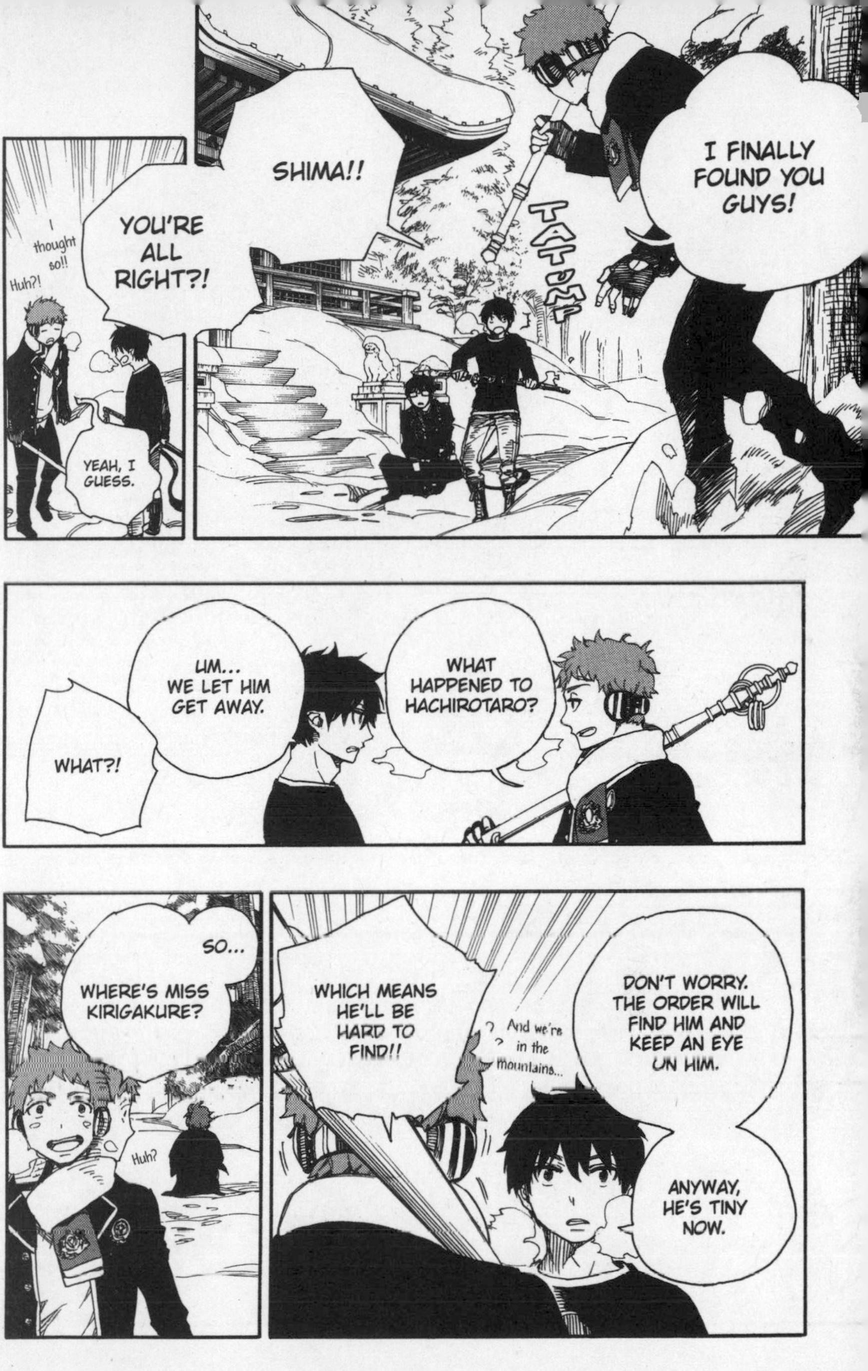
I FINALLY FOUND YOU GUYS!
TATUMP
SHIMA!!
YOU'RE ALL RIGHT?!
I thought so!!
Huh?!
YEAH, I GUESS.
WHAT HAPPENED TO HACHIROTARO?
UM... WE LET HIM GET AWAY.
WHAT?!
DON'T WORRY. THE ORDER WILL FIND HIM AND KEEP AN EYE ON HIM.
ANYWAY, HE'S TINY NOW.
And we're in the mountains...
WHICH MEANS HE'LL BE HARD TO FIND!!
SO...
WHERE'S MISS KIRIGAKURE?
Huh?

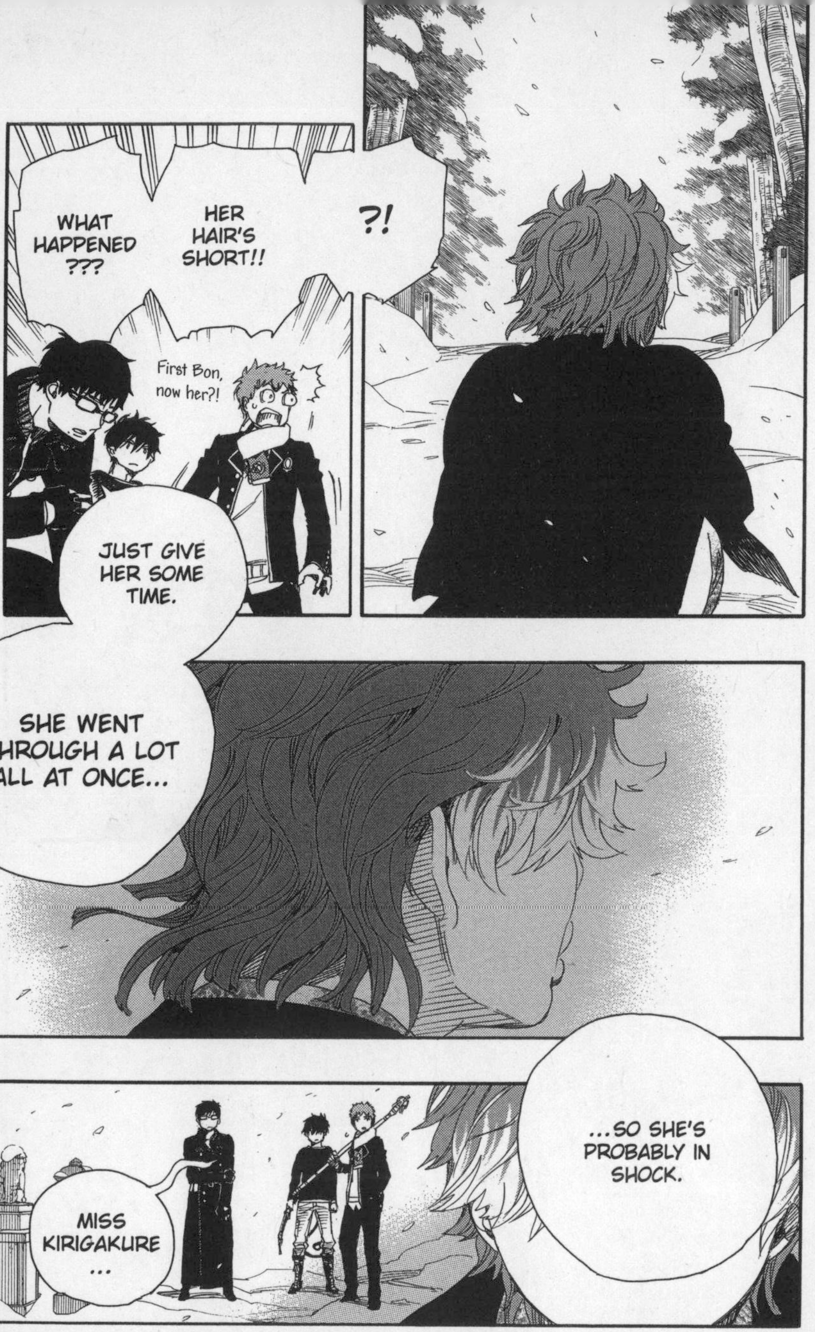
?!
HER HAIR'S SHORT!!
WHAT HAPPENED ???
First Bon, now her?!
JUST GIVE HER SOME TIME.
SHE WENT THROUGH A LOT ALL AT ONCE...
...SO SHE'S PROBABLY IN SHOCK.
MISS KIRIGAKURE ...

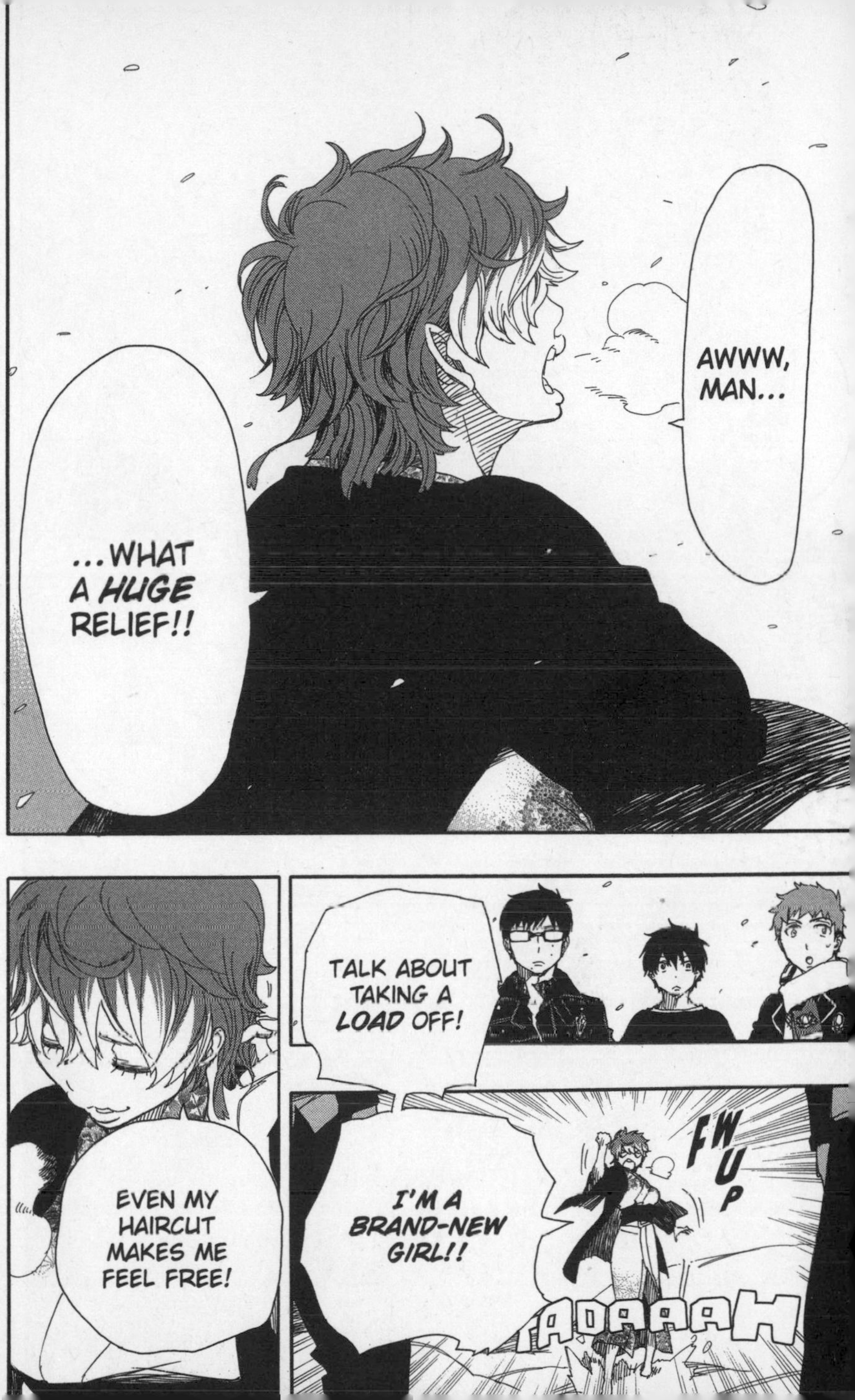
AWWW, MAN...
...WHAT A HUGE RELIEF!!
TALK ABOUT TAKING A LOAD OFF!
FWUP
I'M A BRAND-NEW GIRL!!
TADAAAAH
EVEN MY HAIRCUT MAKES ME FEEL FREE!

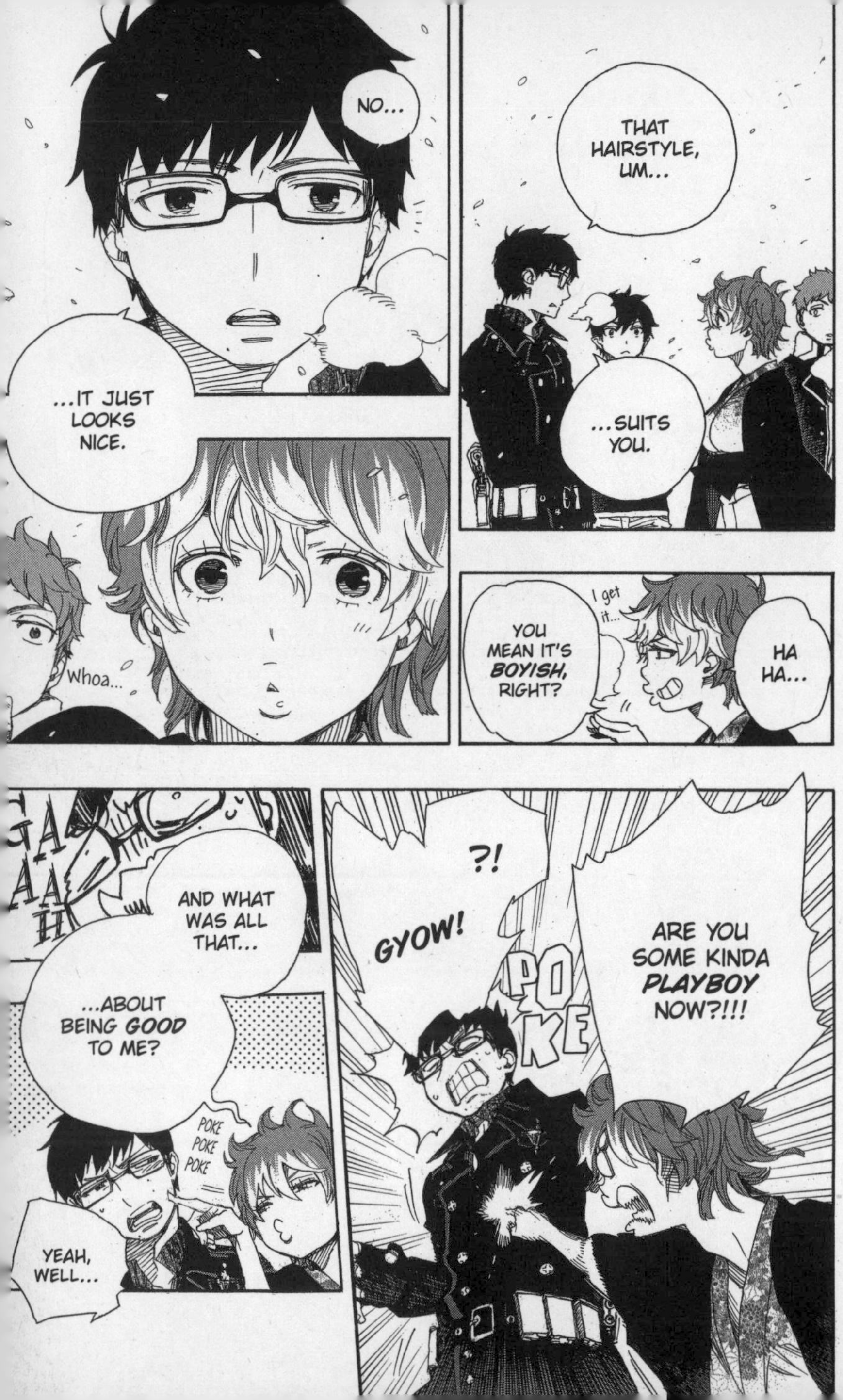
THAT HAIRSTYLE, UM...
...SUITS YOU.
NO...
...IT JUST LOOKS NICE.
HA HA...
I get it...
YOU MEAN IT'S *BOYISH*, RIGHT?
Whoa...
?!
ARE YOU SOME KINDA *PLAYBOY* NOW?!!!
GYOW!
POKE
GAAAH
AND WHAT WAS ALL THAT...
...ABOUT BEING *GOOD* TO ME?
POKE POKE POKE
YEAH, WELL...

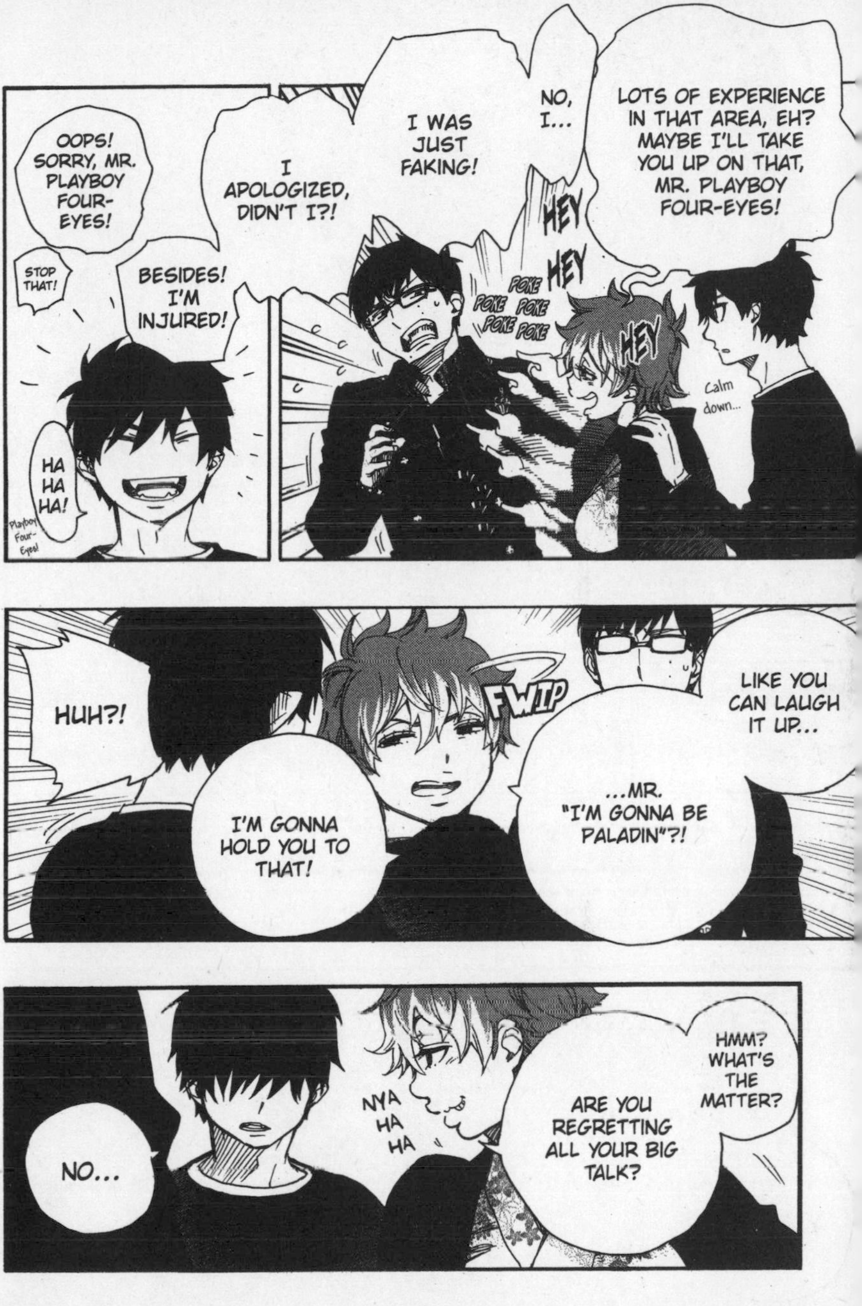
LOTS OF EXPERIENCE IN THAT AREA, EH? MAYBE I'LL TAKE YOU UP ON THAT, MR. PLAYBOY FOUR-EYES!
NO, I...
I WAS JUST FAKING!
HEY HEY
HEY
POKE POKE POKE POKE POKE POKE
Calm down...
I APOLOGIZED, DIDN'T I?!
OOPS! SORRY, MR. PLAYBOY FOUR-EYES!
BESIDES! I'M INJURED!
STOP THAT!
HA HA HA!
Playboy Four-Eyes!
LIKE YOU CAN LAUGH IT UP...
...MR. "I'M GONNA BE PALADIN"?!
FWIP
I'M GONNA HOLD YOU TO THAT!
HUH?!
HMM? WHAT'S THE MATTER?
ARE YOU REGRETTING ALL YOUR BIG TALK?
NYA HA HA
NO...

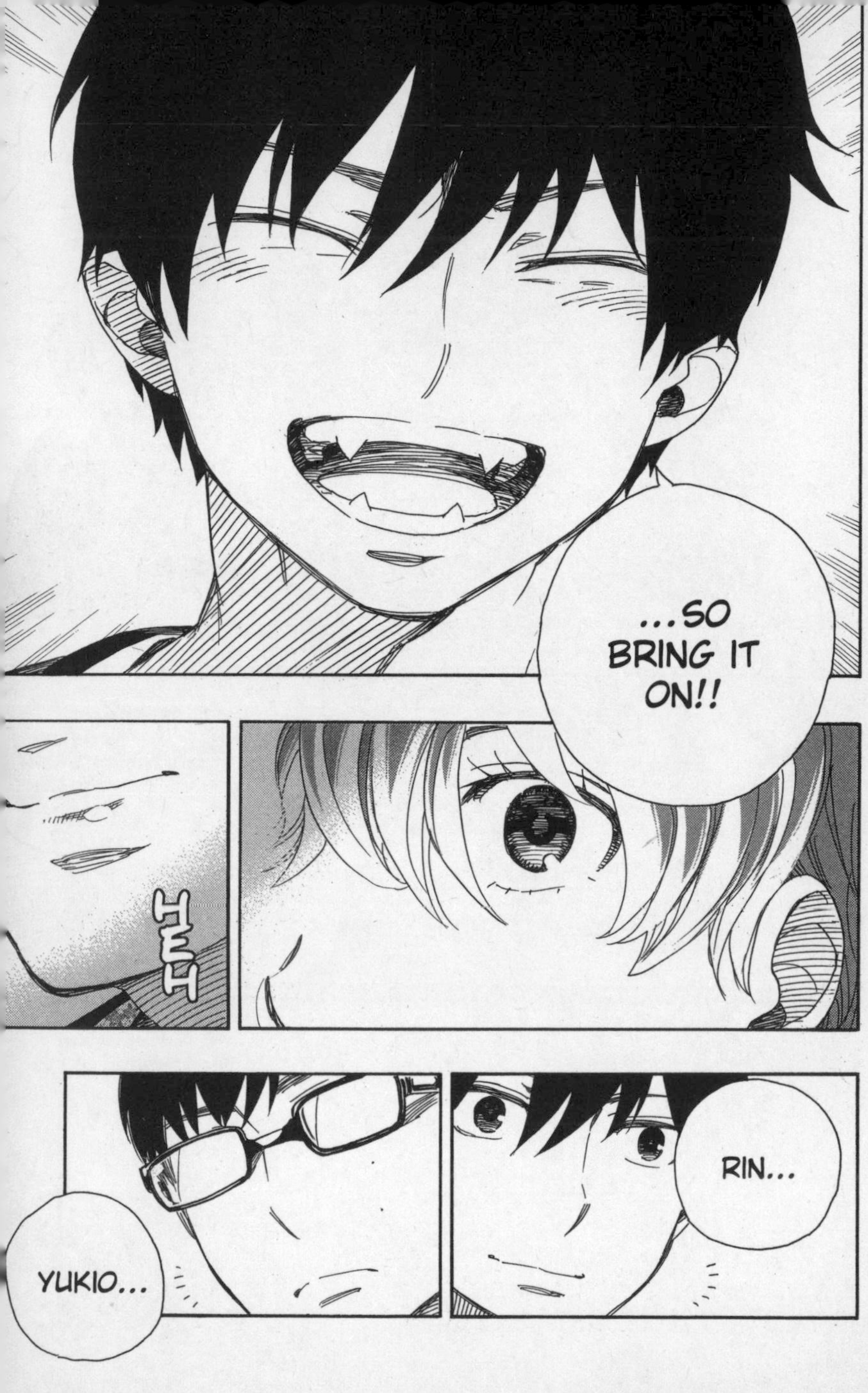
...SO BRING IT ON!!
HEH
RIN...
YUKIO...

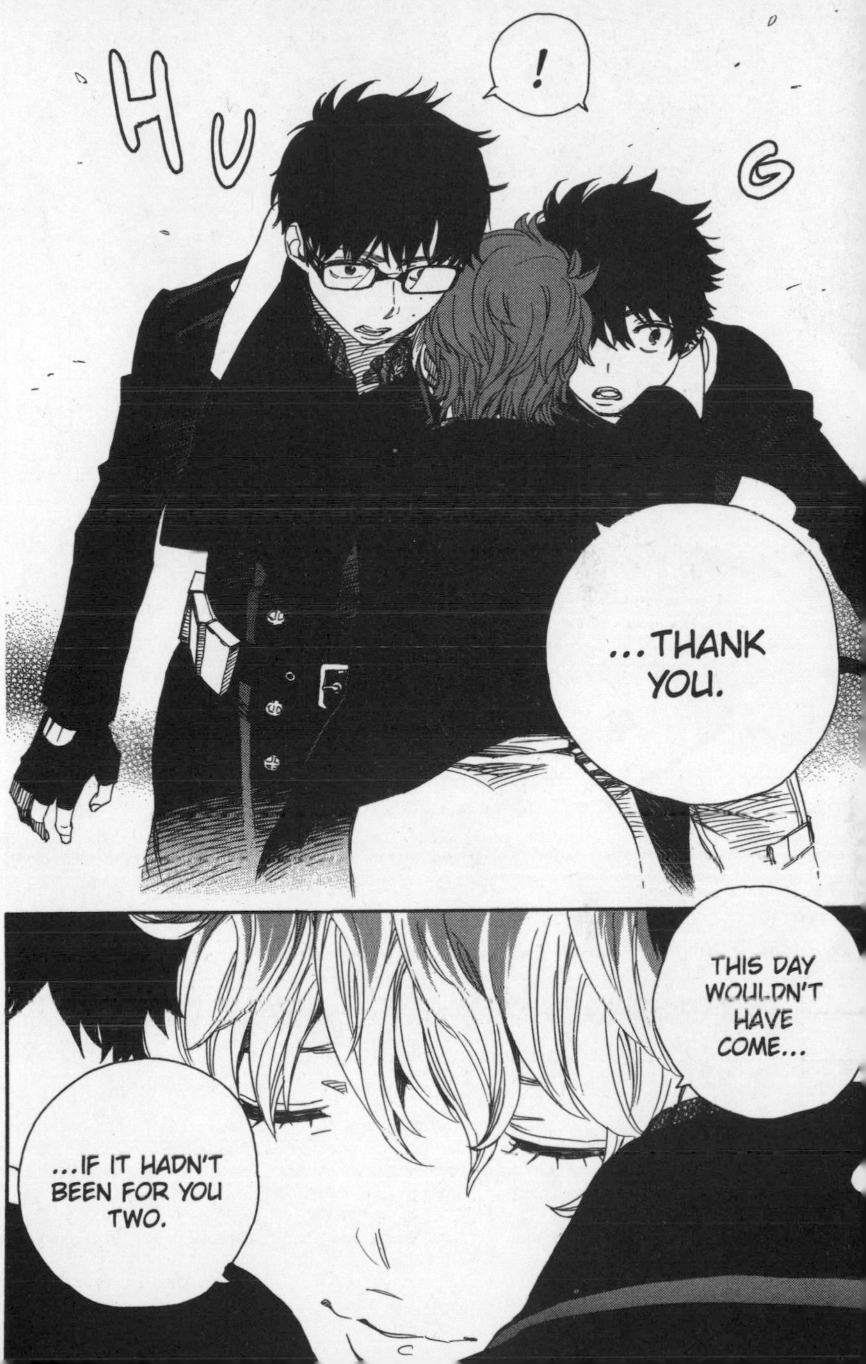
HUG
!
...THANK YOU.
THIS DAY WOULDN'T HAVE COME...
...IF IT HADN'T BEEN FOR YOU TWO.

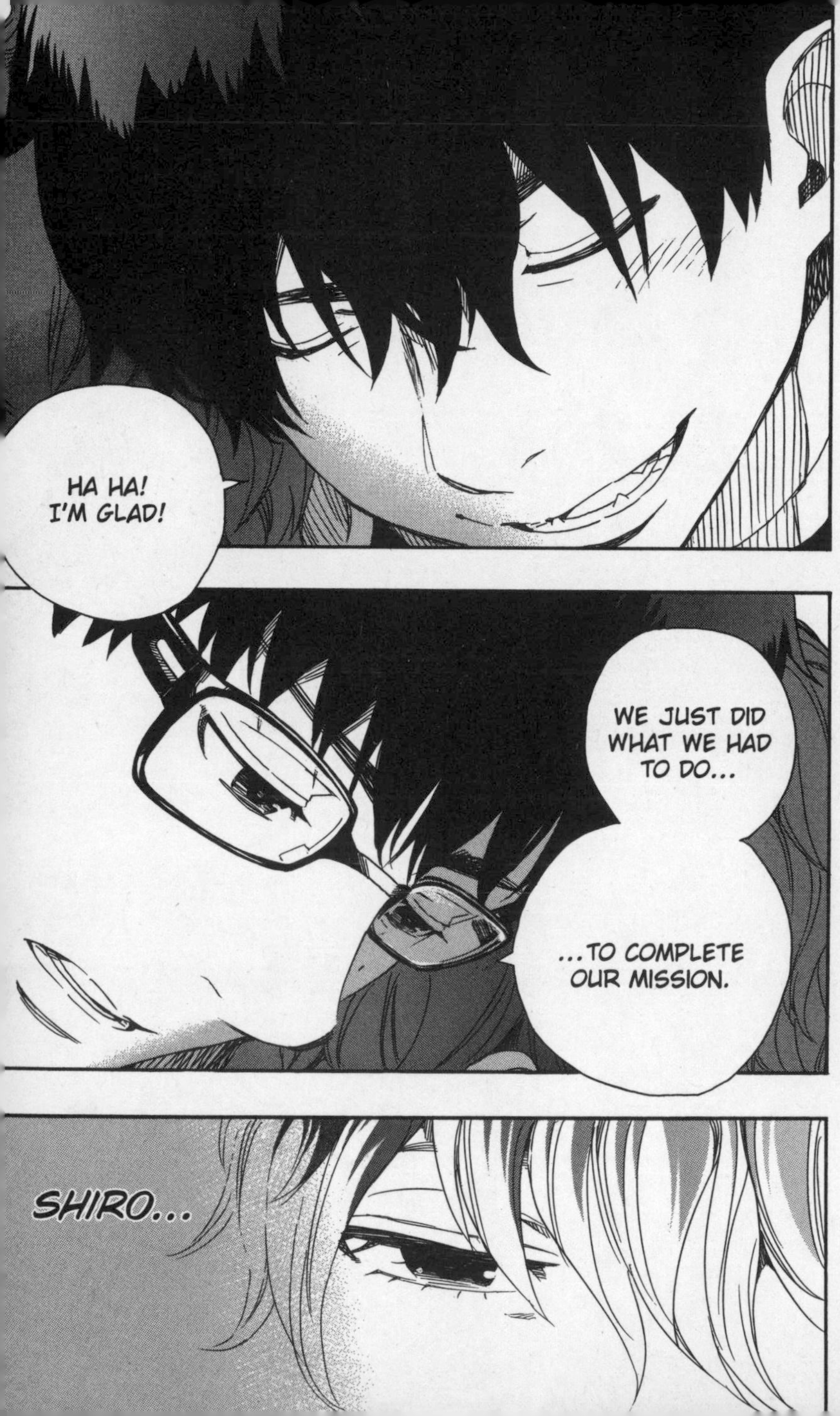
HA HA! I'M GLAD!
WE JUST DID WHAT WE HAD TO DO...
...TO COMPLETE OUR MISSION.
SHIRO...

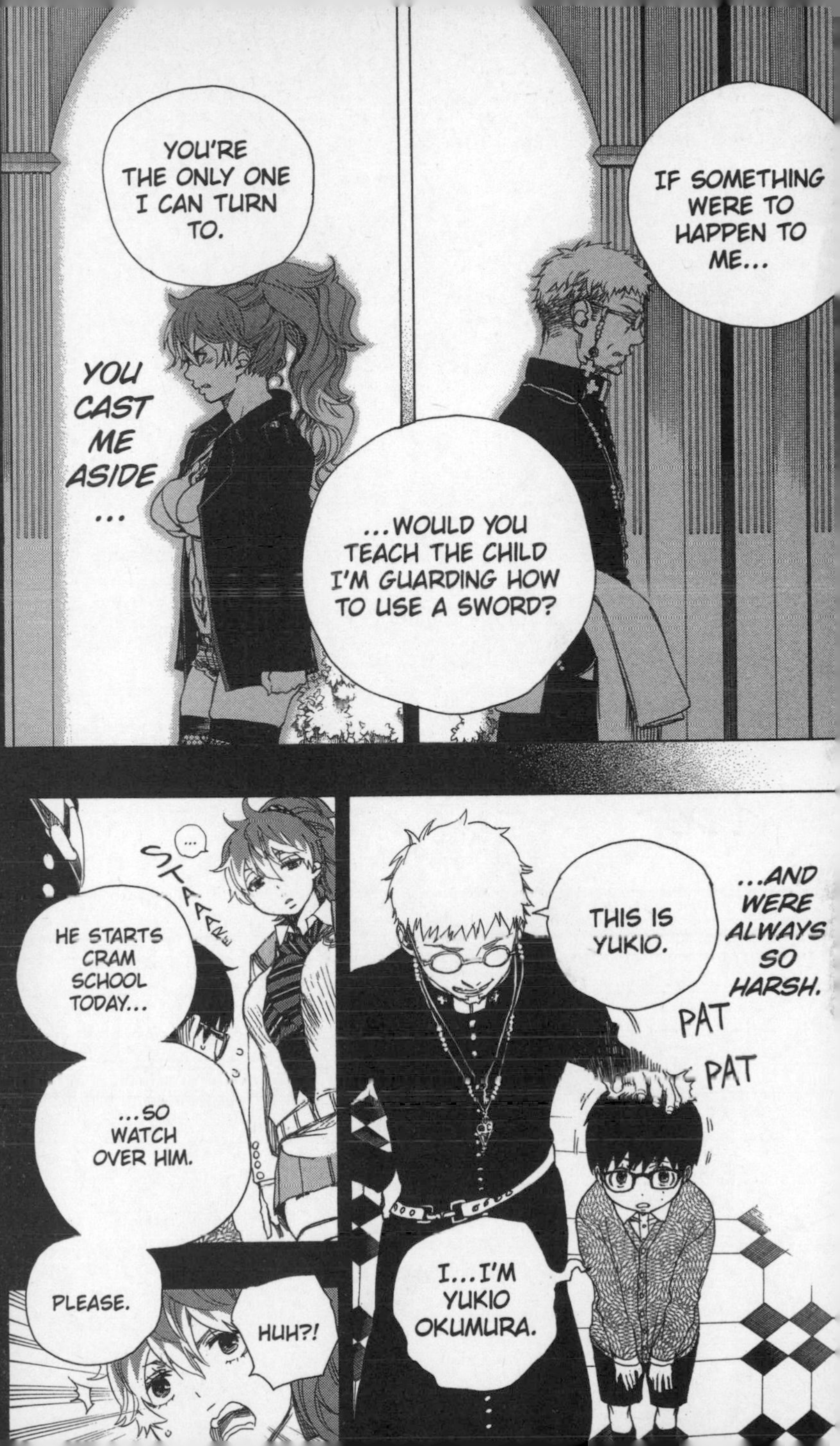
IF SOMETHING WERE TO HAPPEN TO ME...
...WOULD YOU TEACH THE CHILD I'M GUARDING HOW TO USE A SWORD?
YOU'RE THE ONLY ONE I CAN TURN TO.
YOU CAST ME ASIDE...
...AND WERE ALWAYS SO HARSH.
THIS IS YUKIO.
PAT
PAT
I...I'M YUKIO OKUMURA.
...
STAAARE
HE STARTS CRAM SCHOOL TODAY...
...SO WATCH OVER HIM.
PLEASE.
HUH?!

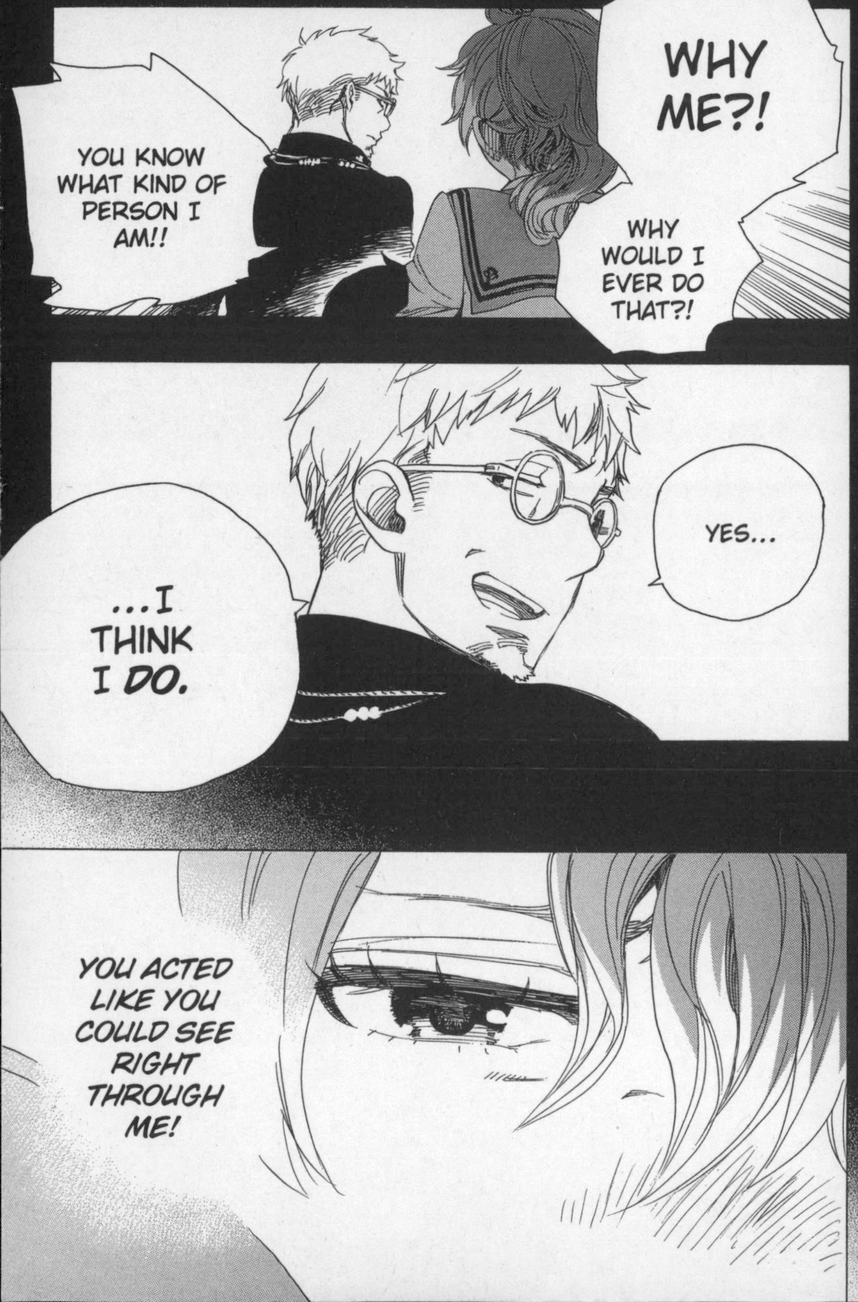
WHY ME?!
WHY WOULD I EVER DO THAT?!
YOU KNOW WHAT KIND OF PERSON I AM!!
YES...
...I THINK I DO.
YOU ACTED LIKE YOU COULD SEE RIGHT THROUGH ME!

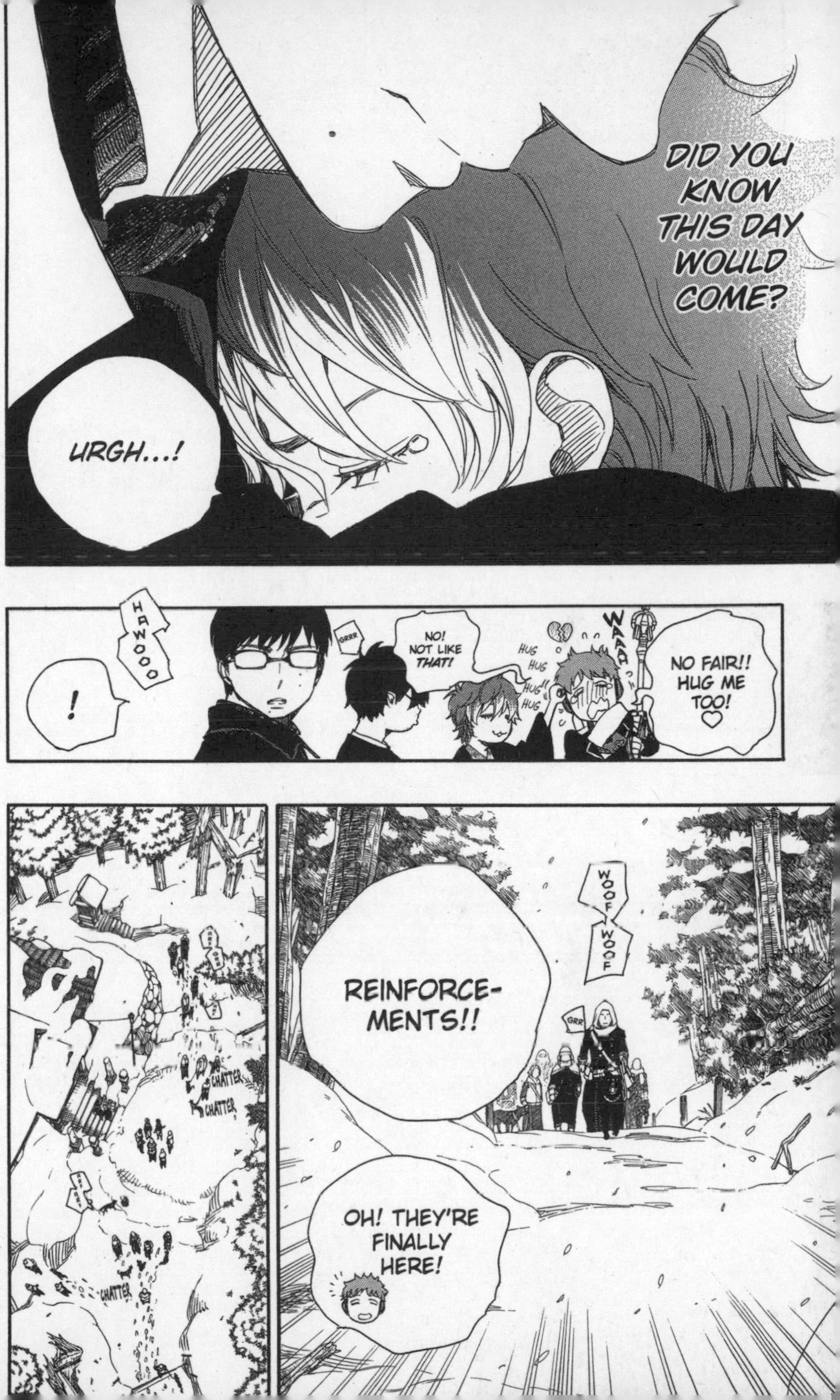
DID YOU KNOW THIS DAY WOULD COME?
URGH...!
NO FAIR!! HUG ME TOO! ♡
WAAAH
HUG HUG HUG HUG
NO! NOT LIKE THAT!
GRRR
HAWOOO
!
WOOF WOOF
GRR
REINFORCE-MENTS!!
OH! THEY'RE FINALLY HERE!
CHATTER CHATTER
CHATTER

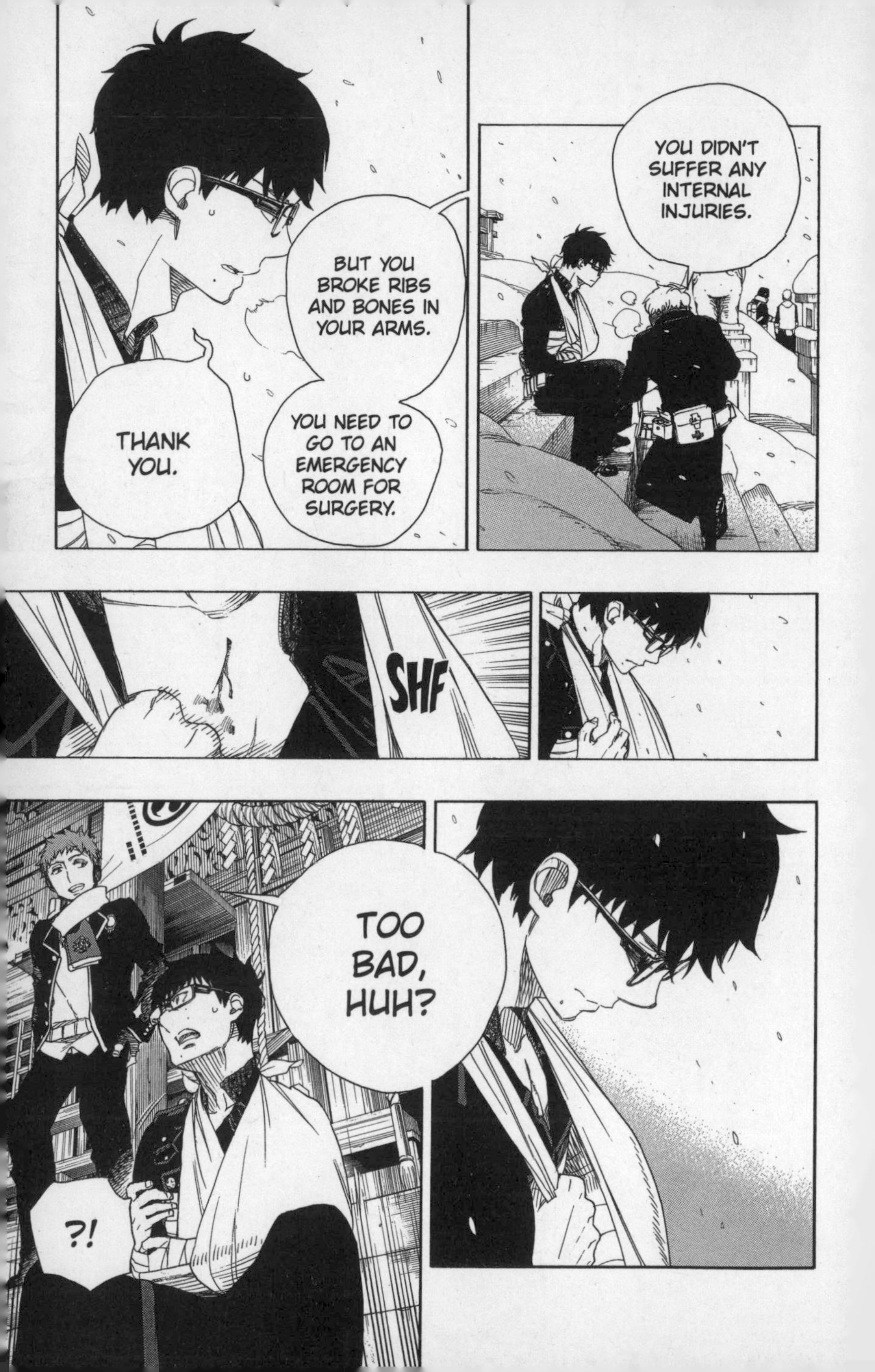
YOU DIDN'T SUFFER ANY INTERNAL INJURIES.
BUT YOU BROKE RIBS AND BONES IN YOUR ARMS.
YOU NEED TO GO TO AN EMERGENCY ROOM FOR SURGERY.
THANK YOU.
SHF
TOO BAD, HUH?
?!

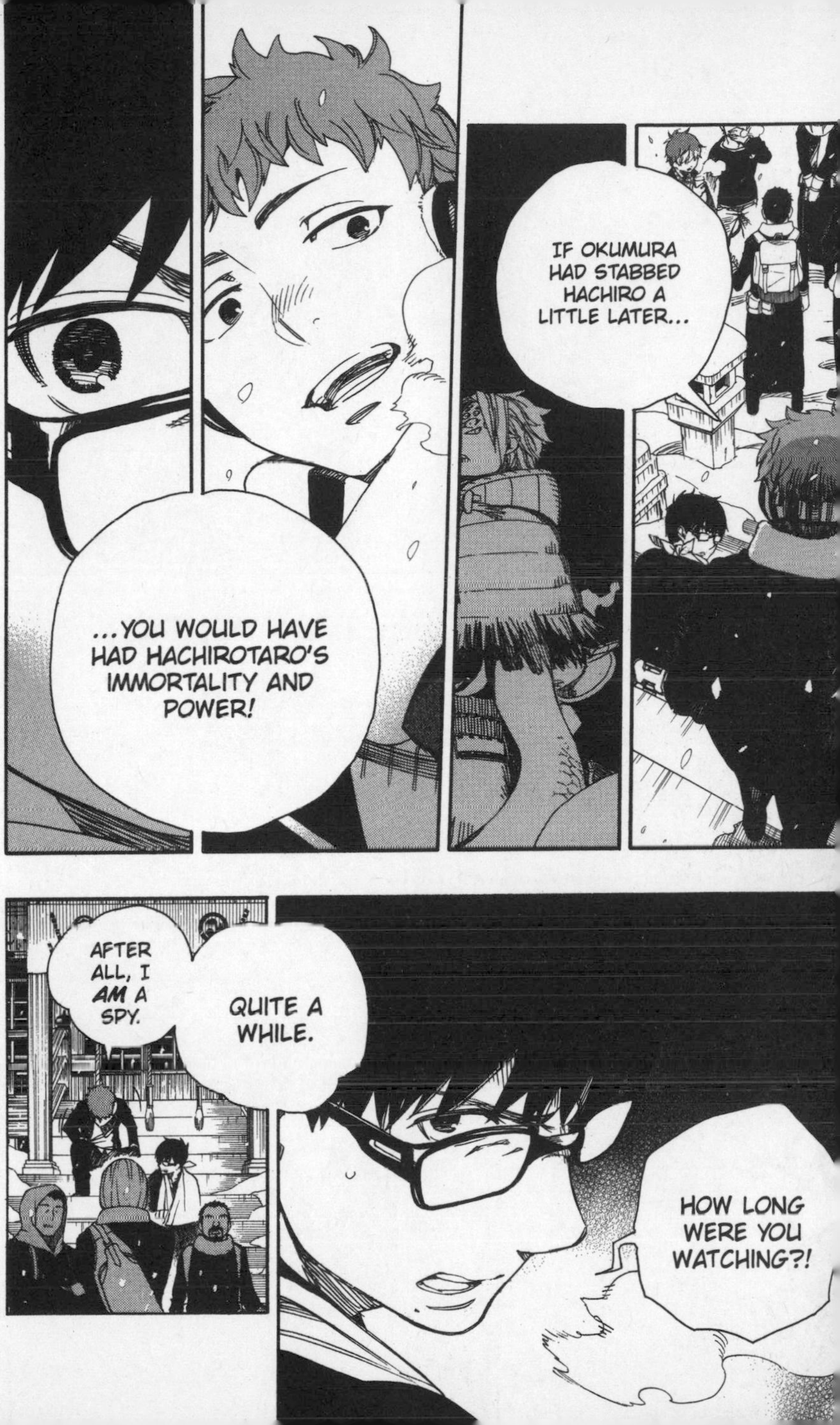
IF OKUMURA HAD STABBED HACHIRO A LITTLE LATER...
...YOU WOULD HAVE HAD HACHIROTARO'S IMMORTALITY AND POWER!
HOW LONG WERE YOU WATCHING?!
QUITE A WHILE.
AFTER ALL, I *AM* A SPY.

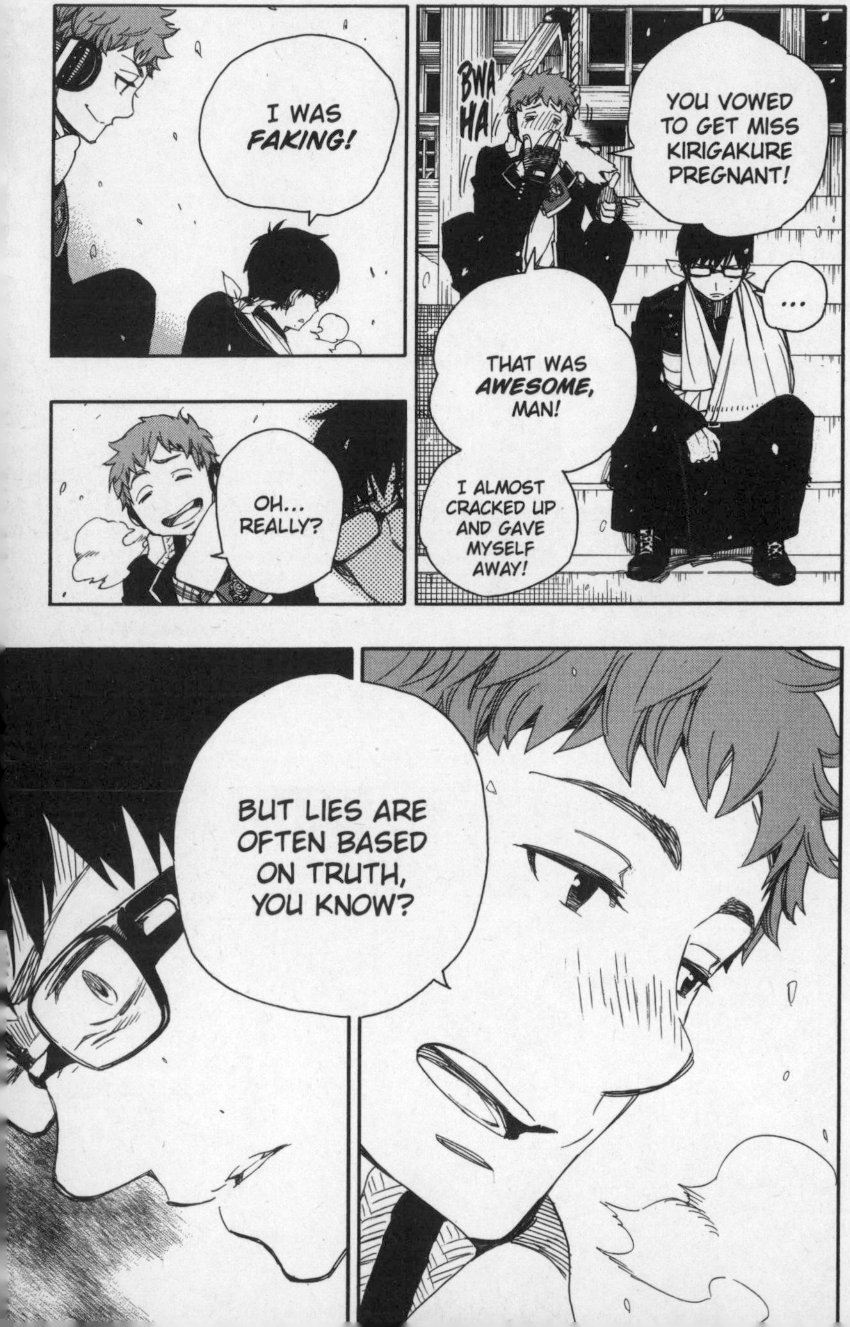
YOU VOWED TO GET MISS KIRIGAKURE PREGNANT!
BWA HA
...
THAT WAS *AWESOME,* MAN!
I ALMOST CRACKED UP AND GAVE MYSELF AWAY!
I WAS *FAKING!*
OH... REALLY?
BUT LIES ARE OFTEN BASED ON TRUTH, YOU KNOW?

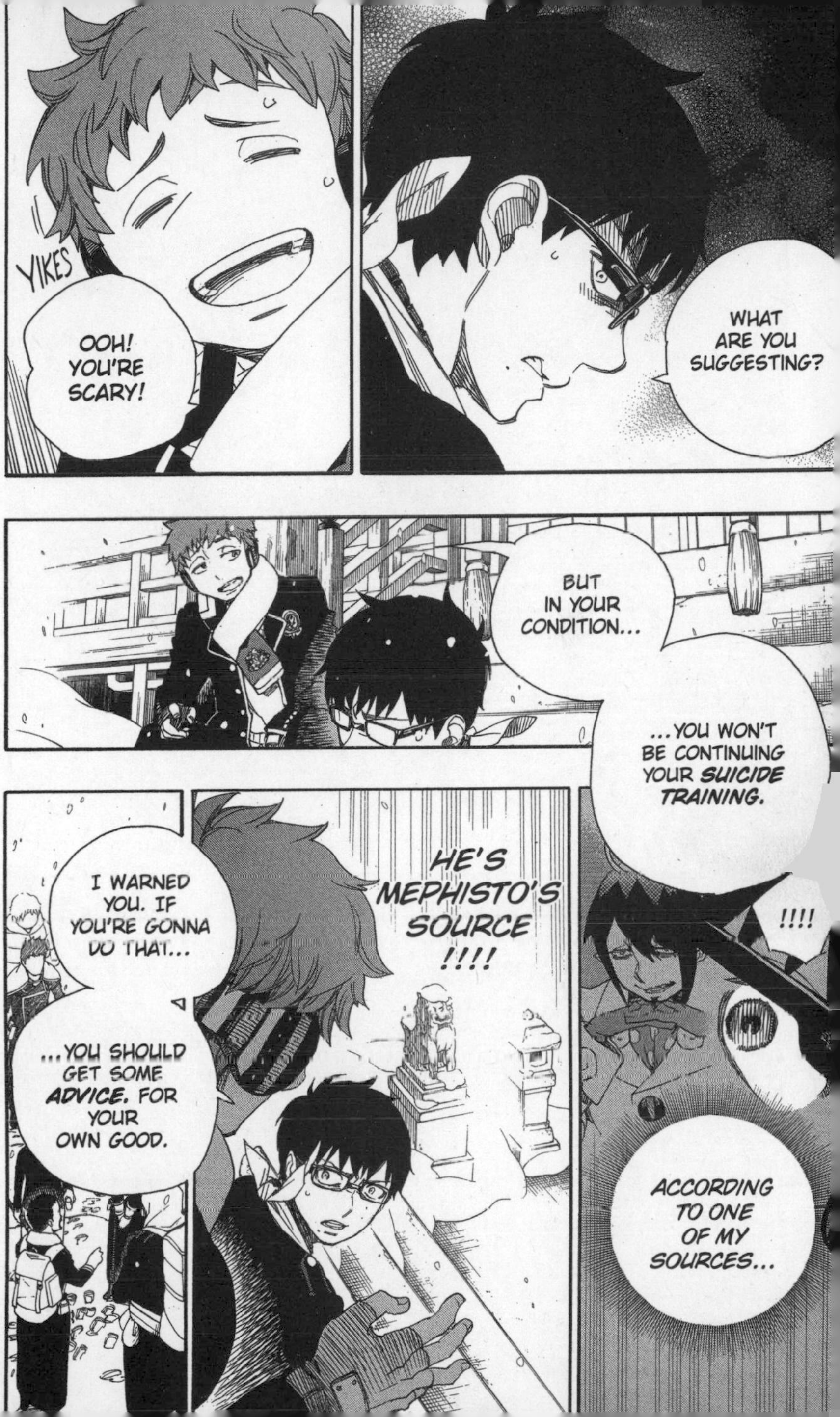
WHAT ARE YOU SUGGESTING?
YIKES
OOH! YOU'RE SCARY!
BUT IN YOUR CONDITION...
...YOU WON'T BE CONTINUING YOUR SUICIDE TRAINING.
!!!!
ACCORDING TO ONE OF MY SOURCES...
HE'S MEPHISTO'S SOURCE !!!!
I WARNED YOU. IF YOU'RE GONNA DO THAT...
...YOU SHOULD GET SOME ADVICE. FOR YOUR OWN GOOD.

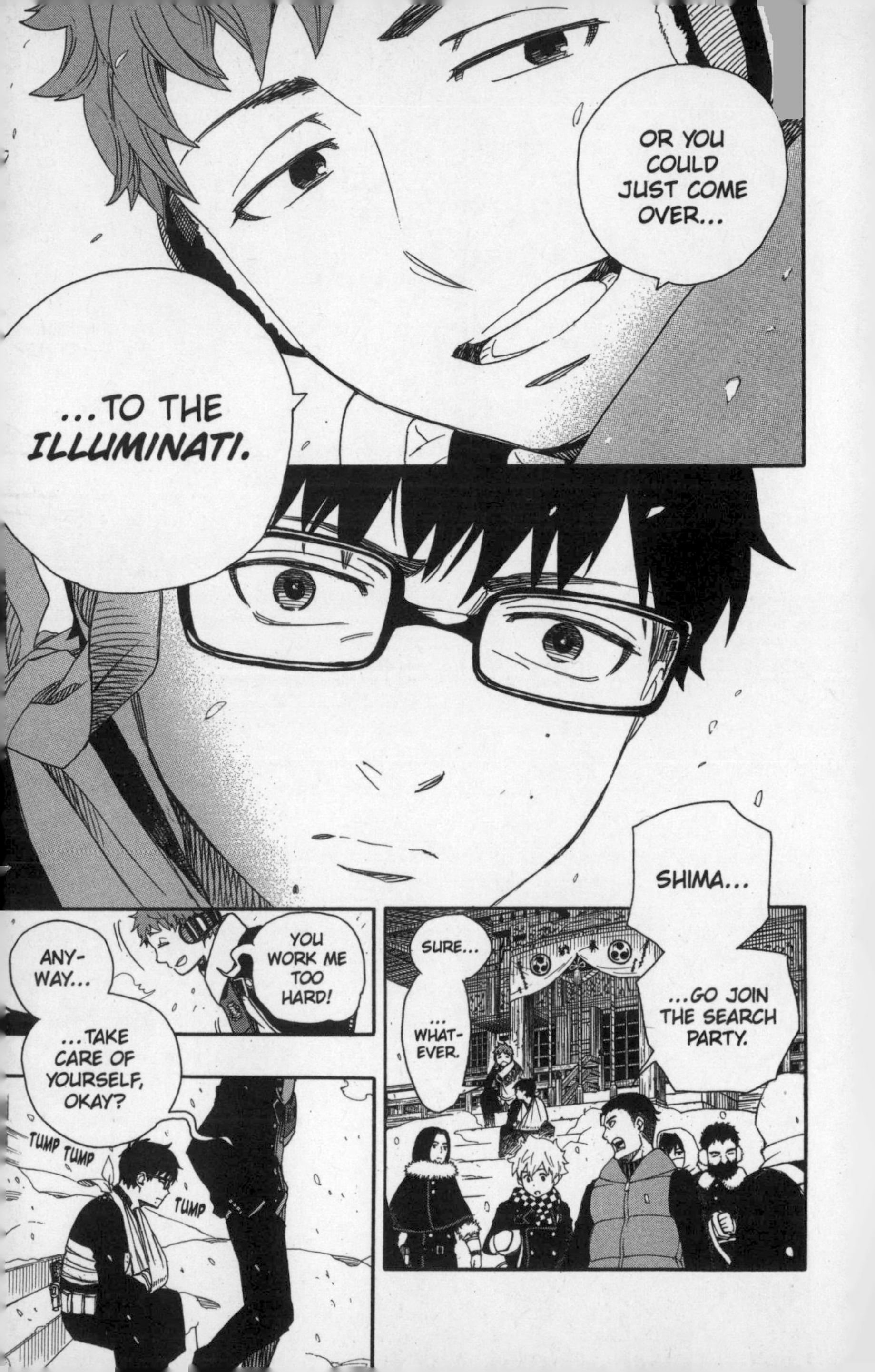
OR YOU COULD JUST COME OVER...
...TO THE *ILLUMINATI.*
SHIMA...
...GO JOIN THE SEARCH PARTY.
SURE...
...WHAT-EVER.
YOU WORK ME TOO HARD!
ANY-WAY...
...TAKE CARE OF YOURSELF, OKAY?
TUMP TUMP
TUMP

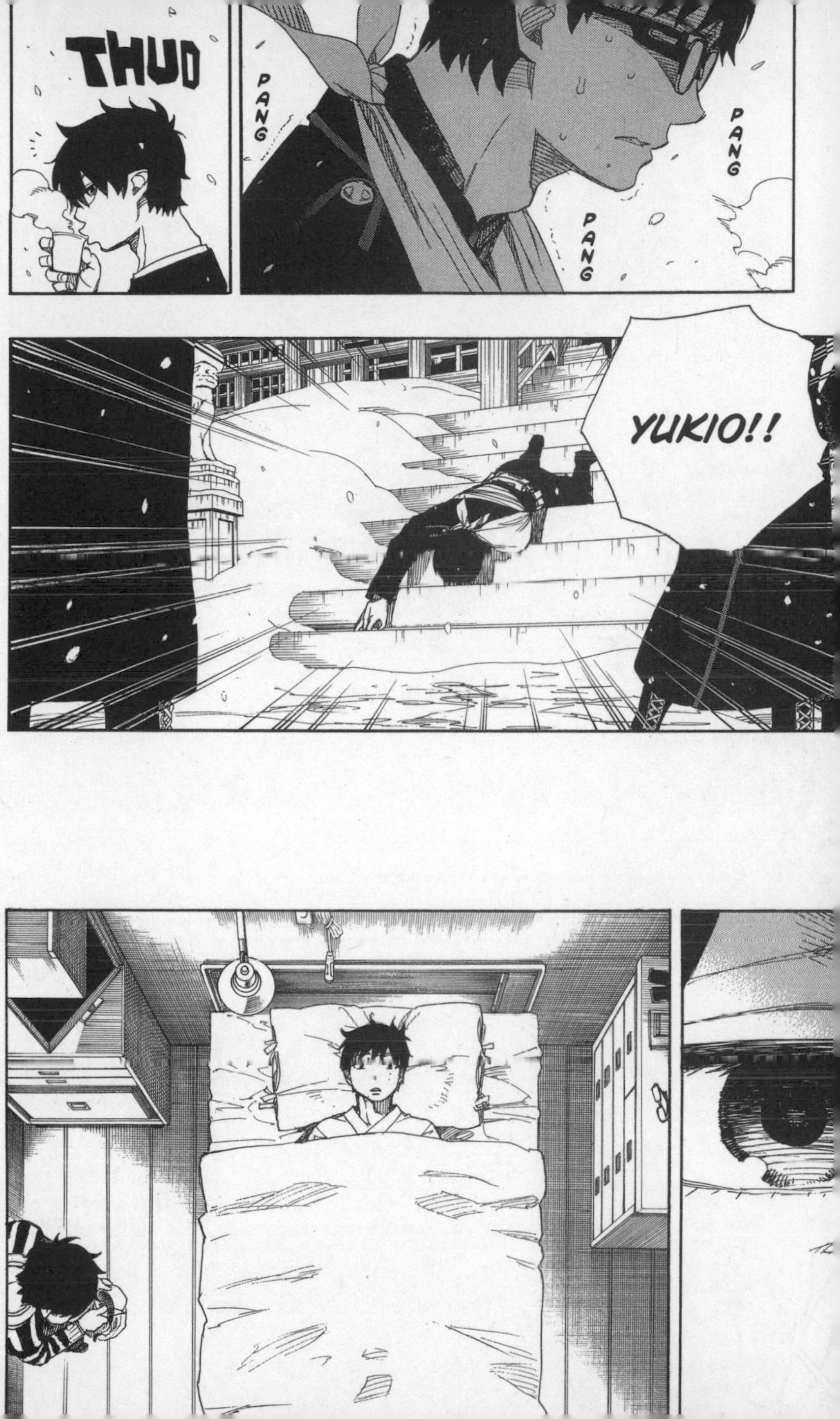
PANG
PANG
PANG
THUD
YUKIO!!

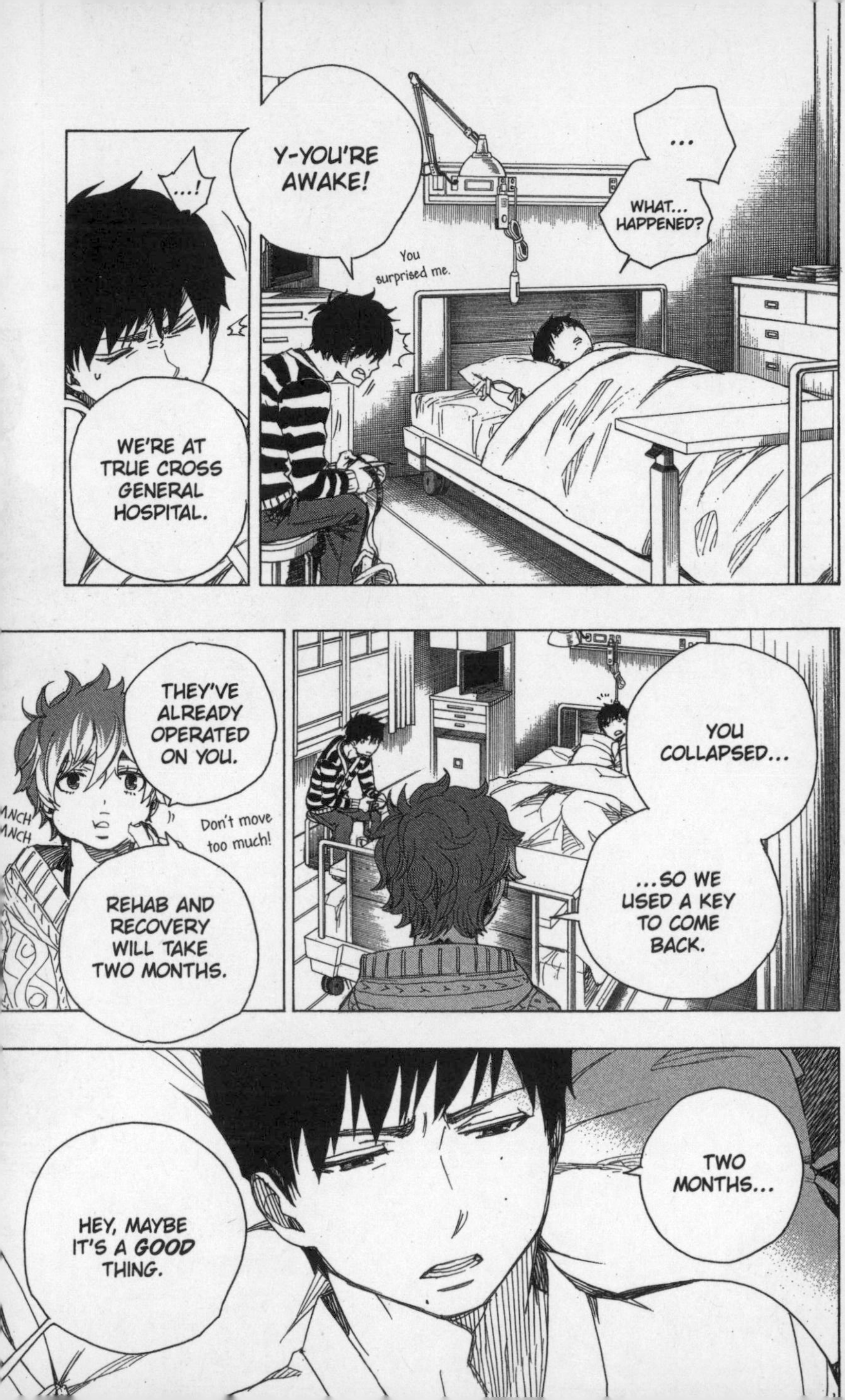
...
WHAT... HAPPENED?
Y-YOU'RE AWAKE!
You surprised me.
...!
WE'RE AT TRUE CROSS GENERAL HOSPITAL.
YOU COLLAPSED...
...SO WE USED A KEY TO COME BACK.
THEY'VE ALREADY OPERATED ON YOU.
Don't move too much!
REHAB AND RECOVERY WILL TAKE TWO MONTHS.
TWO MONTHS...
HEY, MAYBE IT'S A *GOOD* THING.

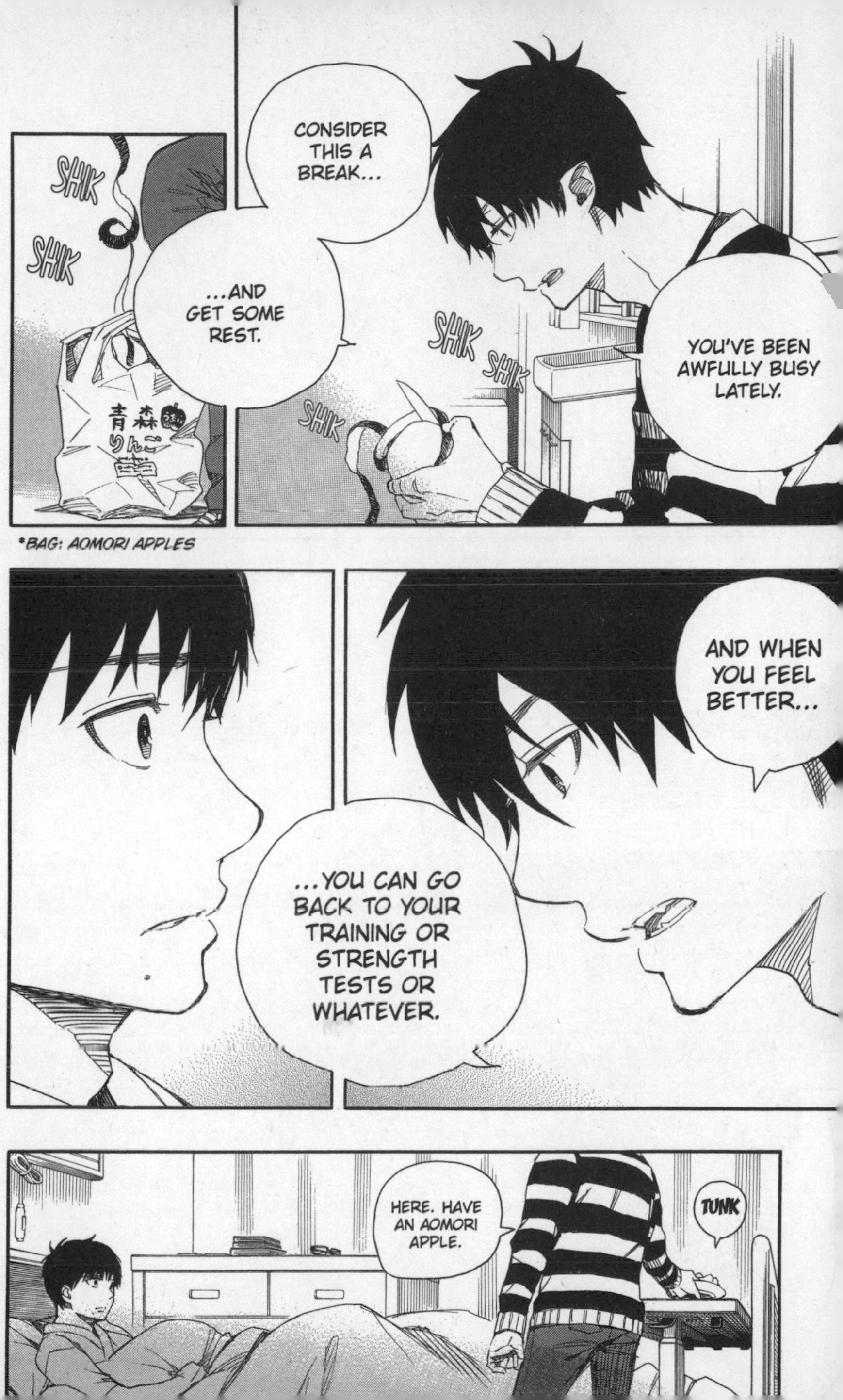
YOU'VE BEEN AWFULLY BUSY LATELY.
CONSIDER THIS A BREAK...
...AND GET SOME REST.
SHIK
SHIK
SHIK
SHIK
SHIK
青森りんご
*BAG: AOMORI APPLES
AND WHEN YOU FEEL BETTER...
...YOU CAN GO BACK TO YOUR TRAINING OR STRENGTH TESTS OR WHATEVER.
TUNK
HERE. HAVE AN AOMORI APPLE.

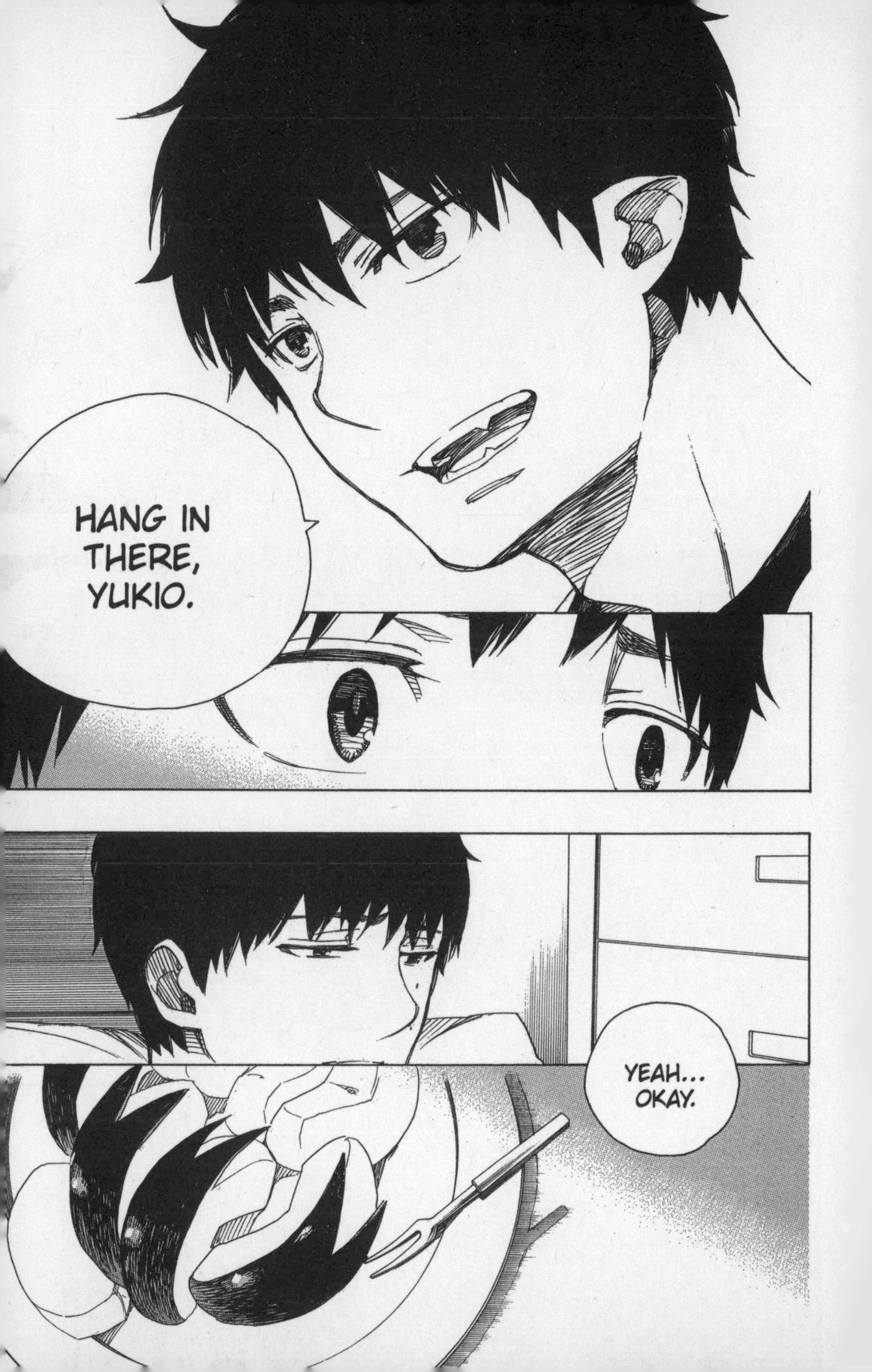
HANG IN THERE, YUKIO.
YEAH... OKAY.

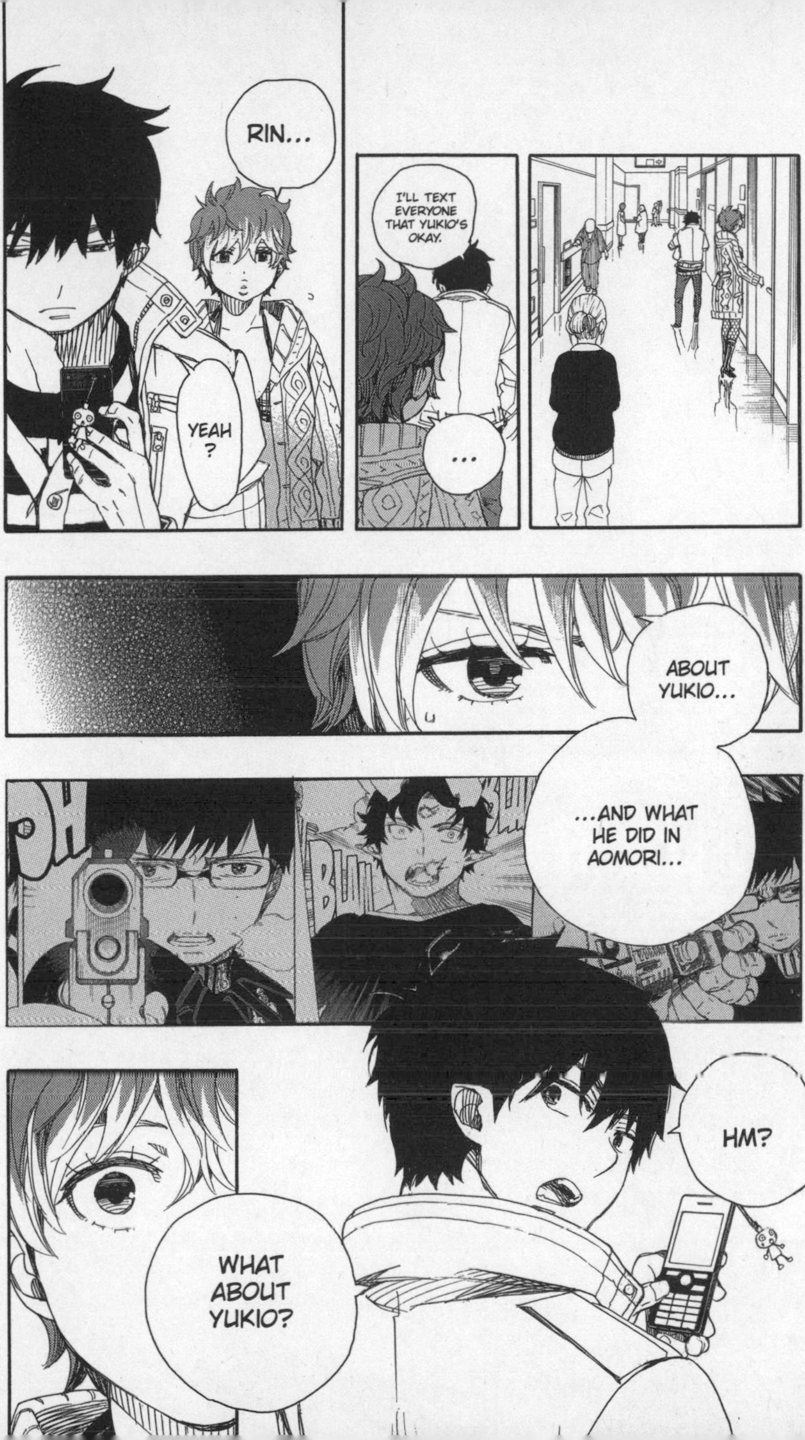
I'LL TEXT EVERYONE THAT YUKIO'S OKAY.
...
RIN...
YEAH?
ABOUT YUKIO...
...AND WHAT HE DID IN AOMORI...
HM?
WHAT ABOUT YUKIO?

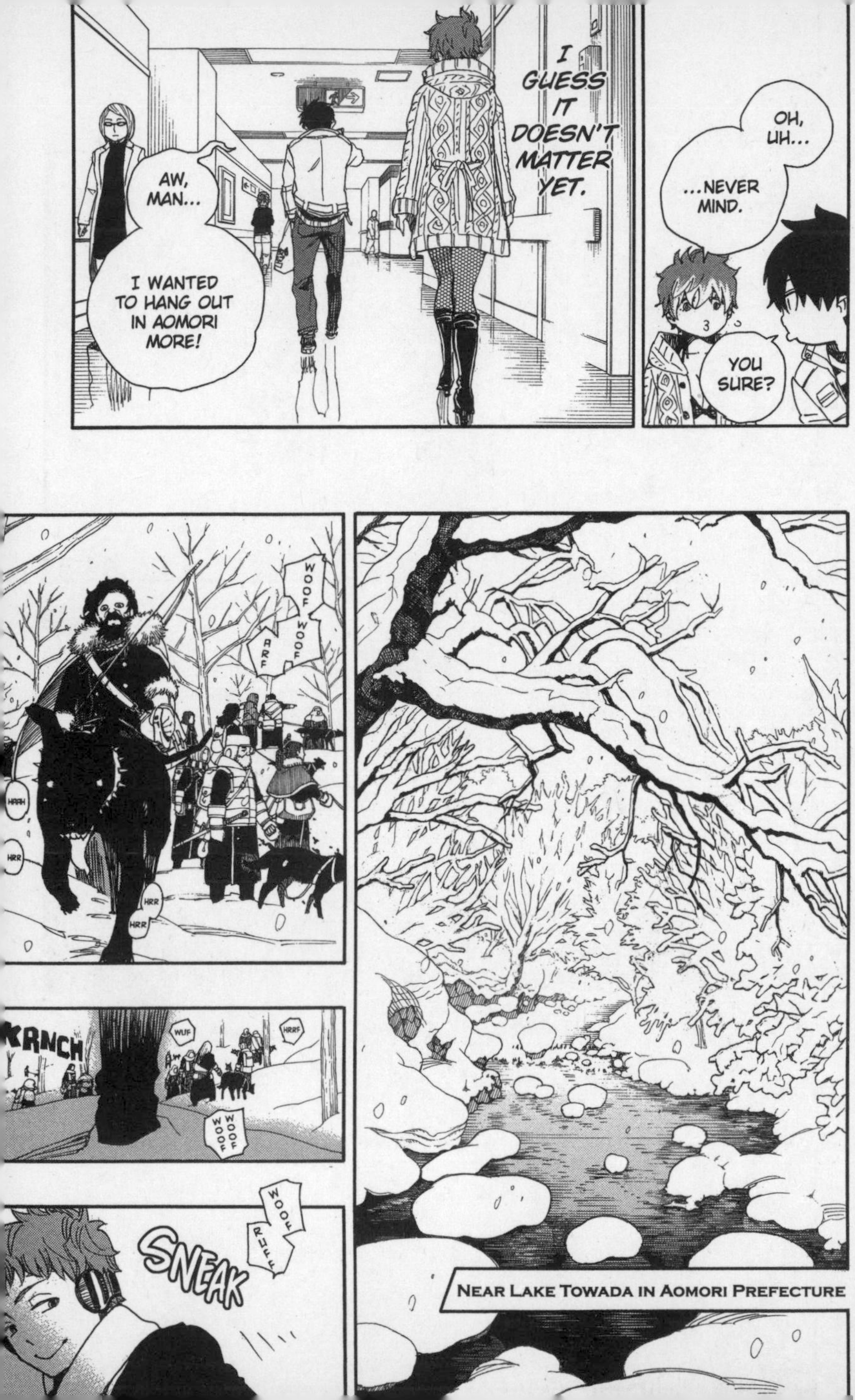
OH, UH...
...NEVER MIND.
YOU SURE?
I GUESS IT DOESN'T MATTER YET.
AW, MAN...
I WANTED TO HANG OUT IN AOMORI MORE!
NEAR LAKE TOWADA IN AOMORI PREFECTURE
WOOF WOOF
ARF
HRAH
HRR
HRR
HRR
WUF
HRRF
KRNCH
WOOF WOOF
WOOF WOOF
WOOF
RUFF
SNEAK

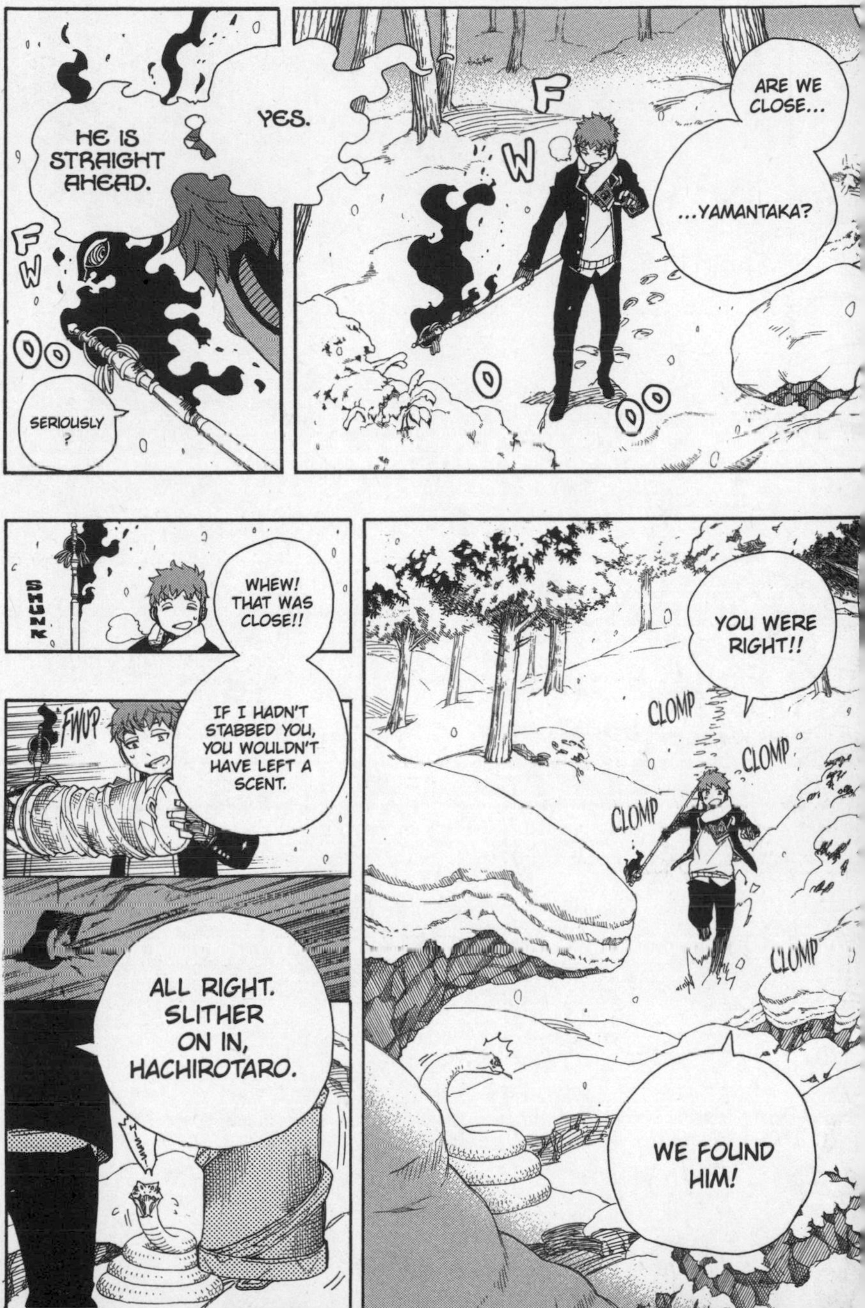
FWOOO
ARE WE CLOSE...
...YAMANTAKA?
YES.
HE IS STRAIGHT AHEAD.
FWOO
SERIOUSLY?
YOU WERE RIGHT!!
CLOMP
CLOMP
CLOMP
CLOMP
WE FOUND HIM!
SHUNK
WHEW! THAT WAS CLOSE!!
FWUP
IF I HADN'T STABBED YOU, YOU WOULDN'T HAVE LEFT A SCENT.
ALL RIGHT. SLITHER ON IN, HACHIROTARO.

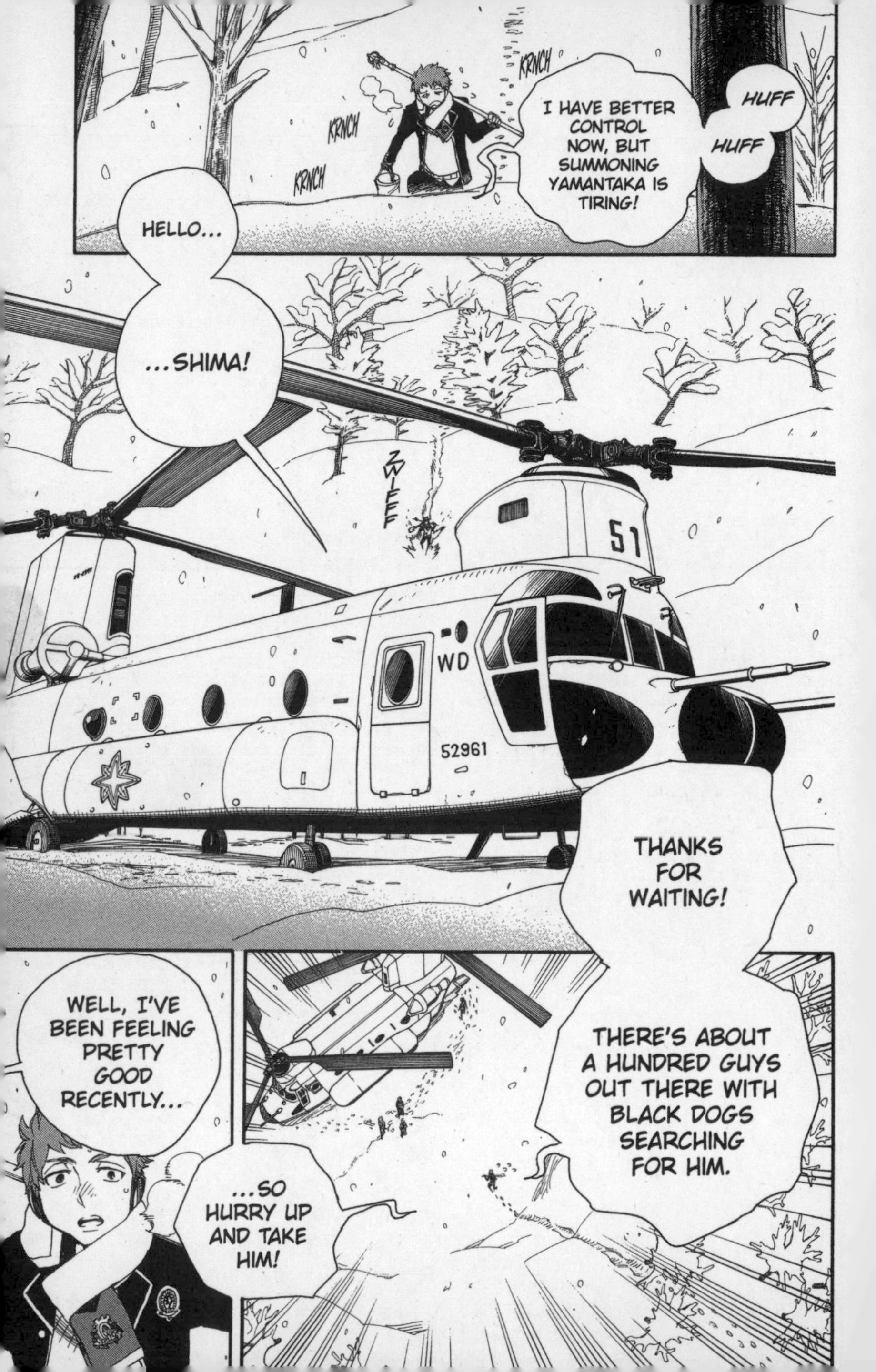
HUFF
HUFF
I HAVE BETTER CONTROL NOW, BUT SUMMONING YAMANTAKA IS TIRING!
KRNCH
KRNCH
KRNCH
HELLO...
...SHIMA!
ZWIFF
51
WD
52961
THANKS FOR WAITING!
THERE'S ABOUT A HUNDRED GUYS OUT THERE WITH BLACK DOGS SEARCHING FOR HIM.
WELL, I'VE BEEN FEELING PRETTY GOOD RECENTLY...
...SO HURRY UP AND TAKE HIM!

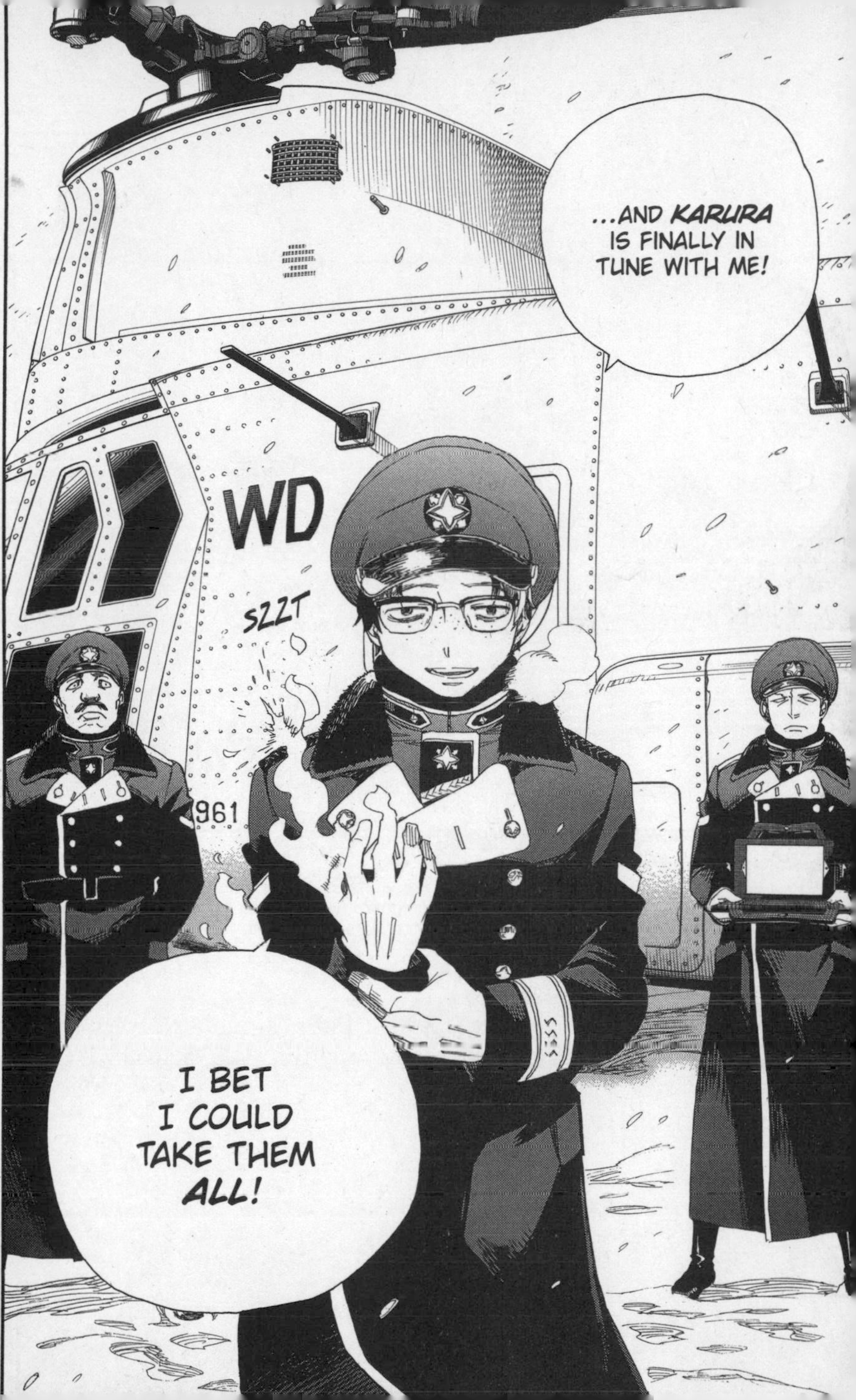
...AND KARURA IS FINALLY IN TUNE WITH ME!
SZZT
I BET I COULD TAKE THEM ALL!

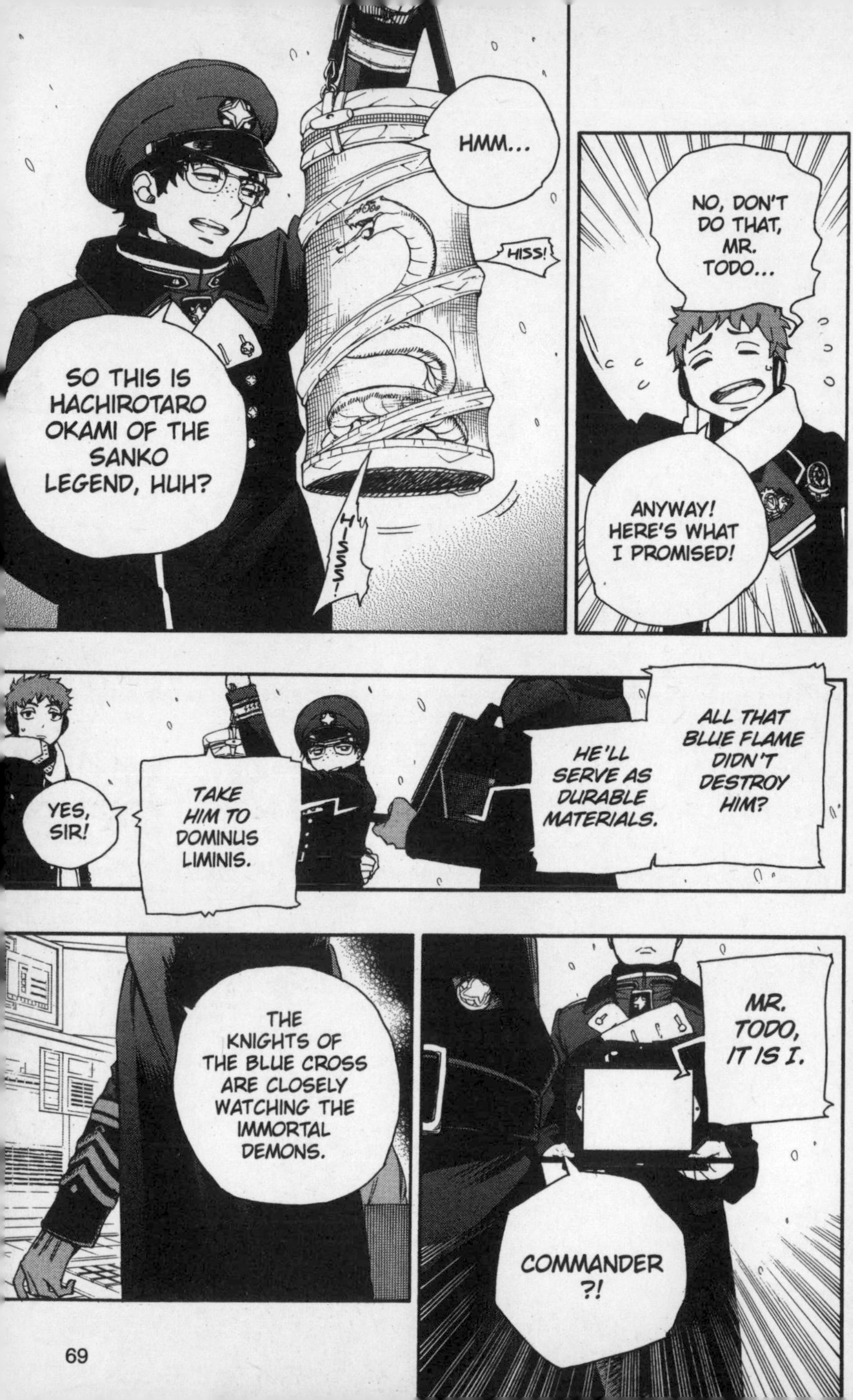
NO, DON'T DO THAT, MR. TODO...
ANYWAY! HERE'S WHAT I PROMISED!
HMM...
HISS!
SO THIS IS HACHIROTARO OKAMI OF THE SANKO LEGEND, HUH?
HISSS!
ALL THAT BLUE FLAME DIDN'T DESTROY HIM?
HE'LL SERVE AS DURABLE MATERIALS.
TAKE HIM TO DOMINUS LIMINIS.
YES, SIR!
MR. TODO, IT IS I.
COMMANDER?!
THE KNIGHTS OF THE BLUE CROSS ARE CLOSELY WATCHING THE IMMORTAL DEMONS.

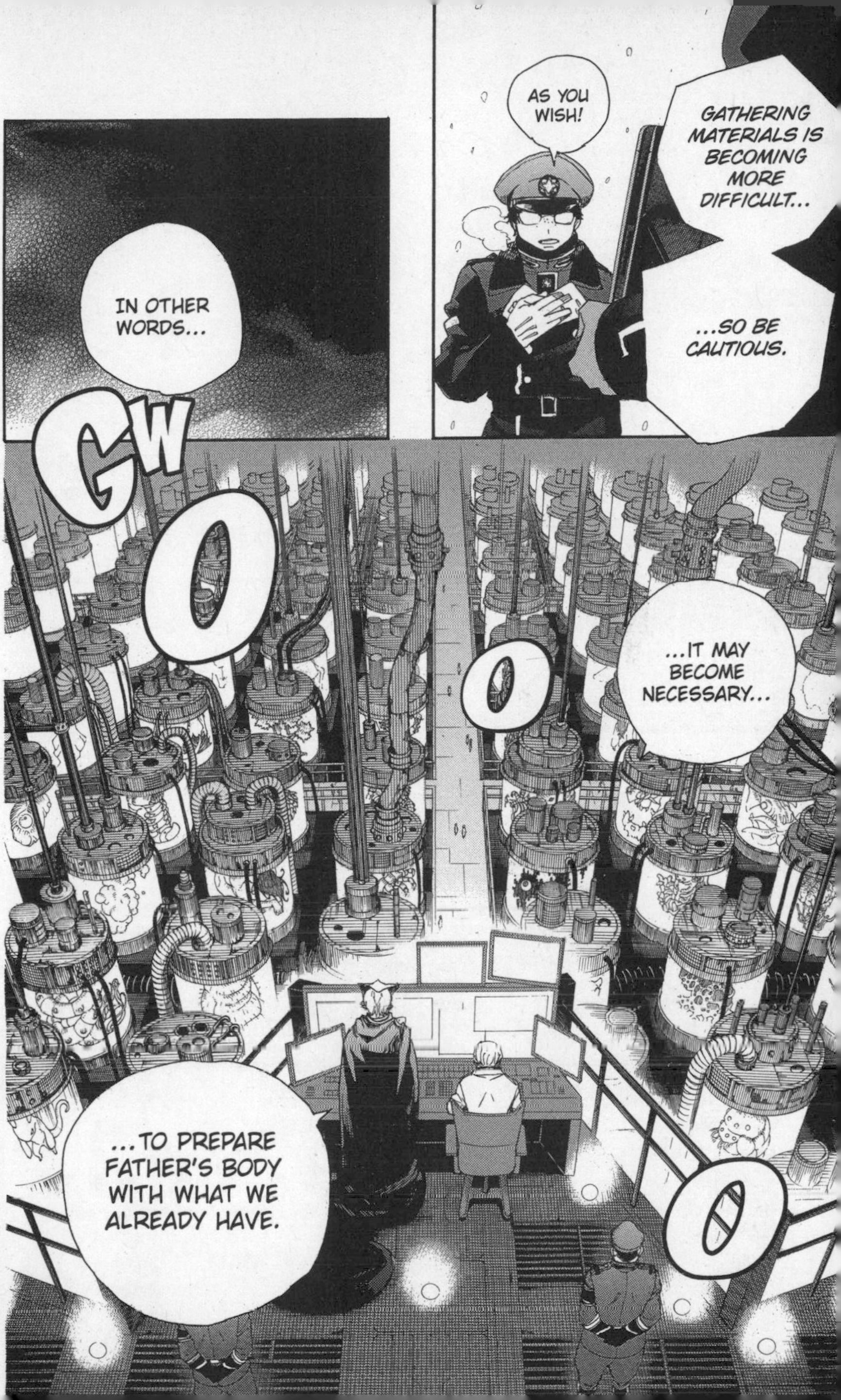
GATHERING MATERIALS IS BECOMING MORE DIFFICULT...
...SO BE CAUTIOUS.
AS YOU WISH!
IN OTHER WORDS...
GWOOO
...IT MAY BECOME NECESSARY...
...TO PREPARE FATHER'S BODY WITH WHAT WE ALREADY HAVE.

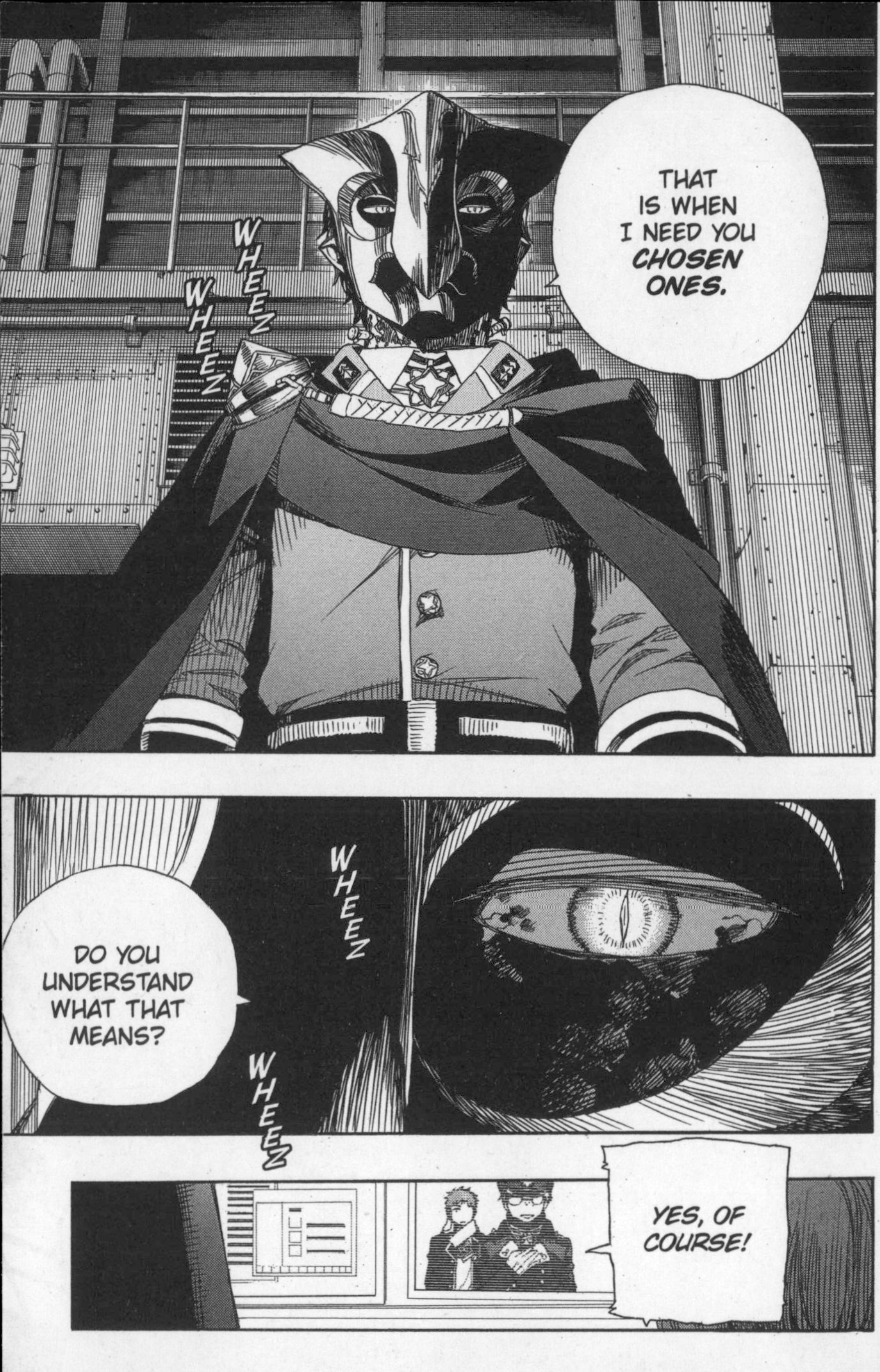
THAT IS WHEN I NEED YOU CHOSEN ONES.
WHEEZ
WHEEZ
WHEEZ
DO YOU UNDERSTAND WHAT THAT MEANS?
WHEEZ
YES, OF COURSE!

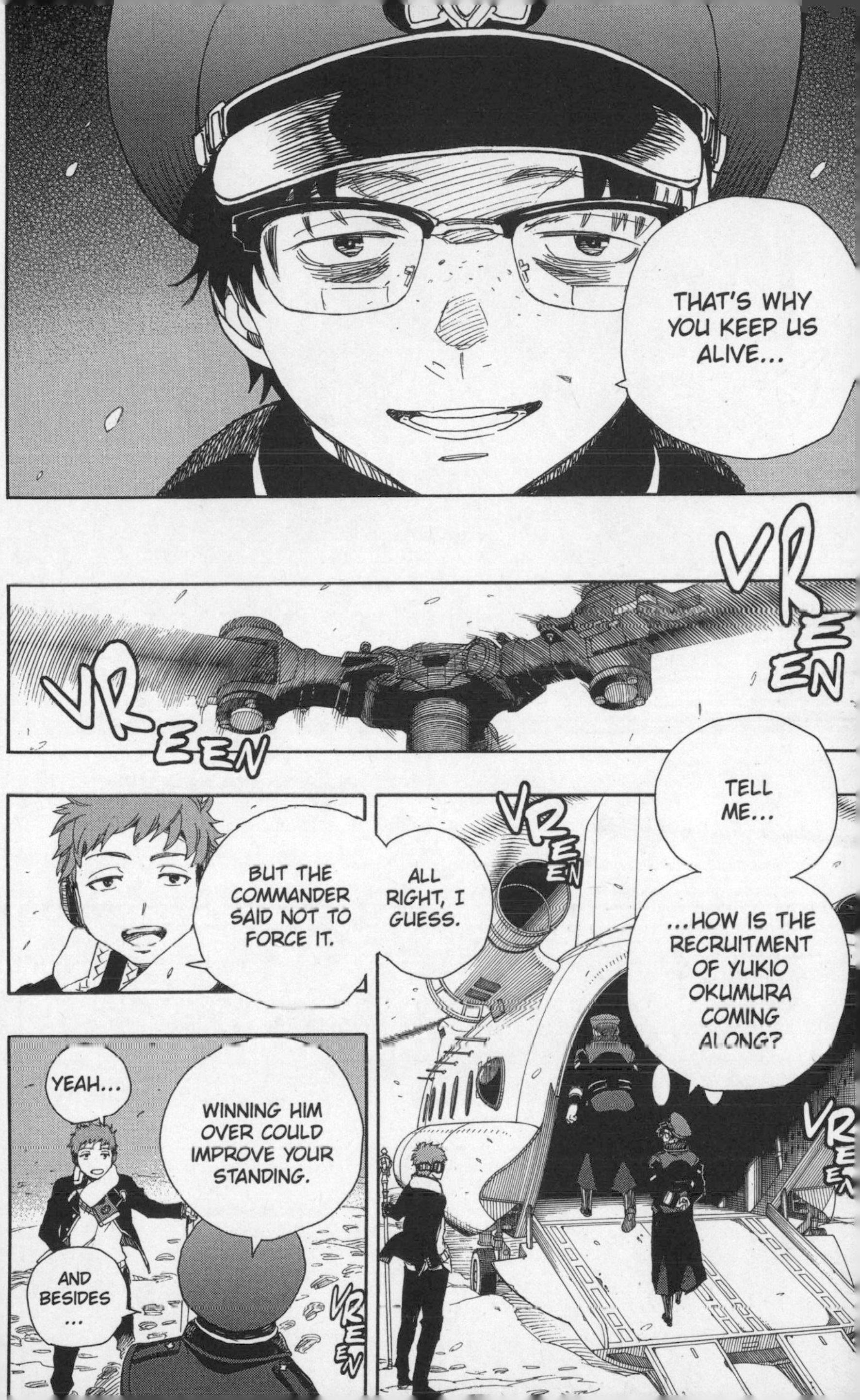
THAT'S WHY YOU KEEP US ALIVE...
VREEN
VREEEN
VREEN
TELL ME...
...HOW IS THE RECRUITMENT OF YUKIO OKUMURA COMING ALONG?
VREEN
ALL RIGHT, I GUESS.
BUT THE COMMANDER SAID NOT TO FORCE IT.
WINNING HIM OVER COULD IMPROVE YOUR STANDING.
YEAH...
AND BESIDES...
VREEN

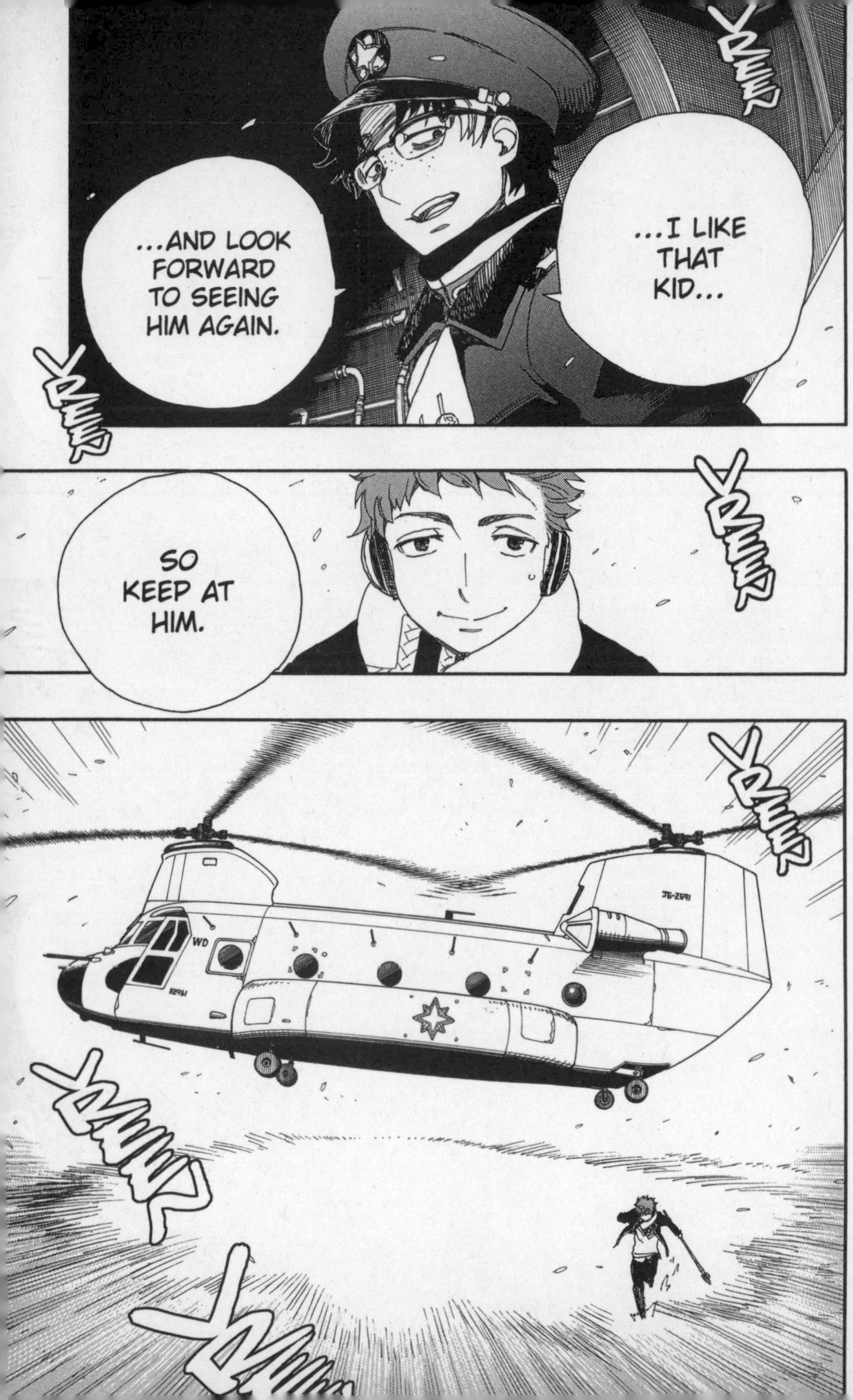
...I LIKE THAT KID...
...AND LOOK FORWARD TO SEEING HIM AGAIN.
SO KEEP AT HIM.

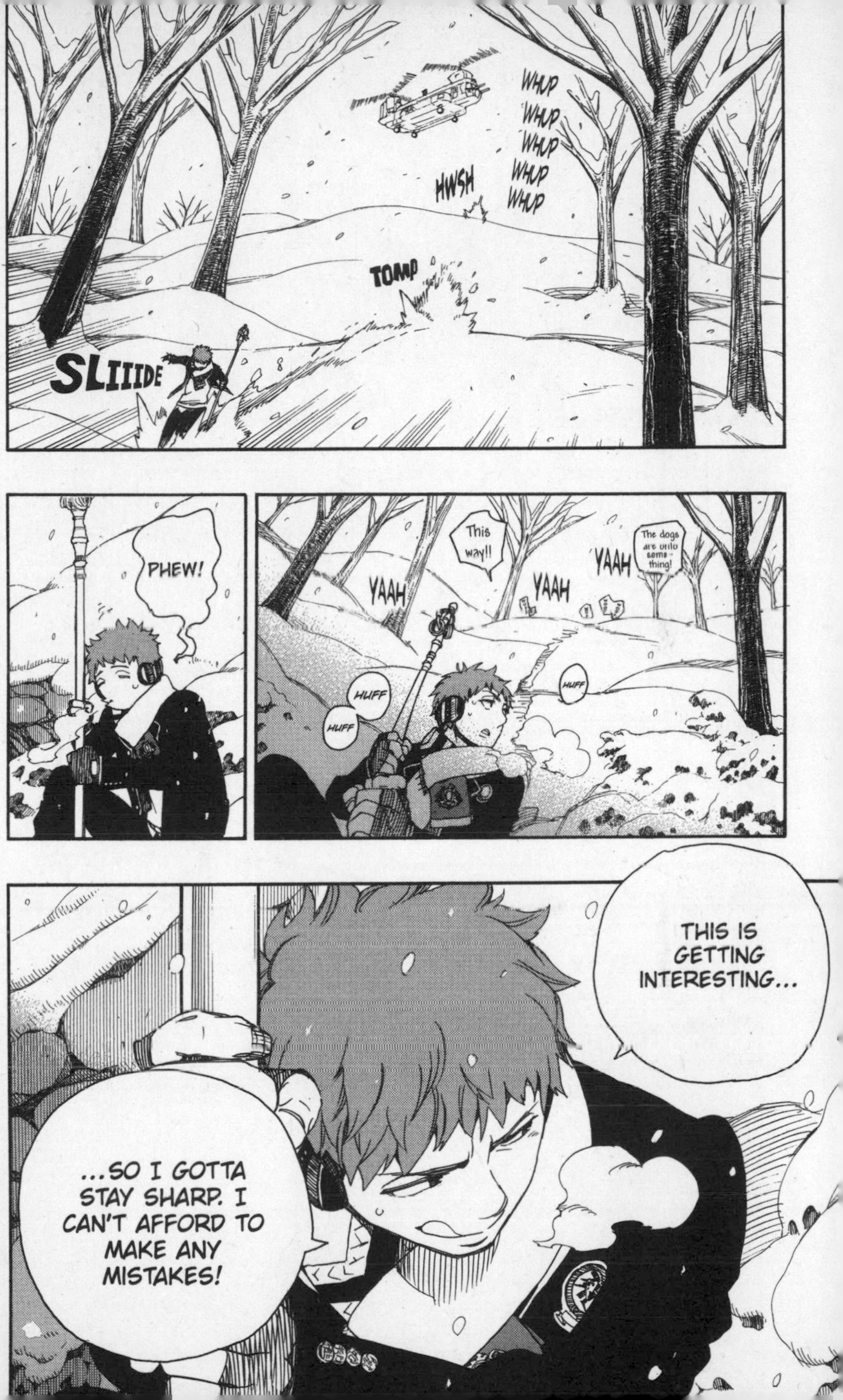
WHUP
WHUP
WHUP
WHUP
WHUP
HWSH
TOMP
SLIIIDE
The dogs are onto some-thing!
YAAH
YAAH
This way!!
YAAH
HUFF
HUFF
HUFF
PHEW!
THIS IS GETTING INTERESTING...
...SO I GOTTA STAY SHARP. I CAN'T AFFORD TO MAKE ANY MISTAKES!

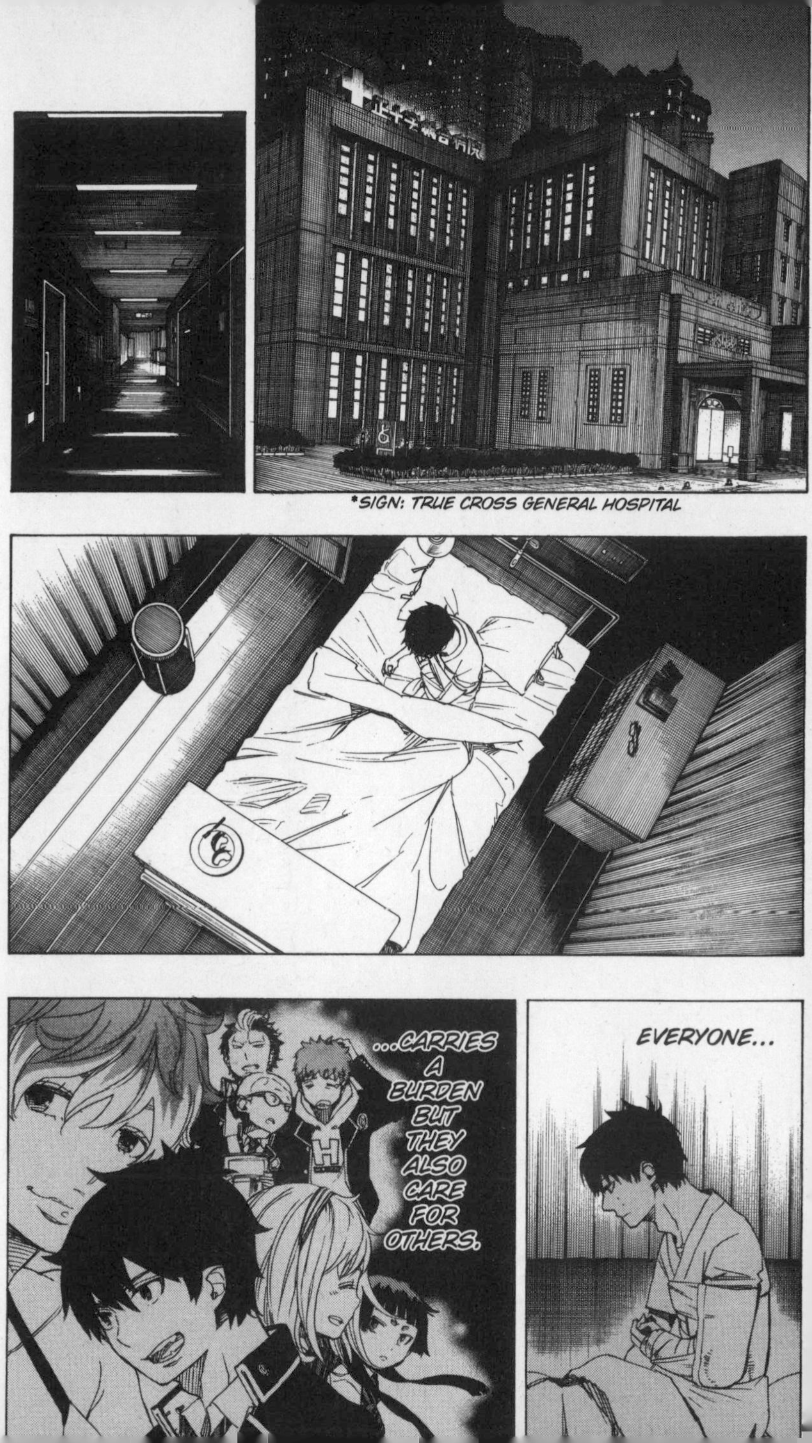
*SIGN: TRUE CROSS GENERAL HOSPITAL
EVERYONE...
...CARRIES A BURDEN BUT THEY ALSO CARE FOR OTHERS.

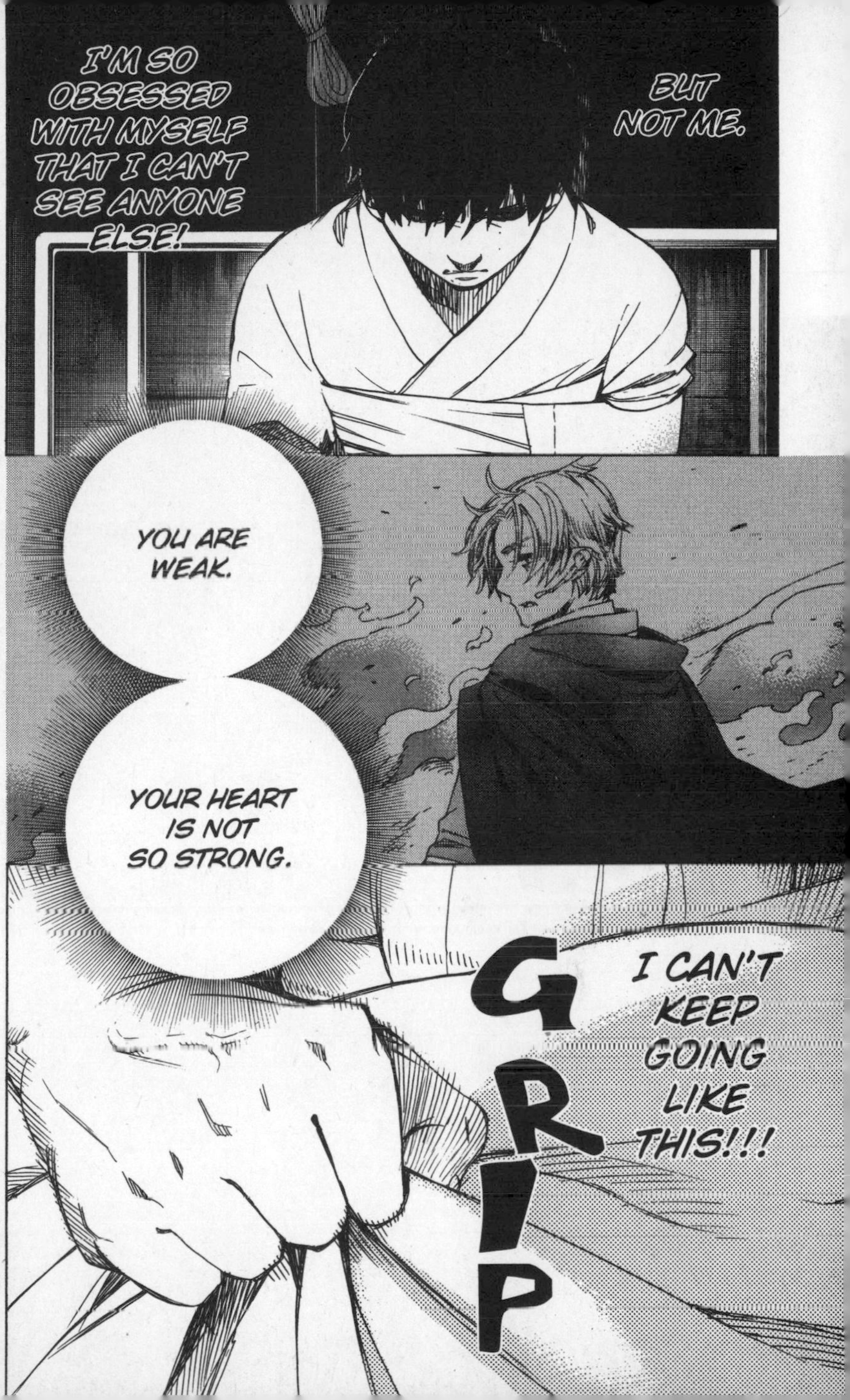
BUT NOT ME.
I'M SO OBSESSED WITH MYSELF THAT I CAN'T SEE ANYONE ELSE!
YOU ARE WEAK.
YOUR HEART IS NOT SO STRONG.
I CAN'T KEEP GOING LIKE THIS!!!
GRIP

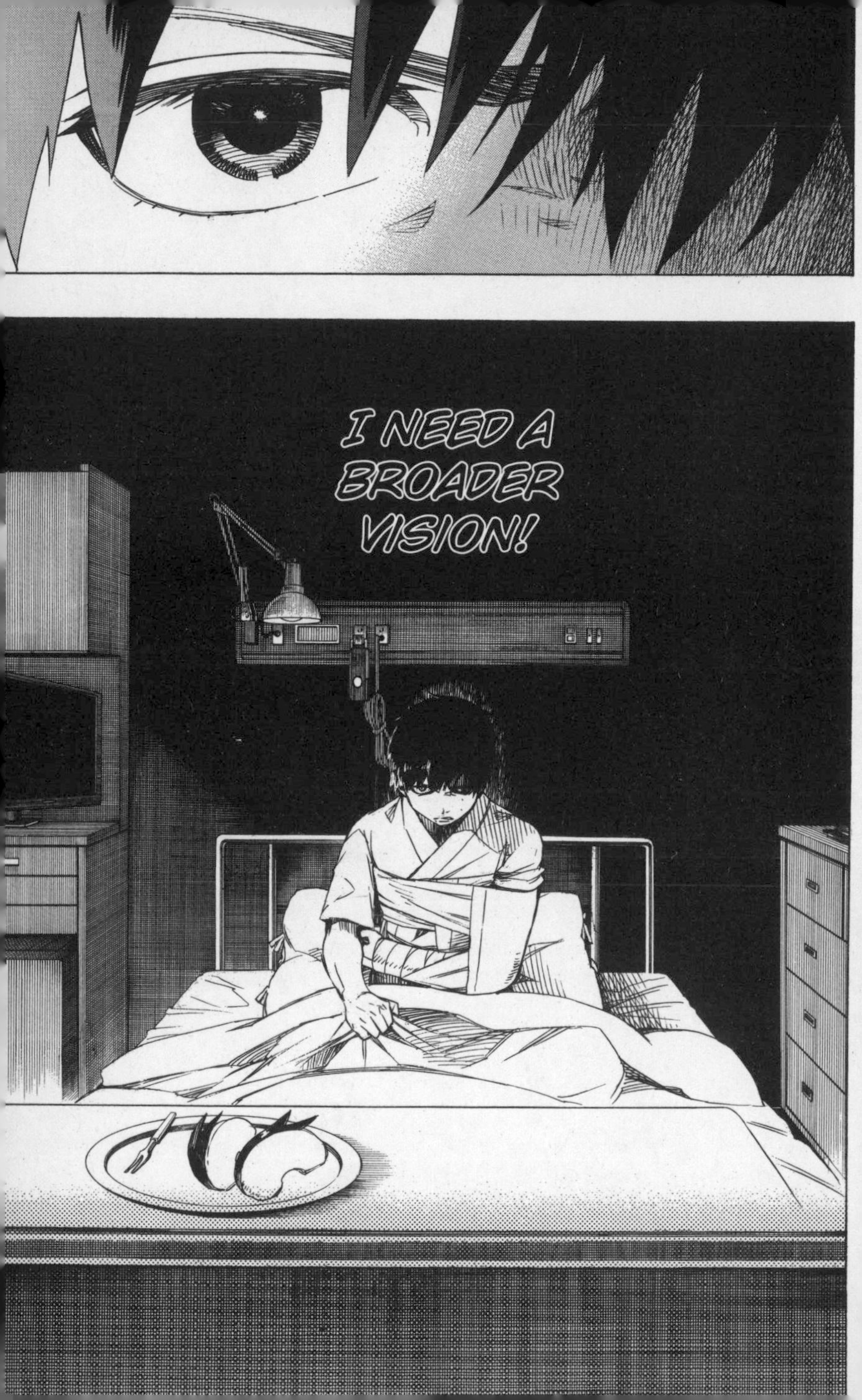
I NEED A BROADER VISION!

BLUE EXORCIST CHAPTER 80: AH, AOMORI WINTER SCENERY

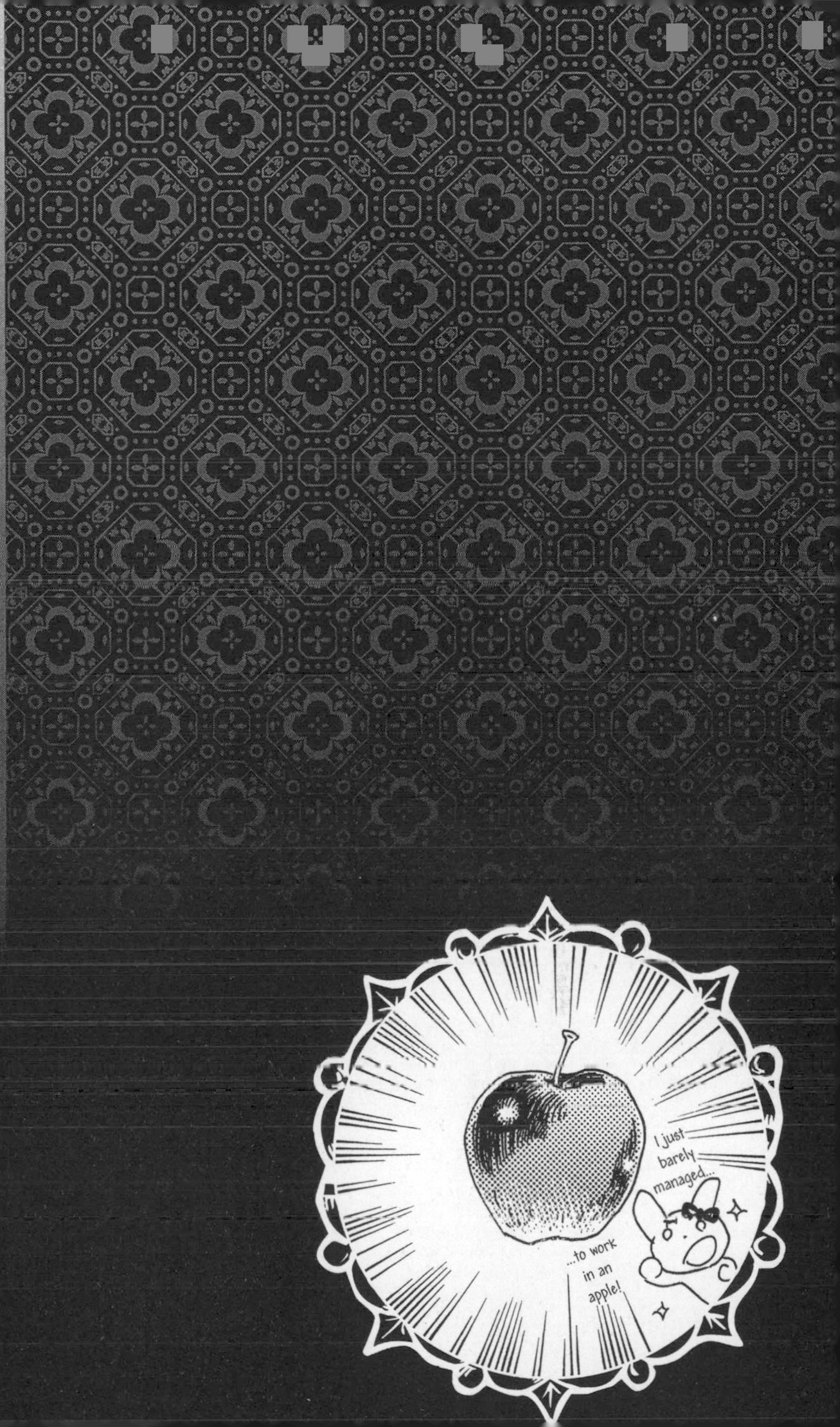

I just barely managed...
...to work in an apple!

Chapter 81: Rhizome

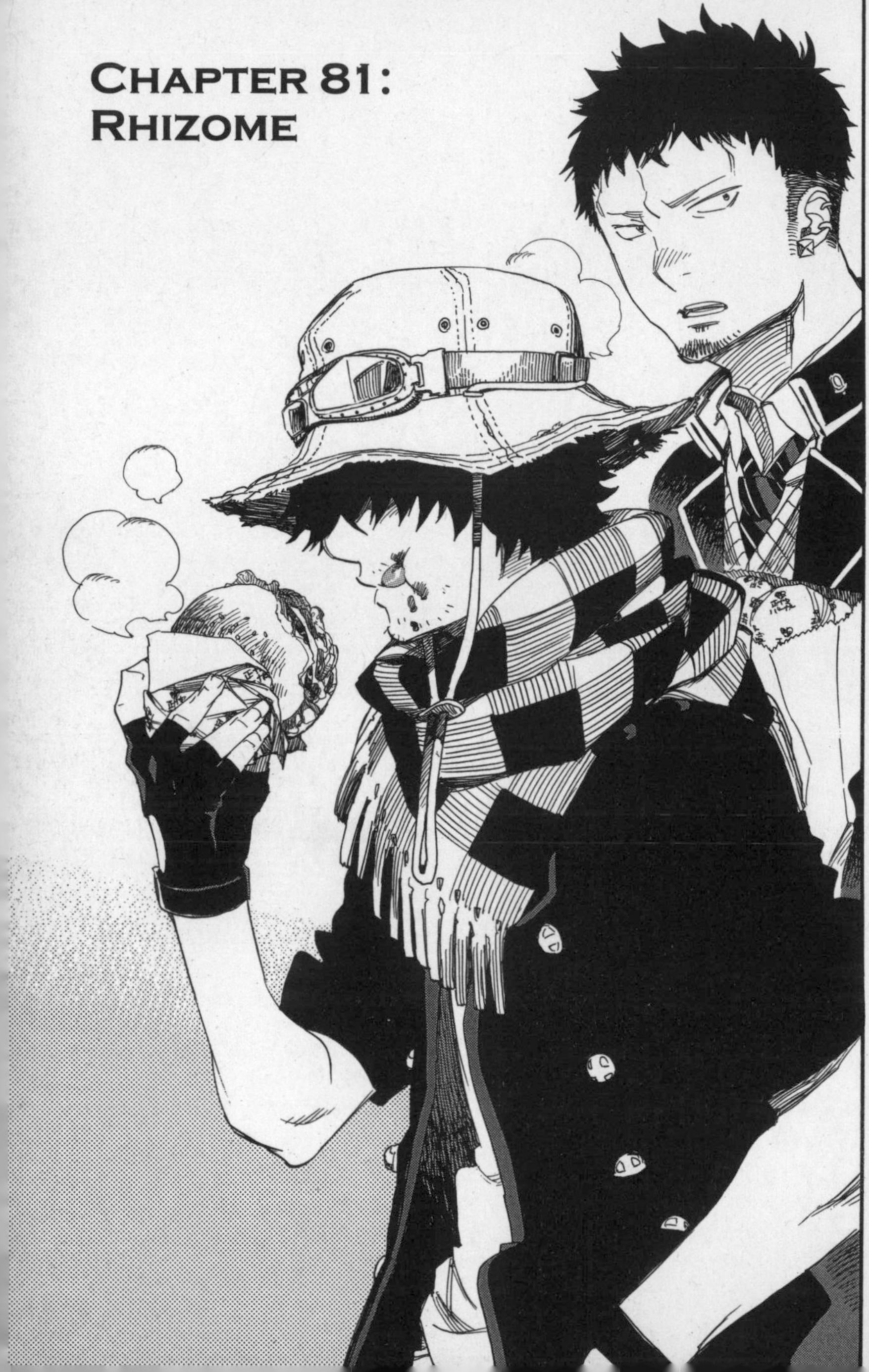

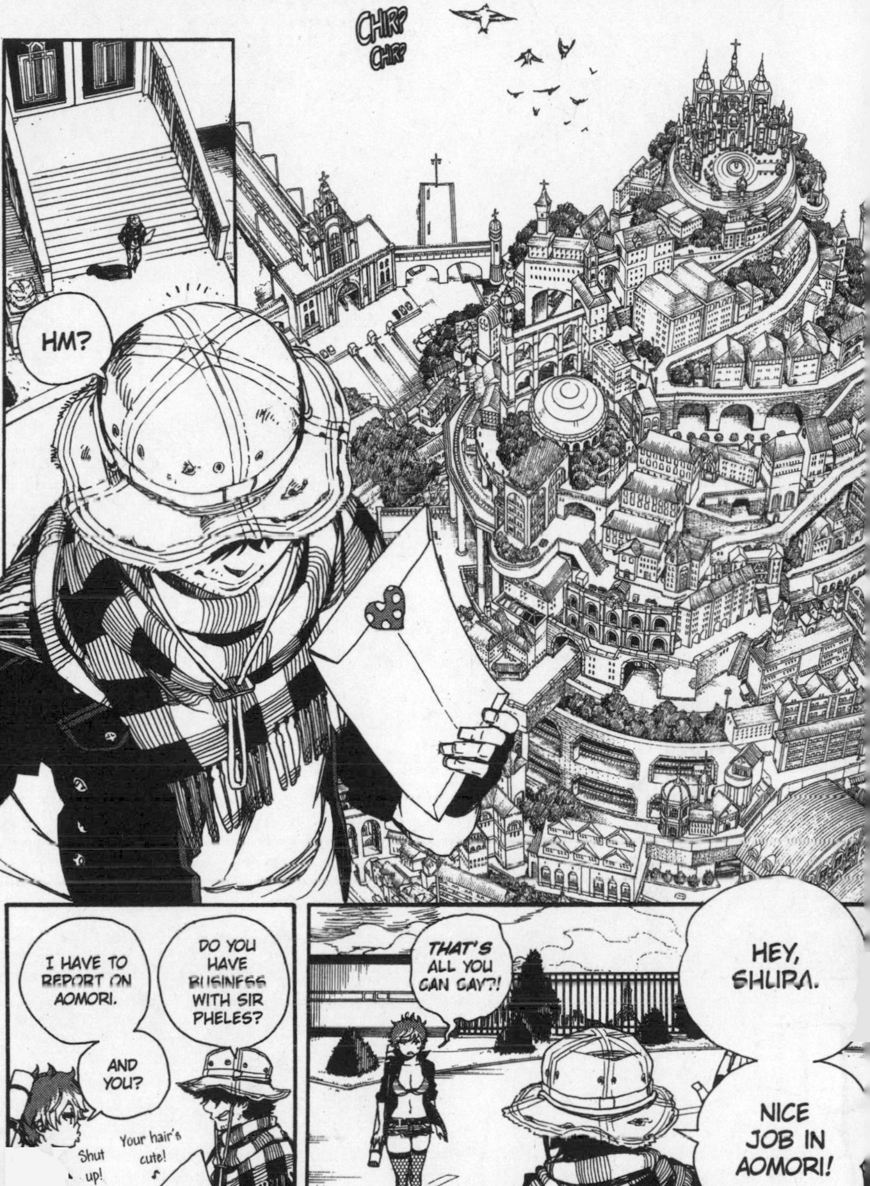
CHIRP CHIRP
HM?
HEY, SHURA.
NICE JOB IN AOMORI!
THAT'S ALL YOU CAN SAY?!
DO YOU HAVE BUSINESS WITH SIR PHELES?
I HAVE TO REPORT ON AOMORI.
AND YOU?
Your hair's cute!
Shut up!

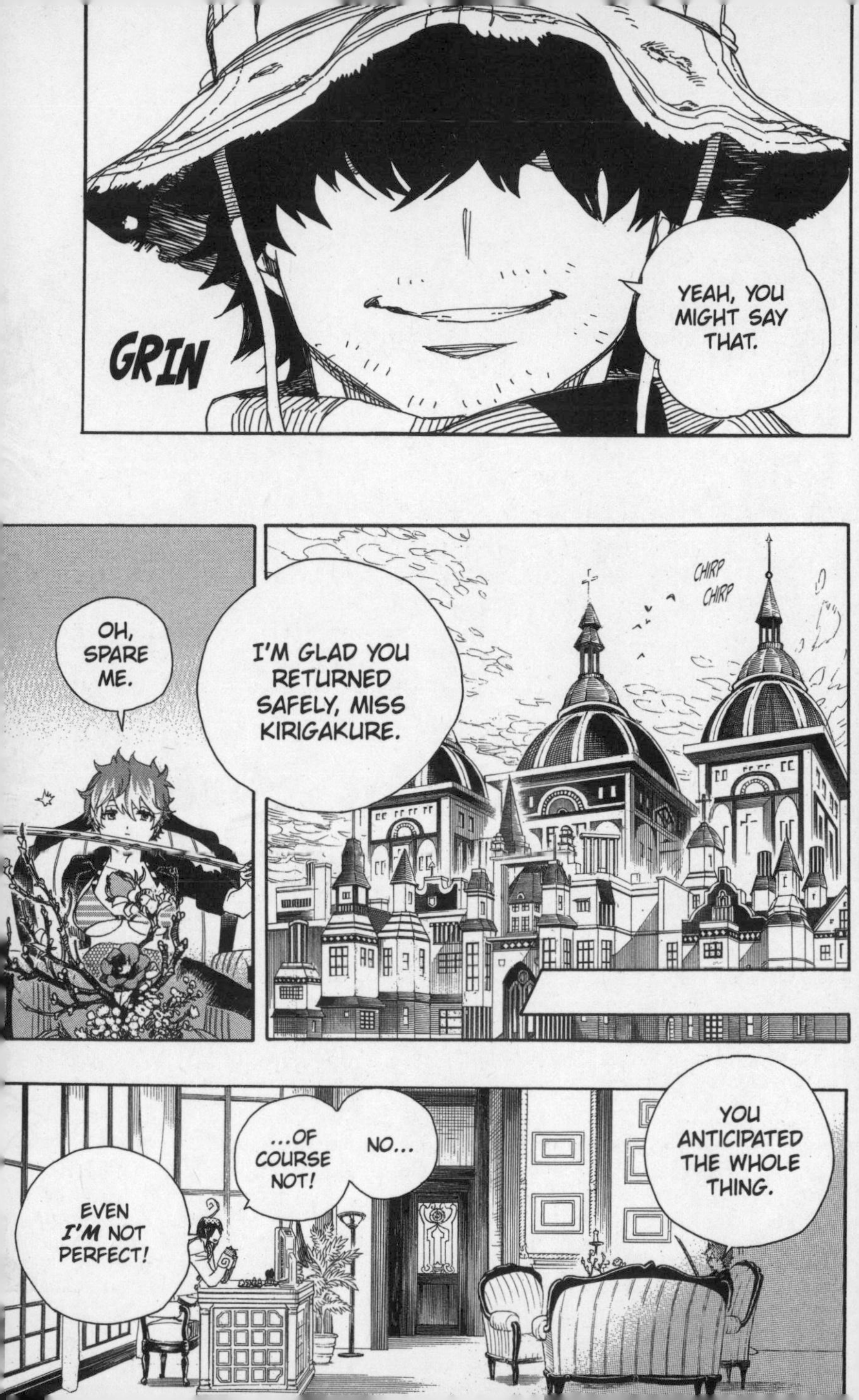
YEAH, YOU MIGHT SAY THAT.
GRIN
CHIRP CHIRP
I'M GLAD YOU RETURNED SAFELY, MISS KIRIGAKURE.
OH, SPARE ME.
YOU ANTICIPATED THE WHOLE THING.
NO...
...OF COURSE NOT!
EVEN *I'M* NOT PERFECT!

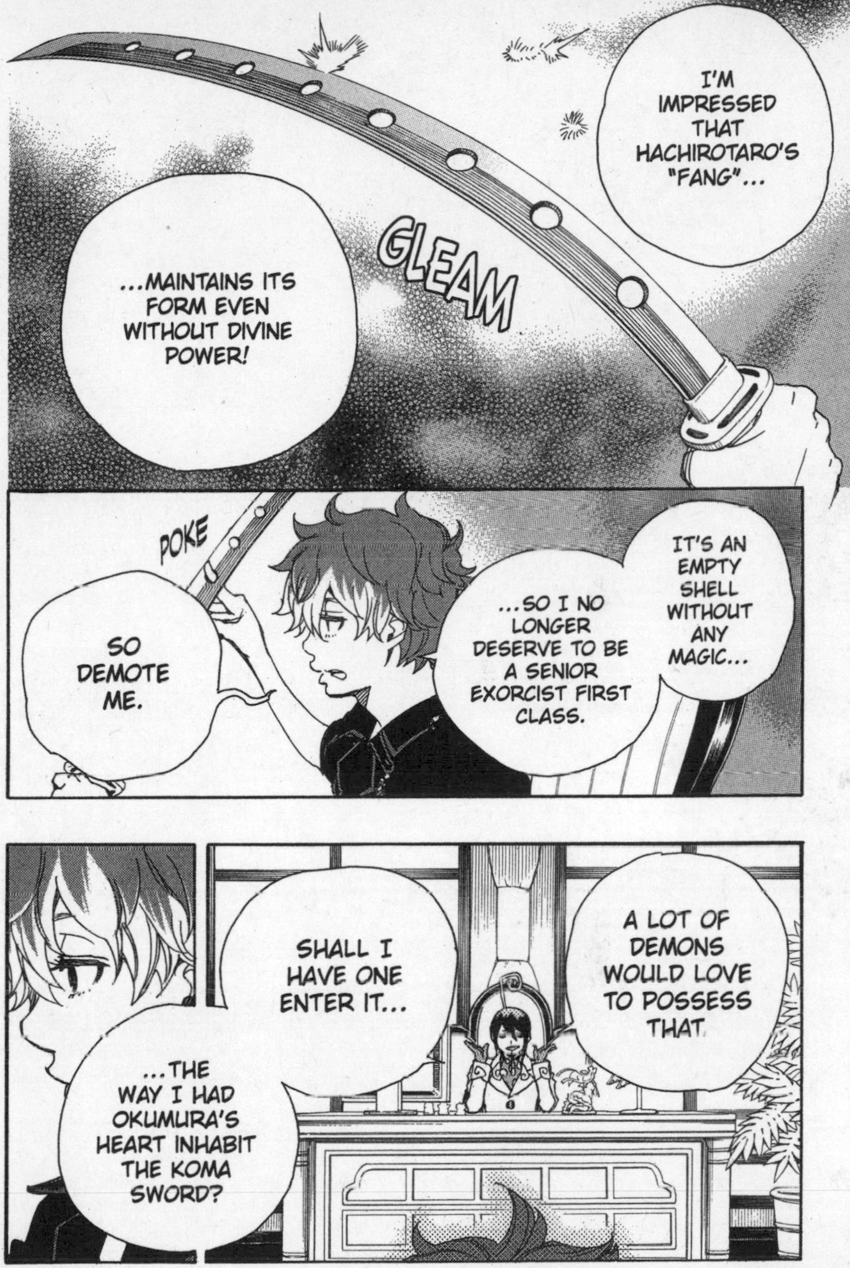
I'M IMPRESSED THAT HACHIROTARO'S "FANG"...
GLEAM
...MAINTAINS ITS FORM EVEN WITHOUT DIVINE POWER!
IT'S AN EMPTY SHELL WITHOUT ANY MAGIC...
...SO I NO LONGER DESERVE TO BE A SENIOR EXORCIST FIRST CLASS.
POKE
SO DEMOTE ME.
A LOT OF DEMONS WOULD LOVE TO POSSESS THAT.
SHALL I HAVE ONE ENTER IT...
...THE WAY I HAD OKUMURA'S HEART INHABIT THE KOMA SWORD?

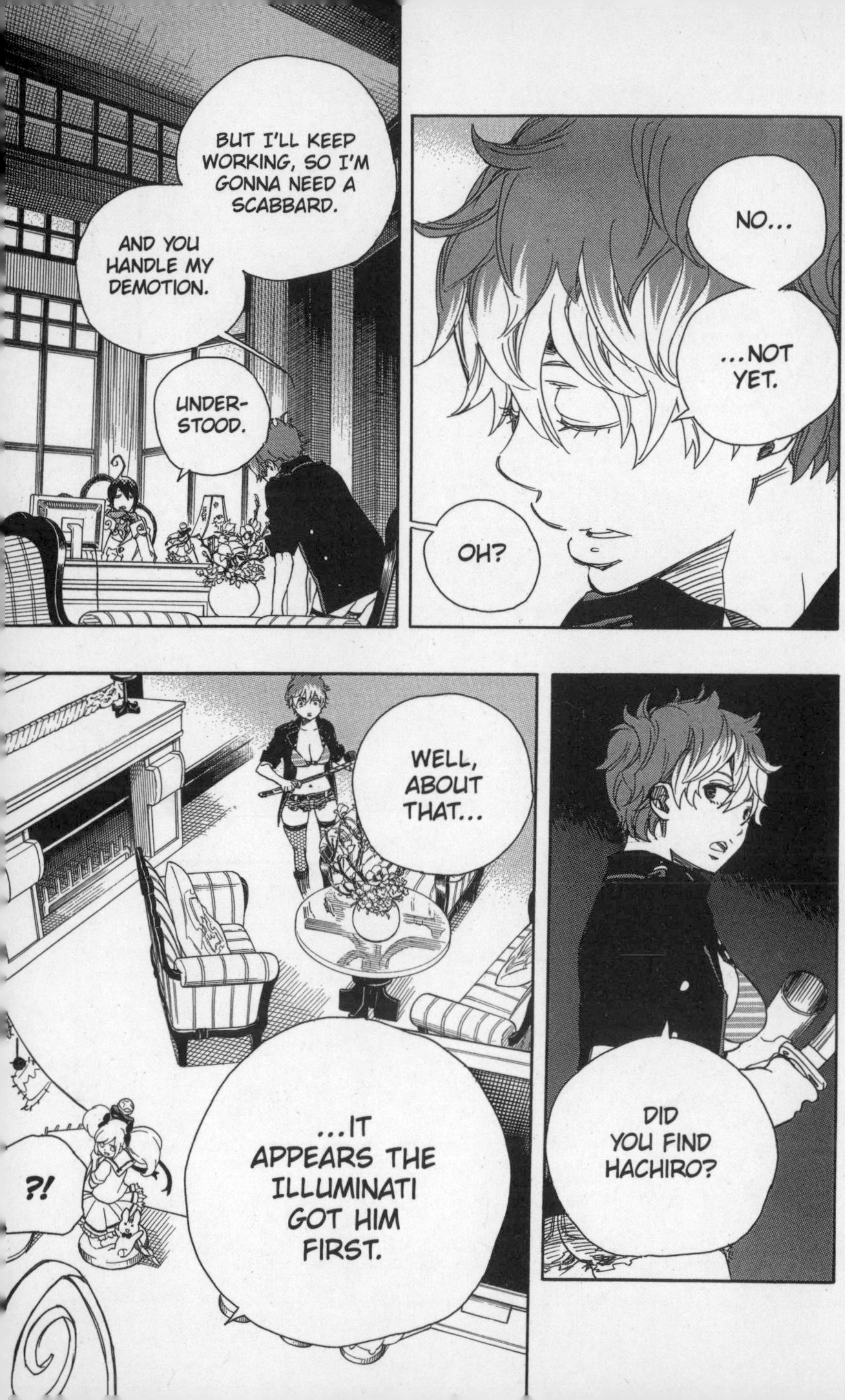
NO...
...NOT YET.
OH?
BUT I'LL KEEP WORKING, SO I'M GONNA NEED A SCABBARD.
AND YOU HANDLE MY DEMOTION.
UNDER-STOOD.
DID YOU FIND HACHIRO?
WELL, ABOUT THAT...
...IT APPEARS THE ILLUMINATI GOT HIM FIRST.
?!

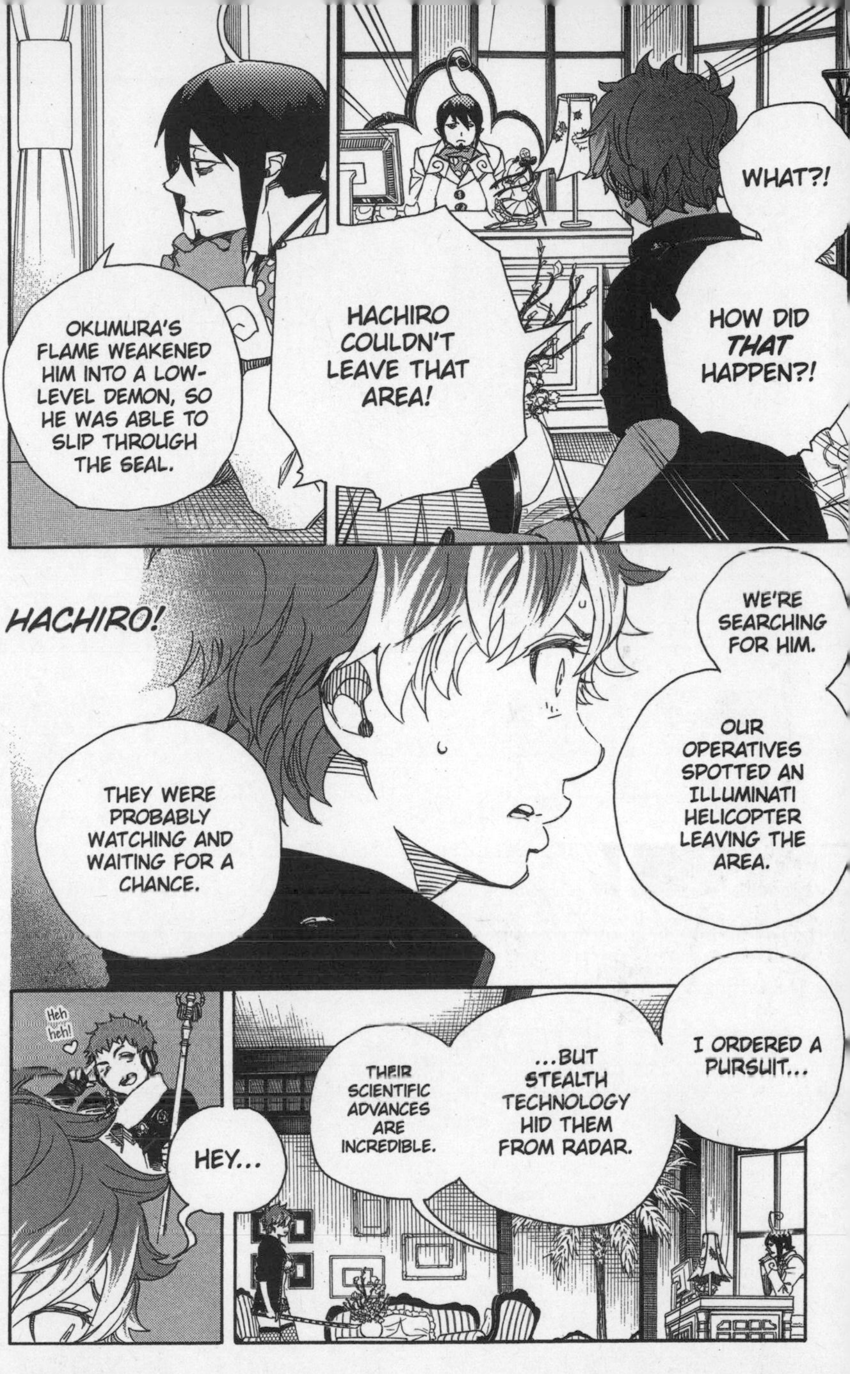

WHAT?!
HOW DID THAT HAPPEN?!
HACHIRO COULDN'T LEAVE THAT AREA!
OKUMURA'S FLAME WEAKENED HIM INTO A LOW-LEVEL DEMON, SO HE WAS ABLE TO SLIP THROUGH THE SEAL.
WE'RE SEARCHING FOR HIM.
OUR OPERATIVES SPOTTED AN ILLUMINATI HELICOPTER LEAVING THE AREA.
HACHIRO!
THEY WERE PROBABLY WATCHING AND WAITING FOR A CHANCE.
I ORDERED A PURSUIT...
...BUT STEALTH TECHNOLOGY HID THEM FROM RADAR.
THEIR SCIENTIFIC ADVANCES ARE INCREDIBLE.
Heh heh!
HEY...

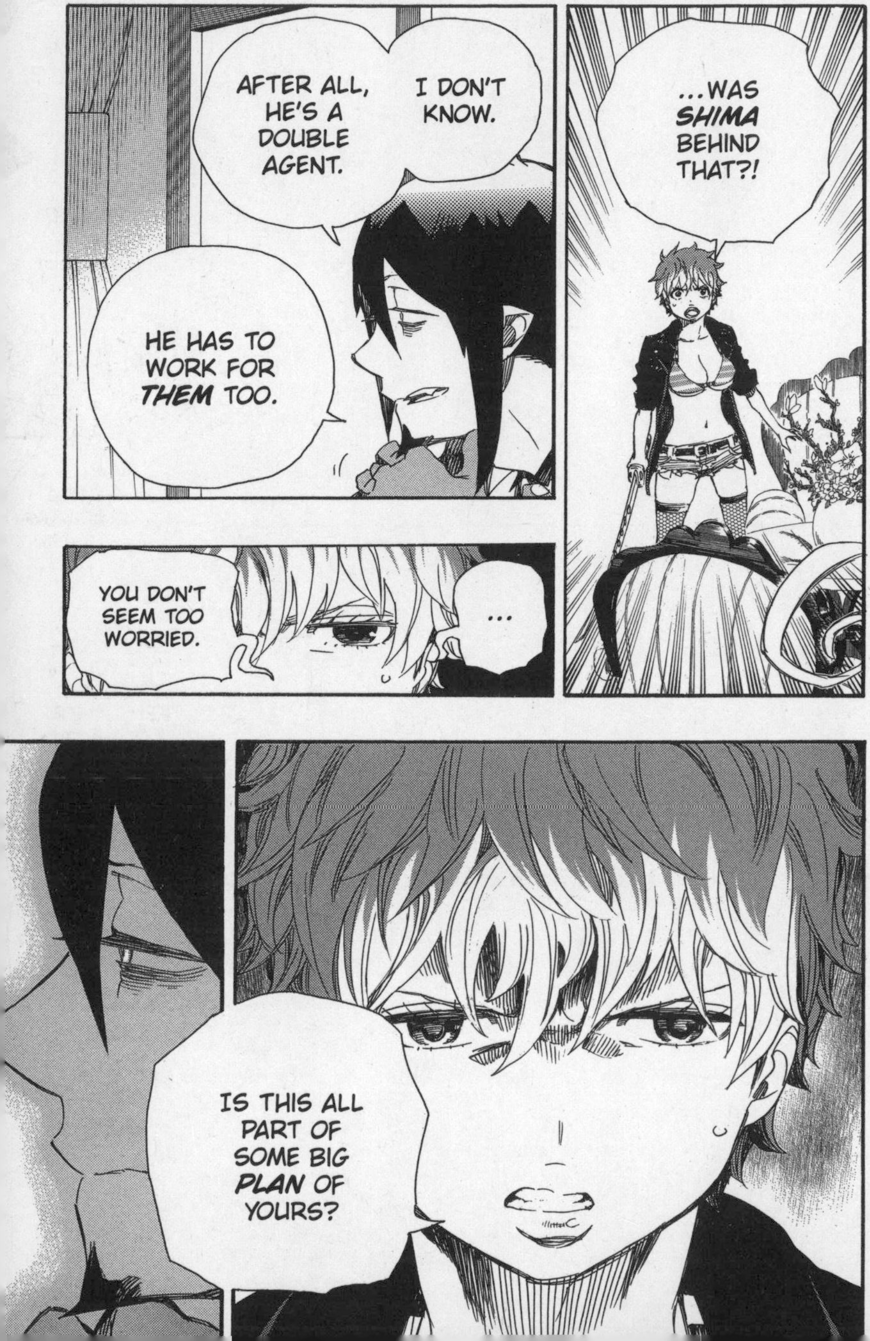
...WAS *SHIMA* BEHIND THAT?!
I DON'T KNOW.
AFTER ALL, HE'S A DOUBLE AGENT.
HE HAS TO WORK FOR *THEM* TOO.
...
YOU DON'T SEEM TOO WORRIED.
IS THIS ALL PART OF SOME BIG *PLAN* OF YOURS?

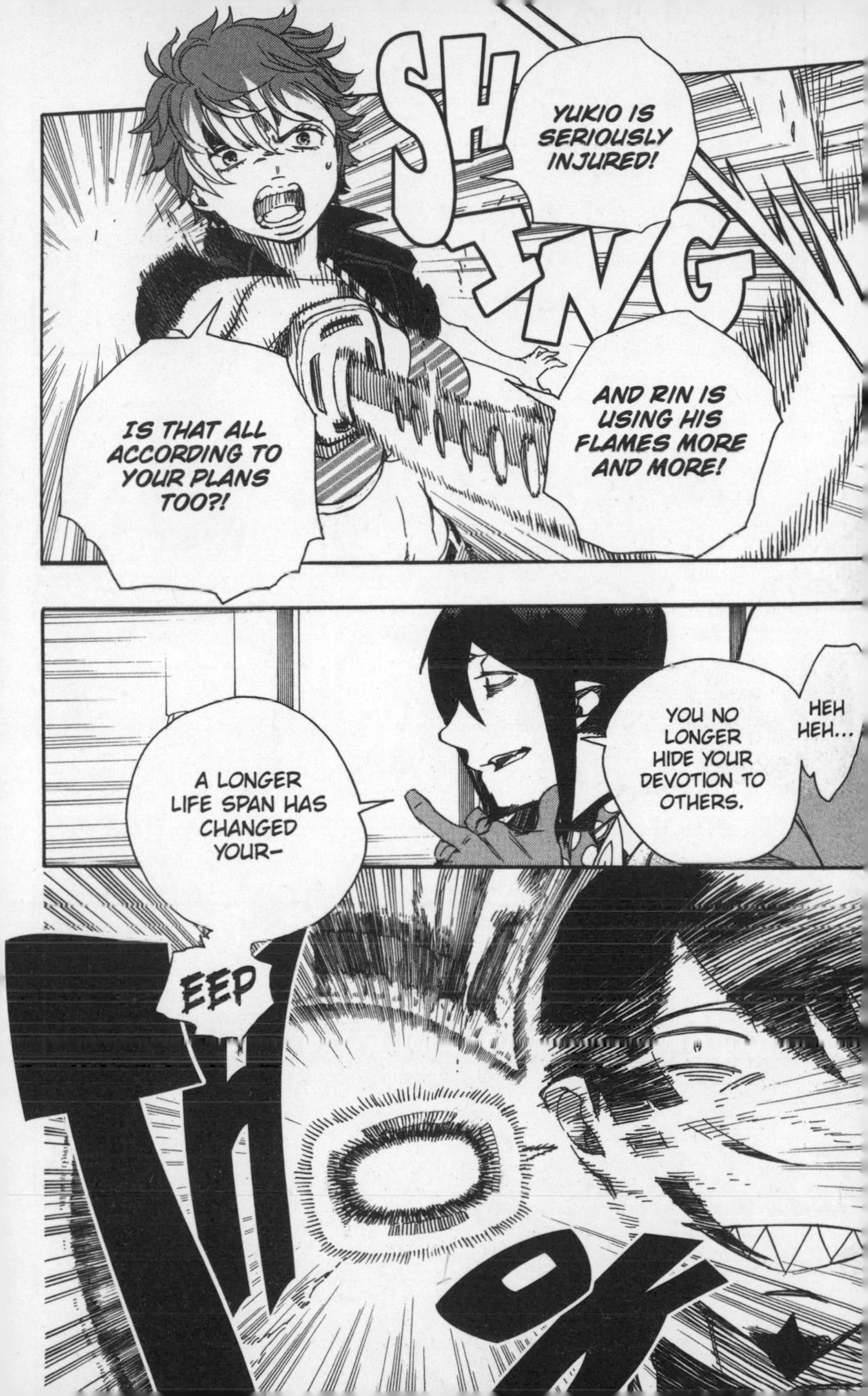
YUKIO IS SERIOUSLY INJURED!
SHING
AND RIN IS USING HIS FLAMES MORE AND MORE!
IS THAT ALL ACCORDING TO YOUR PLANS TOO?!
HEH HEH...
YOU NO LONGER HIDE YOUR DEVOTION TO OTHERS.
A LONGER LIFE SPAN HAS CHANGED YOUR-
EEP

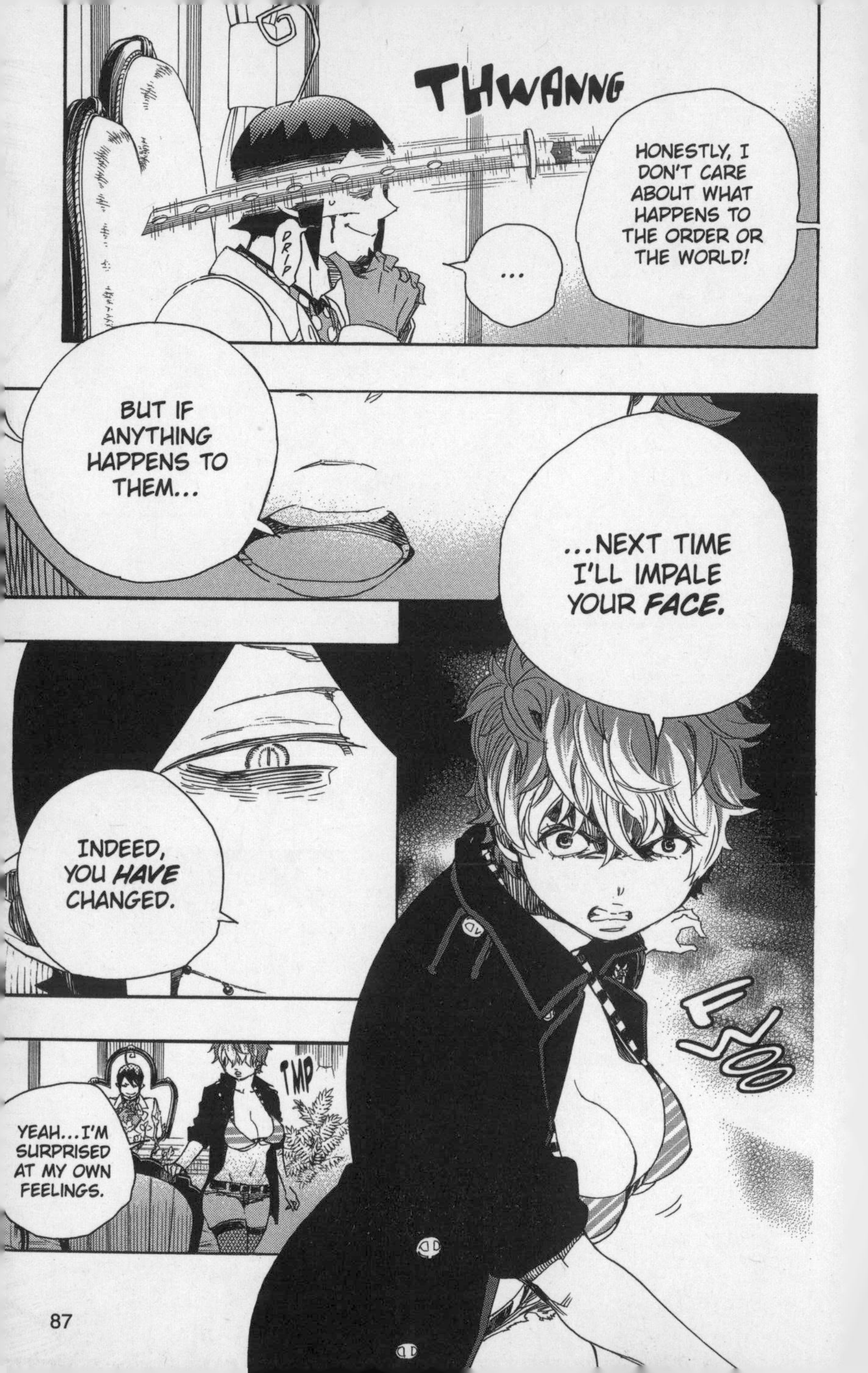
THWANNG
HONESTLY, I DON'T CARE ABOUT WHAT HAPPENS TO THE ORDER OR THE WORLD!
...
DRIP
BUT IF ANYTHING HAPPENS TO THEM...
...NEXT TIME I'LL IMPALE YOUR FACE.
FSHOO
INDEED, YOU HAVE CHANGED.
TMP
YEAH...I'M SURPRISED AT MY OWN FEELINGS.

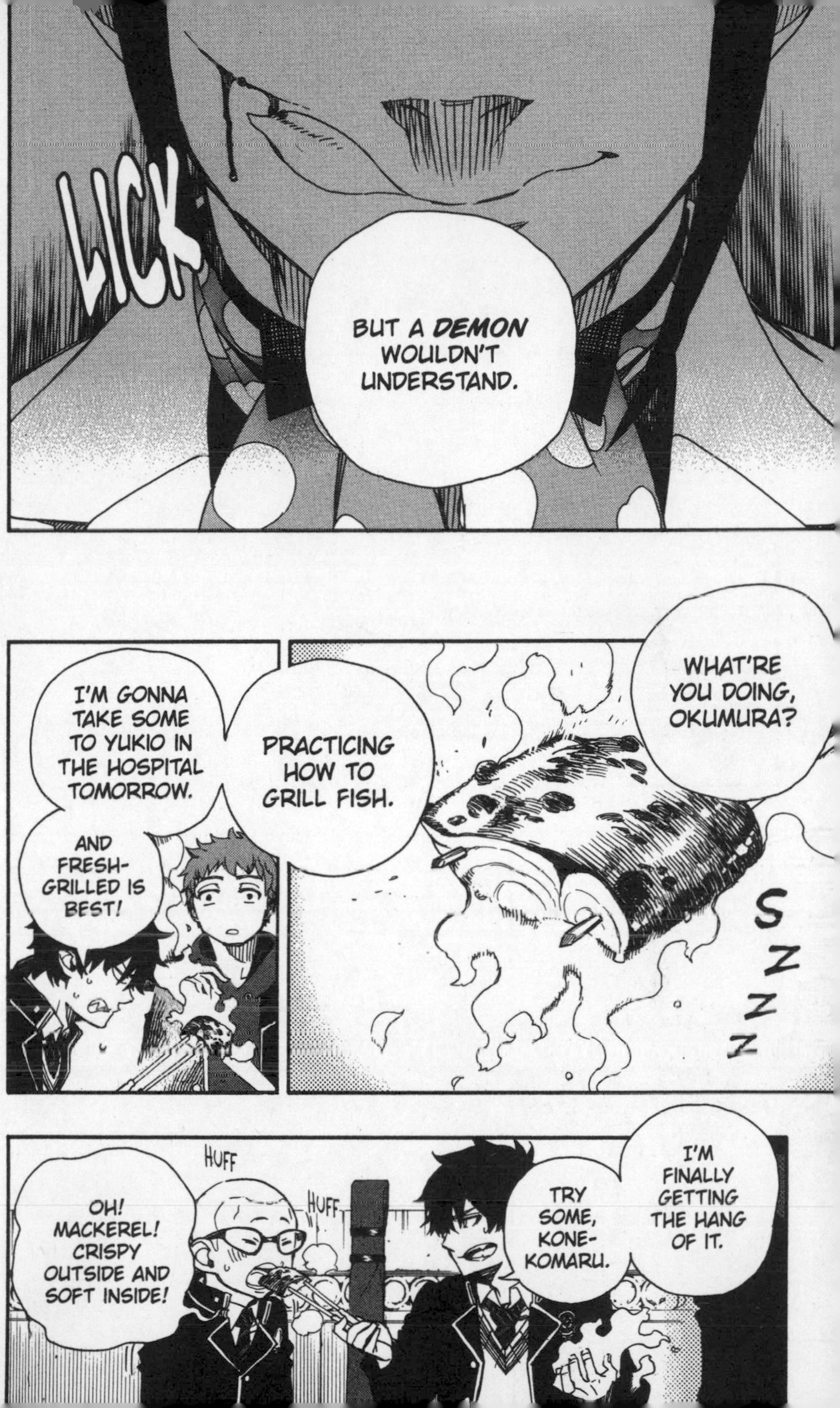
LICK
BUT A *DEMON* WOULDN'T UNDERSTAND.
WHAT'RE YOU DOING, OKUMURA?
SZZZ
PRACTICING HOW TO GRILL FISH.
I'M GONNA TAKE SOME TO YUKIO IN THE HOSPITAL TOMORROW.
AND FRESH-GRILLED IS BEST!
I'M FINALLY GETTING THE HANG OF IT.
TRY SOME, KONE-KOMARU.
HUFF
HUFF
OH! MACKEREL! CRISPY OUTSIDE AND SOFT INSIDE!

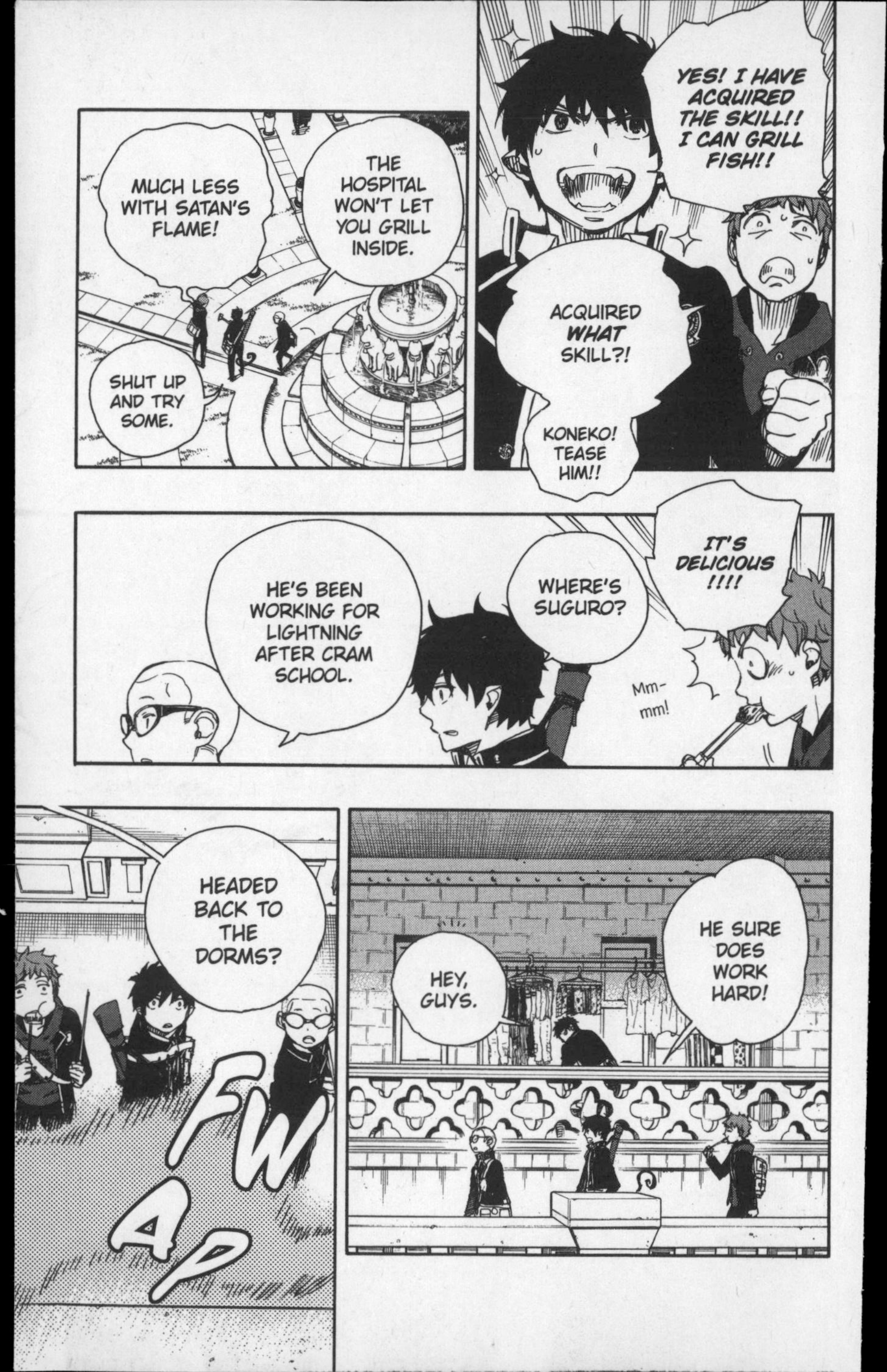
YES! I HAVE ACQUIRED THE SKILL!! I CAN GRILL FISH!!
ACQUIRED WHAT SKILL?!
KONEKO! TEASE HIM!!
THE HOSPITAL WON'T LET YOU GRILL INSIDE.
MUCH LESS WITH SATAN'S FLAME!
SHUT UP AND TRY SOME.
IT'S DELICIOUS !!!!
Mm-mm!
WHERE'S SUGURO?
HE'S BEEN WORKING FOR LIGHTNING AFTER CRAM SCHOOL.
HE SURE DOES WORK HARD!
HEY, GUYS.
HEADED BACK TO THE DORMS?
FWAP

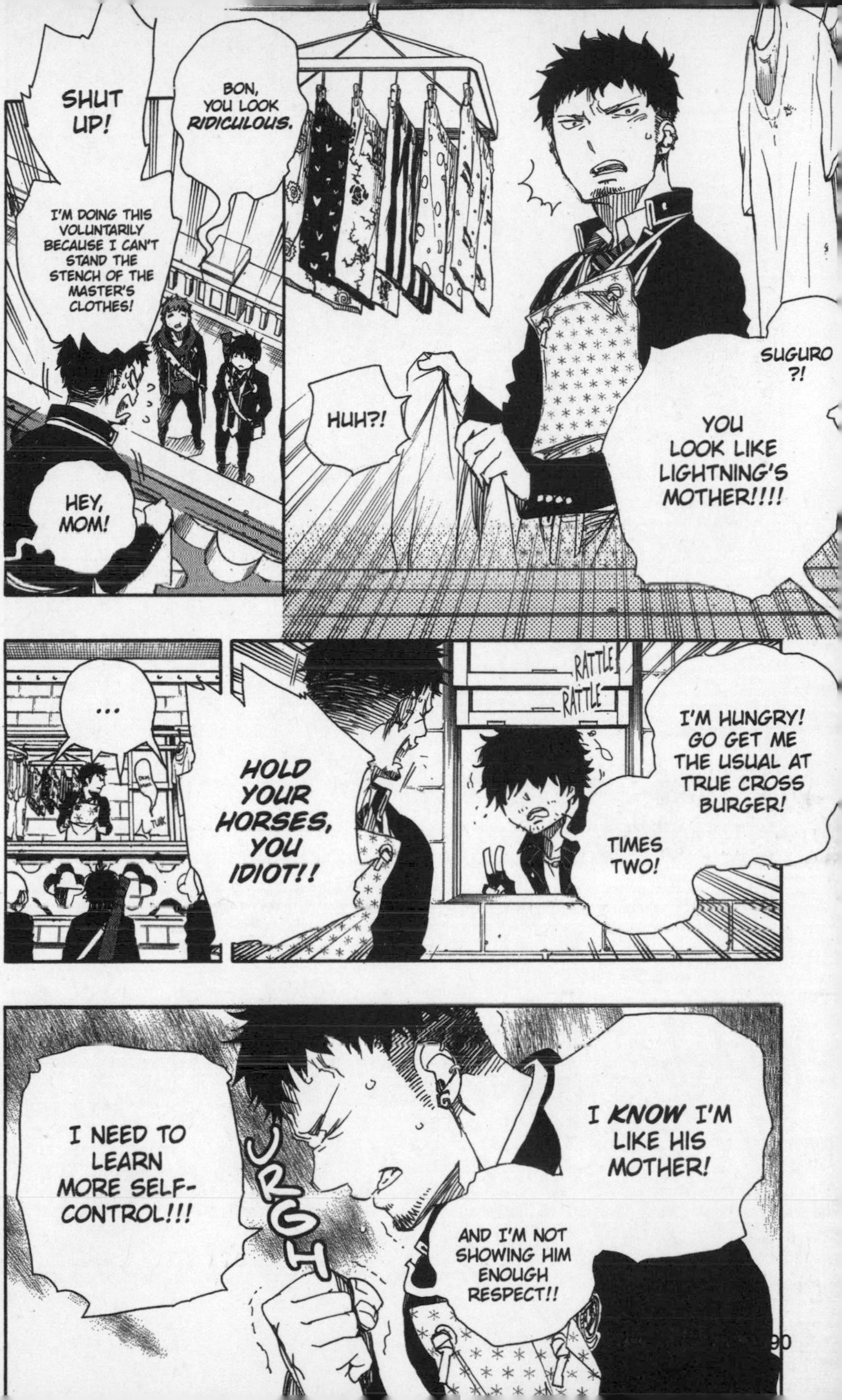
SUGURO ?!
YOU LOOK LIKE LIGHTNING'S MOTHER!!!!
HUH?!
BON, YOU LOOK *RIDICULOUS.*
SHUT UP!
I'M DOING THIS VOLUNTARILY BECAUSE I CAN'T STAND THE STENCH OF THE MASTER'S CLOTHES!
HEY, MOM!
RATTLE
RATTLE
I'M HUNGRY! GO GET ME THE USUAL AT TRUE CROSS BURGER!
TIMES TWO!
HOLD YOUR HORSES, YOU IDIOT!!
...
I *KNOW* I'M LIKE HIS MOTHER!
AND I'M NOT SHOWING HIM ENOUGH RESPECT!!
URGH
I NEED TO LEARN MORE SELF-CONTROL!!!

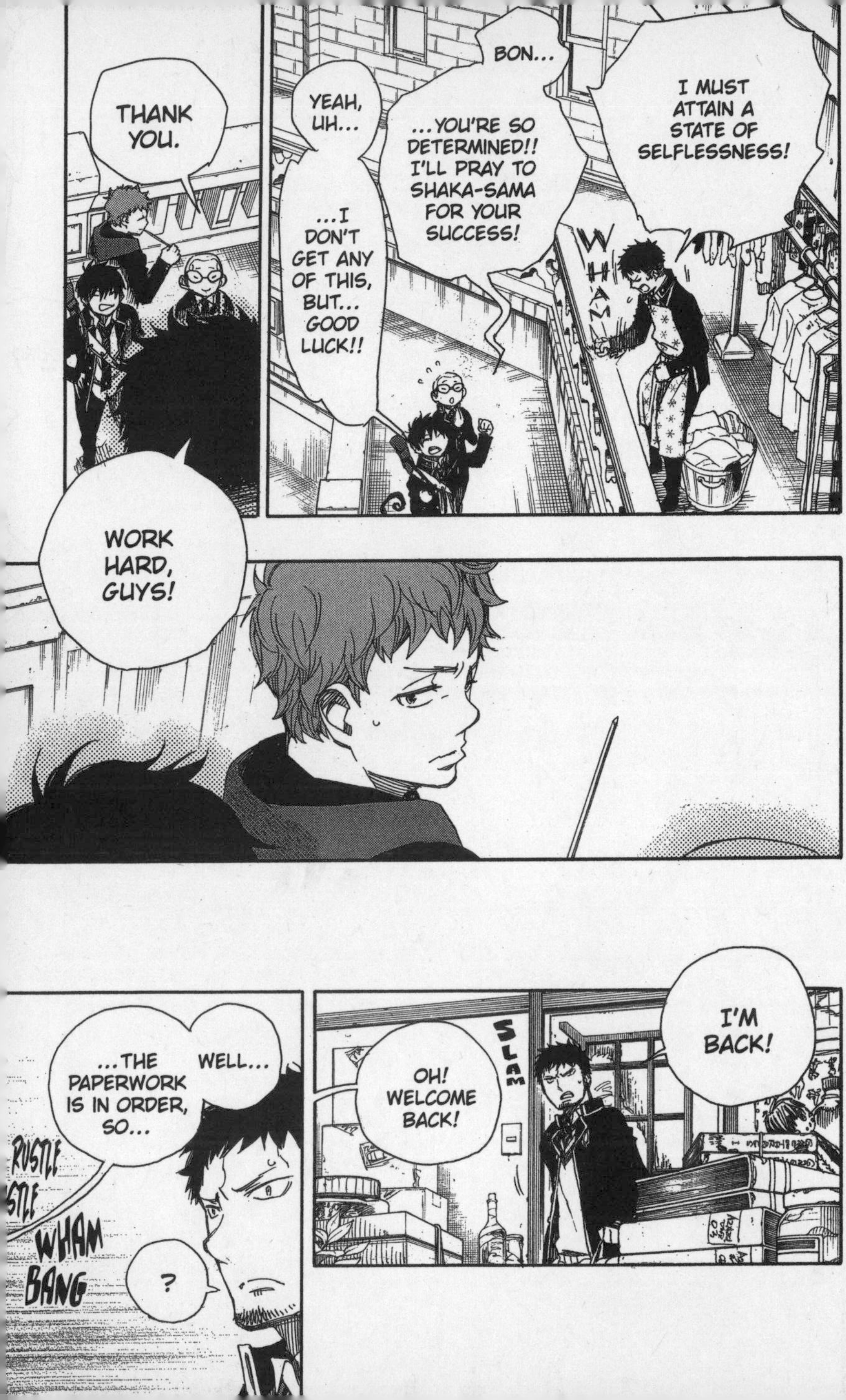

I MUST ATTAIN A STATE OF SELFLESSNESS!
WHAM
BON...
...YOU'RE SO DETERMINED!! I'LL PRAY TO SHAKA-SAMA FOR YOUR SUCCESS!
YEAH, UH...
...I DON'T GET ANY OF THIS, BUT... GOOD LUCK!!
THANK YOU.
WORK HARD, GUYS!
I'M BACK!
SLAM
OH! WELCOME BACK!
WELL...
...THE PAPERWORK IS IN ORDER, SO...
RUSTLE
STLE
WHAM
BANG
?

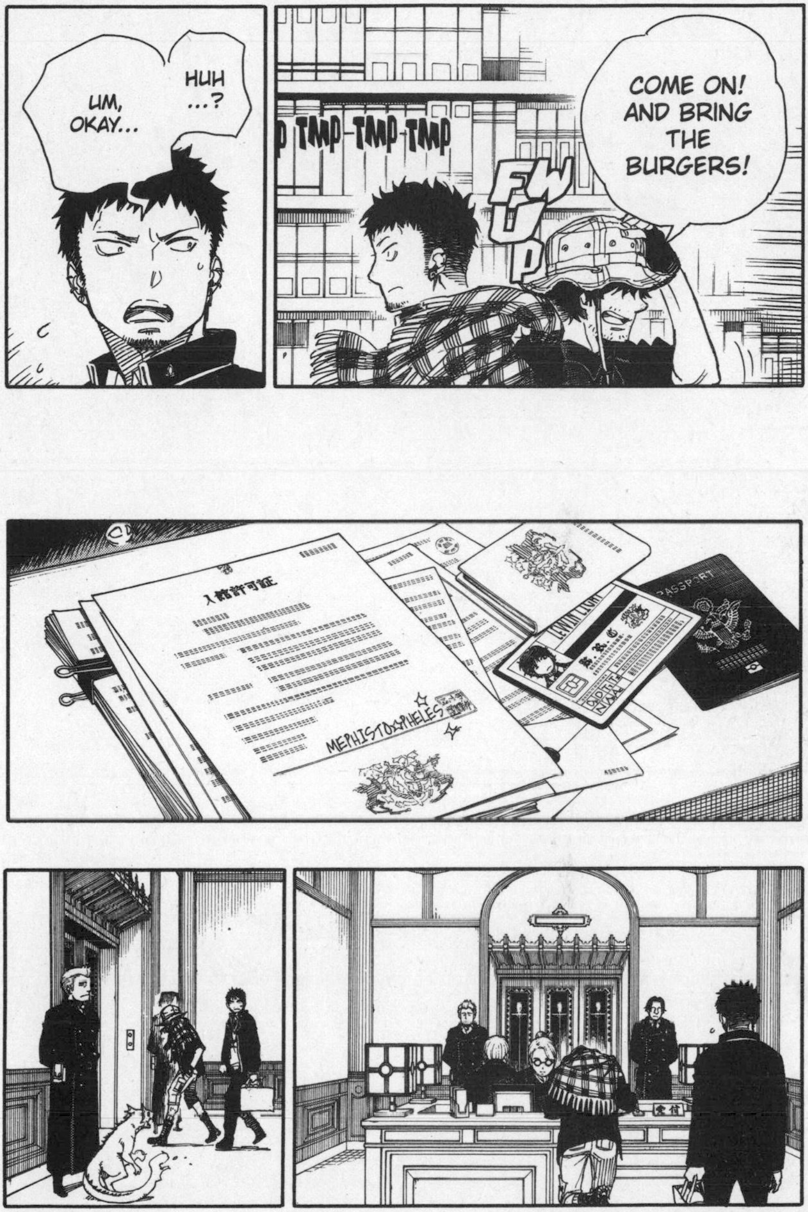
TMP TMP TMP TMP
FWUP
COME ON! AND BRING THE BURGERS!
HUH ...?
UM, OKAY...
入館許可証
MEPHISTOPHELES
LEWIN LIGHT
PASSPORT
受付

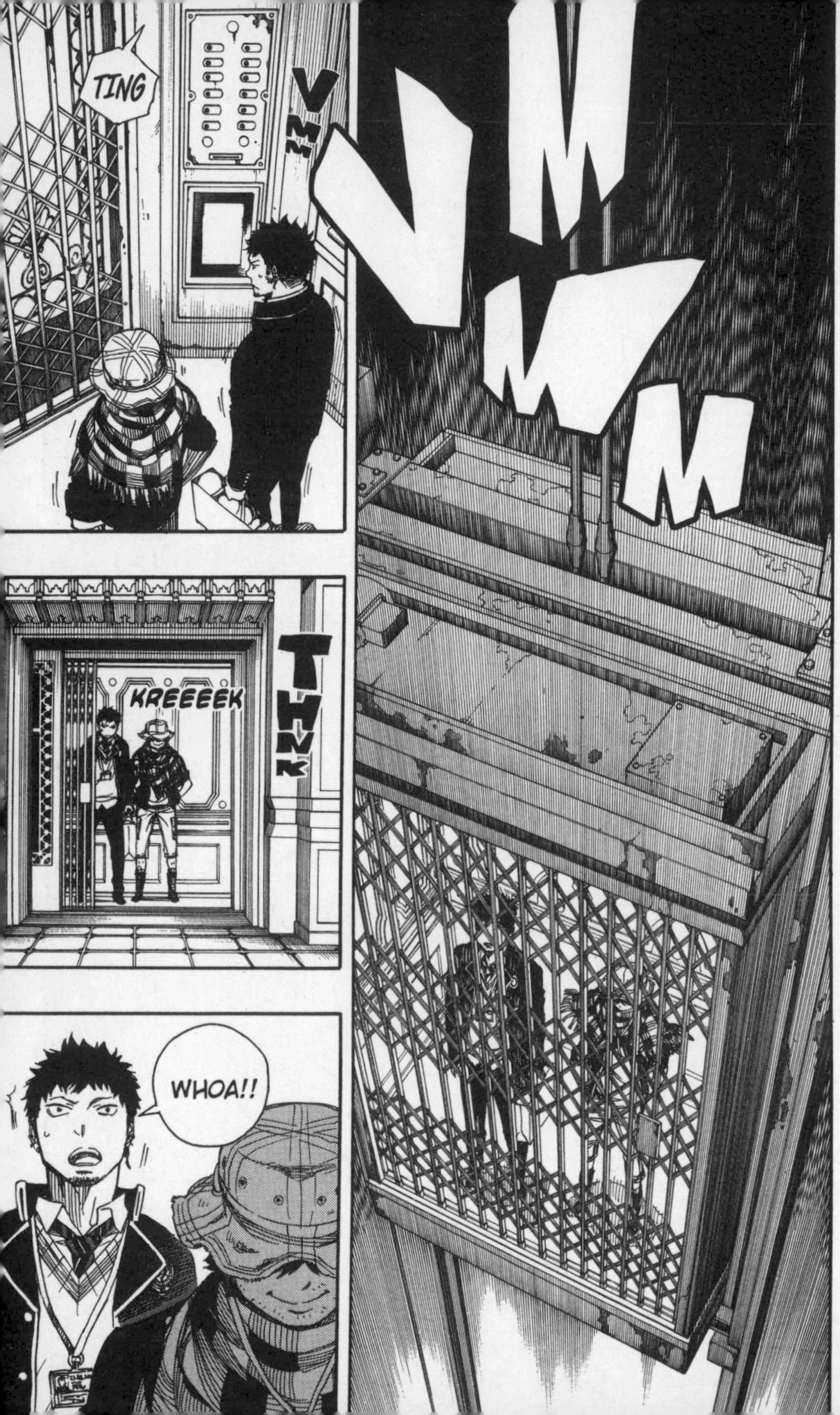
VMMM
TING
VMM
KREEEEK
THNK
WHOA!!

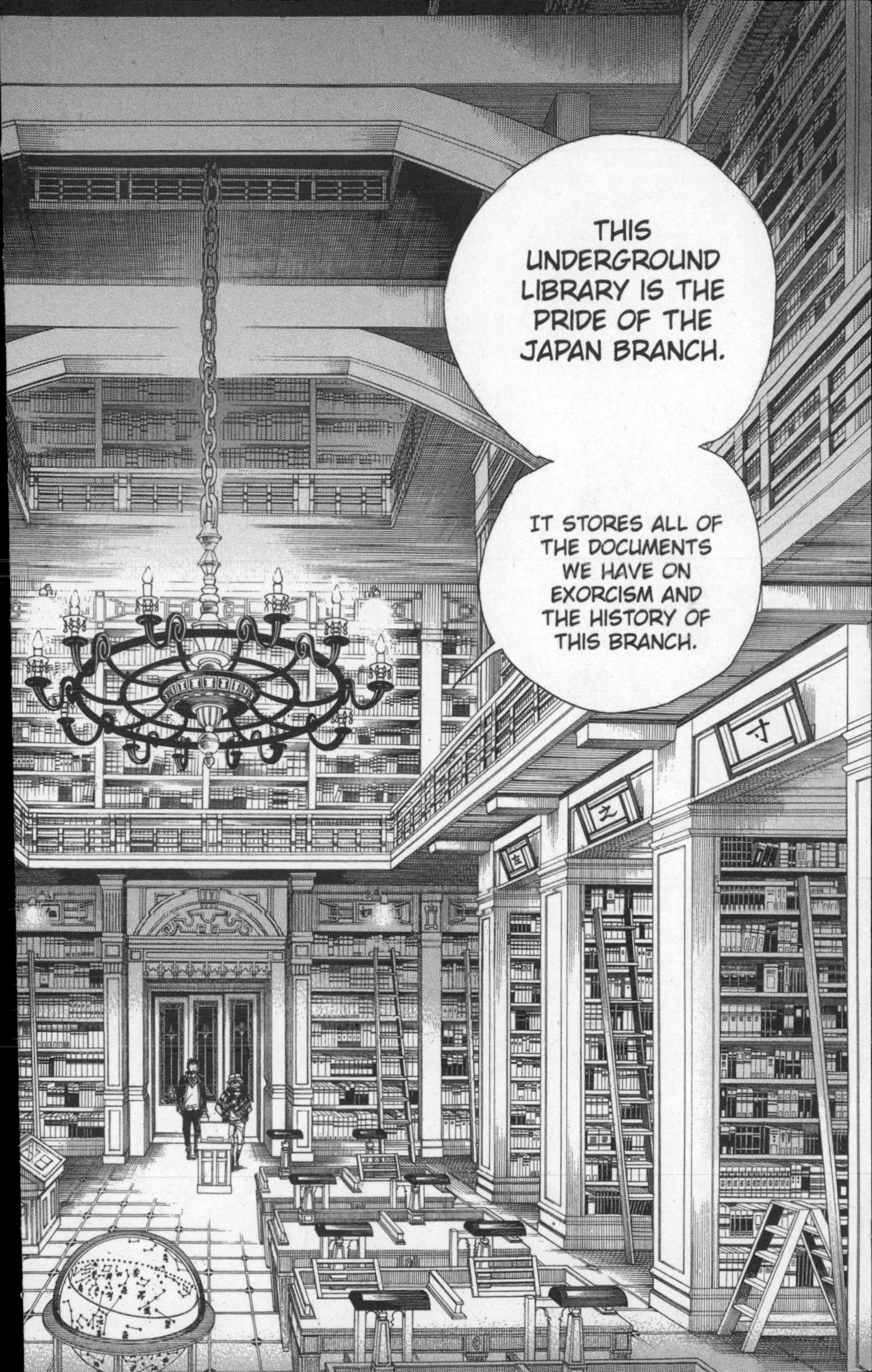
THIS UNDERGROUND LIBRARY IS THE PRIDE OF THE JAPAN BRANCH.
IT STORES ALL OF THE DOCUMENTS WE HAVE ON EXORCISM AND THE HISTORY OF THIS BRANCH.

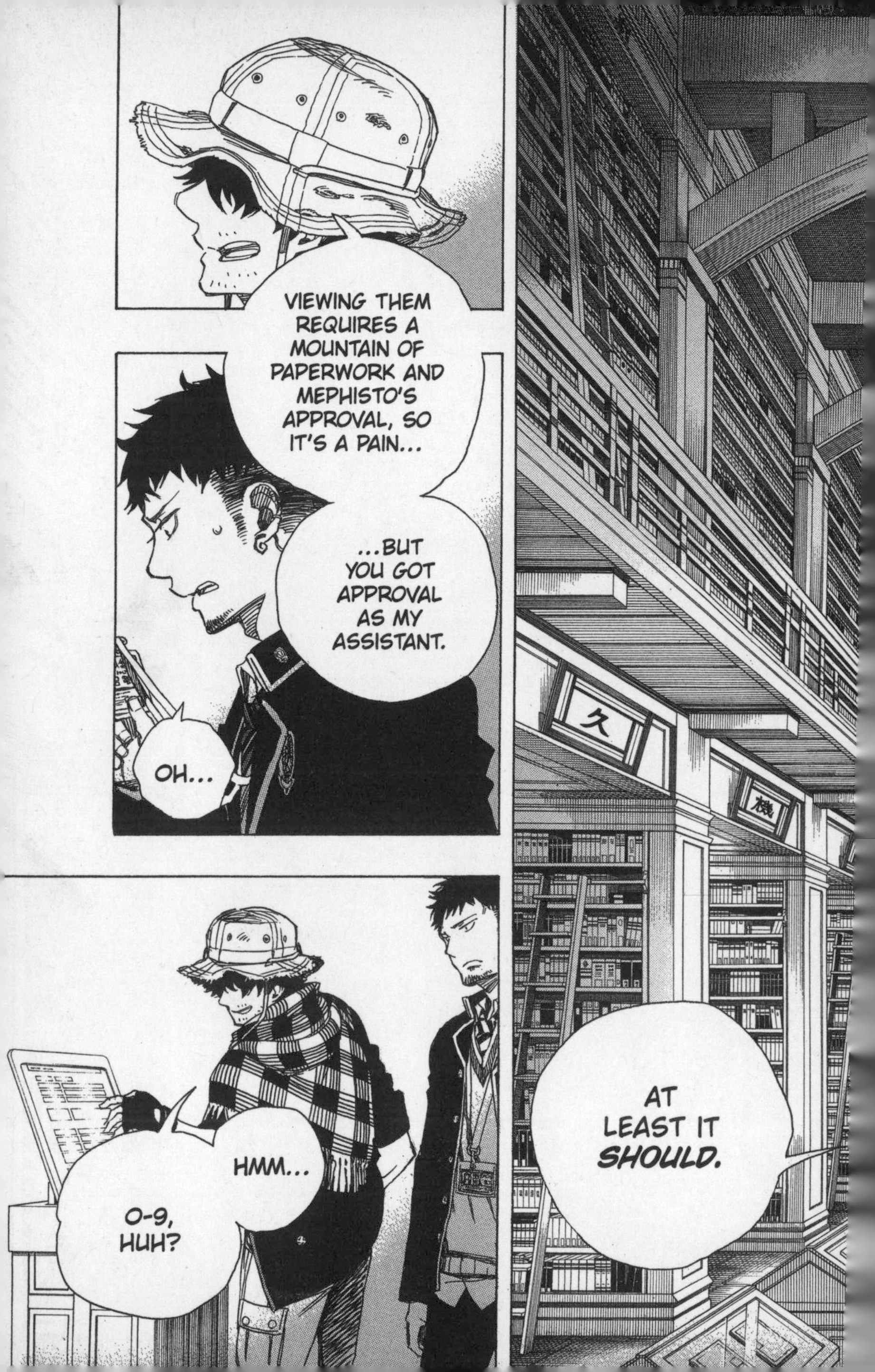
VIEWING THEM REQUIRES A MOUNTAIN OF PAPERWORK AND MEPHISTO'S APPROVAL, SO IT'S A PAIN...
...BUT YOU GOT APPROVAL AS MY ASSISTANT.
OH...
HMM...
O-9, HUH?
AT LEAST IT *SHOULD.*

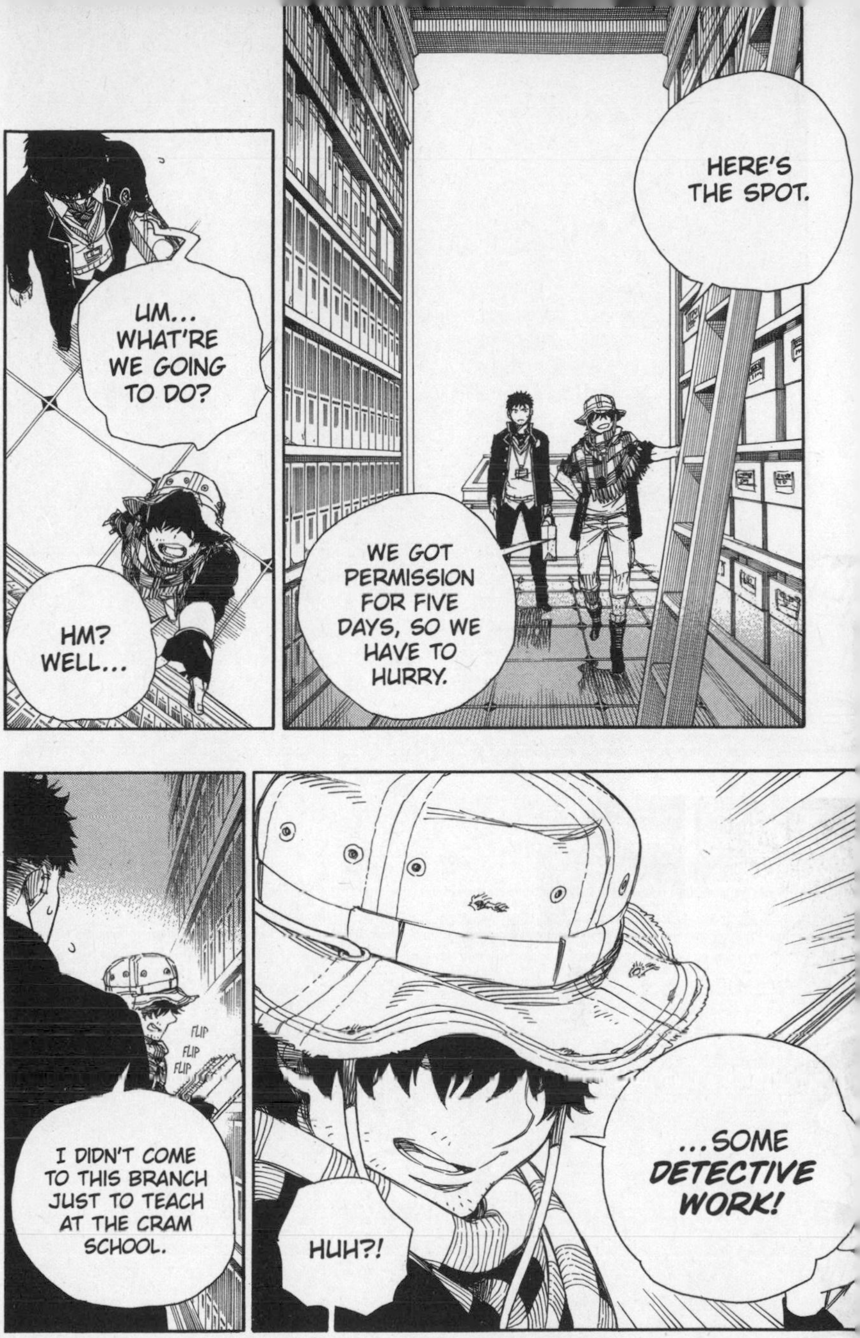
HERE'S THE SPOT.
WE GOT PERMISSION FOR FIVE DAYS, SO WE HAVE TO HURRY.
UM... WHAT'RE WE GOING TO DO?
HM? WELL...
...SOME DETECTIVE WORK!
HUH?!
FLIP FLIP FLIP
I DIDN'T COME TO THIS BRANCH JUST TO TEACH AT THE CRAM SCHOOL.

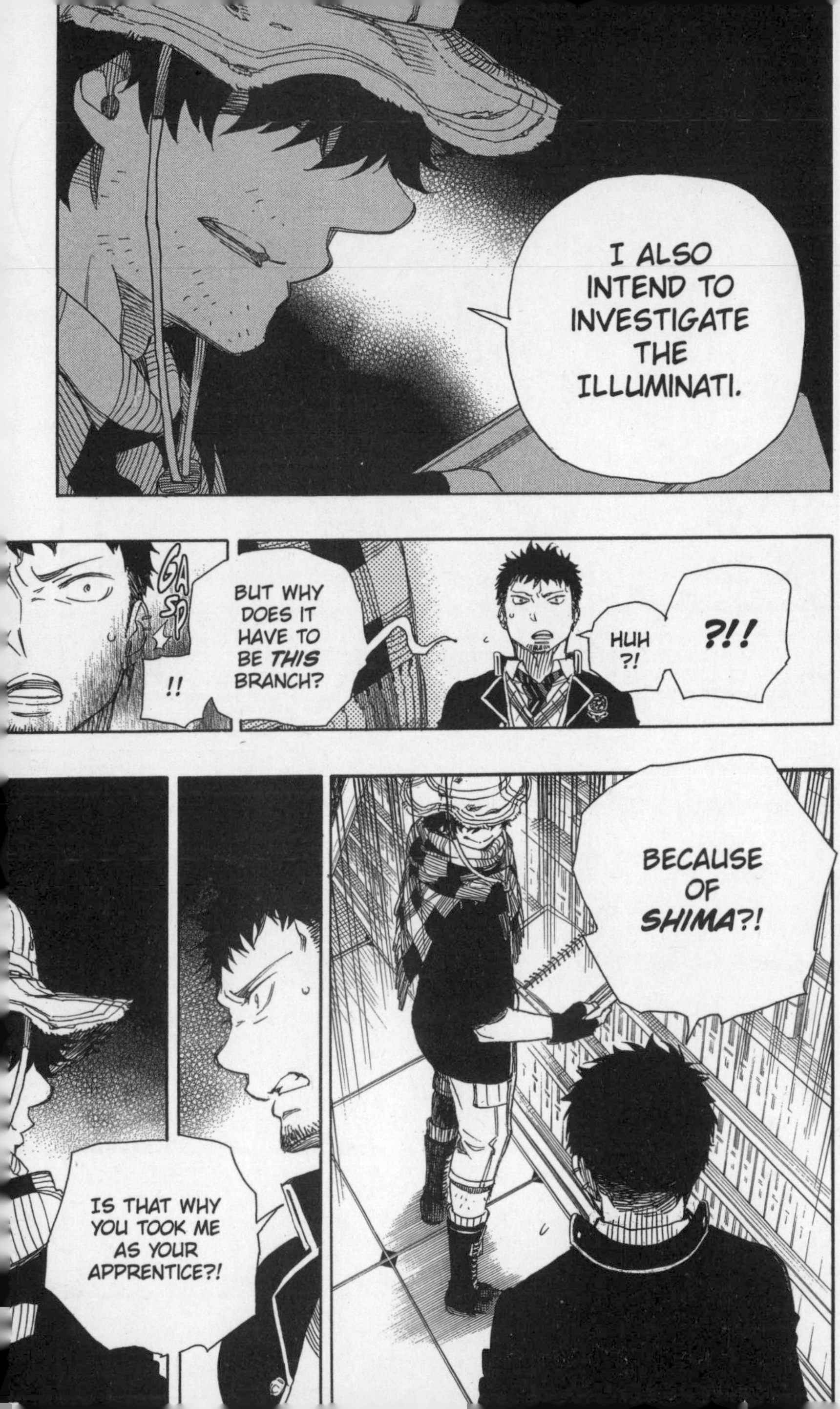
I ALSO INTEND TO INVESTIGATE THE ILLUMINATI.
?!!
HUH ?!
BUT WHY DOES IT HAVE TO BE *THIS* BRANCH?
GASP
!!
BECAUSE OF *SHIMA*?!
IS THAT WHY YOU TOOK ME AS YOUR APPRENTICE?!

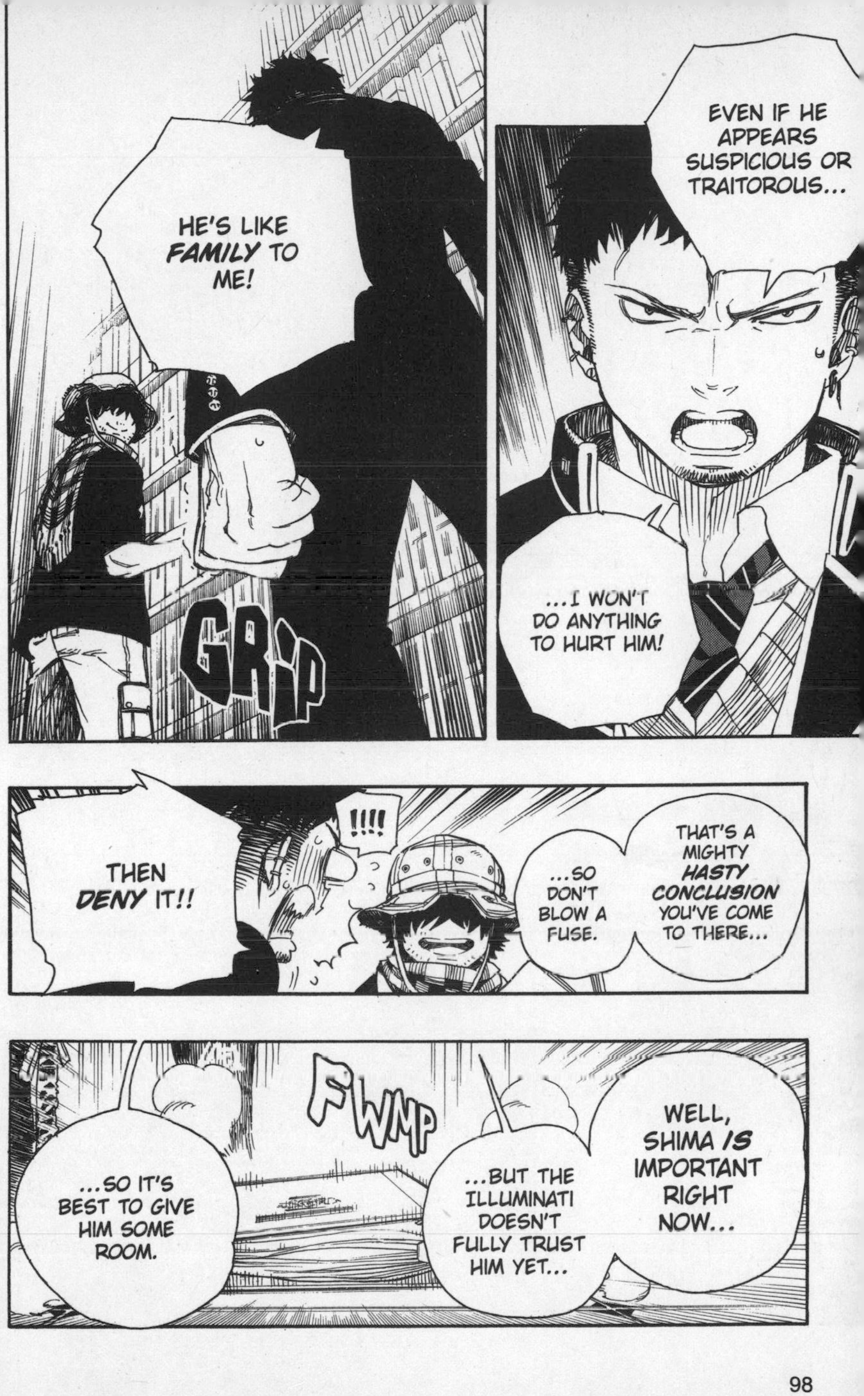
EVEN IF HE APPEARS SUSPICIOUS OR TRAITOROUS...
...I WON'T DO ANYTHING TO HURT HIM!
HE'S LIKE *FAMILY* TO ME!
GRIP
THAT'S A MIGHTY *HASTY CONCLUSION* YOU'VE COME TO THERE...
...SO DON'T BLOW A FUSE.
!!!!
THEN *DENY* IT!!
WELL, SHIMA *IS* IMPORTANT RIGHT NOW...
...BUT THE ILLUMINATI DOESN'T FULLY TRUST HIM YET...
FWMP
...SO IT'S BEST TO GIVE HIM SOME ROOM.

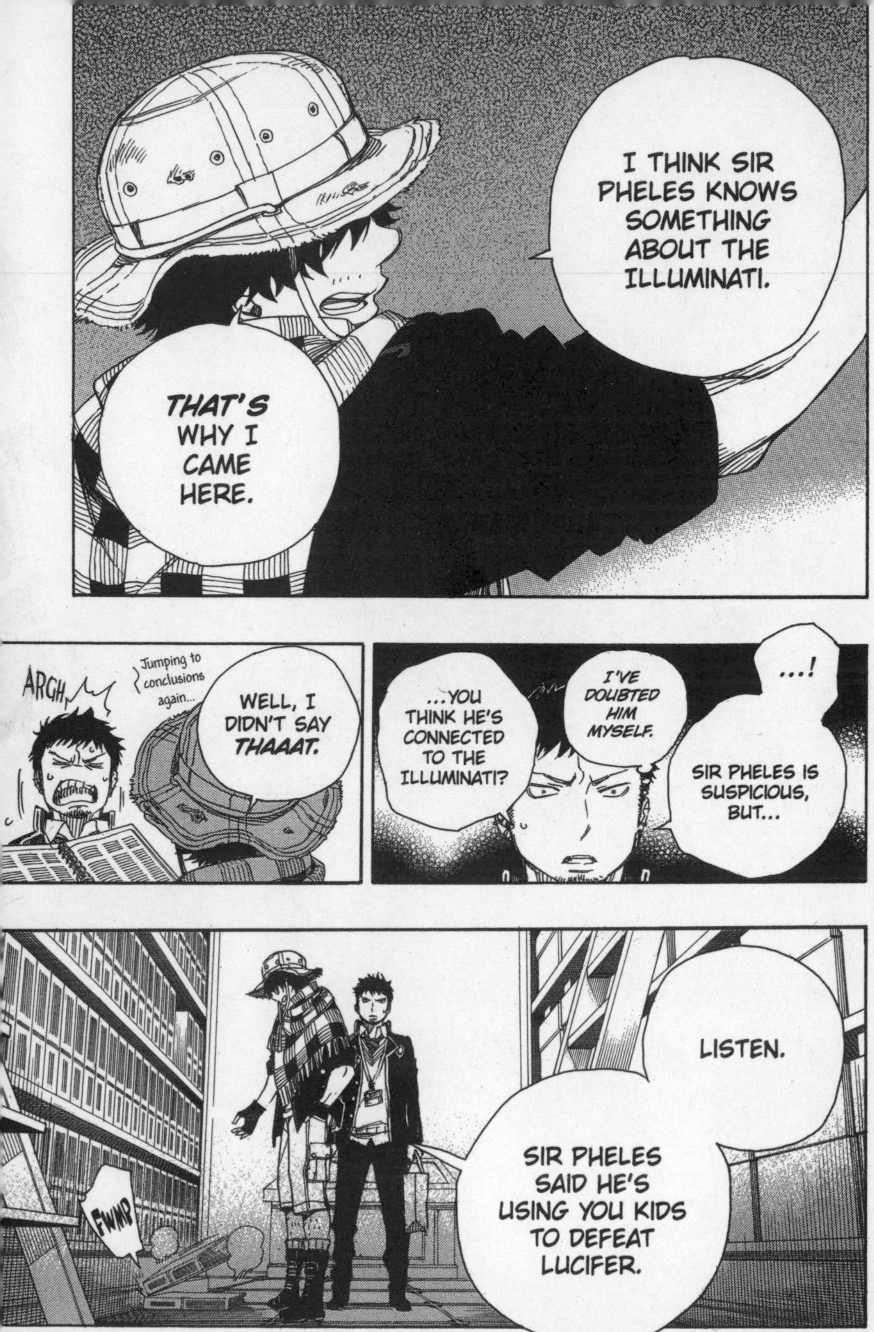
I THINK SIR PHELES KNOWS SOMETHING ABOUT THE ILLUMINATI.
THAT'S WHY I CAME HERE.
...!
SIR PHELES IS SUSPICIOUS, BUT...
I'VE DOUBTED HIM MYSELF.
...YOU THINK HE'S CONNECTED TO THE ILLUMINATI?
WELL, I DIDN'T SAY THAAAT.
Jumping to conclusions again...
ARGH
LISTEN.
SIR PHELES SAID HE'S USING YOU KIDS TO DEFEAT LUCIFER.
FWMP

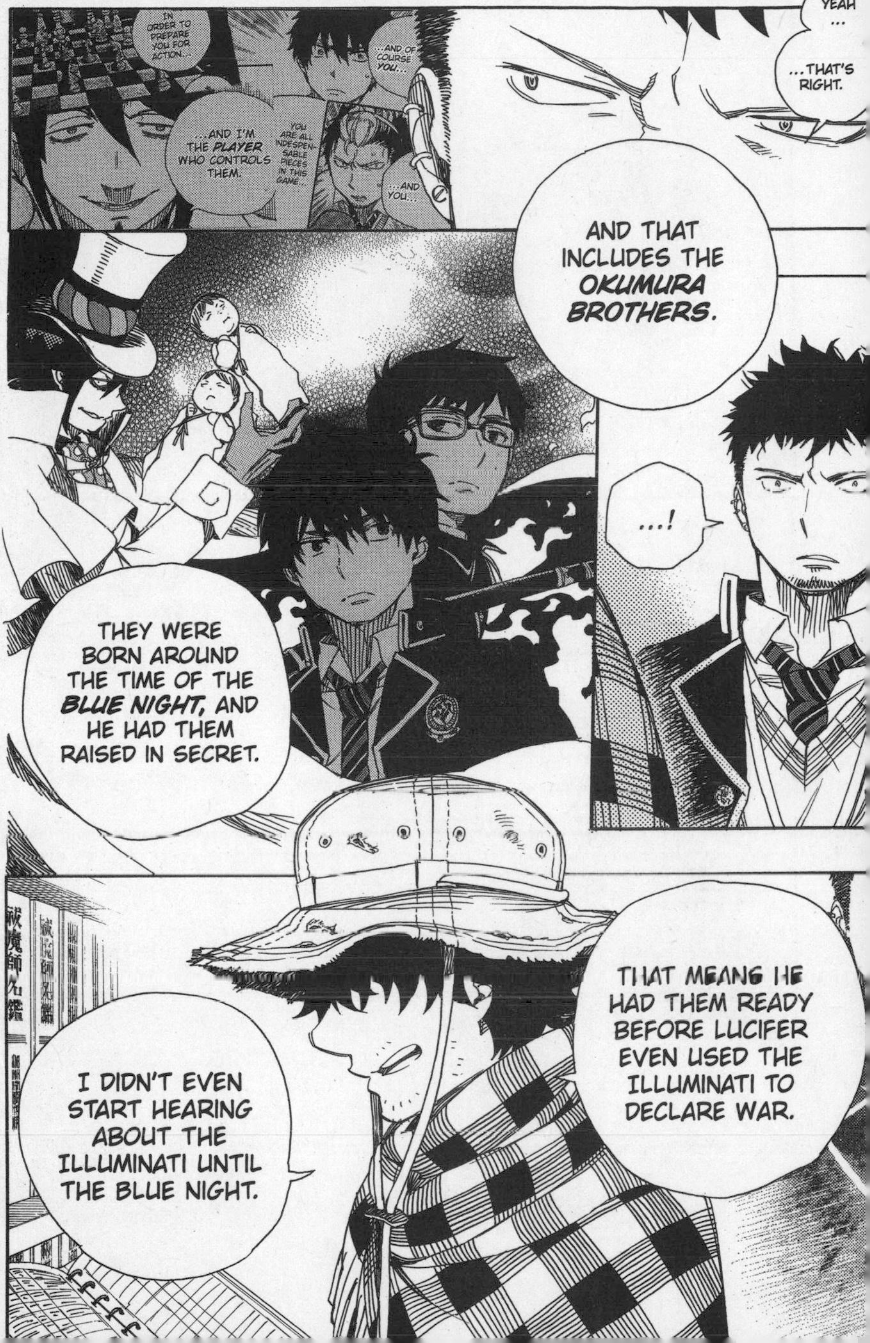
YEAH... ...THAT'S RIGHT.
AND THAT INCLUDES THE OKUMURA BROTHERS.
IN ORDER TO PREPARE YOU FOR ACTION...
...AND OF COURSE YOU...
...AND YOU...
YOU ARE ALL INDESPEN-SABLE PIECES IN THIS GAME...
...AND I'M THE PLAYER WHO CONTROLS THEM.
...!
THEY WERE BORN AROUND THE TIME OF THE BLUE NIGHT, AND HE HAD THEM RAISED IN SECRET.
THAT MEANS HE HAD THEM READY BEFORE LUCIFER EVEN USED THE ILLUMINATI TO DECLARE WAR.
祓魔師名鑑
I DIDN'T EVEN START HEARING ABOUT THE ILLUMINATI UNTIL THE BLUE NIGHT.

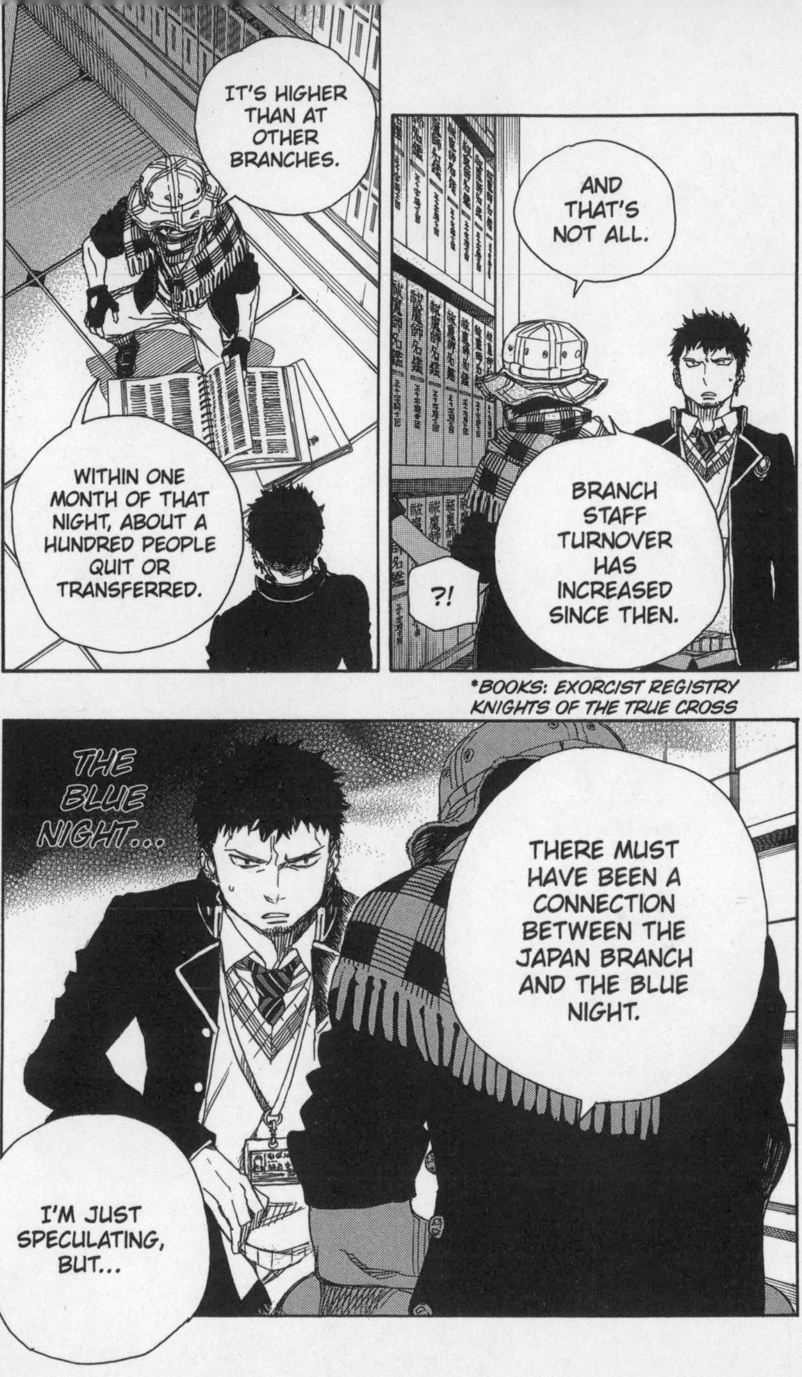
AND THAT'S NOT ALL.
?!
BRANCH STAFF TURNOVER HAS INCREASED SINCE THEN.
IT'S HIGHER THAN AT OTHER BRANCHES.
WITHIN ONE MONTH OF THAT NIGHT, ABOUT A HUNDRED PEOPLE QUIT OR TRANSFERRED.
*BOOKS: EXORCIST REGISTRY KNIGHTS OF THE TRUE CROSS
THERE MUST HAVE BEEN A CONNECTION BETWEEN THE JAPAN BRANCH AND THE BLUE NIGHT.
THE BLUE NIGHT...
I'M JUST SPECULATING, BUT...

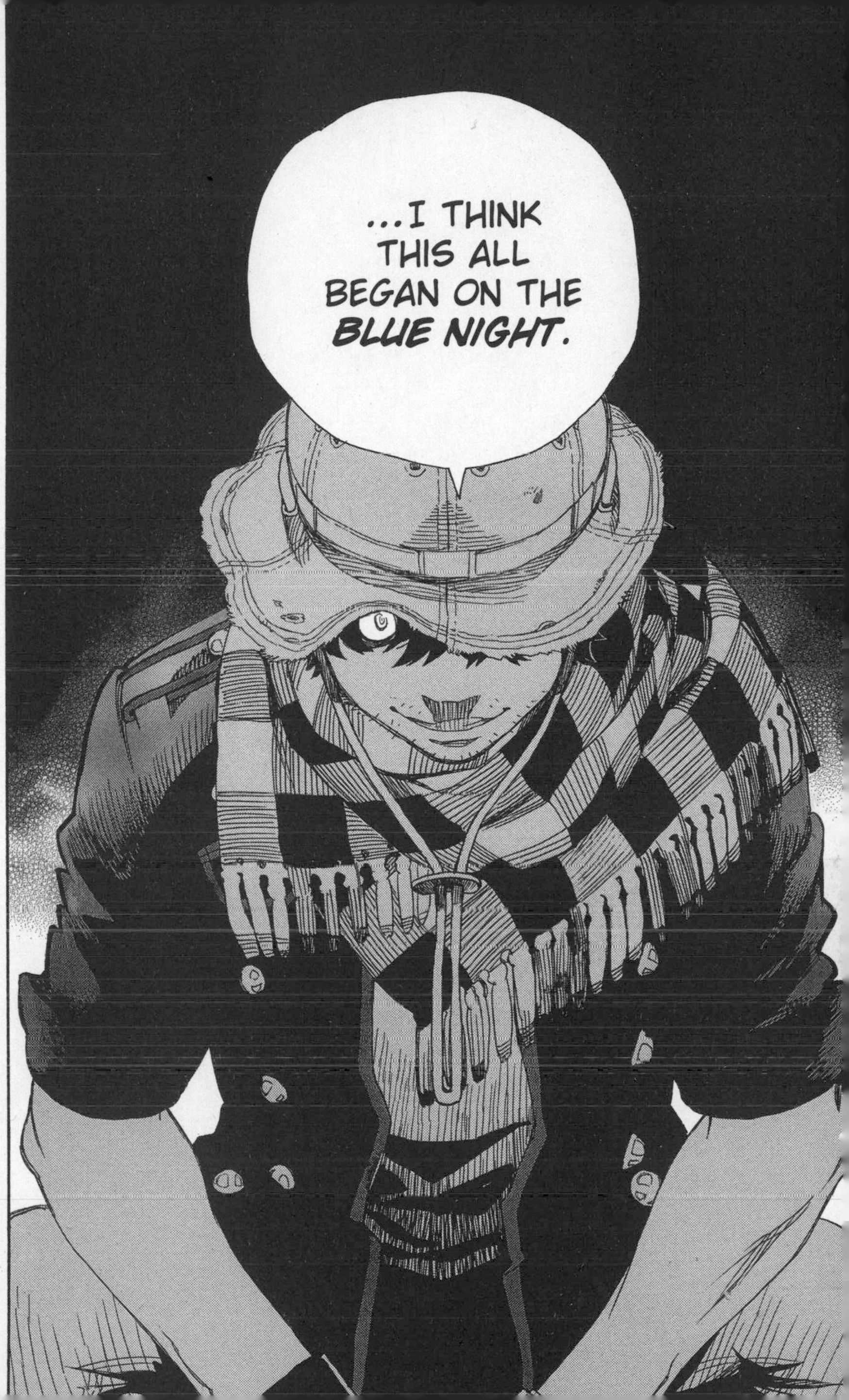
...I THINK THIS ALL BEGAN ON THE *BLUE NIGHT*.

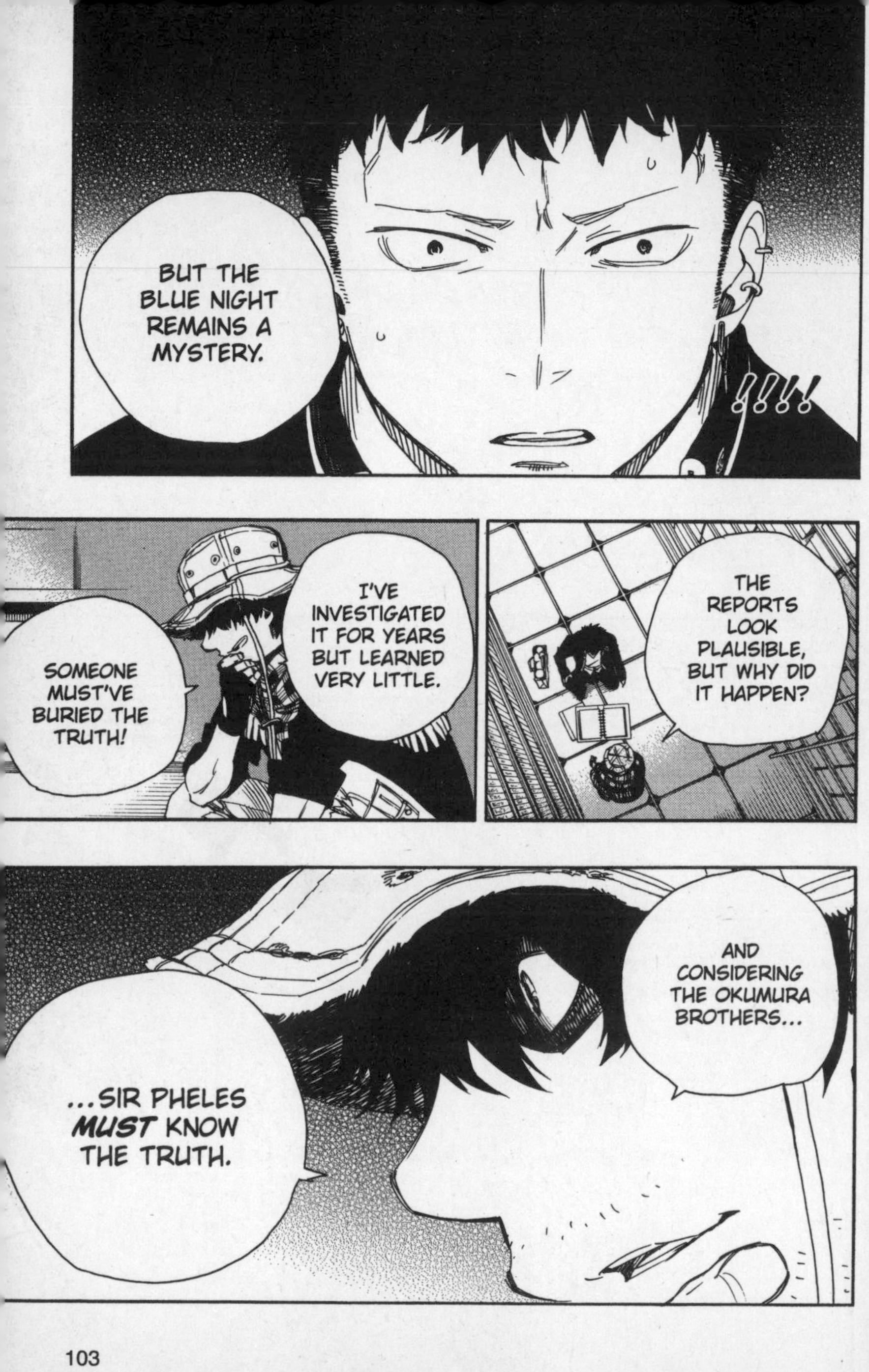
BUT THE BLUE NIGHT REMAINS A MYSTERY.
!!!!
THE REPORTS LOOK PLAUSIBLE, BUT WHY DID IT HAPPEN?
I'VE INVESTIGATED IT FOR YEARS BUT LEARNED VERY LITTLE.
SOMEONE MUST'VE BURIED THE TRUTH!
AND CONSIDERING THE OKUMURA BROTHERS...
...SIR PHELES *MUST* KNOW THE TRUTH.

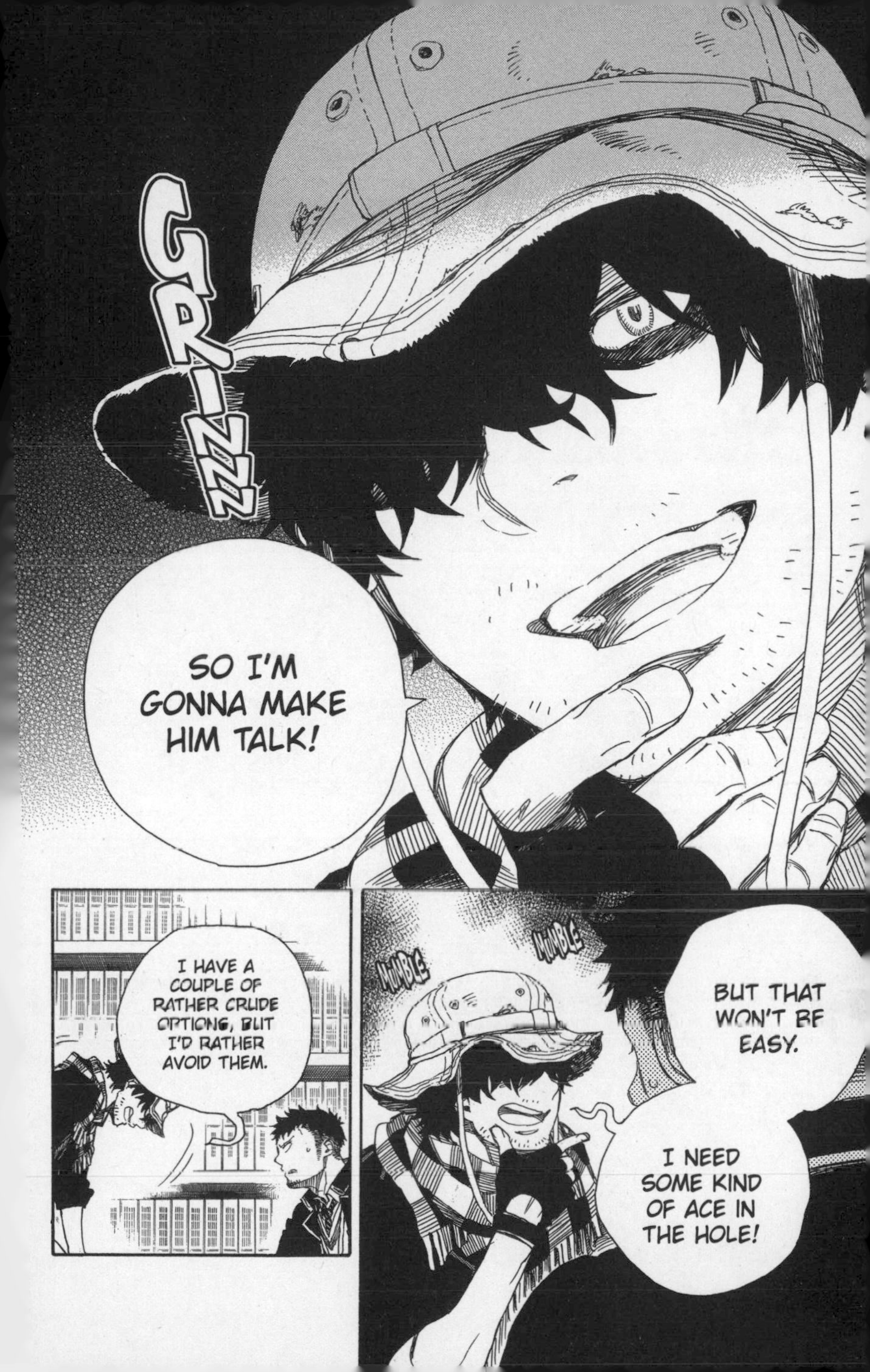
GRINNN
SO I'M GONNA MAKE HIM TALK!
MUMBLE
MUMBLE
BUT THAT WON'T BE EASY.
I NEED SOME KIND OF ACE IN THE HOLE!
I HAVE A COUPLE OF RATHER CRUDE OPTIONS, BUT I'D RATHER AVOID THEM.

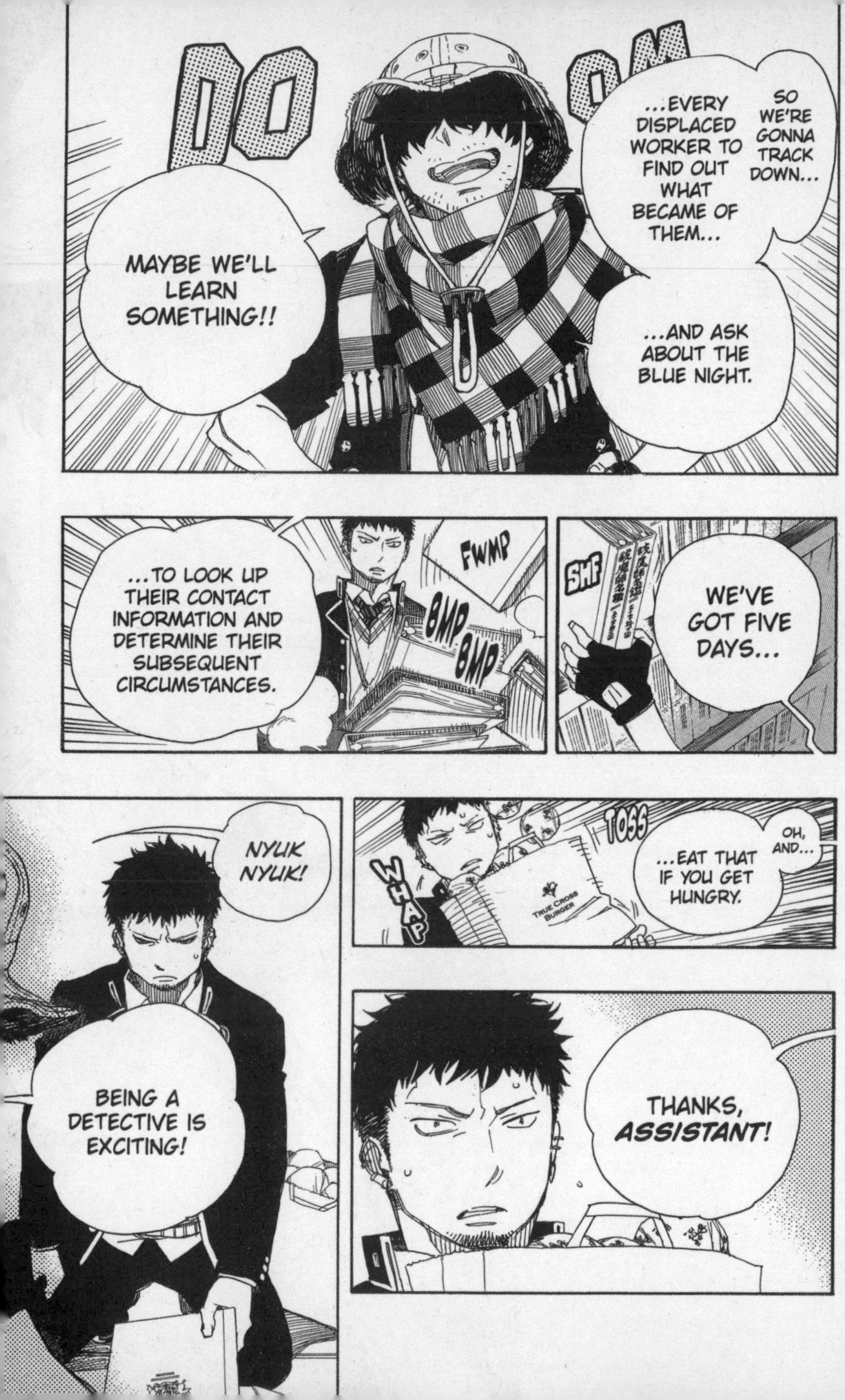
DOOM
SO WE'RE GONNA TRACK DOWN...
...EVERY DISPLACED WORKER TO FIND OUT WHAT BECAME OF THEM...
...AND ASK ABOUT THE BLUE NIGHT.
MAYBE WE'LL LEARN SOMETHING!!
SHF
WE'VE GOT FIVE DAYS...
FWMP
BMP BMP
...TO LOOK UP THEIR CONTACT INFORMATION AND DETERMINE THEIR SUBSEQUENT CIRCUMSTANCES.
OH, AND...
TOSS
...EAT THAT IF YOU GET HUNGRY.
TRUE CROSS BURGER
WHAP
THANKS, ***ASSISTANT***!
NYUK NYUK!
BEING A DETECTIVE IS EXCITING!

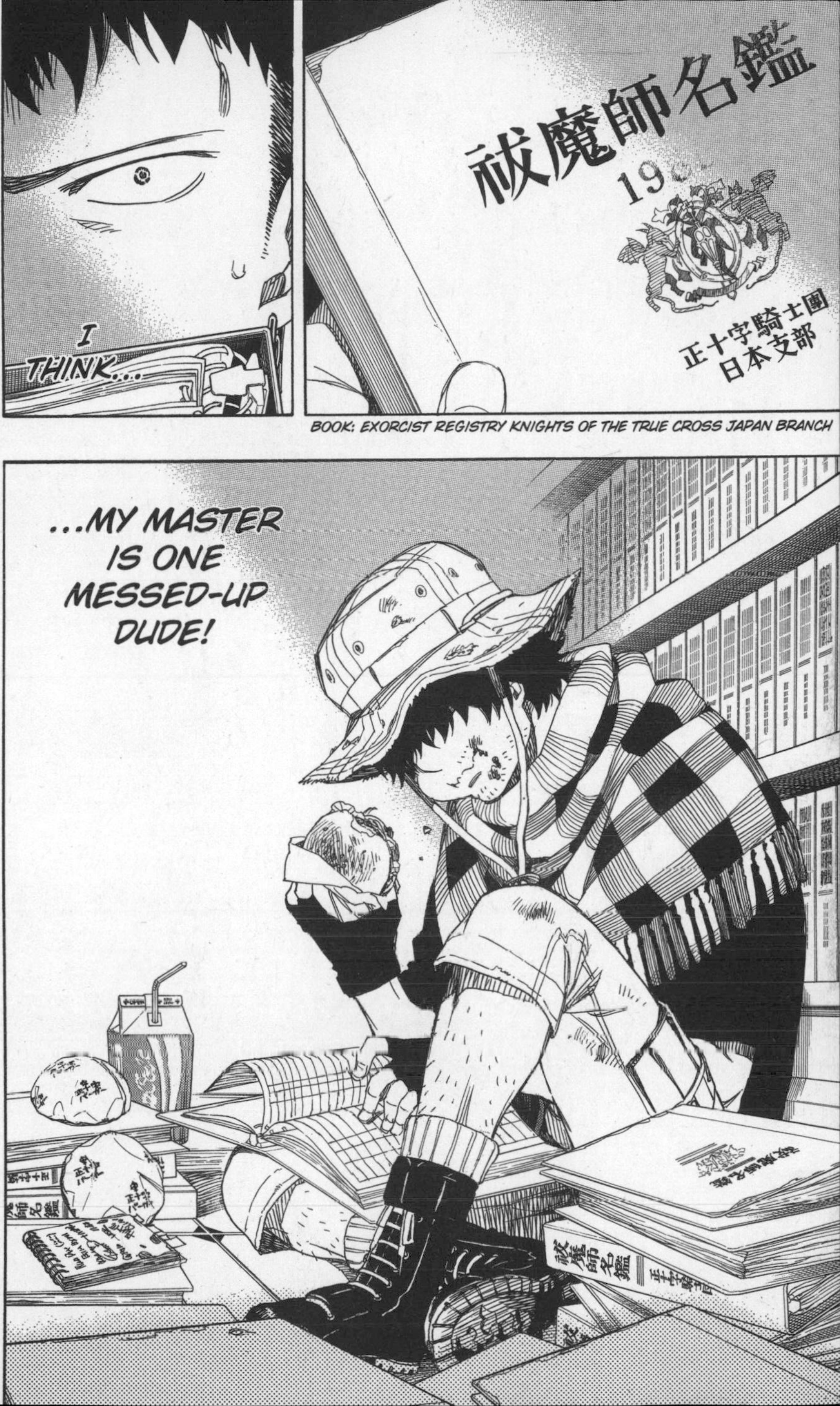
祓魔師名鑑
正十字騎士團
日本支部
BOOK: EXORCIST REGISTRY KNIGHTS OF THE TRUE CROSS JAPAN BRANCH
I THINK...
...MY MASTER IS ONE MESSED-UP DUDE!

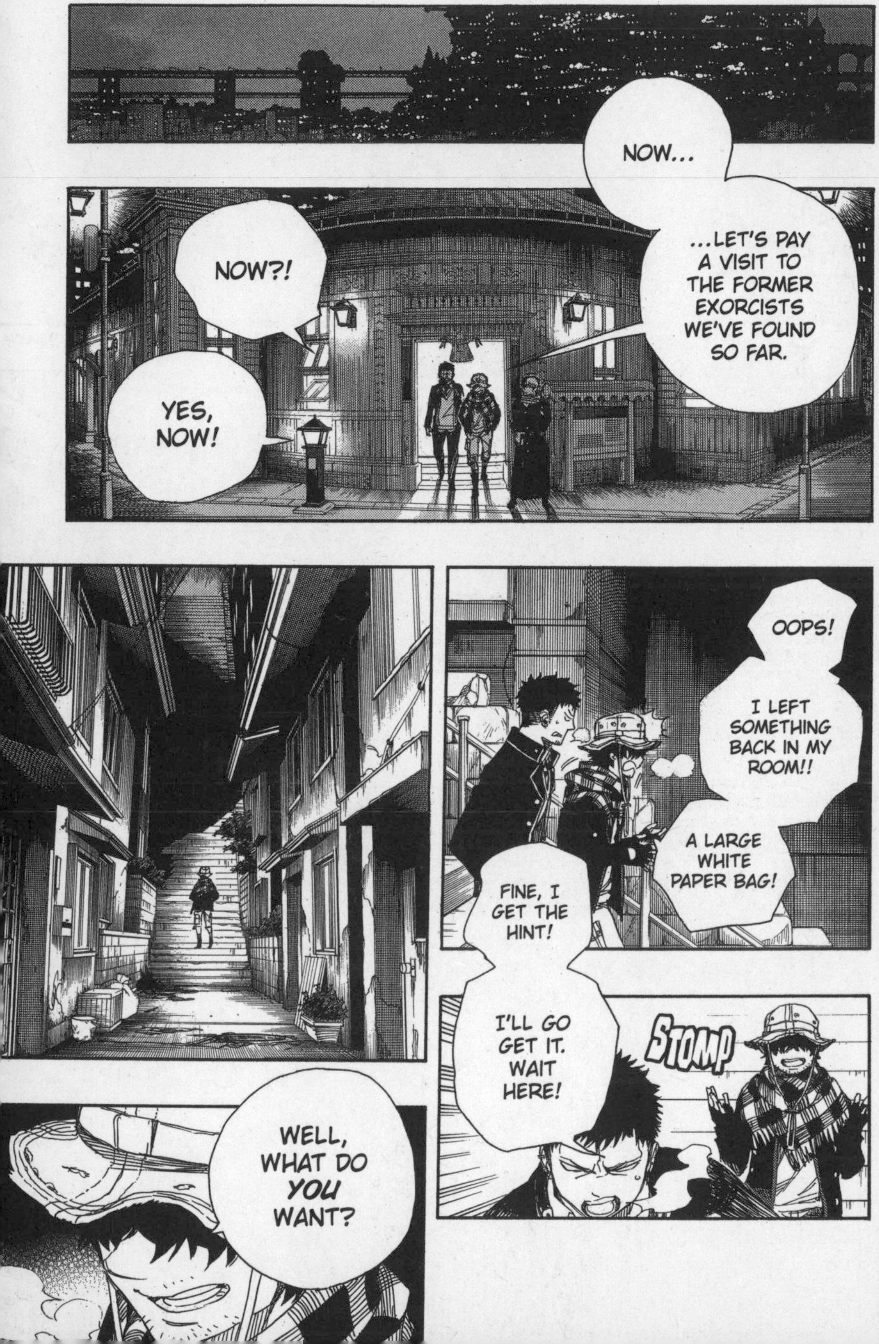
NOW...
...LET'S PAY A VISIT TO THE FORMER EXORCISTS WE'VE FOUND SO FAR.
NOW?!
YES, NOW!
OOPS!
I LEFT SOMETHING BACK IN MY ROOM!!
A LARGE WHITE PAPER BAG!
FINE, I GET THE HINT!
I'LL GO GET IT. WAIT HERE!
STOMP
WELL, WHAT DO *YOU* WANT?

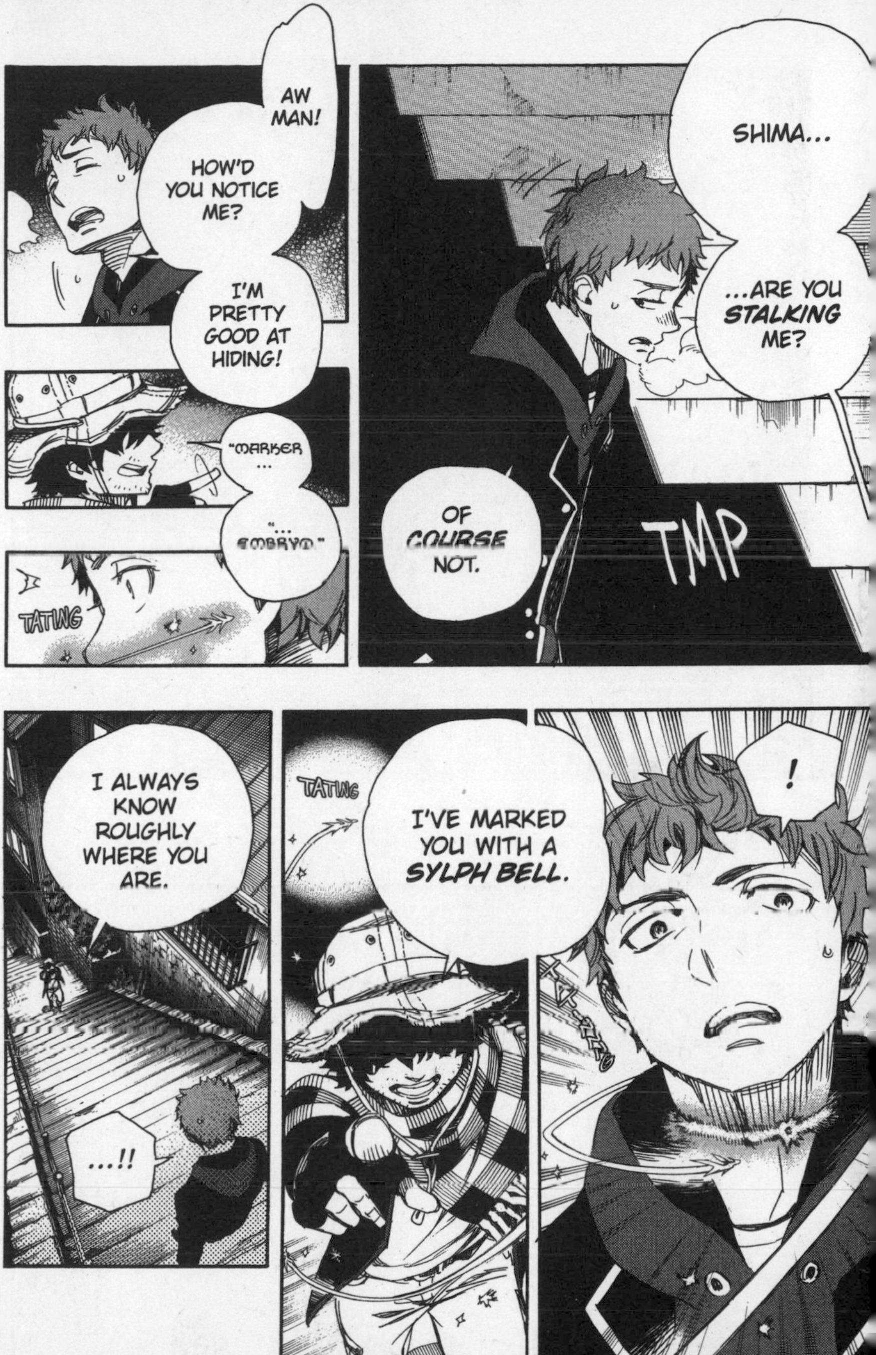
SHIMA...
...ARE YOU STALKING ME?
OF COURSE NOT.
TMP
AW MAN!
HOW'D YOU NOTICE ME?
I'M PRETTY GOOD AT HIDING!
"MARKER...
"...EMBRYO."
TATING
!
TATING
I'VE MARKED YOU WITH A SYLPH BELL.
I ALWAYS KNOW ROUGHLY WHERE YOU ARE.
...!!

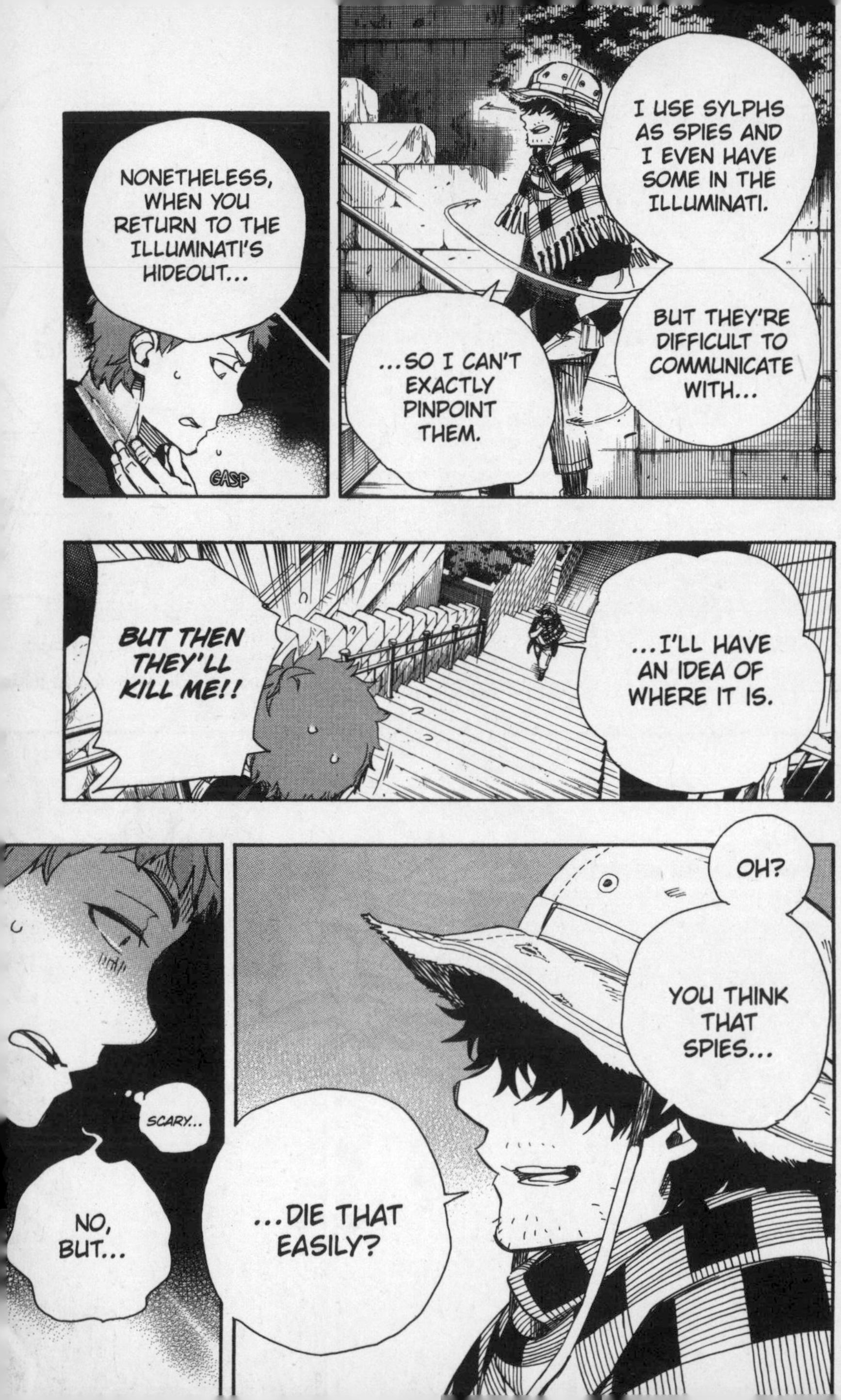
I USE SYLPHS AS SPIES AND I EVEN HAVE SOME IN THE ILLUMINATI.
BUT THEY'RE DIFFICULT TO COMMUNICATE WITH...
...SO I CAN'T EXACTLY PINPOINT THEM.
NONETHELESS, WHEN YOU RETURN TO THE ILLUMINATI'S HIDEOUT...
GASP
...I'LL HAVE AN IDEA OF WHERE IT IS.
BUT THEN THEY'LL KILL ME!!
OH?
YOU THINK THAT SPIES...
...DIE THAT EASILY?
SCARY...
NO, BUT...

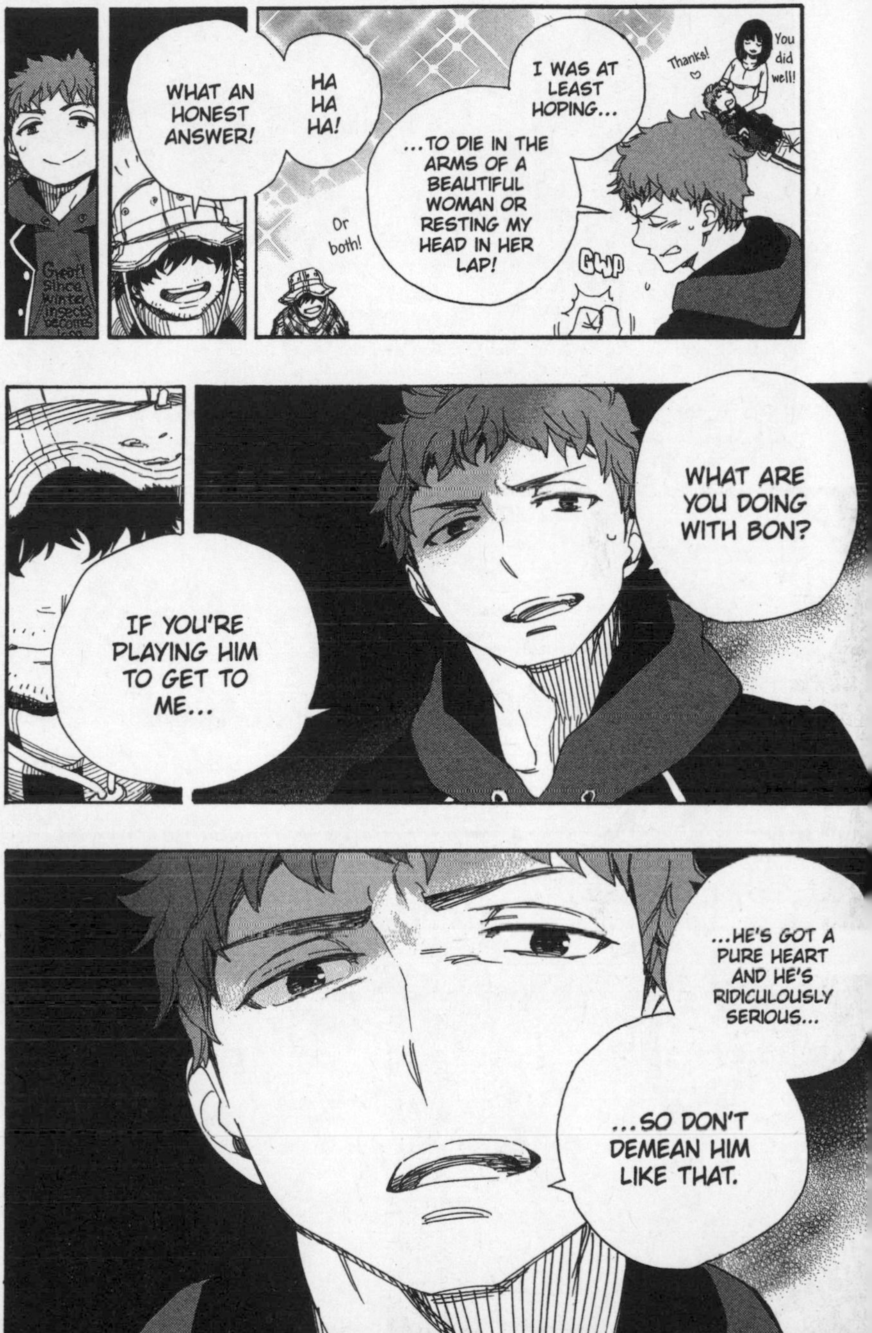
You did well!
Thanks! ♡
I WAS AT LEAST HOPING...
...TO DIE IN THE ARMS OF A BEAUTIFUL WOMAN OR RESTING MY HEAD IN HER LAP!
GWP
Or both!
HA HA HA!
WHAT AN HONEST ANSWER!
Great! Since winter insects become
WHAT ARE YOU DOING WITH BON?
IF YOU'RE PLAYING HIM TO GET TO ME...
...HE'S GOT A PURE HEART AND HE'S RIDICULOUSLY SERIOUS...
...SO DON'T DEMEAN HIM LIKE THAT.

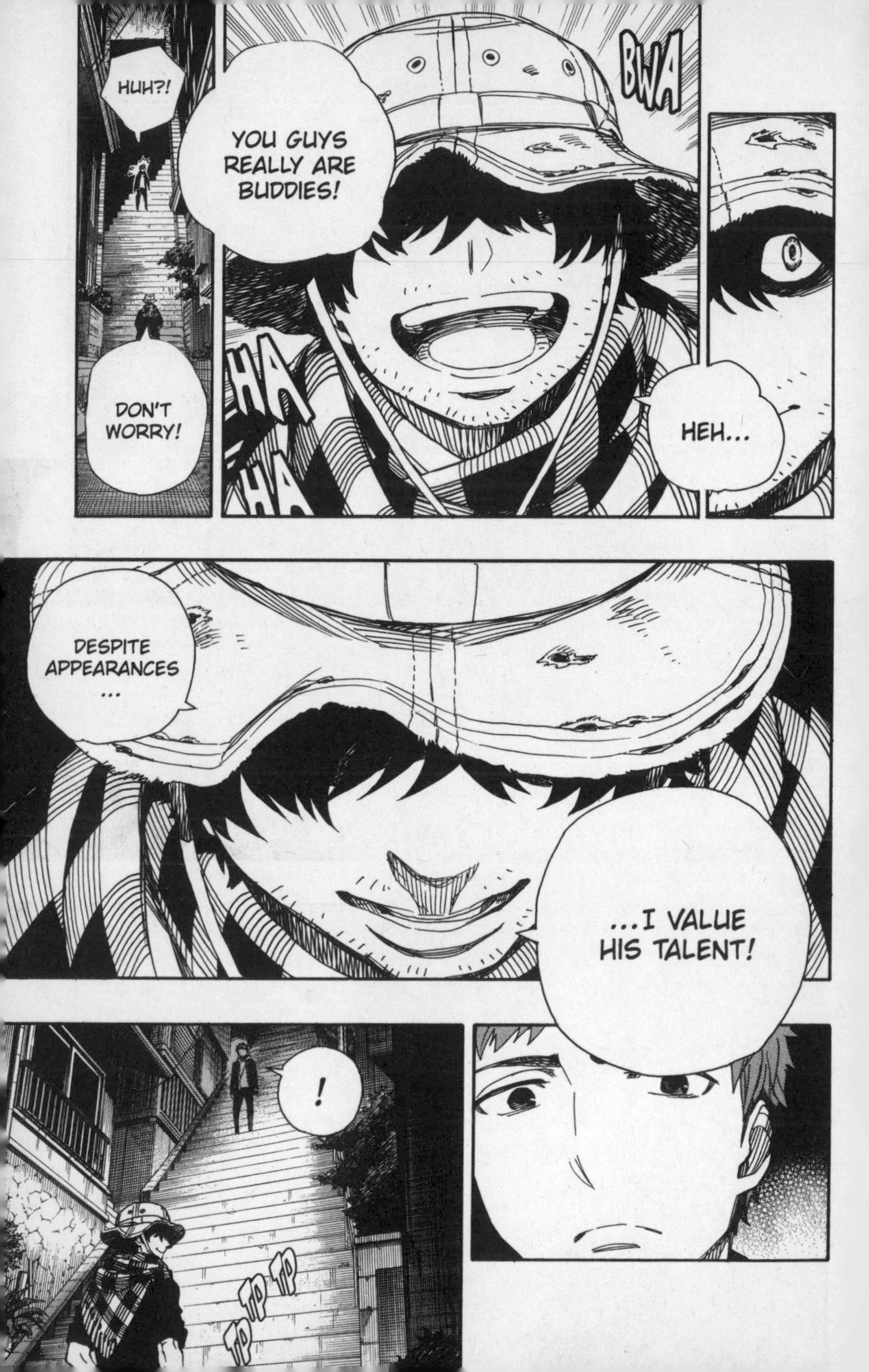
HEH...
BWA
YOU GUYS REALLY ARE BUDDIES!
HA HA
HUH?!
DON'T WORRY!
DESPITE APPEARANCES ...
...I VALUE HIS TALENT!
!
TP TP TP TP

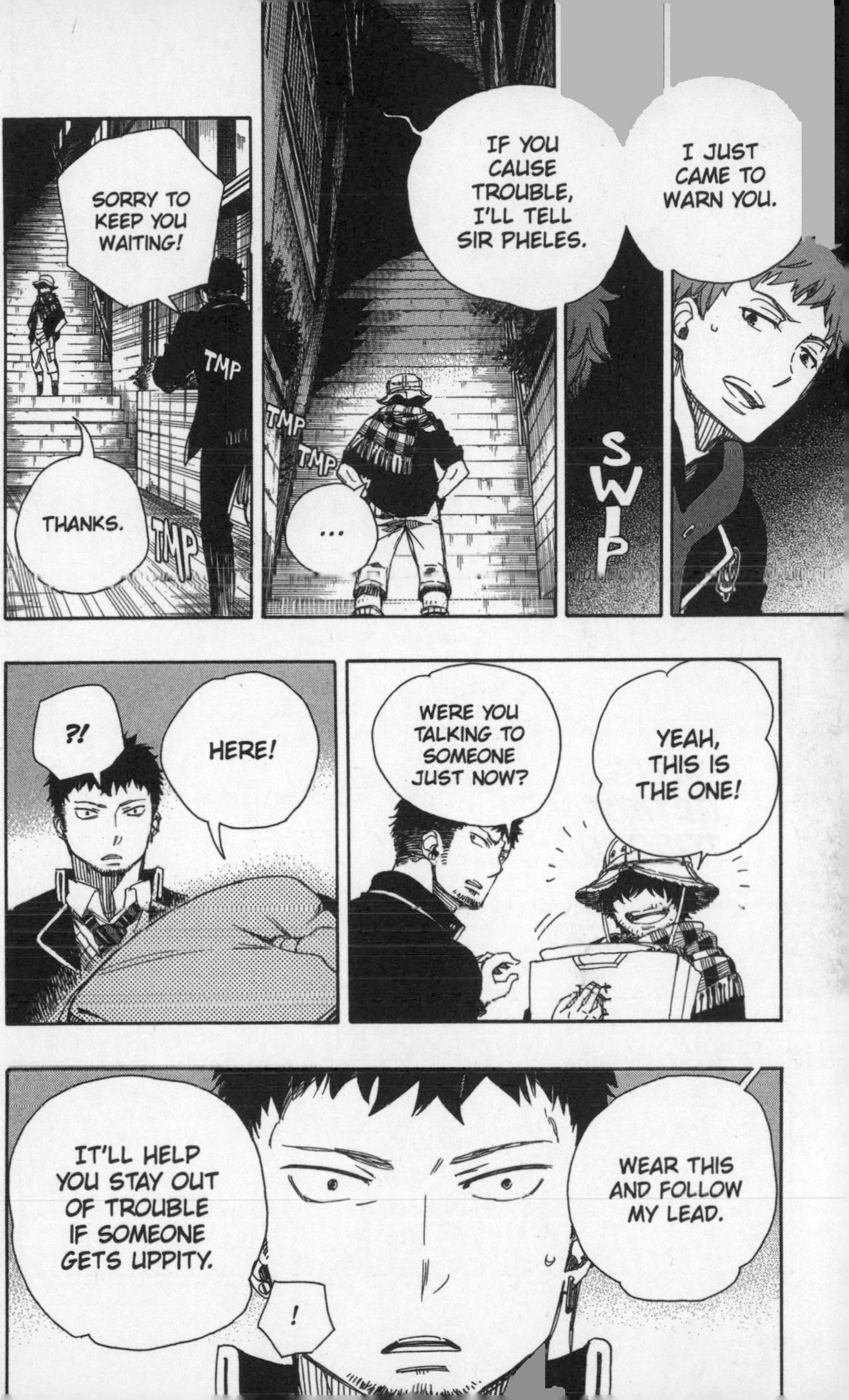
I JUST CAME TO WARN YOU.
IF YOU CAUSE TROUBLE, I'LL TELL SIR PHELES.
SWIP
TMP
TMP
...
SORRY TO KEEP YOU WAITING!
TMP
THANKS.
TMP
YEAH, THIS IS THE ONE!
WERE YOU TALKING TO SOMEONE JUST NOW?
HERE!
?!
WEAR THIS AND FOLLOW MY LEAD.
IT'LL HELP YOU STAY OUT OF TROUBLE IF SOMEONE GETS UPPITY.
!

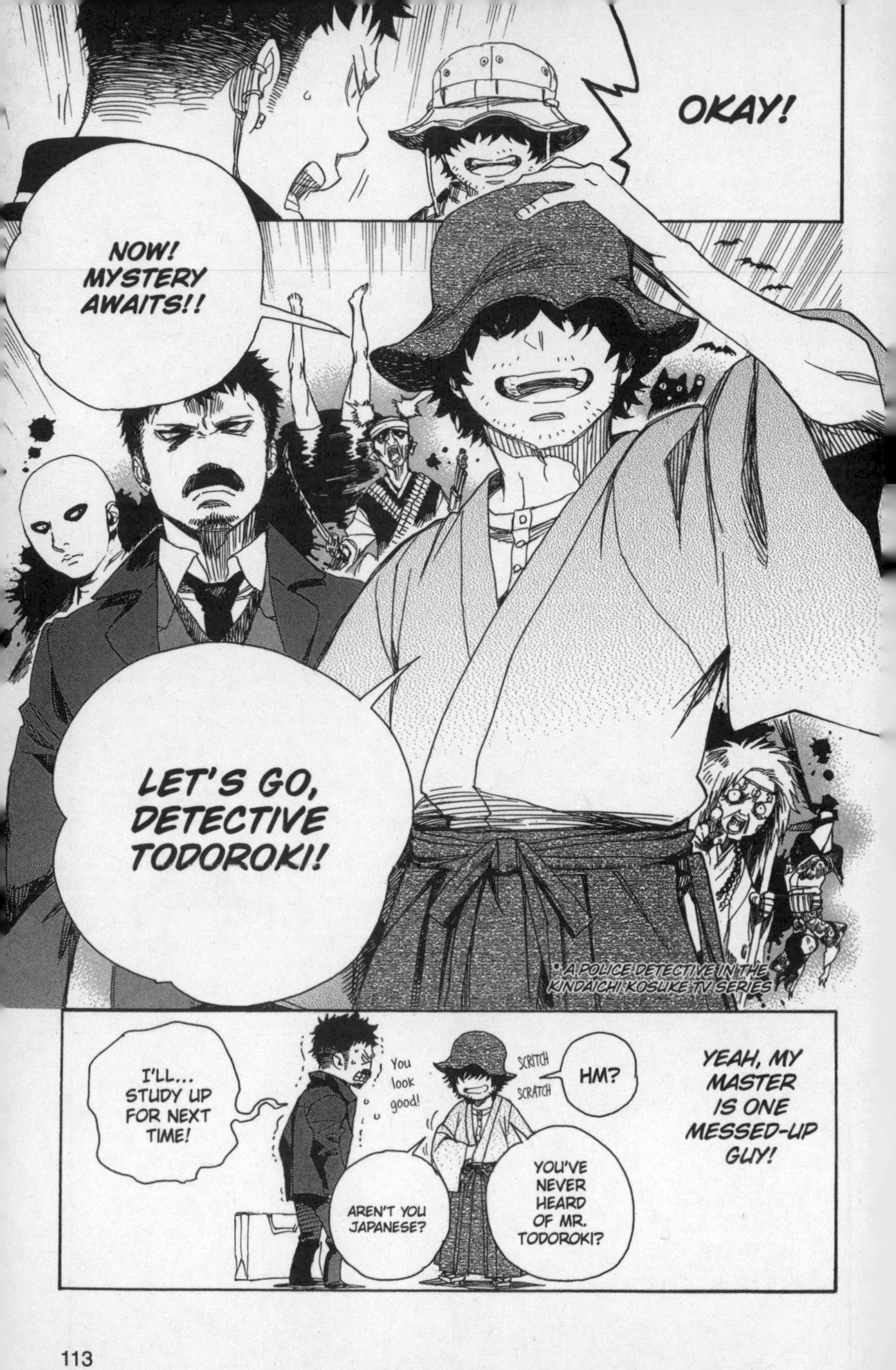
OKAY!
NOW! MYSTERY AWAITS!!
LET'S GO, DETECTIVE TODOROKI!
* A POLICE DETECTIVE IN THE KINDAICHI KOSUKE TV SERIES
YEAH, MY MASTER IS ONE MESSED-UP GUY!
HM?
SCRITCH
SCRATCH
YOU'VE NEVER HEARD OF MR. TODOROKI?
AREN'T YOU JAPANESE?
You look good!
I'LL... STUDY UP FOR NEXT TIME!

Blue Exorcist Chapter 81: Rhizome

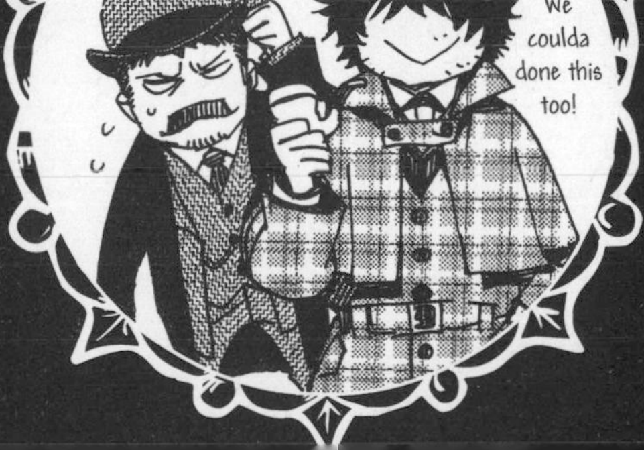
We coulda done this too!
I get a mustache again?

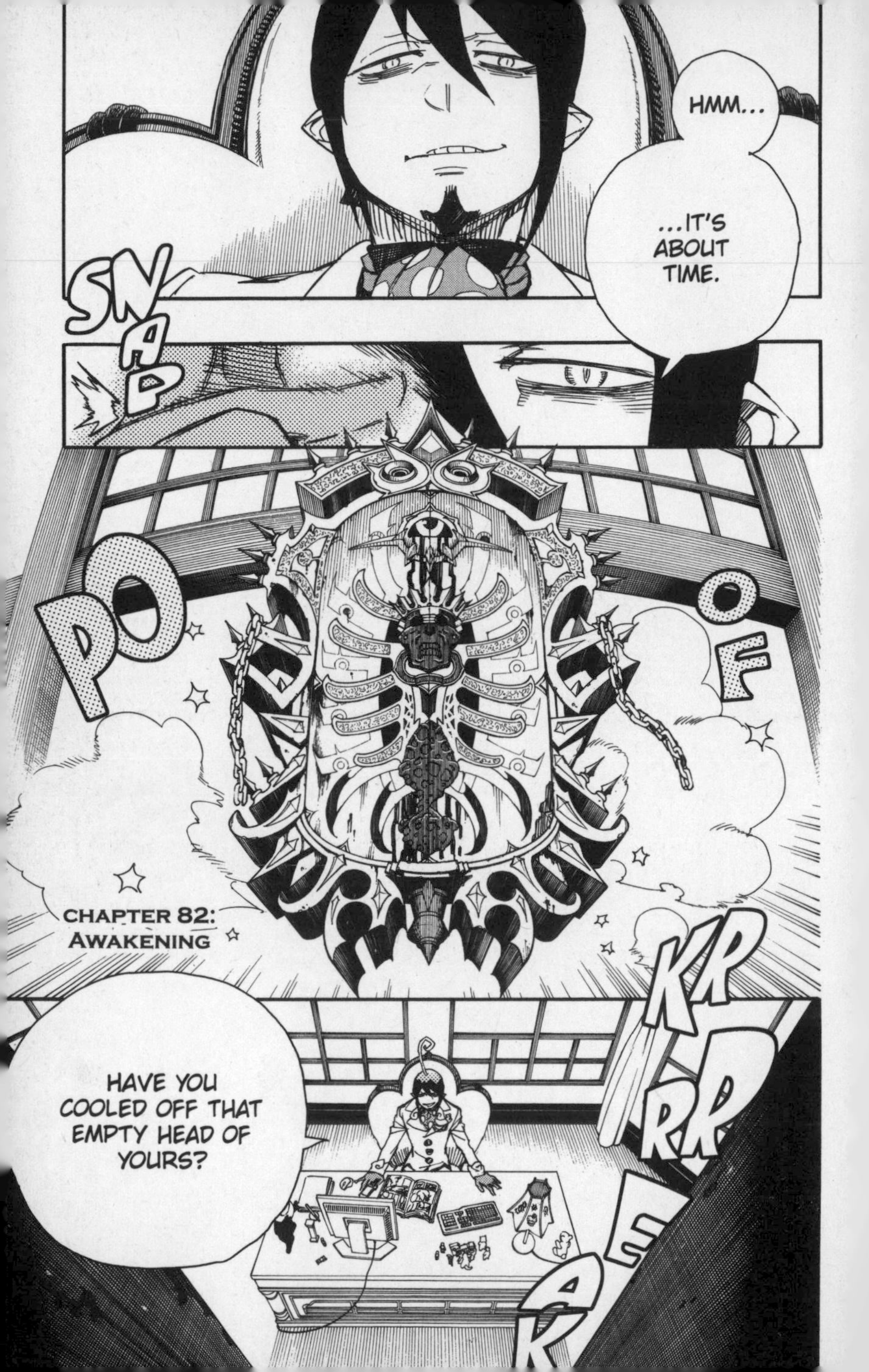
HMM...
...IT'S ABOUT TIME.
SNAP
POOF
CHAPTER 82: AWAKENING
KRRREAK
HAVE YOU COOLED OFF THAT EMPTY HEAD OF YOURS?

Chapter 82: Awakening

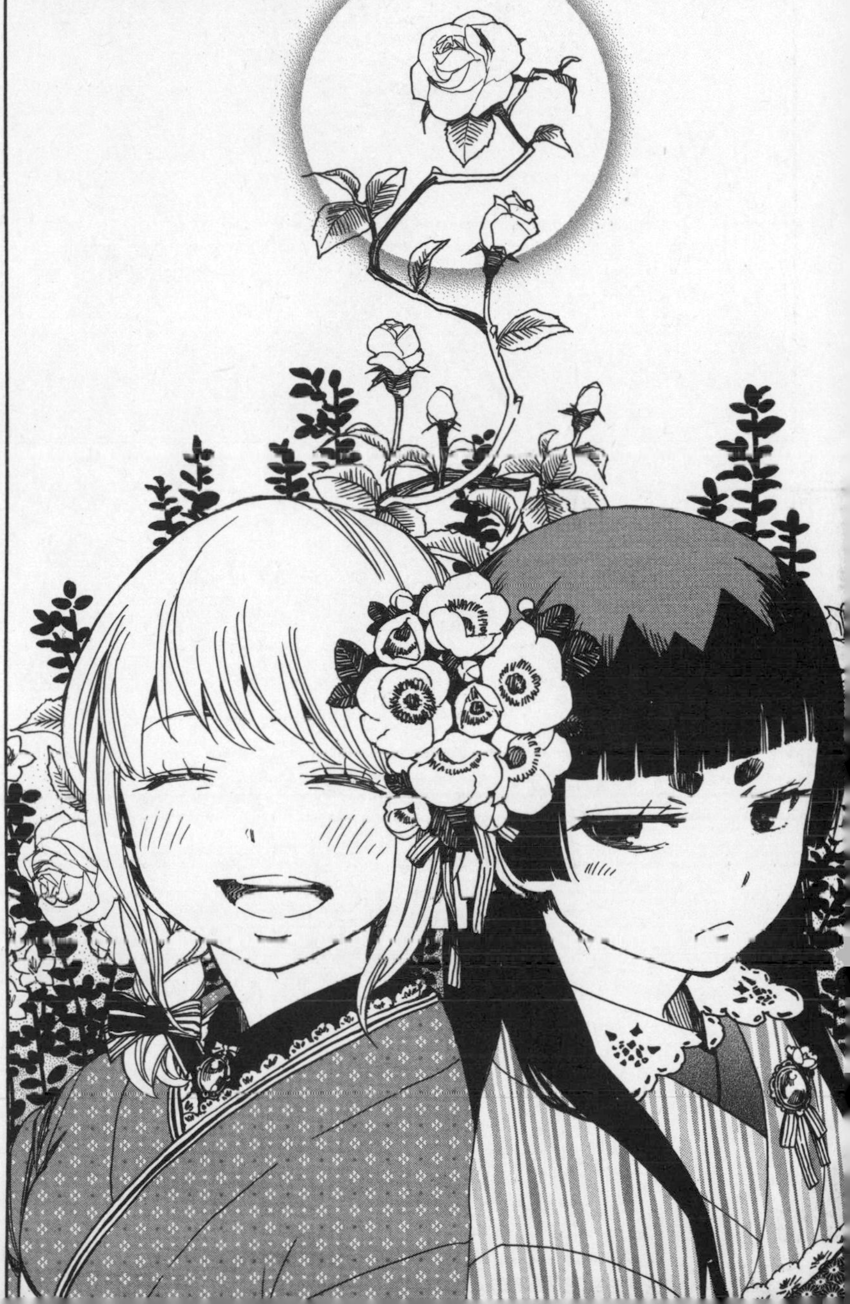

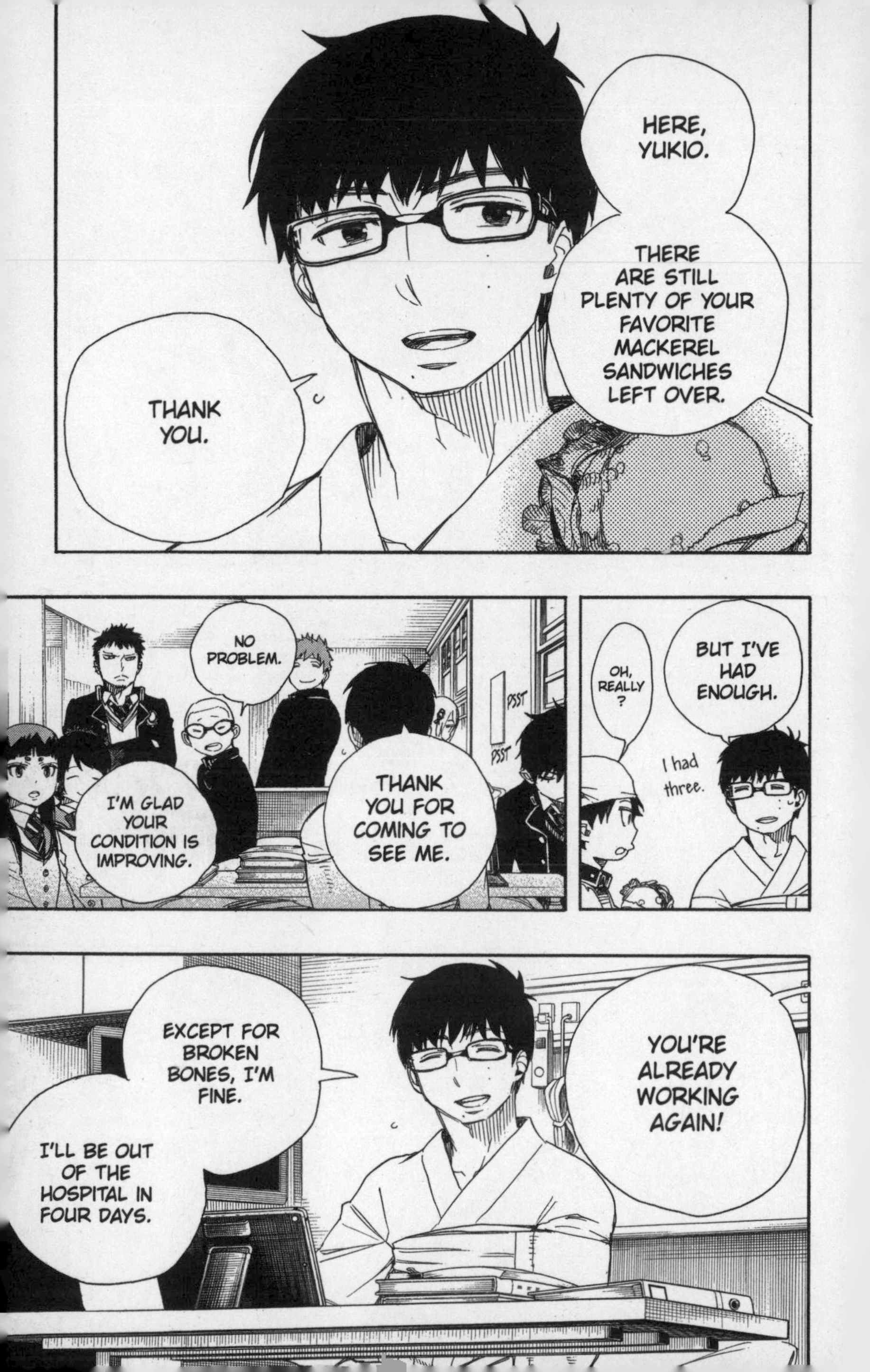
HERE, YUKIO.
THERE ARE STILL PLENTY OF YOUR FAVORITE MACKEREL SANDWICHES LEFT OVER.
THANK YOU.
BUT I'VE HAD ENOUGH.
OH, REALLY?
I had three.
PSST
PSST
NO PROBLEM.
THANK YOU FOR COMING TO SEE ME.
I'M GLAD YOUR CONDITION IS IMPROVING.
YOU'RE ALREADY WORKING AGAIN!
EXCEPT FOR BROKEN BONES, I'M FINE.
I'LL BE OUT OF THE HOSPITAL IN FOUR DAYS.

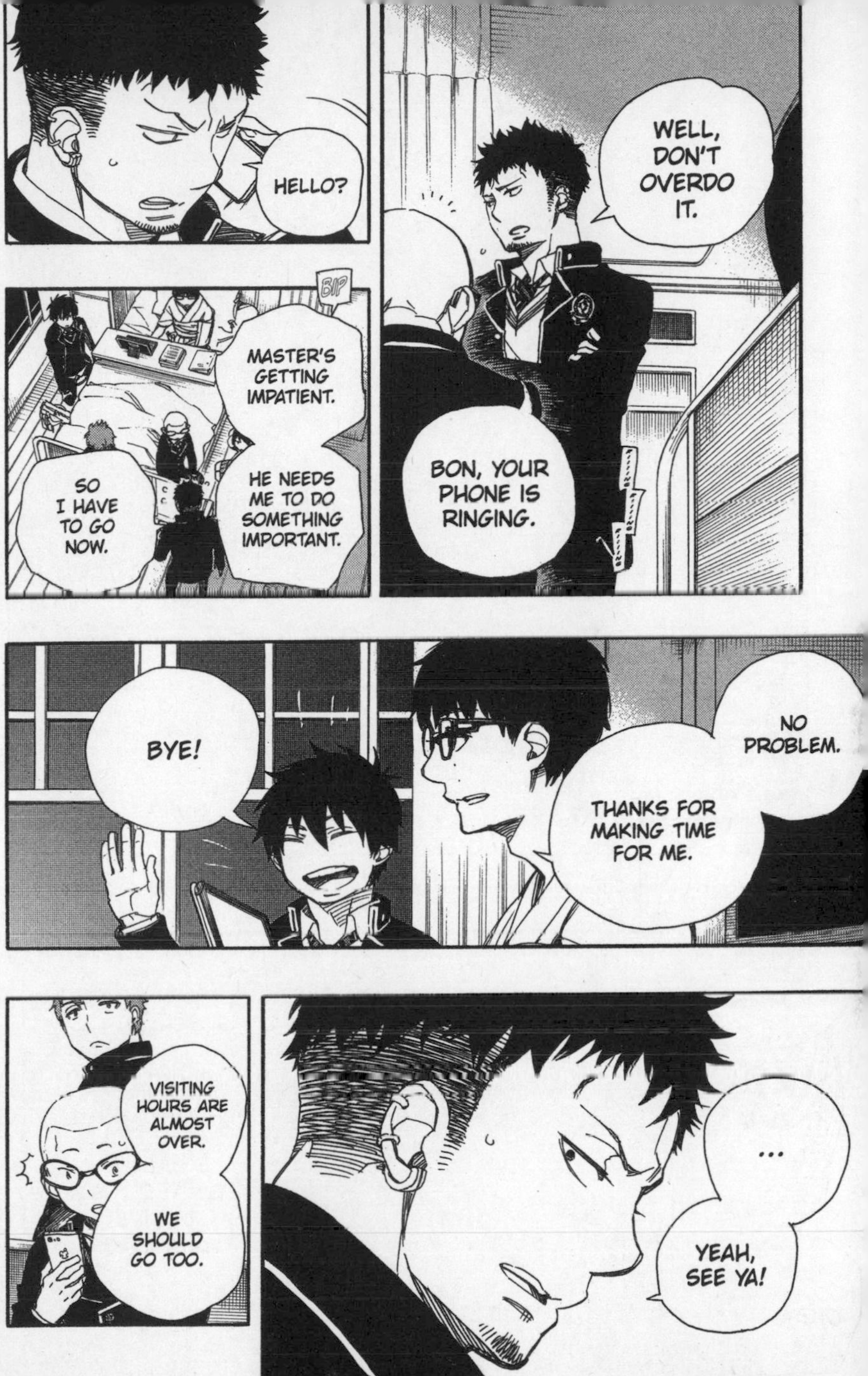
WELL, DON'T OVERDO IT.
BON, YOUR PHONE IS RINGING.
HELLO?
BIP
MASTER'S GETTING IMPATIENT.
HE NEEDS ME TO DO SOMETHING IMPORTANT.
SO I HAVE TO GO NOW.
NO PROBLEM.
THANKS FOR MAKING TIME FOR ME.
BYE!
...
YEAH, SEE YA!
VISITING HOURS ARE ALMOST OVER.
WE SHOULD GO TOO.

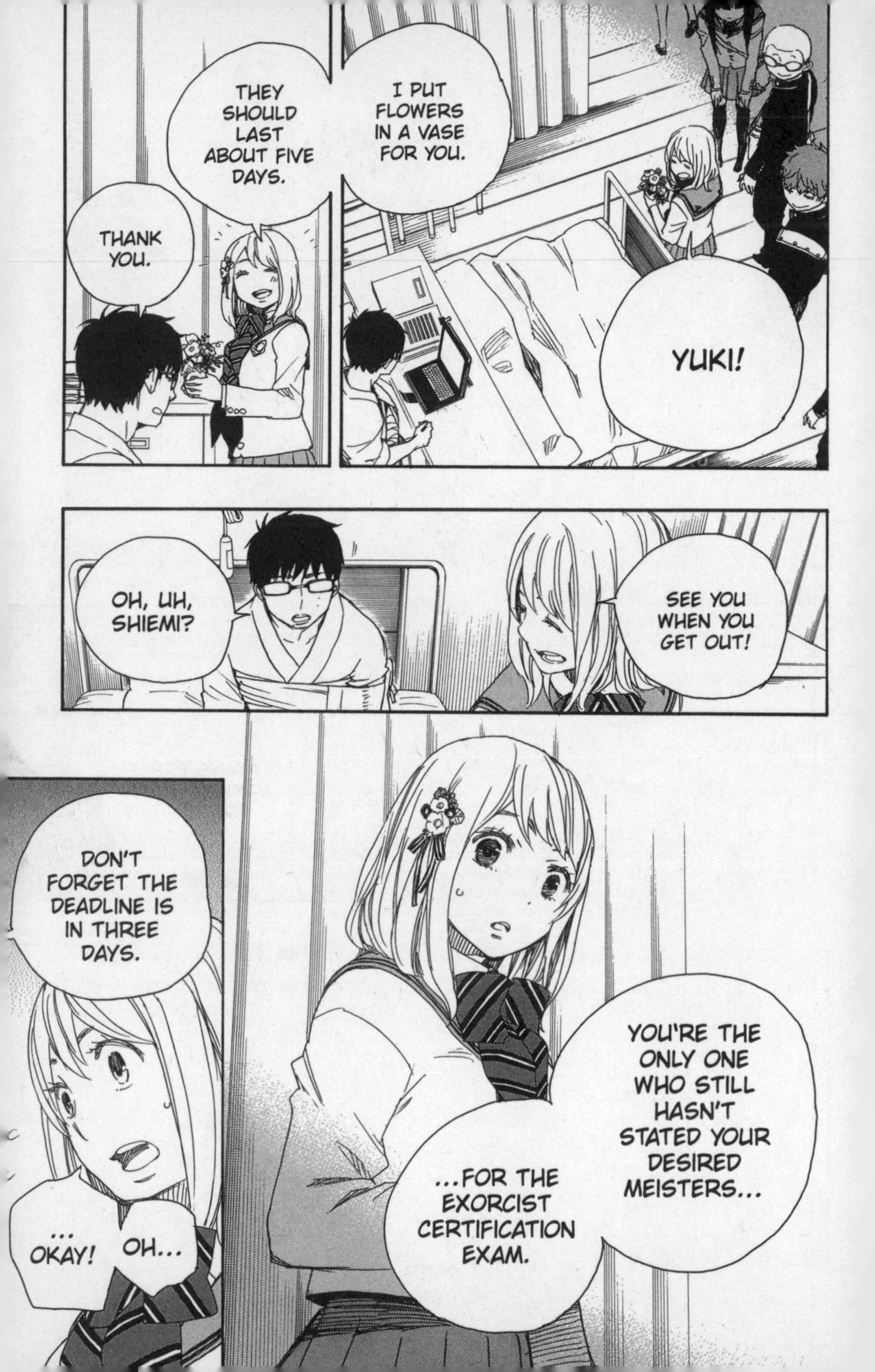
YUKI!
I PUT FLOWERS IN A VASE FOR YOU.
THEY SHOULD LAST ABOUT FIVE DAYS.
THANK YOU.
SEE YOU WHEN YOU GET OUT!
OH, UH, SHIEMI?
YOU'RE THE ONLY ONE WHO STILL HASN'T STATED YOUR DESIRED MEISTERS...
...FOR THE EXORCIST CERTIFICATION EXAM.
DON'T FORGET THE DEADLINE IS IN THREE DAYS.
OH...
... OKAY!

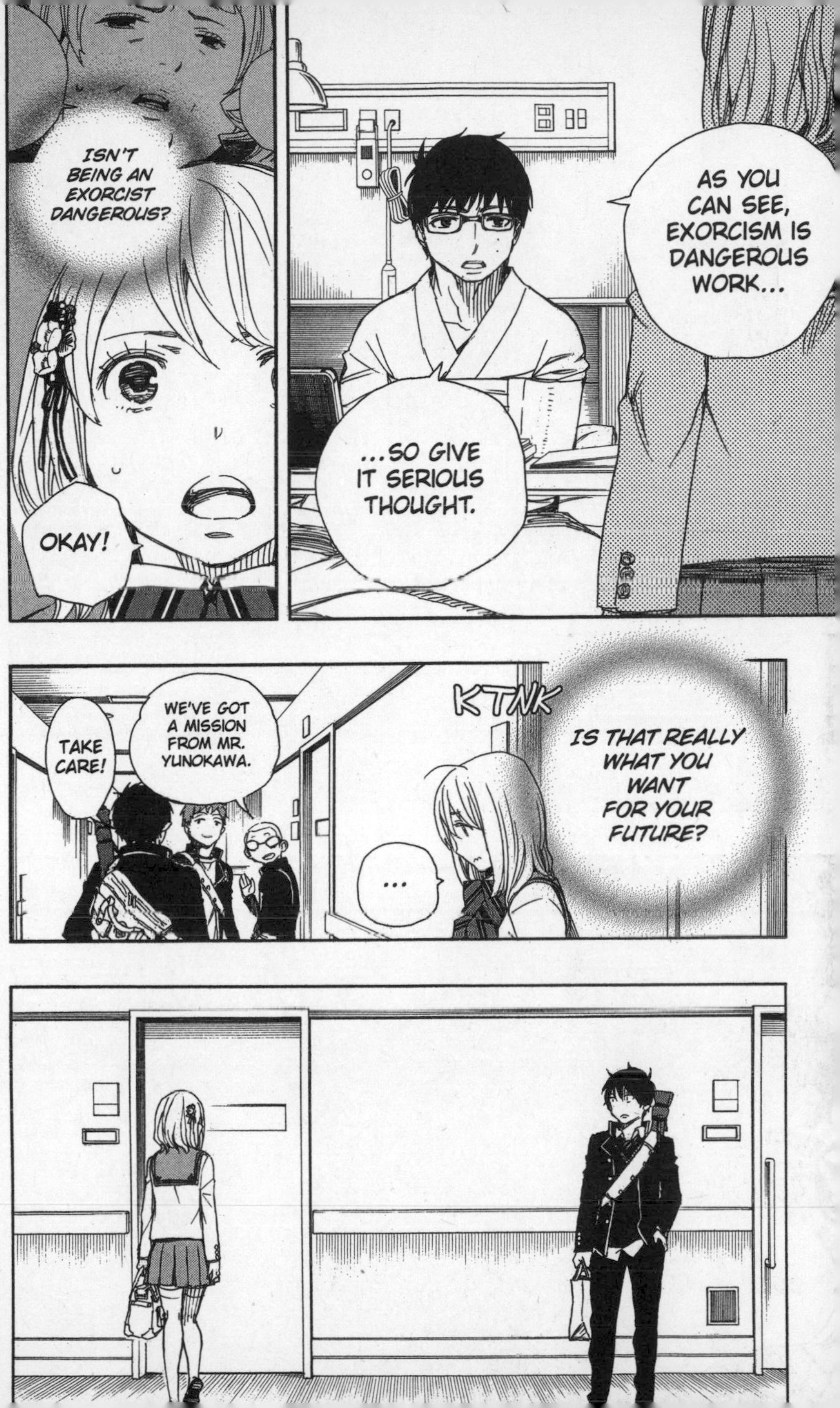
AS YOU CAN SEE, EXORCISM IS DANGEROUS WORK...
...SO GIVE IT SERIOUS THOUGHT.
ISN'T BEING AN EXORCIST DANGEROUS?
OKAY!
IS THAT REALLY WHAT YOU WANT FOR YOUR FUTURE?
KTNK
...
WE'VE GOT A MISSION FROM MR. YUNOKAWA.
TAKE CARE!

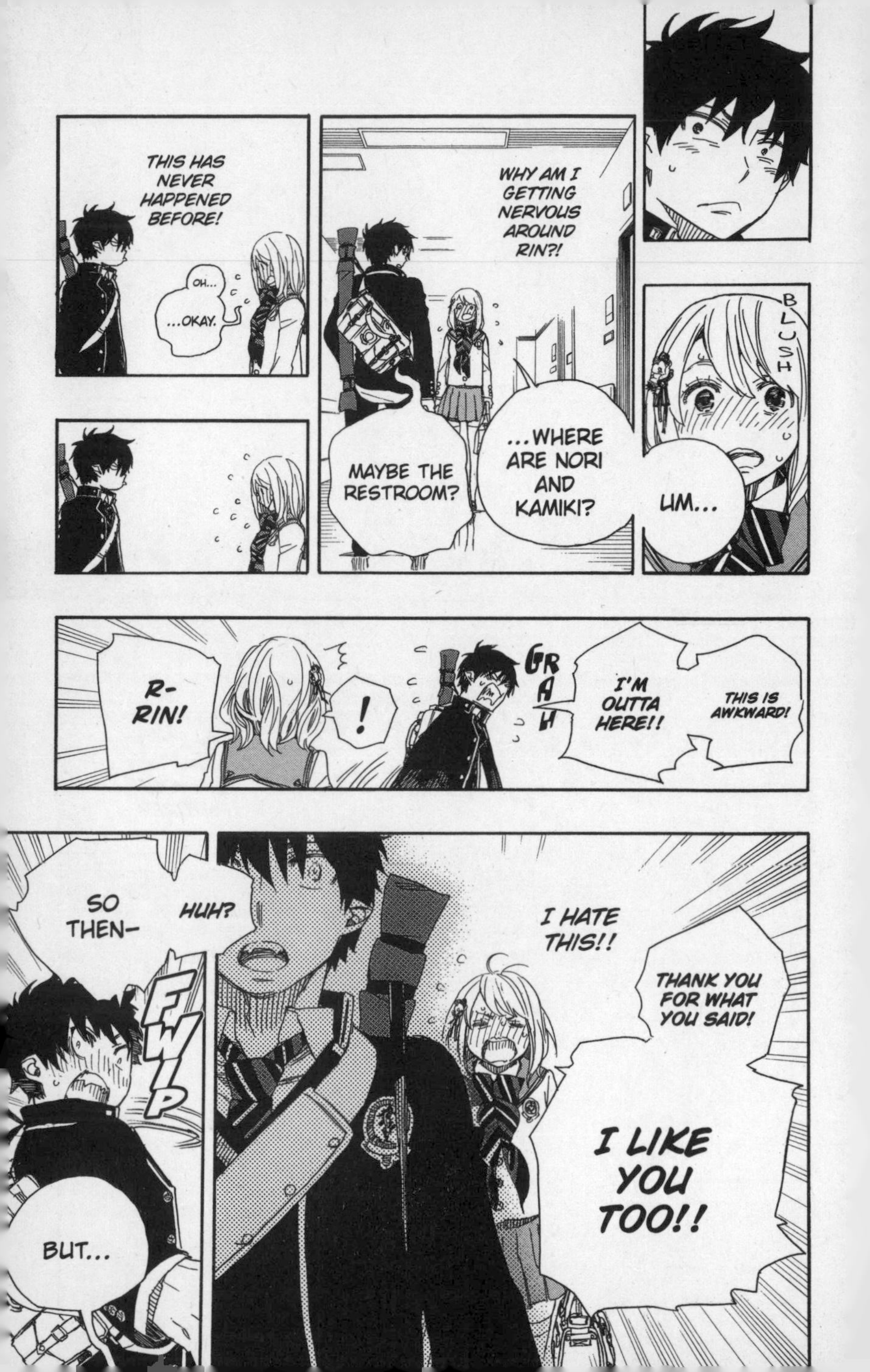
BLUSH
UM...
WHY AM I GETTING NERVOUS AROUND RIN?!
...WHERE ARE NORI AND KAMIKI?
MAYBE THE RESTROOM?
THIS HAS NEVER HAPPENED BEFORE!
OH...
...OKAY.
THIS IS AWKWARD!
I'M OUTTA HERE!!
GRAH
!
R-RIN!
THANK YOU FOR WHAT YOU SAID!
I HATE THIS!!
I LIKE YOU TOO!!
HUH?
SO THEN-
FWIP
BUT...

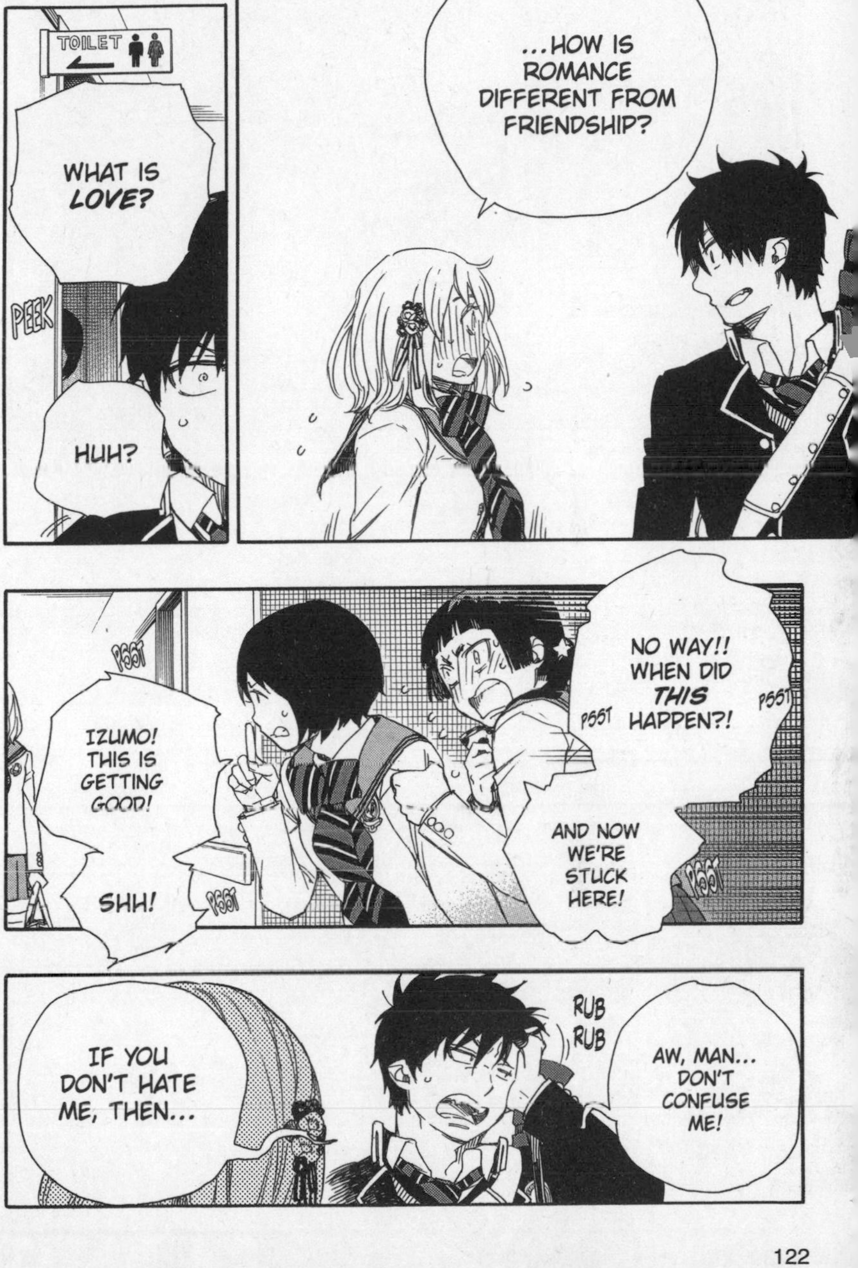
...HOW IS ROMANCE DIFFERENT FROM FRIENDSHIP?
TOILET
WHAT IS LOVE?
PEEK
HUH?
PSST
NO WAY!! WHEN DID THIS HAPPEN?!
PSST
AND NOW WE'RE STUCK HERE!
PSST
PSST
IZUMO! THIS IS GETTING GOOD!
SHH!
PSST
AW, MAN... DON'T CONFUSE ME!
RUB RUB
IF YOU DON'T HATE ME, THEN...

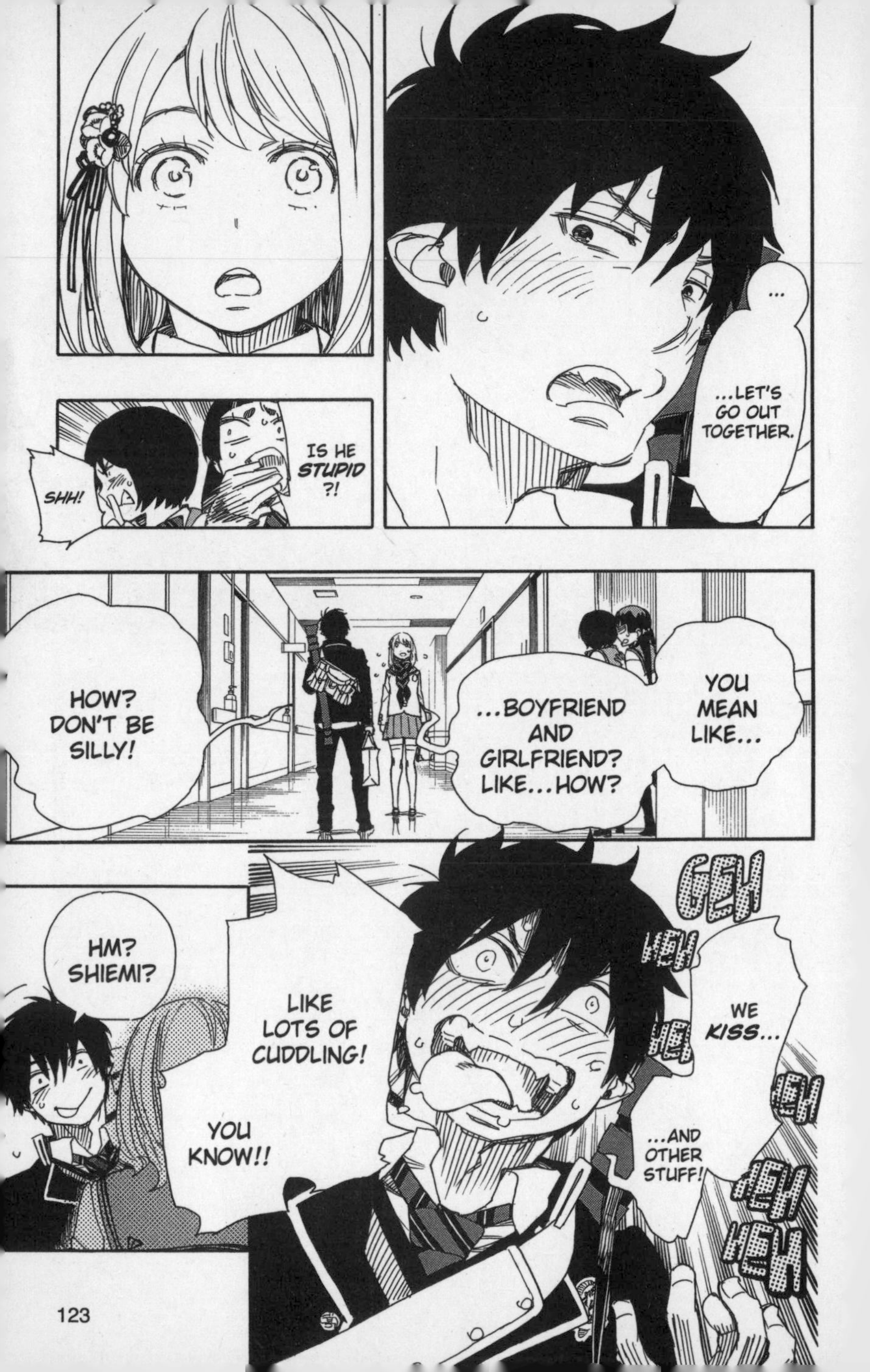
...
...LET'S GO OUT TOGETHER.
IS HE STUPID?!
SHH!
YOU MEAN LIKE...
...BOYFRIEND AND GIRLFRIEND? LIKE...HOW?
HOW? DON'T BE SILLY!
GEH
HEH
HEH
HEH
HEH
HEH
WE KISS...
...AND OTHER STUFF!
LIKE LOTS OF CUDDLING!
YOU KNOW!!
HM? SHIEMI?

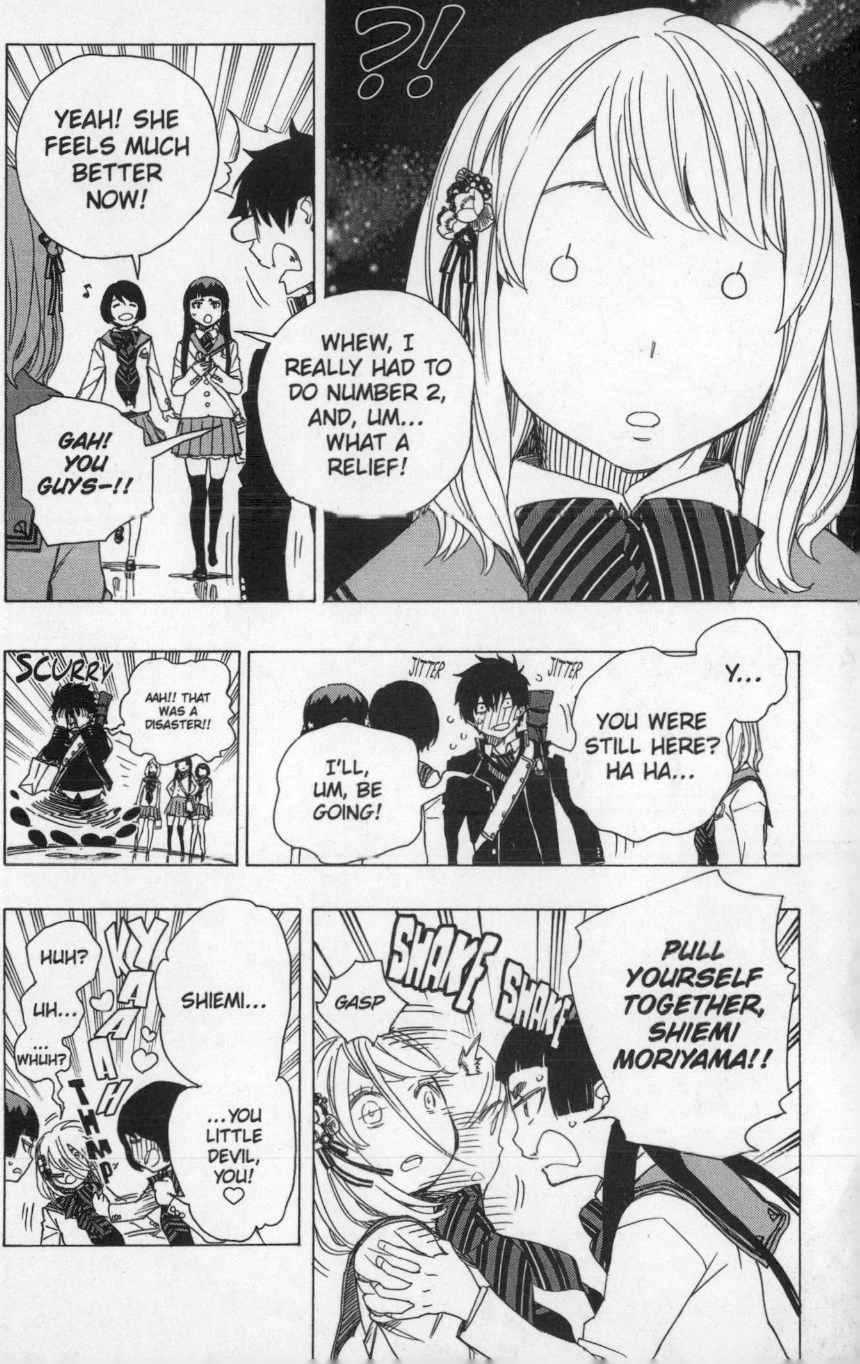
?!
WHEW, I REALLY HAD TO DO NUMBER 2, AND, UM... WHAT A RELIEF!
YEAH! SHE FEELS MUCH BETTER NOW!
GAH! YOU GUYS--!!
JITTER
JITTER
Y... YOU WERE STILL HERE? HA HA...
I'LL, UM, BE GOING!
SCURRY
AAH!! THAT WAS A DISASTER!!
SHAKE
SHAKE
PULL YOURSELF TOGETHER, SHIEMI MORIYAMA!!
GASP
KYAAAAH
SHIEMI...
...YOU LITTLE DEVIL, YOU!
HUH?
UH...
...WHUH?
THMP

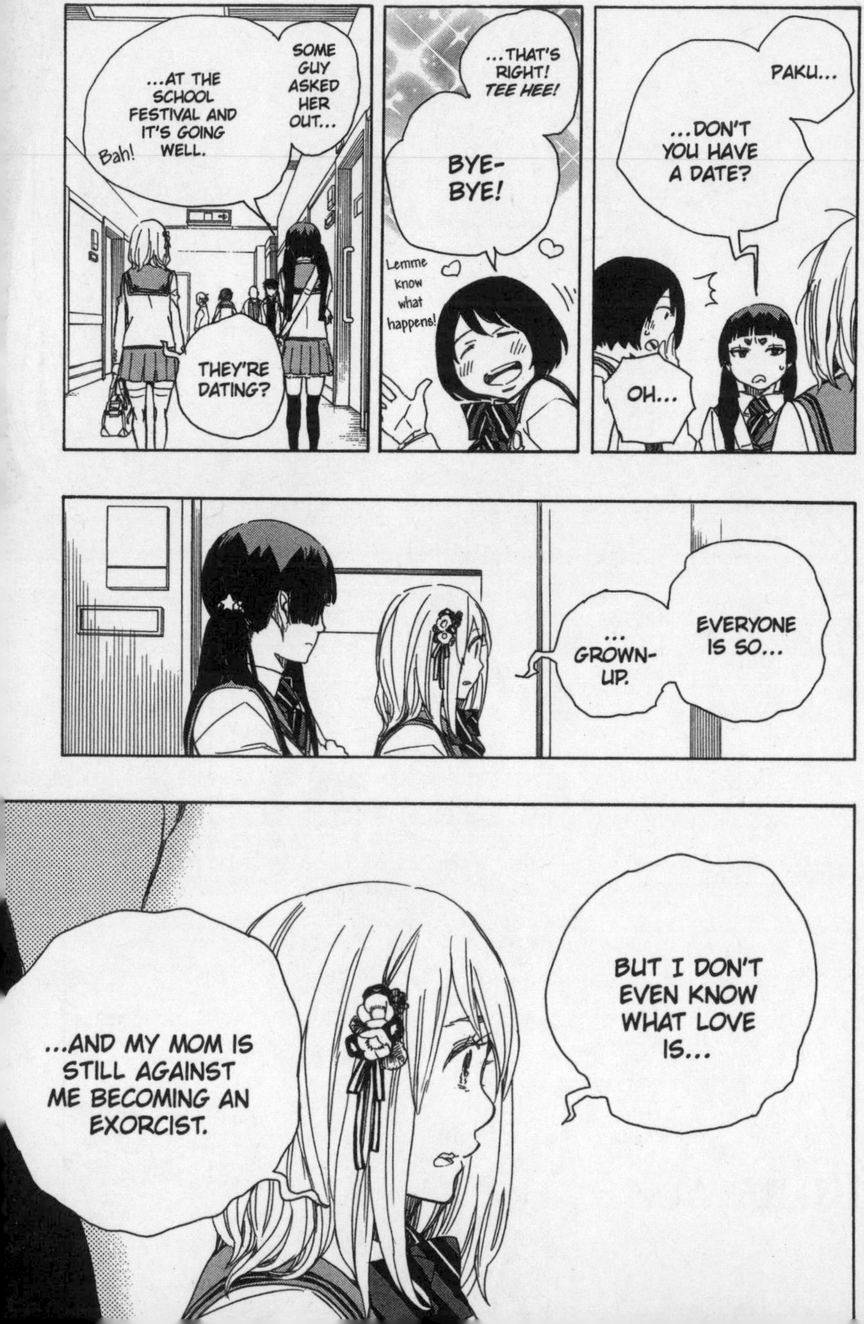
PAKU...
...DON'T YOU HAVE A DATE?
OH...
...THAT'S RIGHT! TEE HEE!
BYE-BYE!
Lemme know what happens!
SOME GUY ASKED HER OUT...
...AT THE SCHOOL FESTIVAL AND IT'S GOING WELL.
Bah!
THEY'RE DATING?
EVERYONE IS SO...
...GROWN-UP.
BUT I DON'T EVEN KNOW WHAT LOVE IS...
...AND MY MOM IS STILL AGAINST ME BECOMING AN EXORCIST.

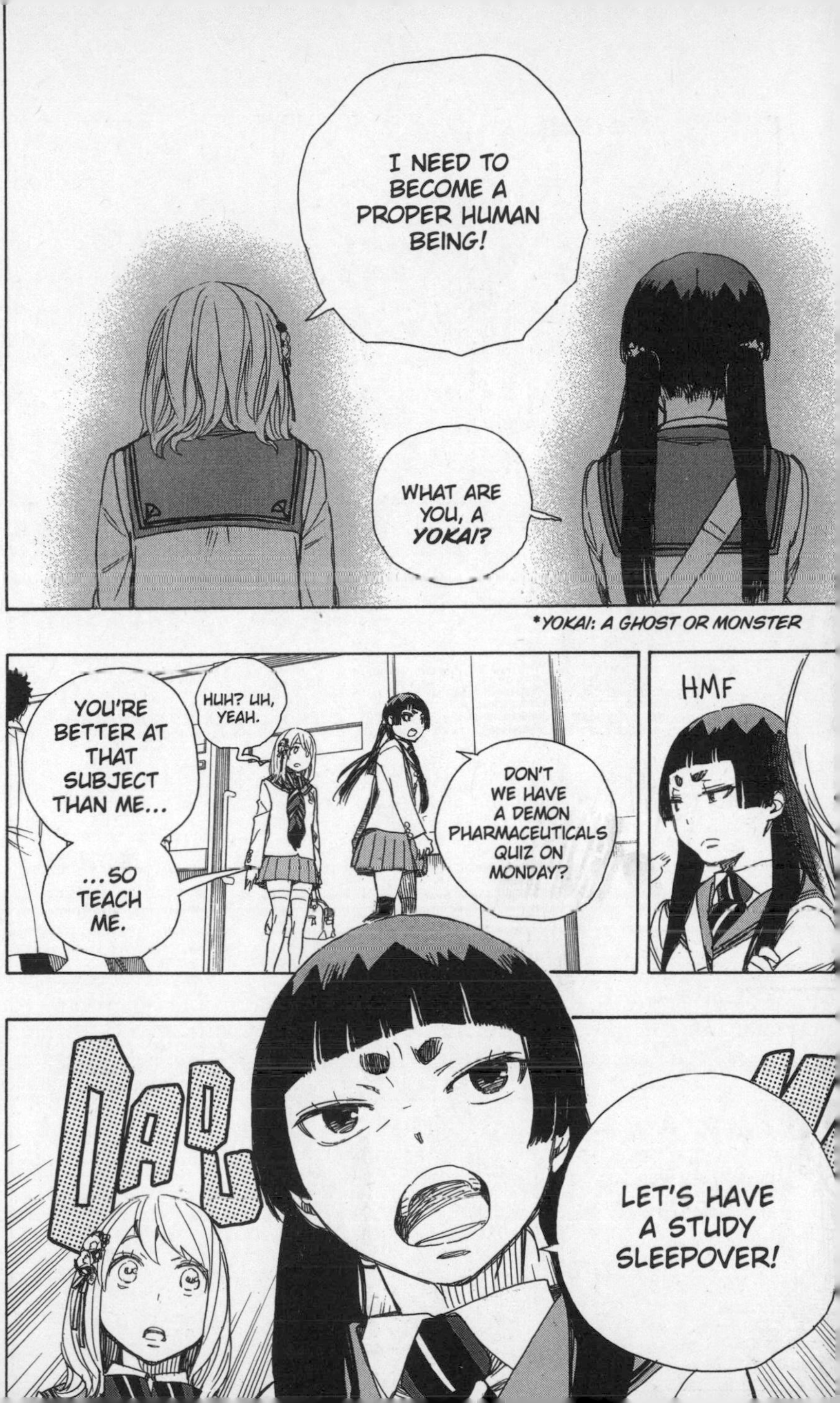
I NEED TO BECOME A PROPER HUMAN BEING!
WHAT ARE YOU, A *YOKAI*?
*YOKAI: A GHOST OR MONSTER
HMF
DON'T WE HAVE A DEMON PHARMACEUTICALS QUIZ ON MONDAY?
HUH? UH, YEAH.
YOU'RE BETTER AT THAT SUBJECT THAN ME...
...SO TEACH ME.
LET'S HAVE A STUDY SLEEPOVER!

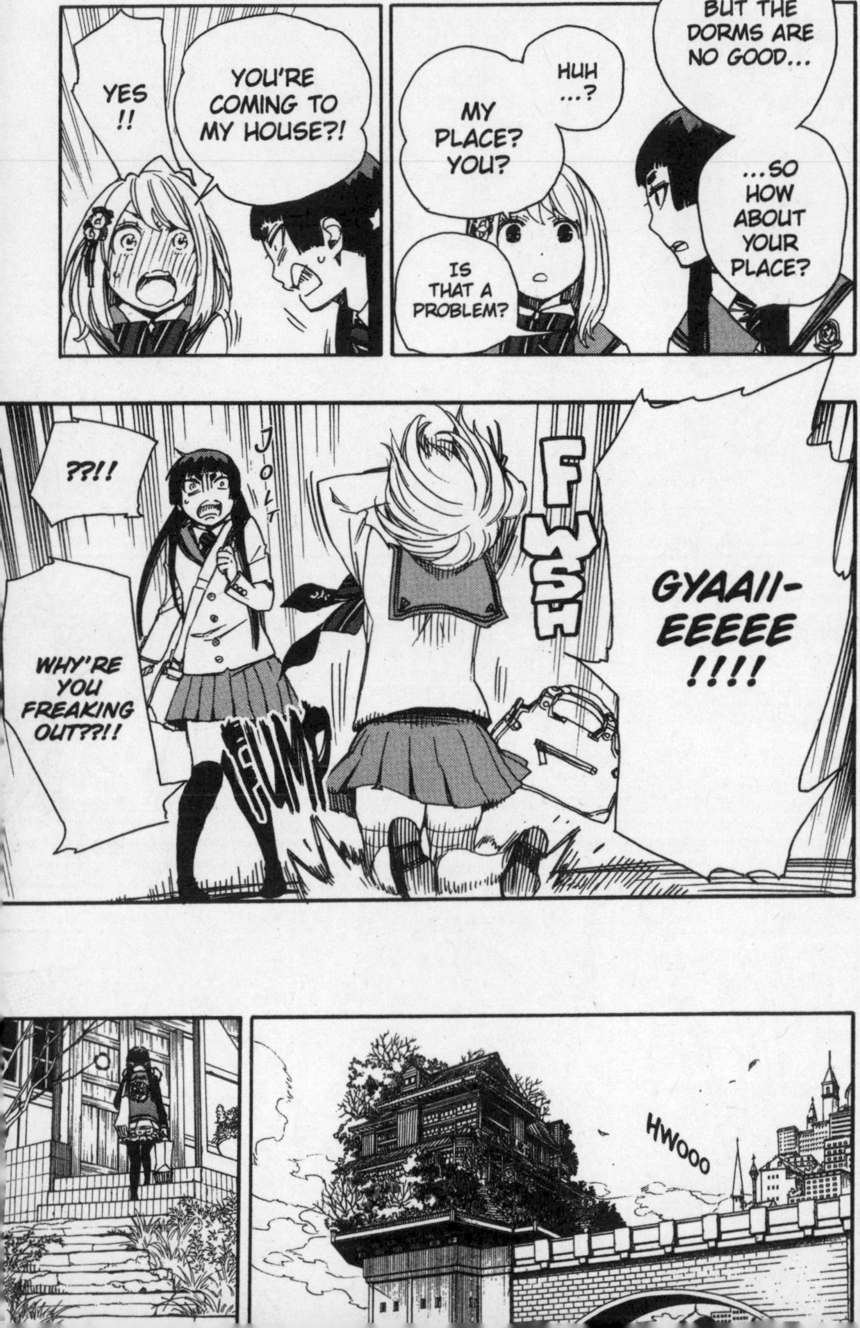
BUT THE DORMS ARE NO GOOD...
...SO HOW ABOUT YOUR PLACE?
HUH ...?
MY PLACE? YOU?
IS THAT A PROBLEM?
YOU'RE COMING TO MY HOUSE?!
YES !!
GYAAII-EEEEE !!!!
FWSH
JOLT
??!!
FUMP
WHY'RE YOU FREAKING OUT??!!
HWOOO

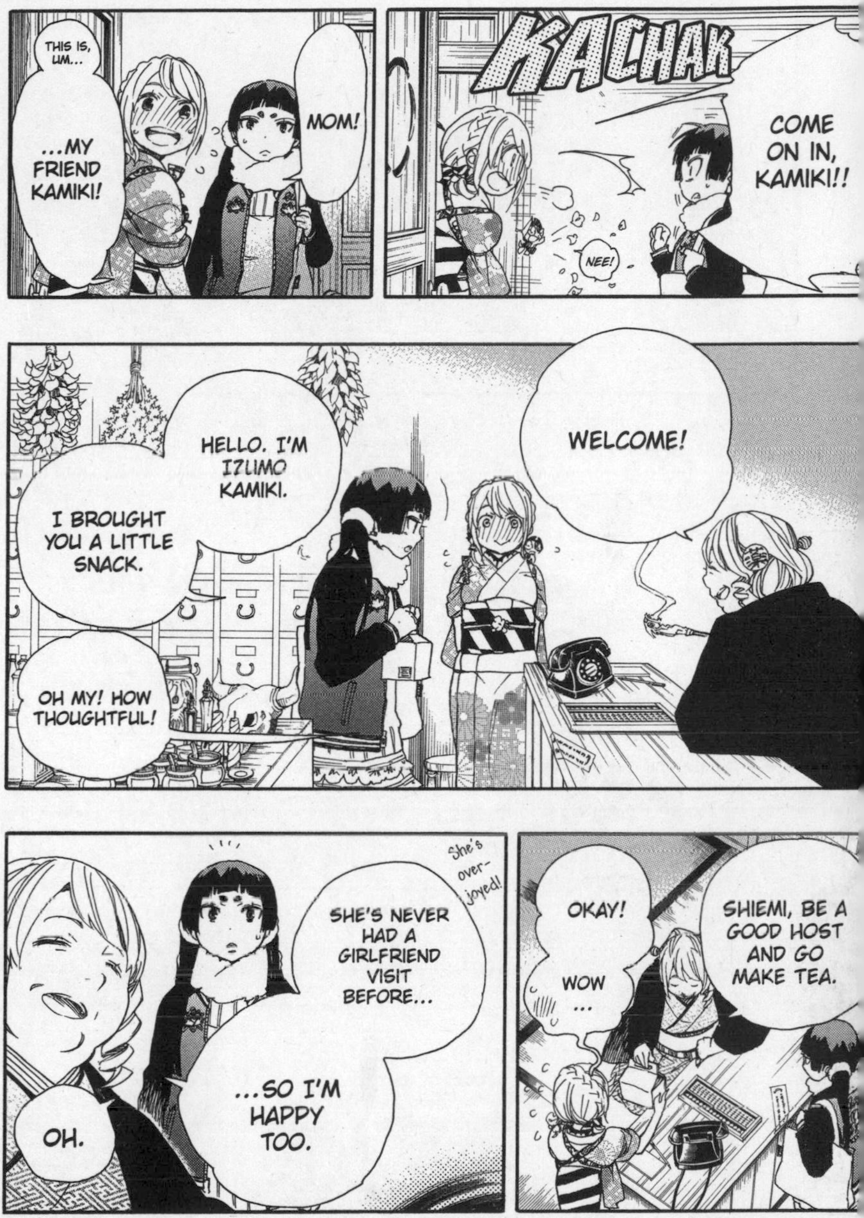
KACHAK
COME ON IN, KAMIKI!!
NEE!
MOM!
THIS IS, UM...
...MY FRIEND KAMIKI!
WELCOME!
HELLO. I'M IZUMO KAMIKI.
I BROUGHT YOU A LITTLE SNACK.
OH MY! HOW THOUGHTFUL!
SHIEMI, BE A GOOD HOST AND GO MAKE TEA.
OKAY!
WOW...
She's over-joyed!
SHE'S NEVER HAD A GIRLFRIEND VISIT BEFORE...
...SO I'M HAPPY TOO.
OH.

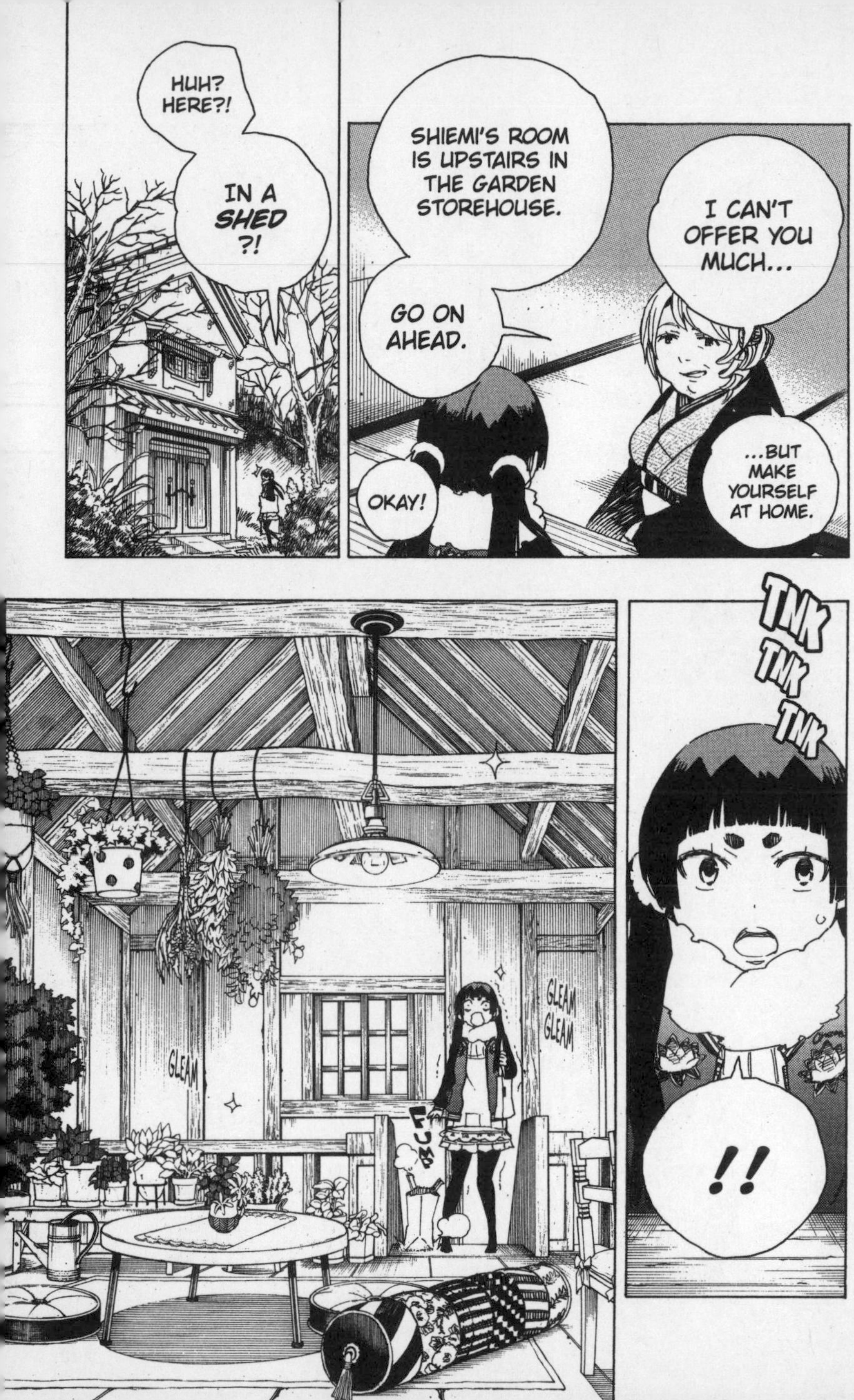
SHIEMI'S ROOM IS UPSTAIRS IN THE GARDEN STOREHOUSE.
GO ON AHEAD.
I CAN'T OFFER YOU MUCH...
...BUT MAKE YOURSELF AT HOME.
OKAY!
HUH? HERE?!
IN A SHED ?!
TNK TNK TNK
!!
GLEAM GLEAM
GLEAM
FUMP

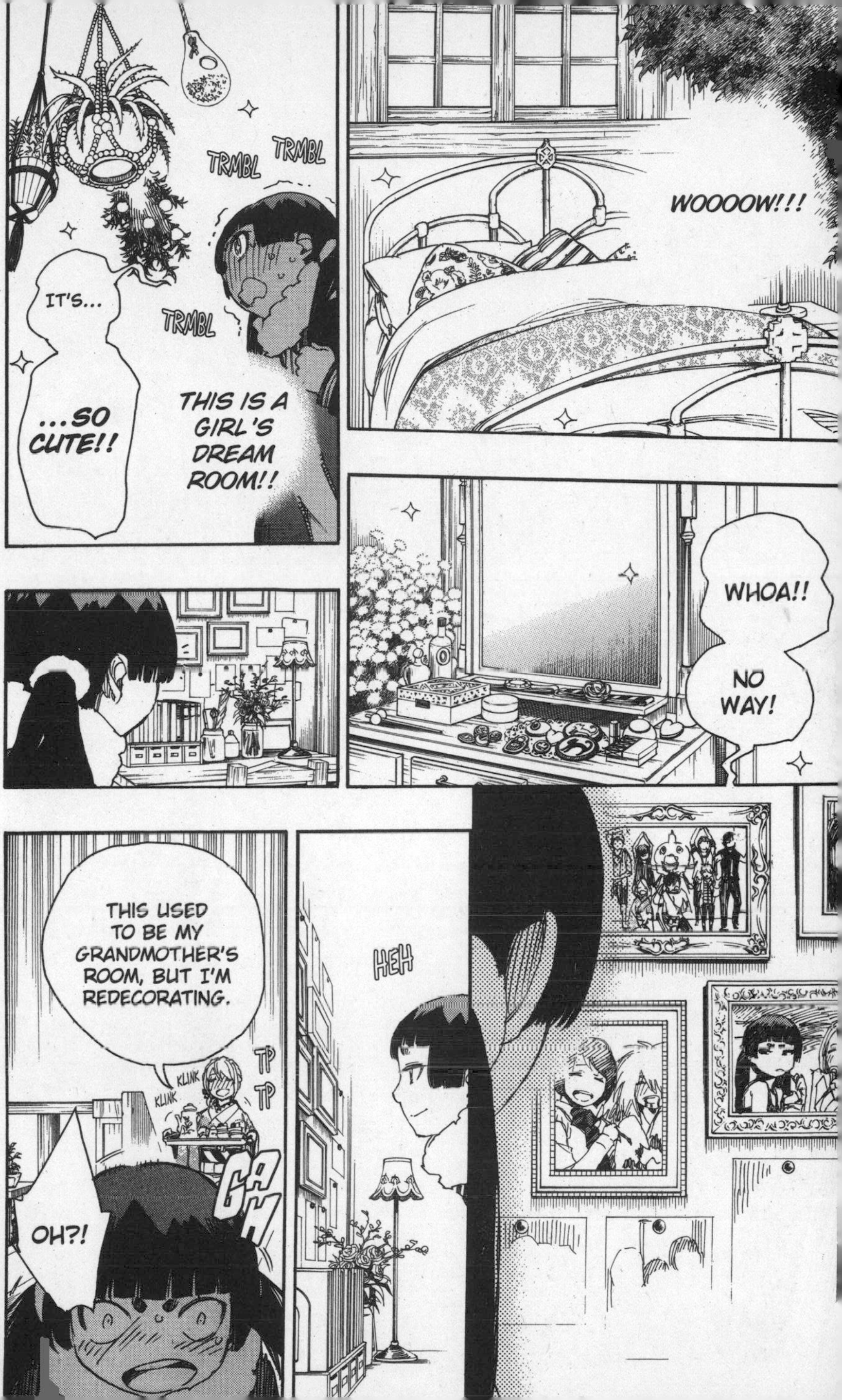
WOOOOW!!!
TRMBL
TRMBL
IT'S...
...SO CUTE!!
TRMBL
THIS IS A GIRL'S DREAM ROOM!!
WHOA!!
NO WAY!
HEH
THIS USED TO BE MY GRANDMOTHER'S ROOM, BUT I'M REDECORATING.
KLINK
KLINK
TP TP
GACH
OH?!

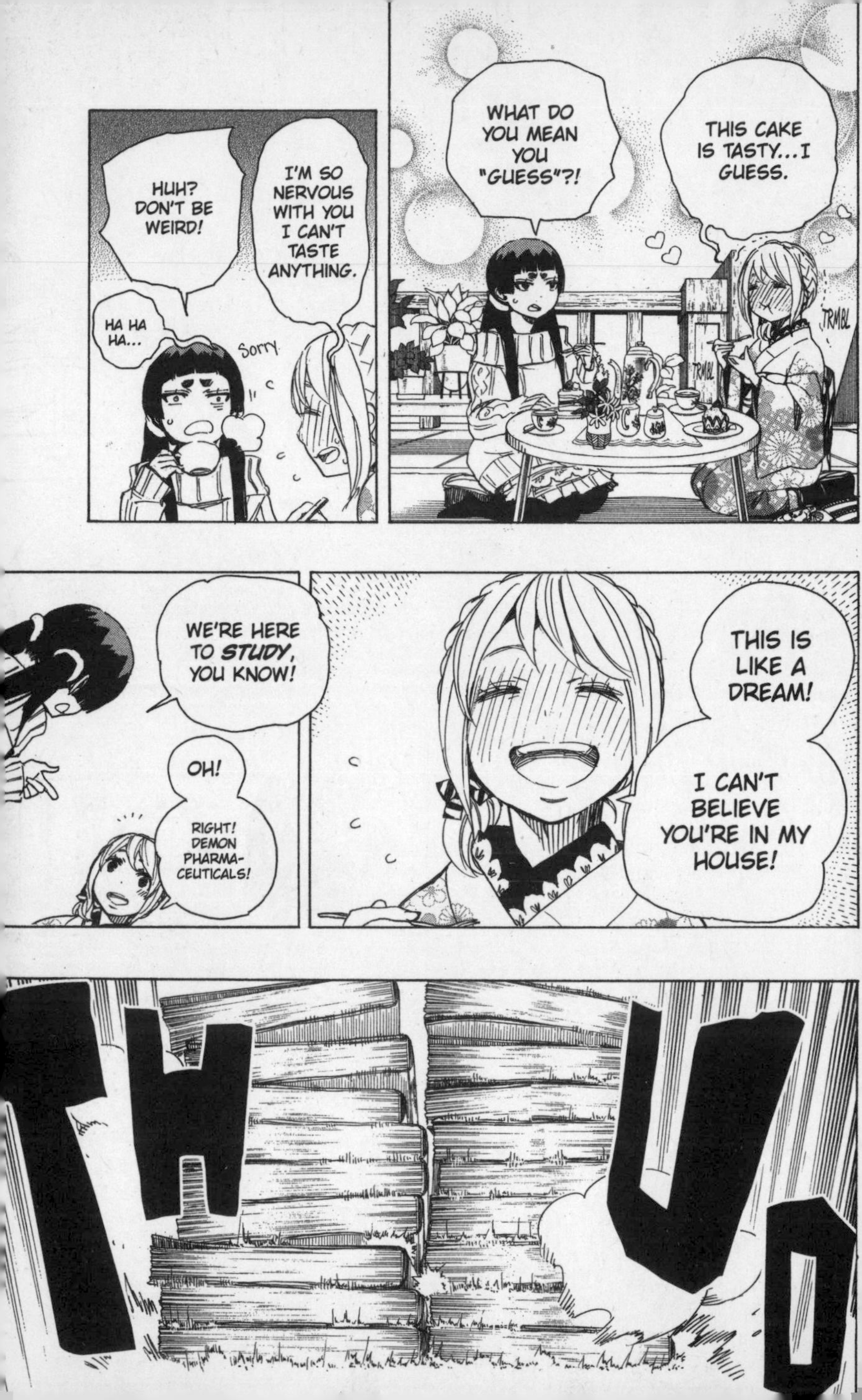
THIS CAKE IS TASTY...I GUESS.
TRMBL
TRMBL
WHAT DO YOU MEAN YOU "GUESS"?!
I'M SO NERVOUS WITH YOU I CAN'T TASTE ANYTHING.
Sorry
HUH? DON'T BE WEIRD!
HA HA HA...
THIS IS LIKE A DREAM!
I CAN'T BELIEVE YOU'RE IN MY HOUSE!
WE'RE HERE TO *STUDY*, YOU KNOW!
OH!
RIGHT! DEMON PHARMA-CEUTICALS!
THUD

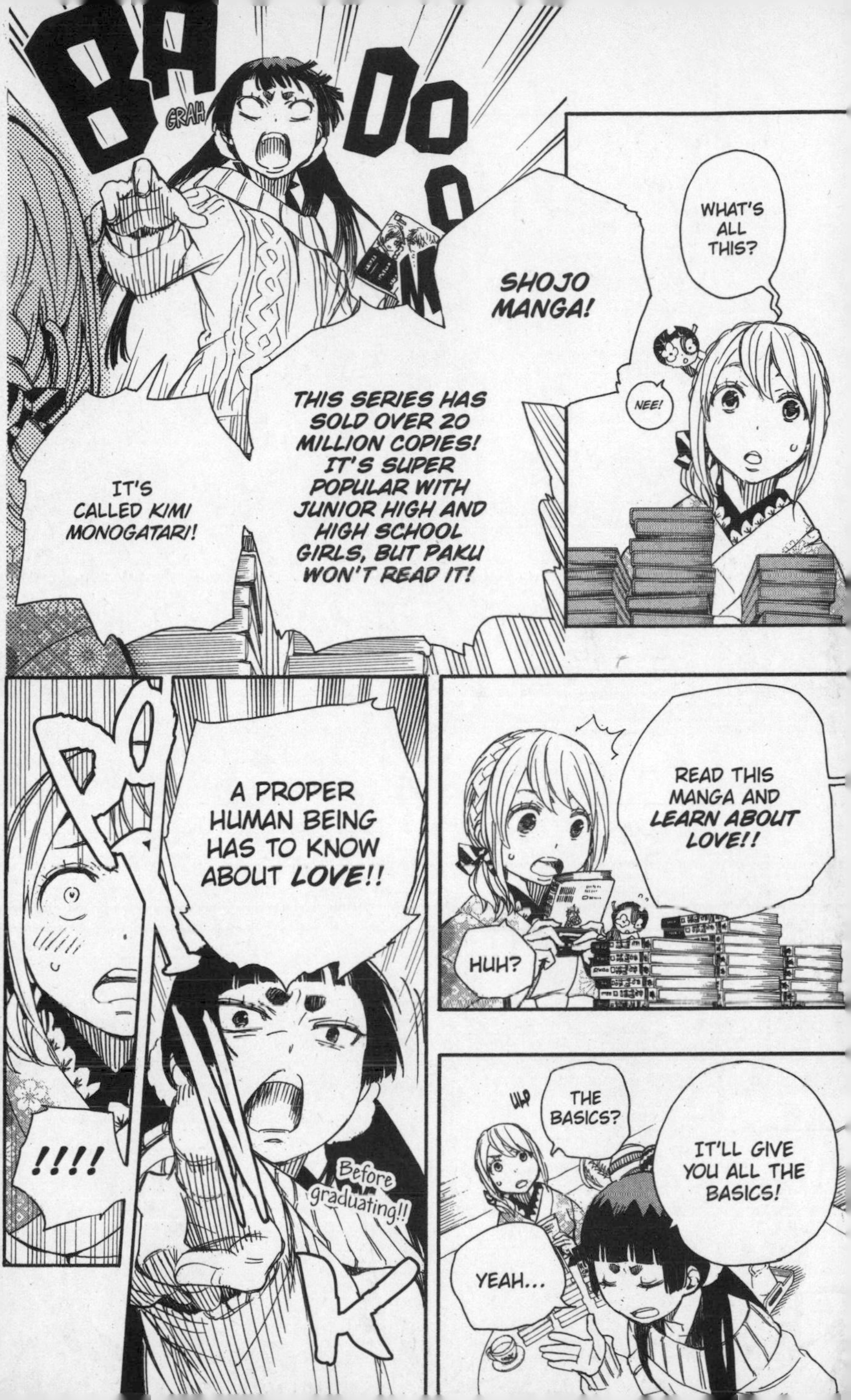
WHAT'S ALL THIS?
NEE!
SHOJO MANGA!
BADOOM
GRAH
THIS SERIES HAS SOLD OVER 20 MILLION COPIES! IT'S SUPER POPULAR WITH JUNIOR HIGH AND HIGH SCHOOL GIRLS, BUT PAKU WON'T READ IT!
IT'S CALLED KIMI MONOGATARI!
READ THIS MANGA AND LEARN ABOUT LOVE!!
HUH?
IT'LL GIVE YOU ALL THE BASICS!
UHP
THE BASICS?
YEAH...
A PROPER HUMAN BEING HAS TO KNOW ABOUT LOVE!!
Before graduating!!
!!!!

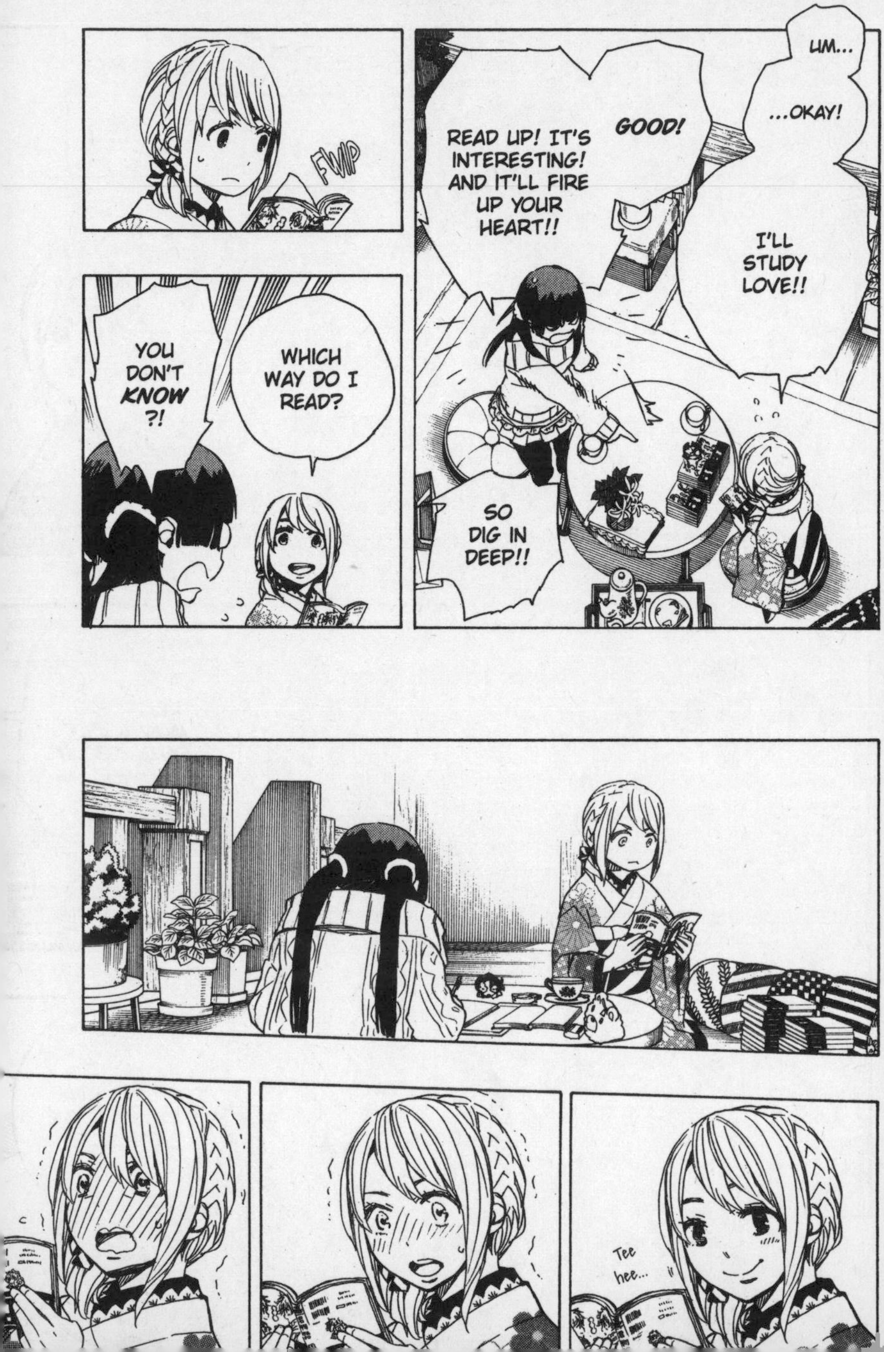
UM...
...OKAY!
GOOD!
READ UP! IT'S INTERESTING! AND IT'LL FIRE UP YOUR HEART!!
I'LL STUDY LOVE!!
SO DIG IN DEEP!!
FWIP
WHICH WAY DO I READ?
YOU DON'T KNOW?!
Tee hee...

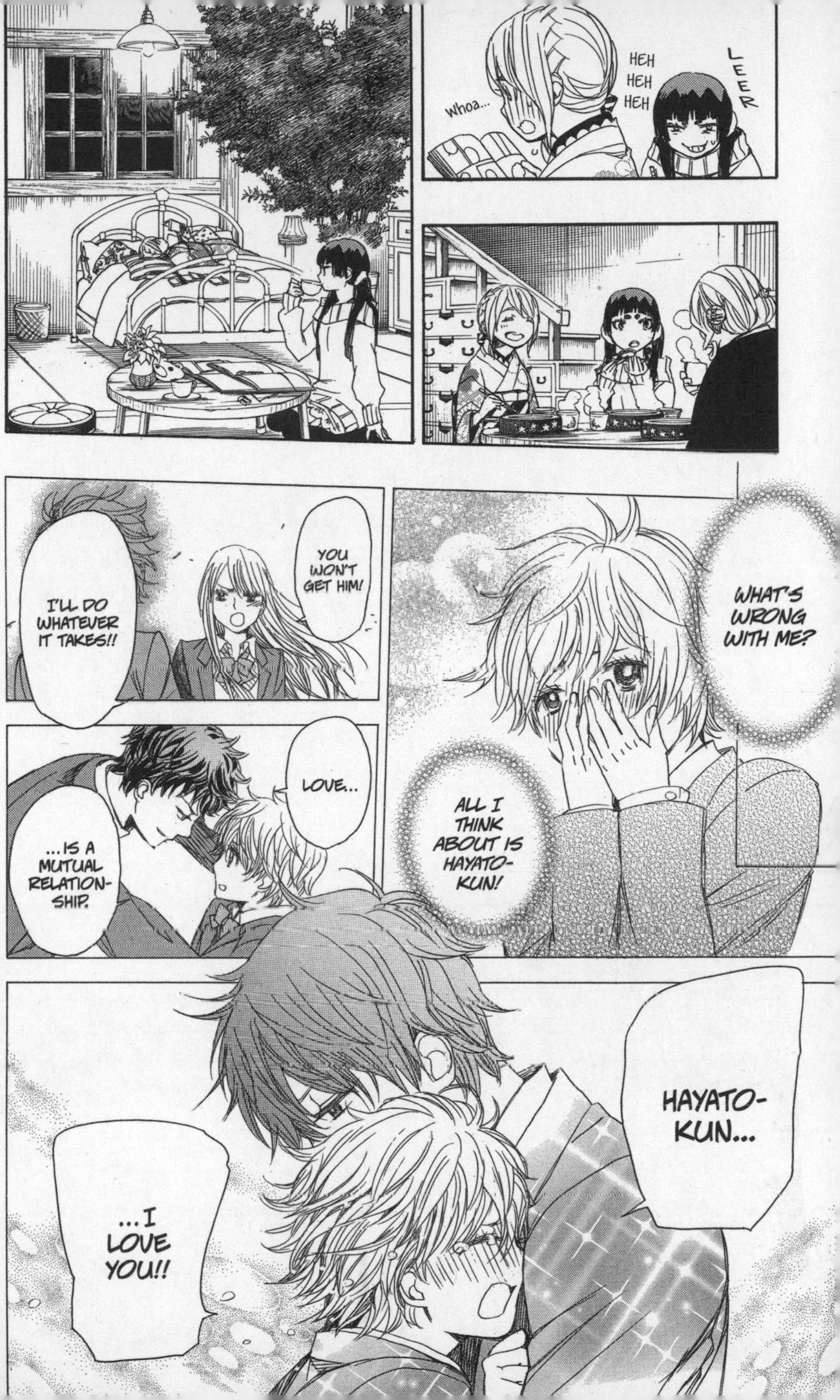

LEER
HEH HEH HEH
Whoa...
WHAT'S WRONG WITH ME?
ALL I THINK ABOUT IS HAYATO-KUN!
YOU WON'T GET HIM!
I'LL DO WHATEVER IT TAKES!!
LOVE...
...IS A MUTUAL RELATIONSHIP.
HAYATO-KUN...
...I LOVE YOU!!

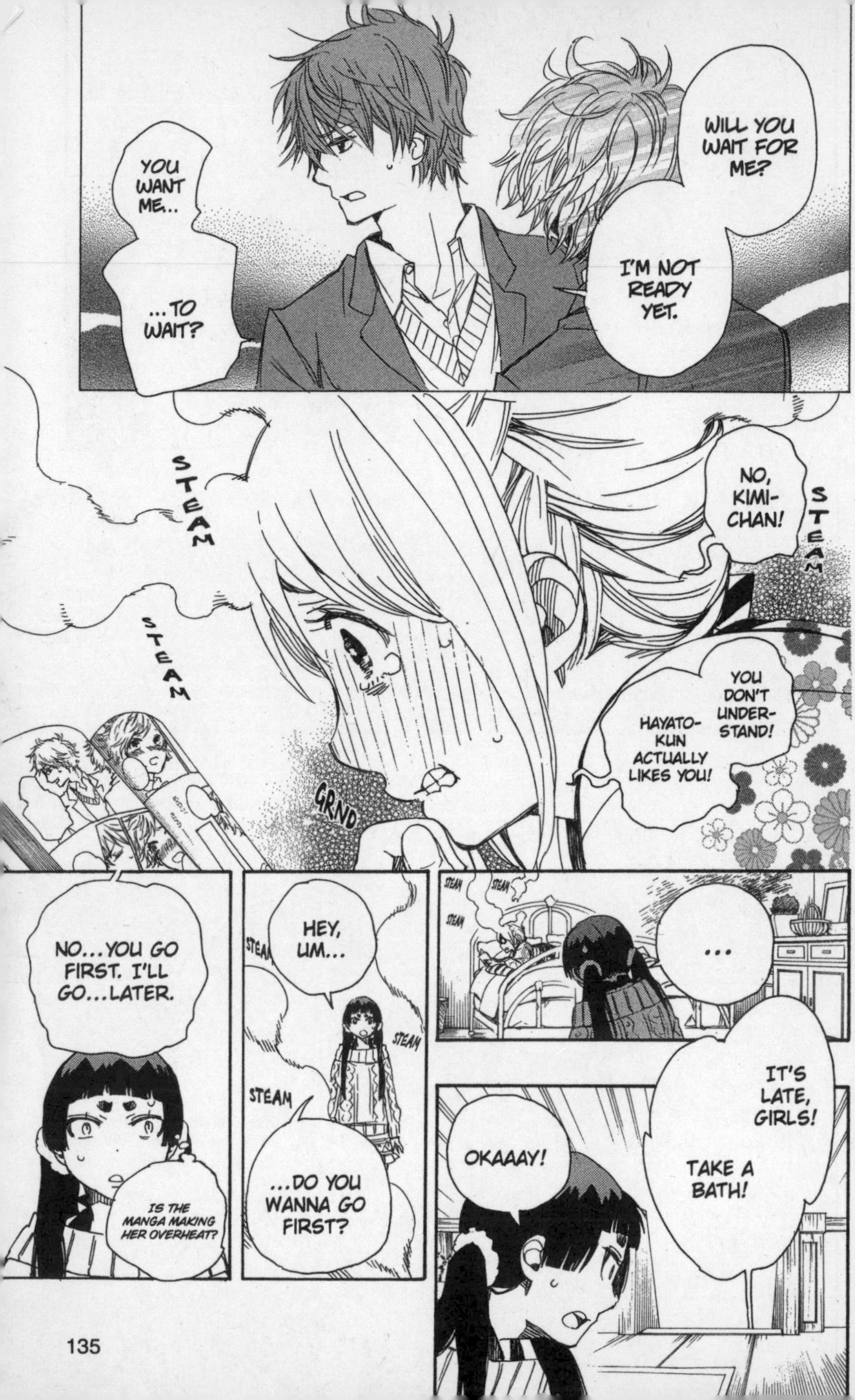
WILL YOU WAIT FOR ME?
I'M NOT READY YET.
YOU WANT ME...
...TO WAIT?
NO, KIMI-CHAN!
STEAM
YOU DON'T UNDERSTAND!
HAYATO-KUN ACTUALLY LIKES YOU!
STEAM
STEAM
GRND
STEAM
STEAM
STEAM
...
IT'S LATE, GIRLS!
TAKE A BATH!
OKAAAY!
HEY, UM...
STEAM
STEAM
STEAM
...DO YOU WANNA GO FIRST?
NO...YOU GO FIRST. I'LL GO...LATER.
IS THE MANGA MAKING HER OVERHEAT?

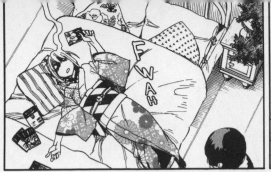
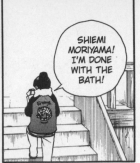

SHIEMI MORIYAMA! I'M DONE WITH THE BATH!

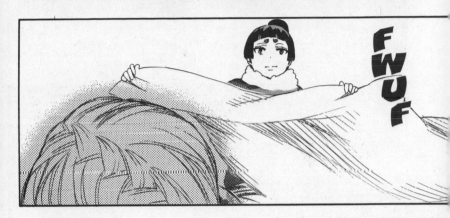

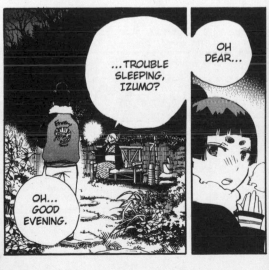

...TROUBLE SLEEPING, IZUMO?

OH DEAR...

OH... GOOD EVENING.

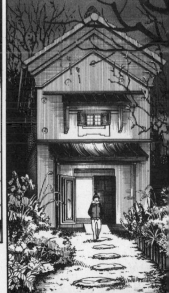

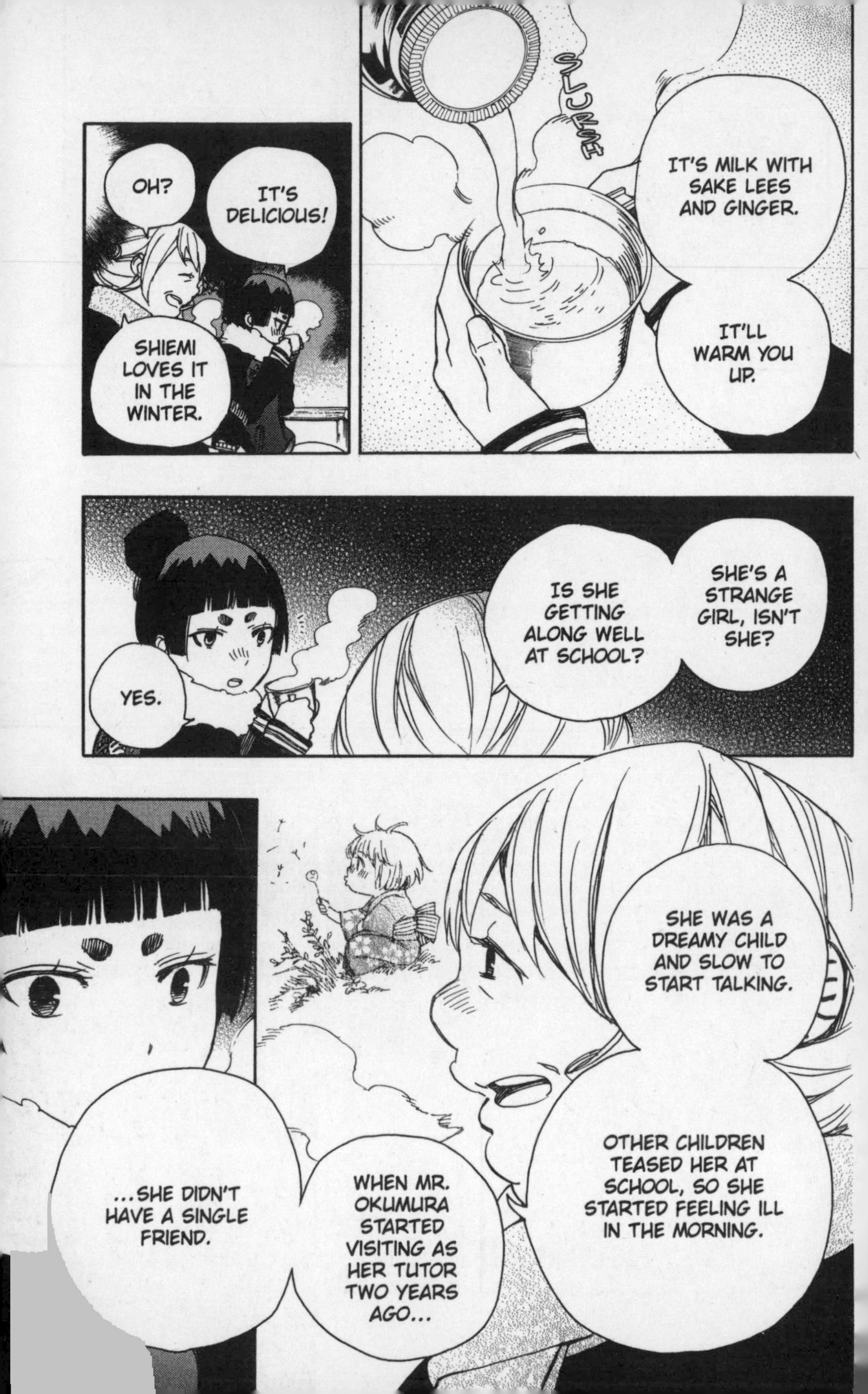
SLURSH
IT'S MILK WITH SAKE LEES AND GINGER.
IT'LL WARM YOU UP.
IT'S DELICIOUS!
OH?
SHIEMI LOVES IT IN THE WINTER.
SHE'S A STRANGE GIRL, ISN'T SHE?
IS SHE GETTING ALONG WELL AT SCHOOL?
YES.
SHE WAS A DREAMY CHILD AND SLOW TO START TALKING.
OTHER CHILDREN TEASED HER AT SCHOOL, SO SHE STARTED FEELING ILL IN THE MORNING.
WHEN MR. OKUMURA STARTED VISITING AS HER TUTOR TWO YEARS AGO...
...SHE DIDN'T HAVE A SINGLE FRIEND.

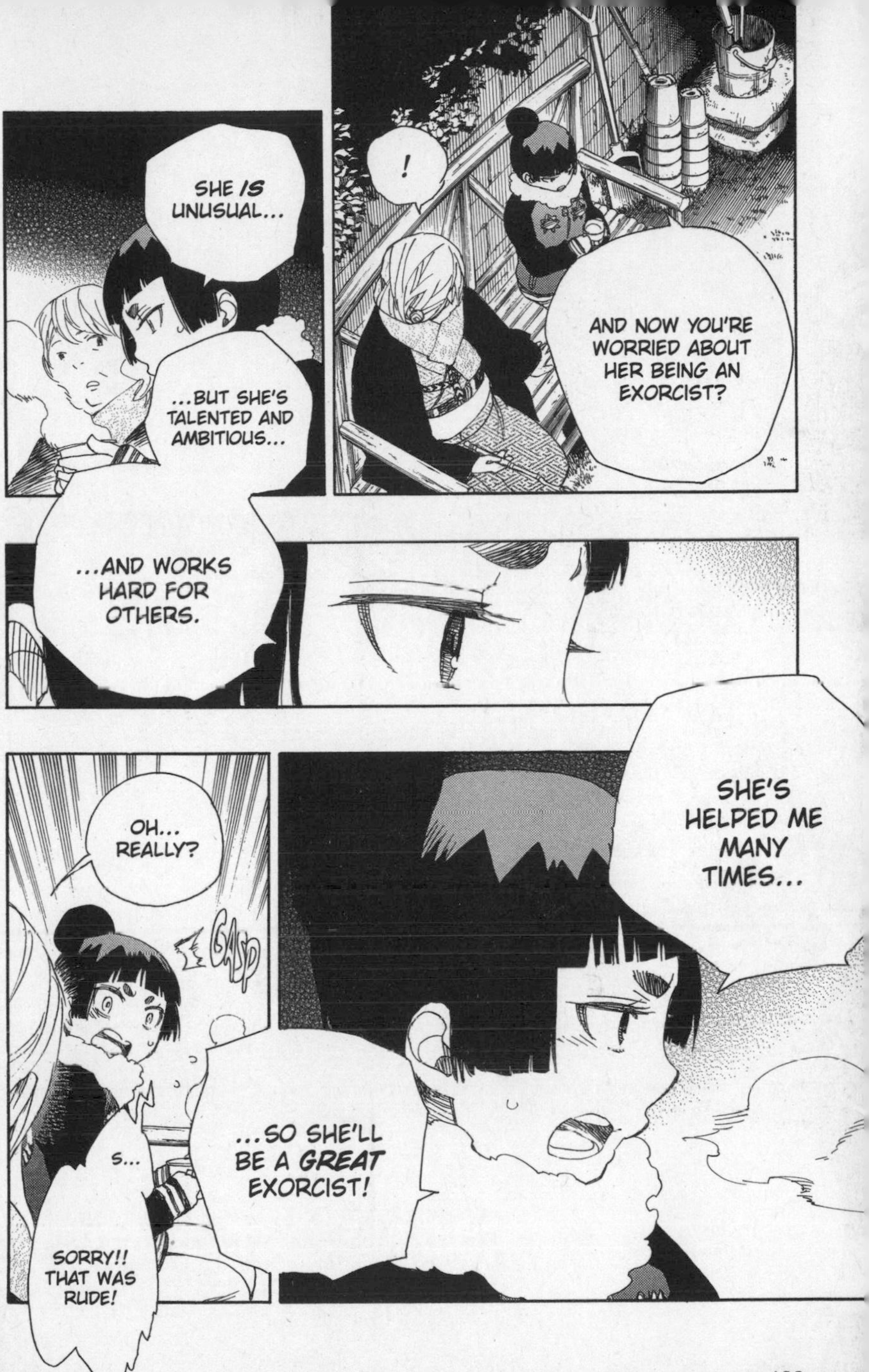
!
AND NOW YOU'RE WORRIED ABOUT HER BEING AN EXORCIST?
SHE IS UNUSUAL...
...BUT SHE'S TALENTED AND AMBITIOUS...
...AND WORKS HARD FOR OTHERS.
SHE'S HELPED ME MANY TIMES...
...SO SHE'LL BE A GREAT EXORCIST!
OH... REALLY?
GASP
S...
SORRY!! THAT WAS RUDE!

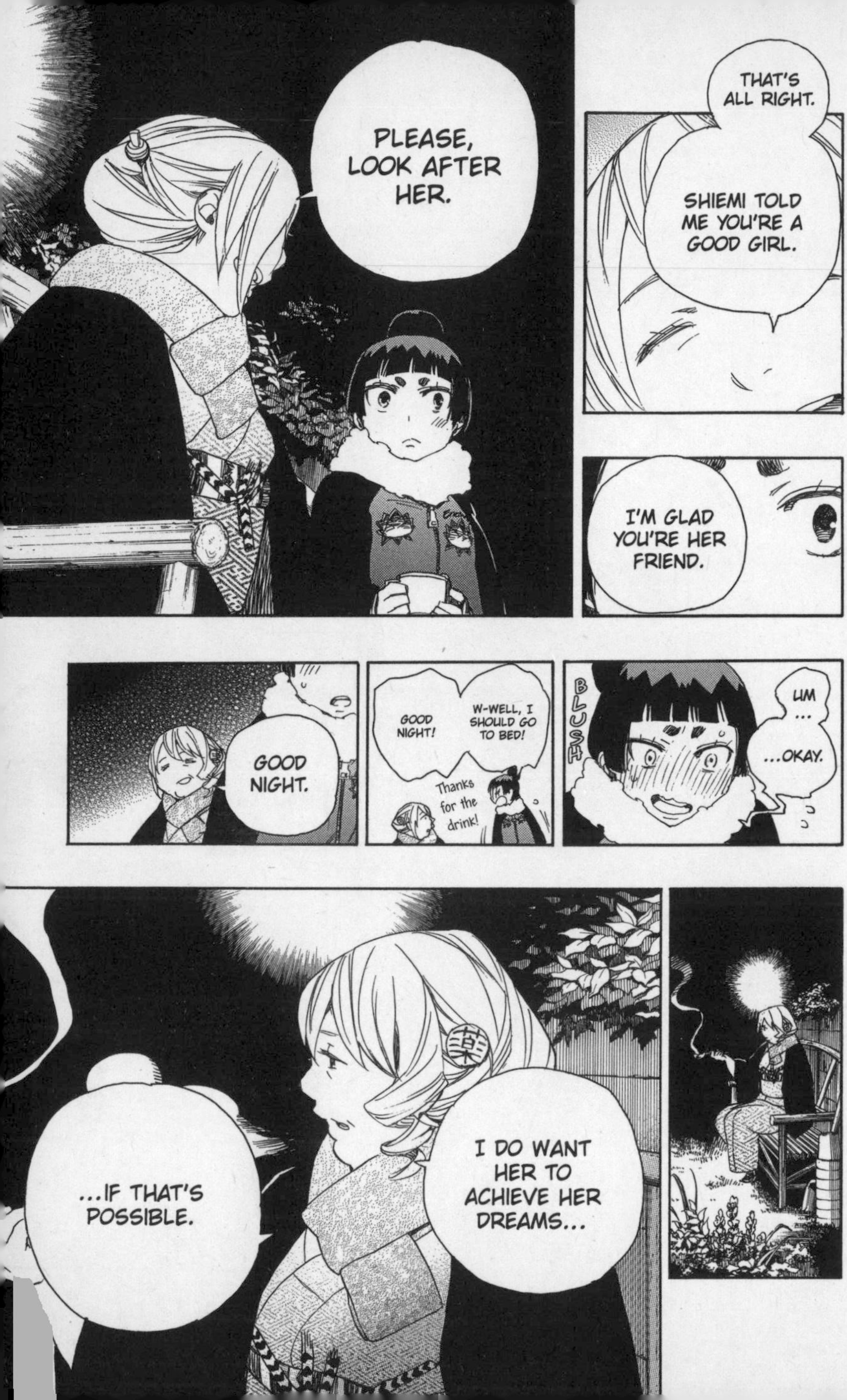
THAT'S ALL RIGHT.
SHIEMI TOLD ME YOU'RE A GOOD GIRL.
I'M GLAD YOU'RE HER FRIEND.
PLEASE, LOOK AFTER HER.
BLUSH
UM ... ...OKAY.
W-WELL, I SHOULD GO TO BED!
GOOD NIGHT!
Thanks for the drink!
GOOD NIGHT.
I DO WANT HER TO ACHIEVE HER DREAMS...
...IF THAT'S POSSIBLE.

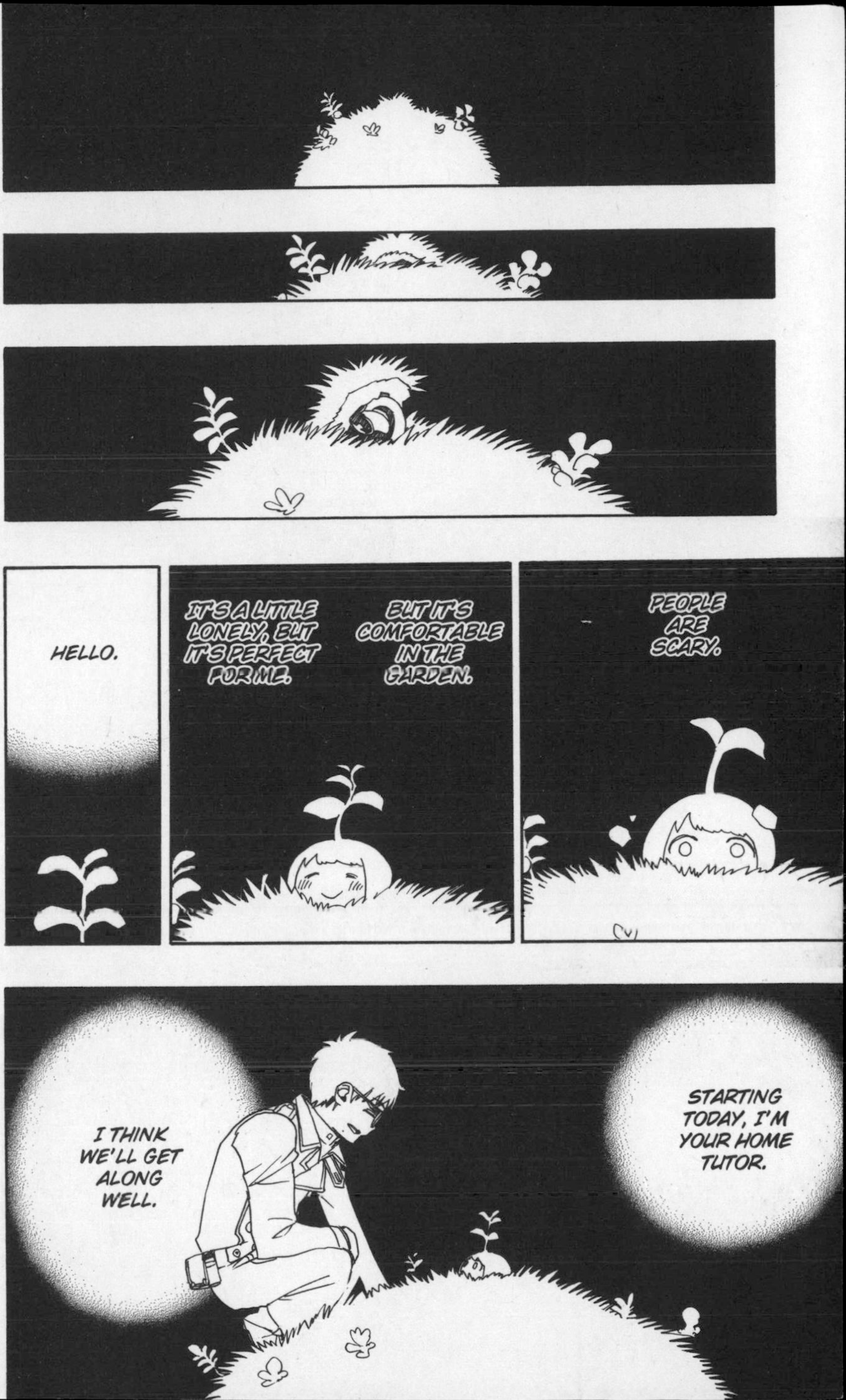
PEOPLE ARE SCARY.
BUT IT'S COMFORTABLE IN THE GARDEN.
IT'S A LITTLE LONELY, BUT IT'S PERFECT FOR ME.
HELLO.
STARTING TODAY, I'M YOUR HOME TUTOR.
I THINK WE'LL GET ALONG WELL.

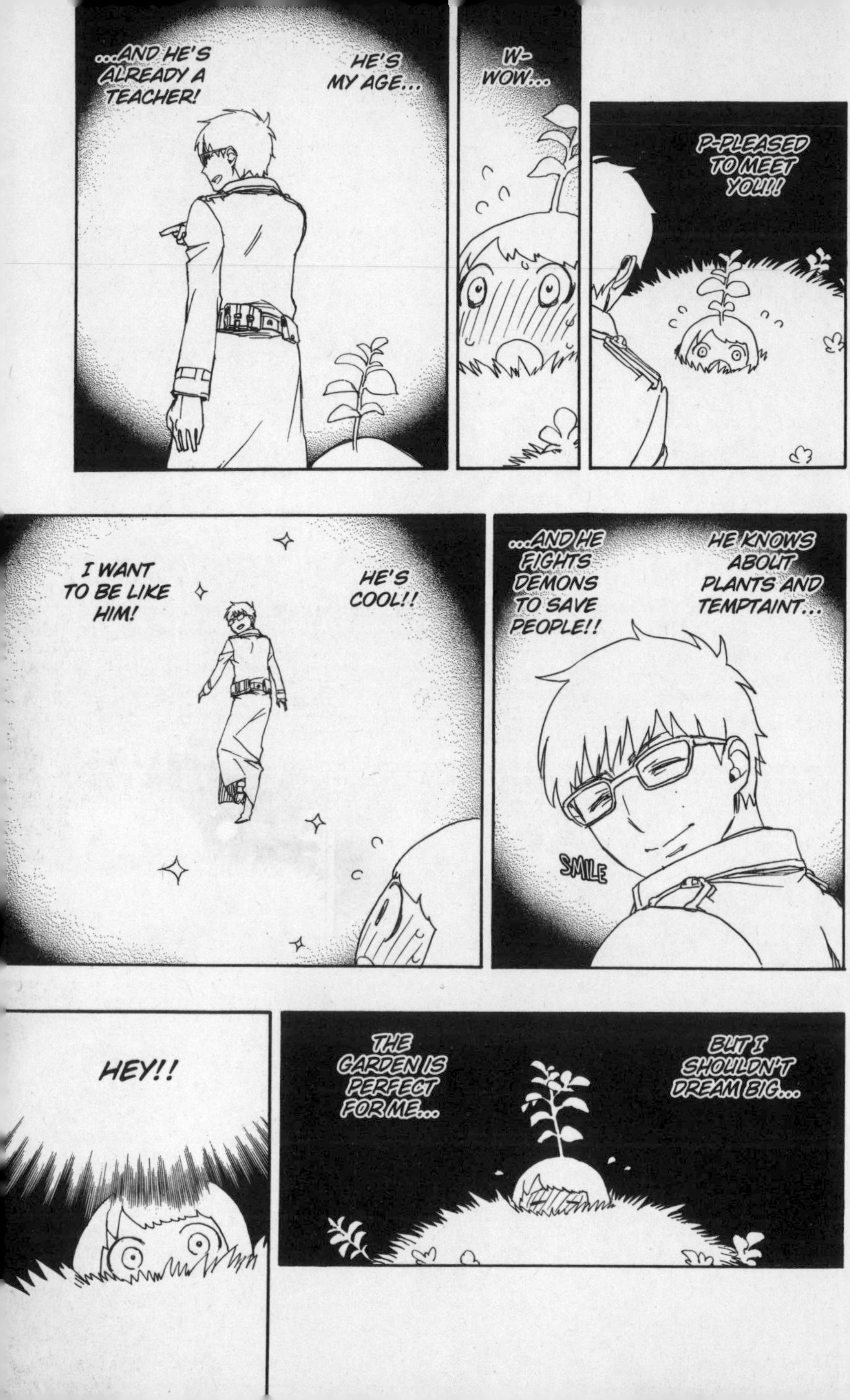
P-PLEASED TO MEET YOU!!
W- WOW...
HE'S MY AGE...
...AND HE'S ALREADY A TEACHER!
HE KNOWS ABOUT PLANTS AND TEMPTAINT...
...AND HE FIGHTS DEMONS TO SAVE PEOPLE!!
SMILE
HE'S COOL!!
I WANT TO BE LIKE HIM!
BUT I SHOULDN'T DREAM BIG...
THE GARDEN IS PERFECT FOR ME...
HEY!!

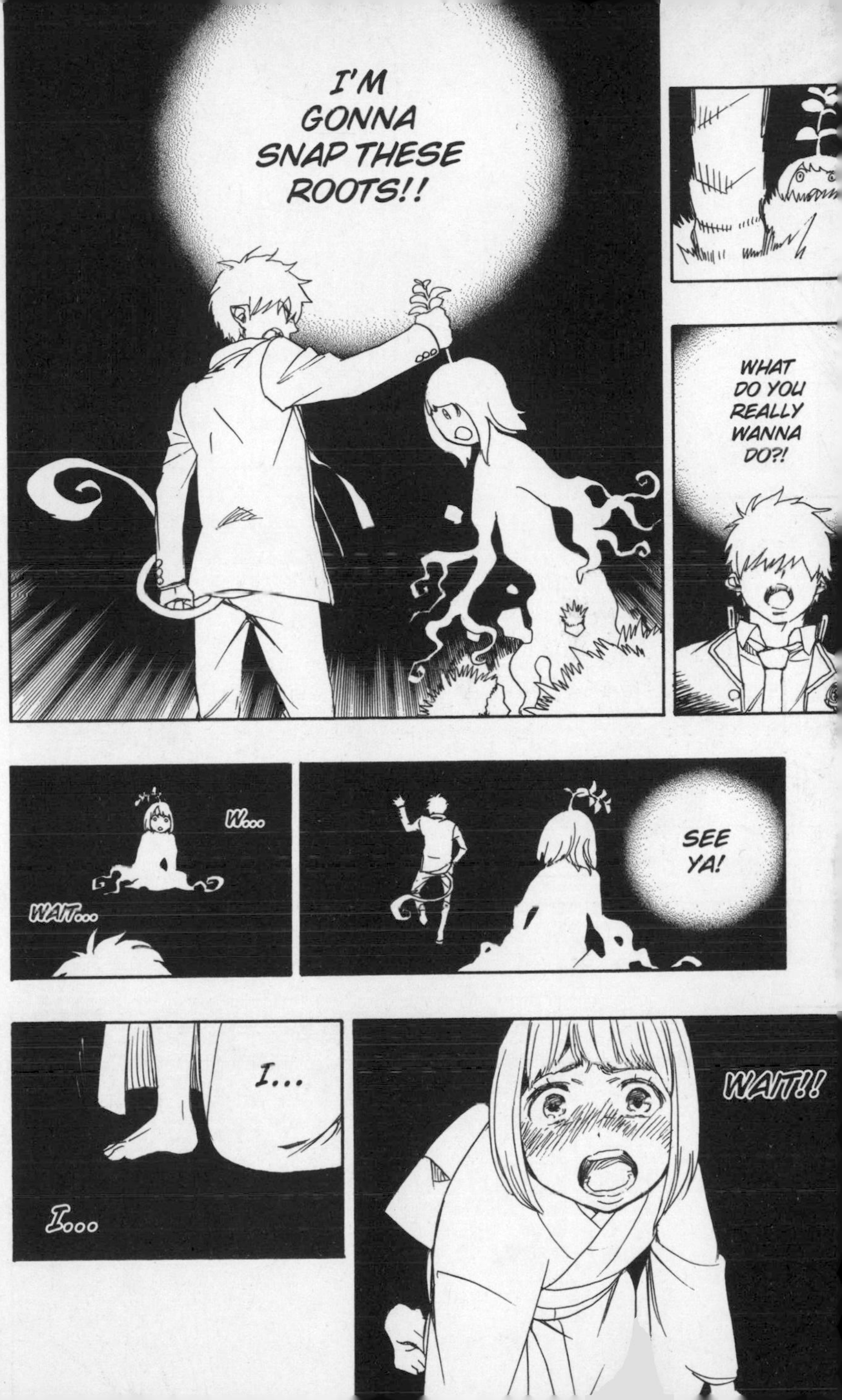
WHAT DO YOU REALLY WANNA DO?!
I'M GONNA SNAP THESE ROOTS!!
SEE YA!
W...
WAIT...
WAIT!!
I...
I...

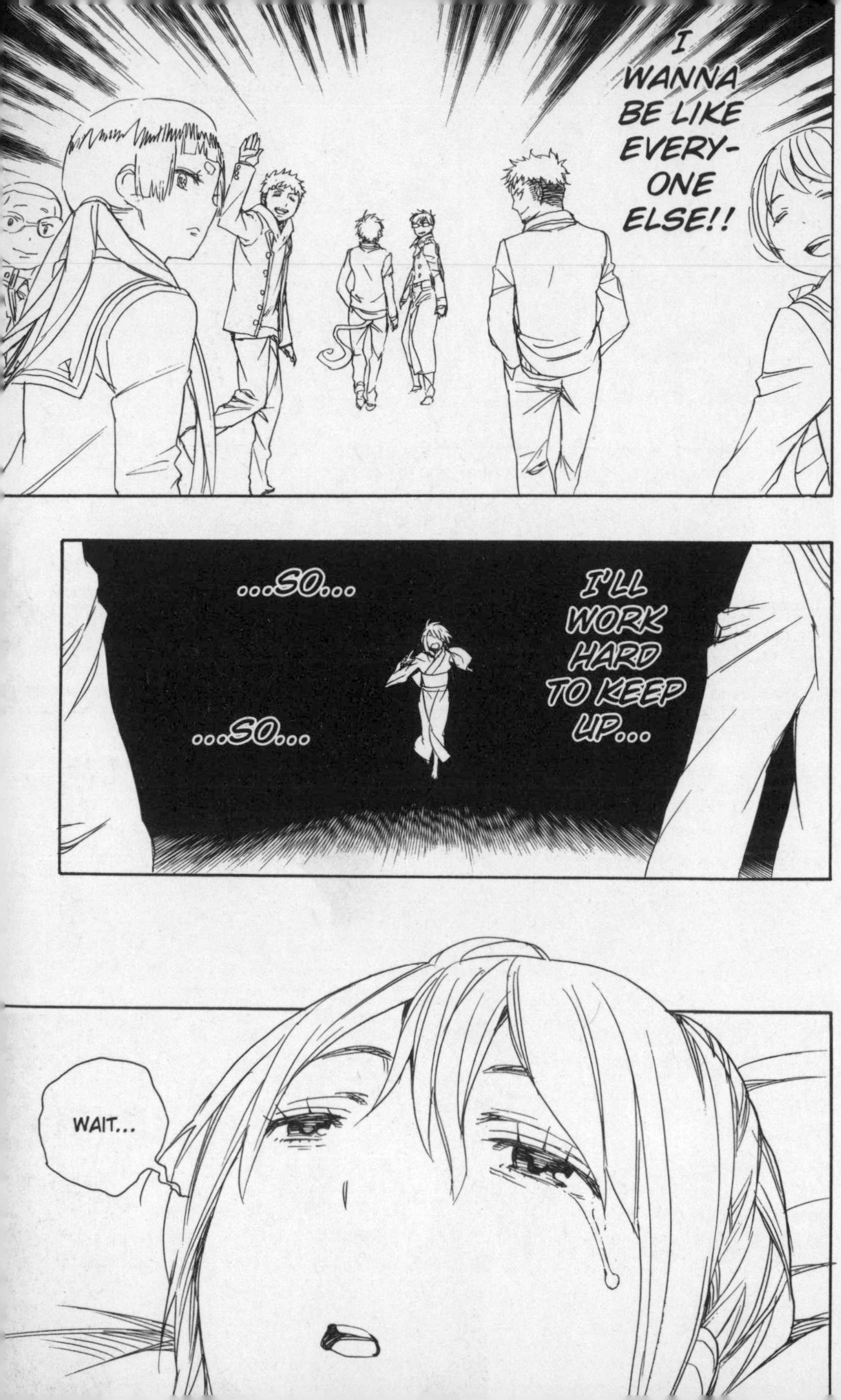
I WANNA BE LIKE EVERY-ONE ELSE!!
I'LL WORK HARD TO KEEP UP...
...SO...
...SO...
WAIT...

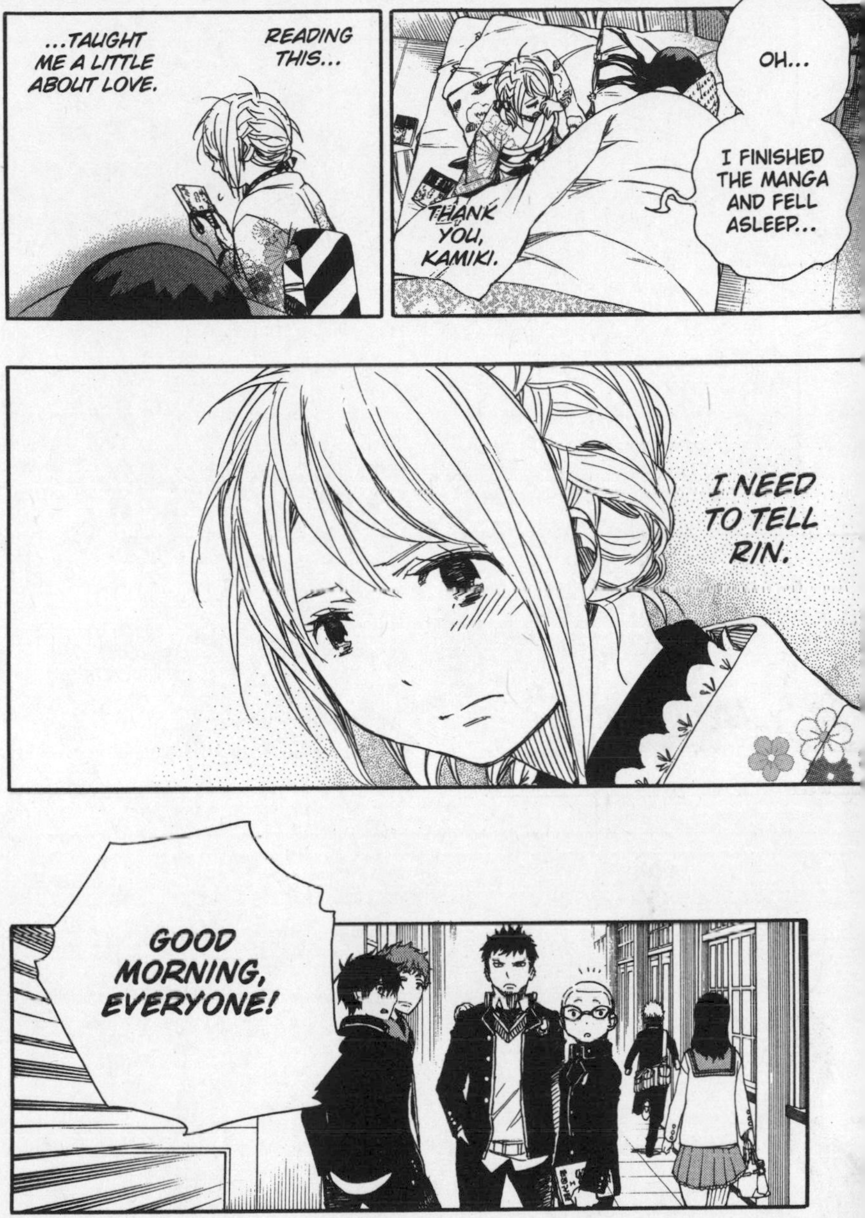
OH...
I FINISHED THE MANGA AND FELL ASLEEP...
THANK YOU, KAMIKI.
READING THIS...
...TAUGHT ME A LITTLE ABOUT LOVE.
I NEED TO TELL RIN.
GOOD MORNING, EVERYONE!

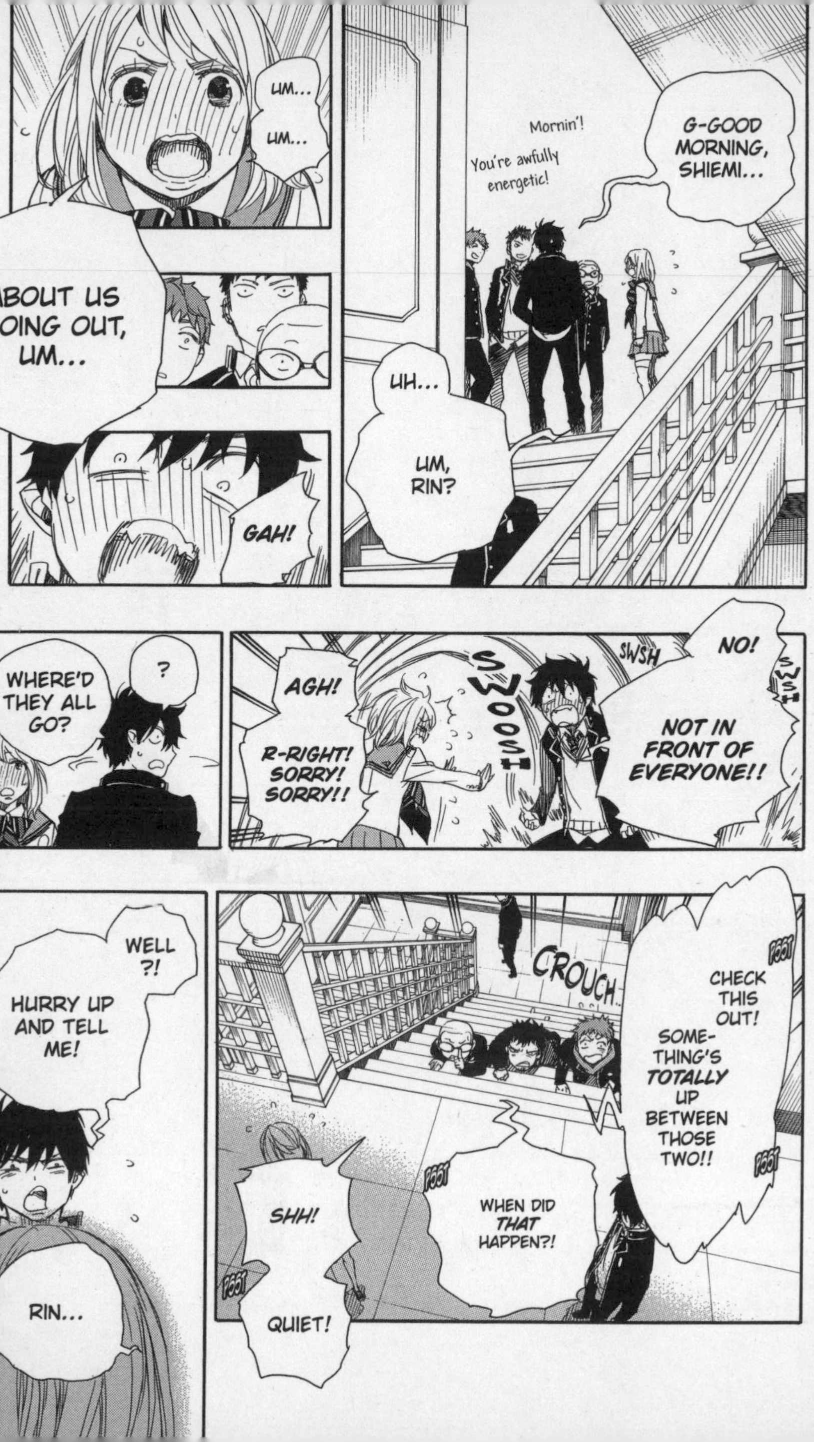
G-GOOD MORNING, SHIEMI...
Mornin'!
You're awfully energetic!
UH...
UM, RIN?
UM...
UM...
ABOUT US GOING OUT, UM...
GAH!
NO!
SWSH
SWSH
NOT IN FRONT OF EVERYONE!!
SWOOSH
AGH!
R-RIGHT! SORRY! SORRY!!
?
WHERE'D THEY ALL GO?
PSST
CHECK THIS OUT!
SOME-THING'S *TOTALLY* UP BETWEEN THOSE TWO!!
CROUCH
PSST
WHEN DID *THAT* HAPPEN?!
PSST
SHH!
PSST
QUIET!
WELL?!
HURRY UP AND TELL ME!
RIN...

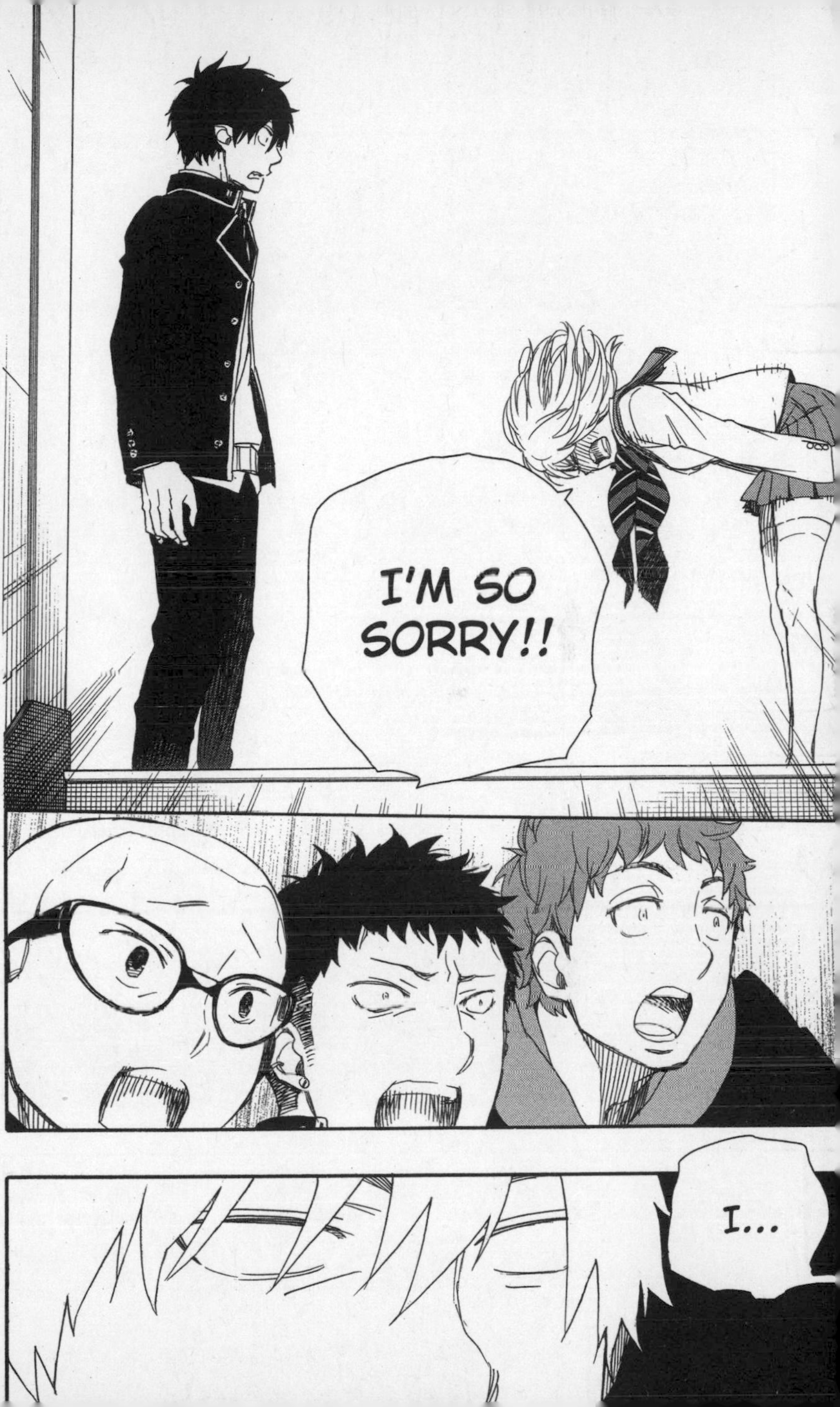
I'M SO SORRY!!
I...

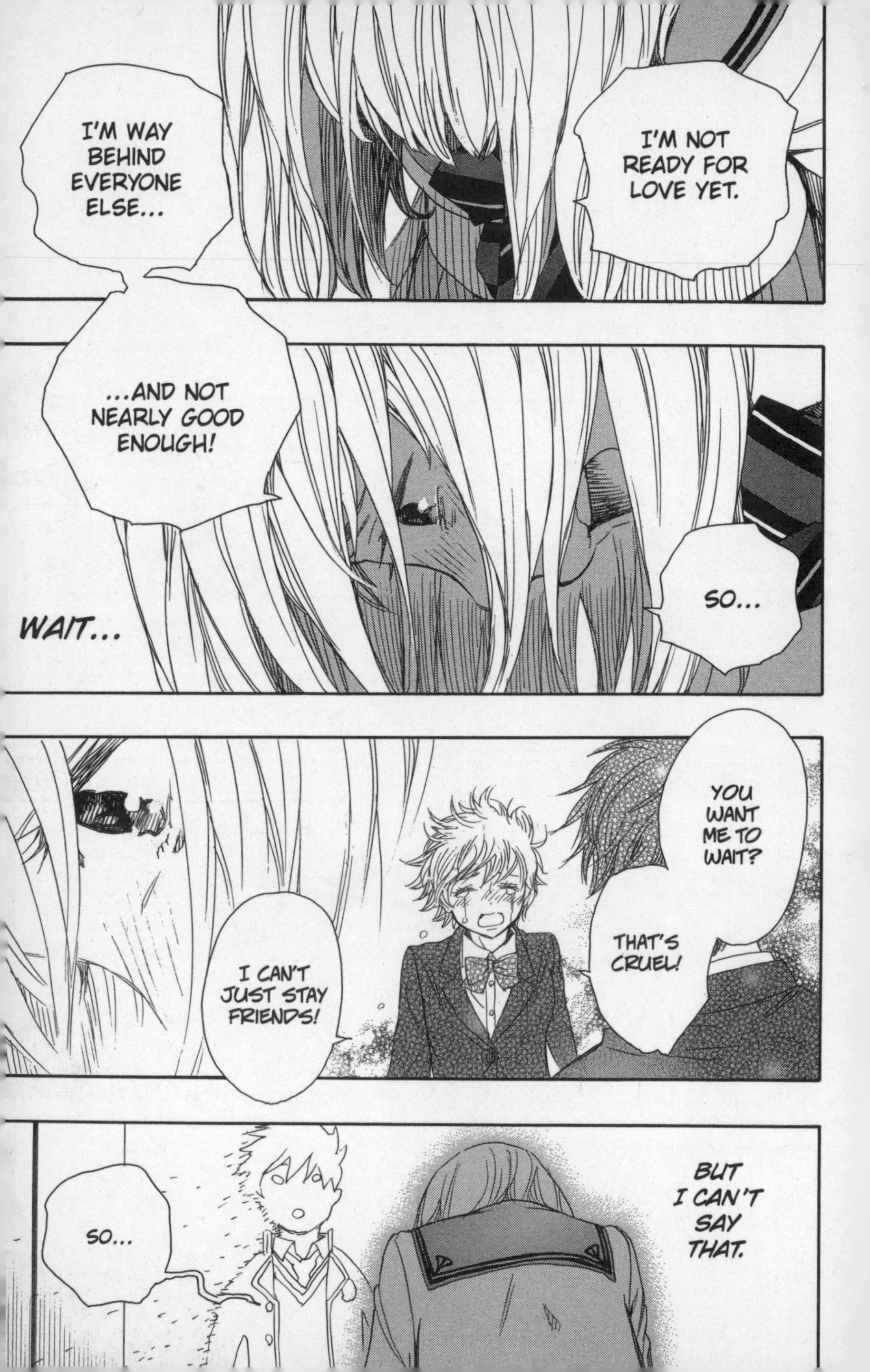
I'M NOT READY FOR LOVE YET.
I'M WAY BEHIND EVERYONE ELSE...
...AND NOT NEARLY GOOD ENOUGH!
SO...
WAIT...
YOU WANT ME TO WAIT?
THAT'S CRUEL!
I CAN'T JUST STAY FRIENDS!
BUT I CAN'T SAY THAT.
SO...

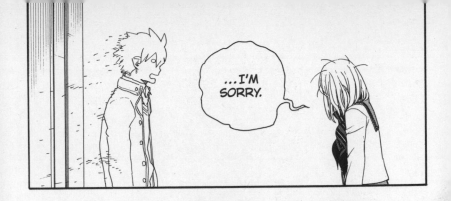

...I'M SORRY.

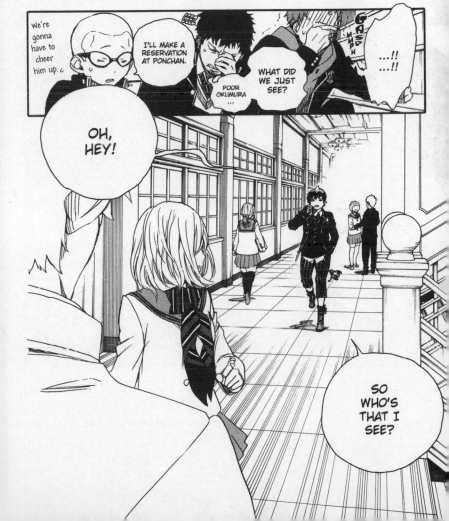

We're gonna have to cheer him up.

I'LL MAKE A RESERVATION AT PONCHAN.

POOR OKUMURA...

WHAT DID WE JUST SEE?

...!! ...!!

OH, HEY!

SO WHO'S THAT I SEE?

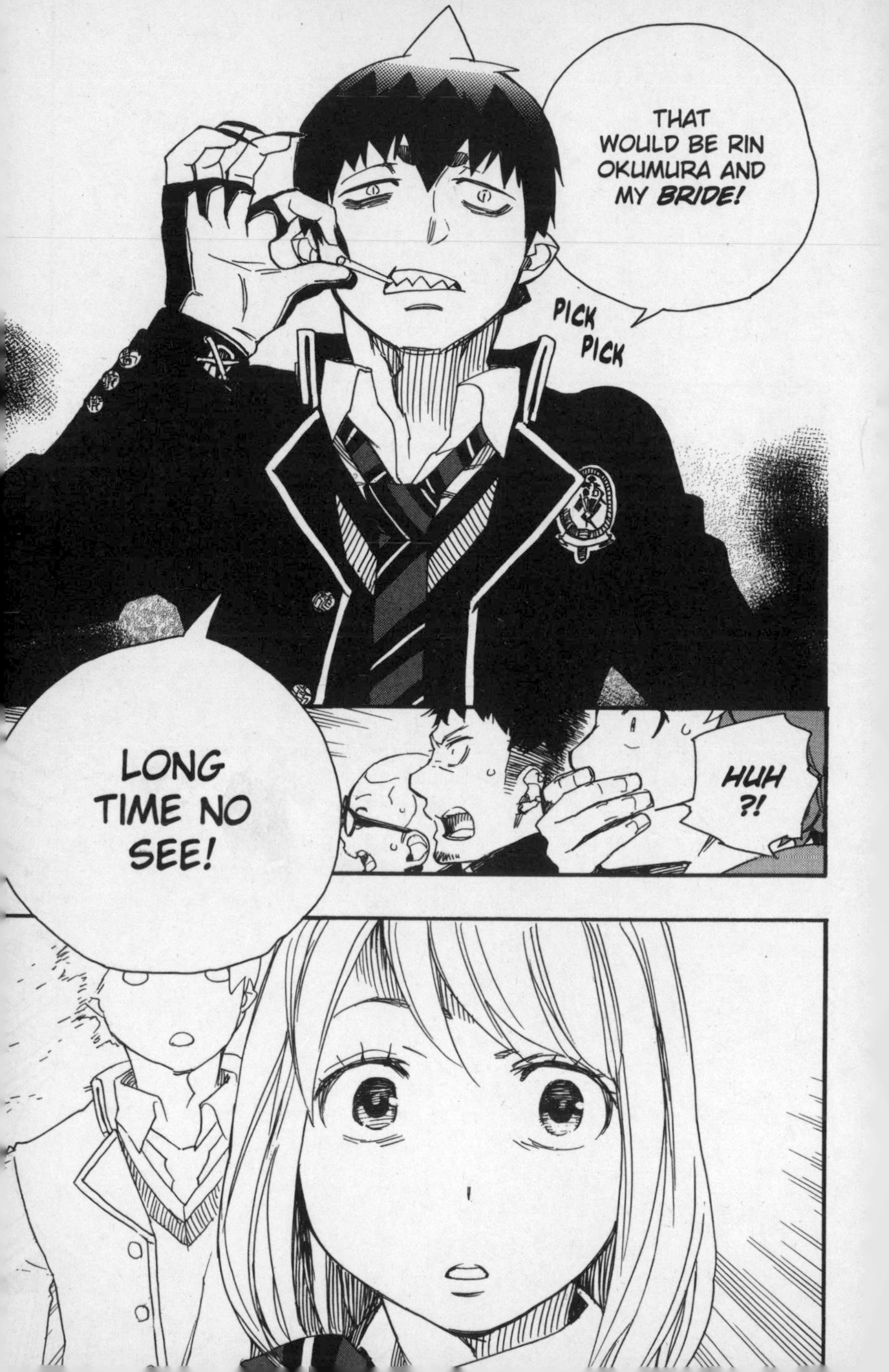
THAT WOULD BE RIN OKUMURA AND MY BRIDE!
PICK PICK
HUH ?!
LONG TIME NO SEE!

BLUE EXORCIST CHAPTER 82: AWAKENING

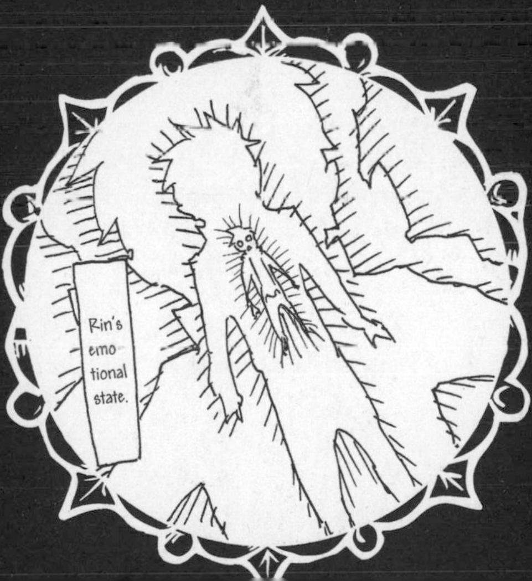
Rin's emo-tional state.

Chapter 83: Sprout

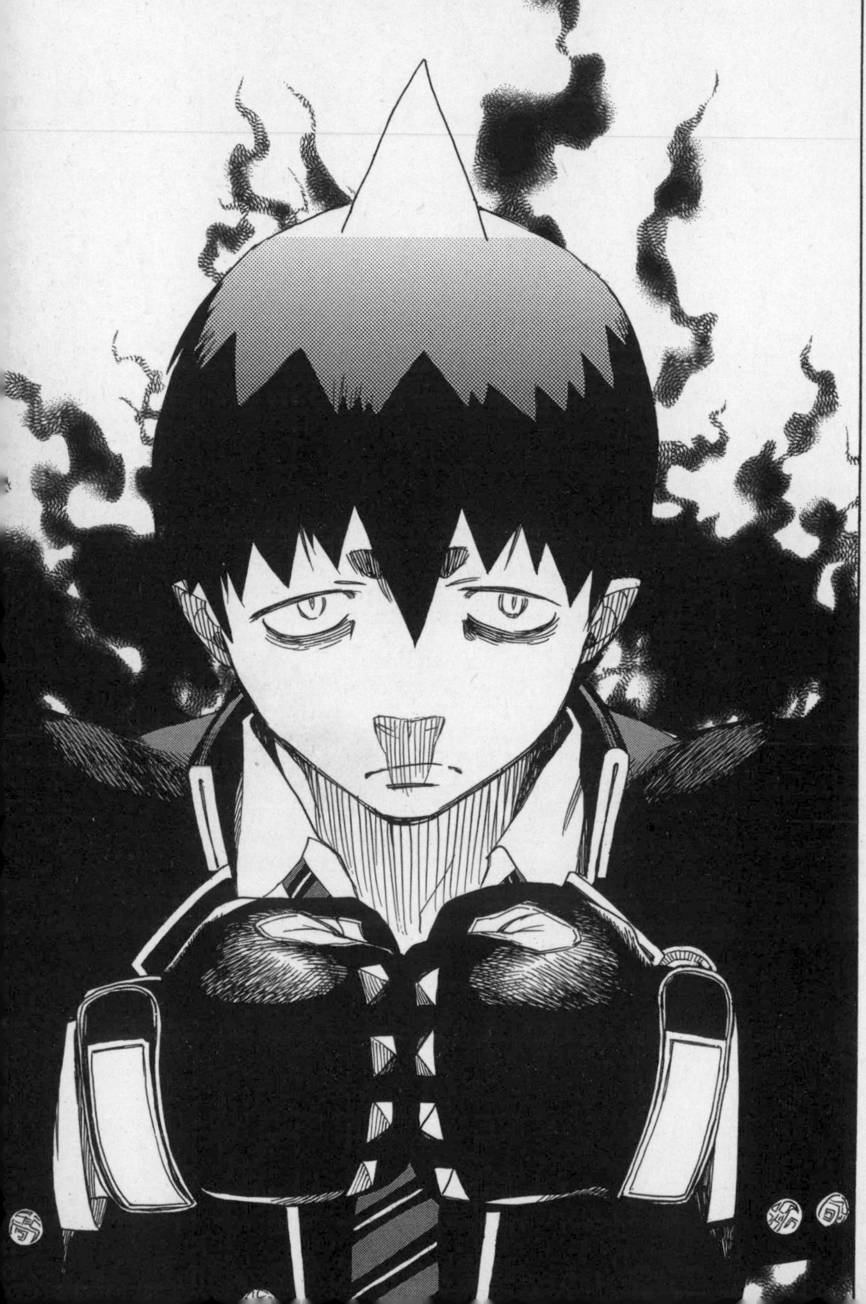

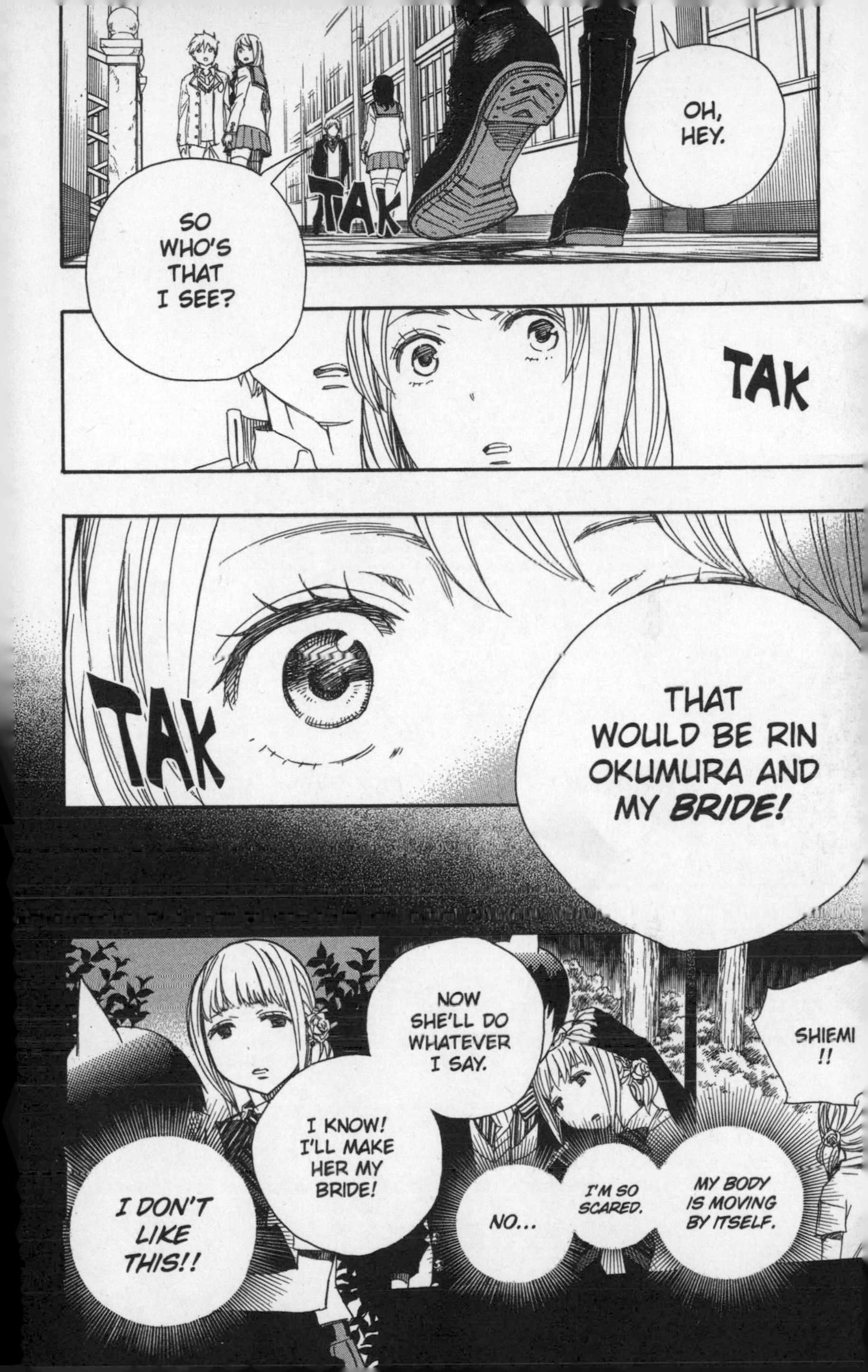
OH, HEY.
TAK
SO WHO'S THAT I SEE?
TAK
THAT WOULD BE RIN OKUMURA AND MY *BRIDE!*
TAK
SHIEMI !!
NOW SHE'LL DO WHATEVER I SAY.
MY BODY IS MOVING BY ITSELF.
I'M SO SCARED.
NO...
I KNOW! I'LL MAKE HER MY BRIDE!
I DON'T LIKE THIS!!

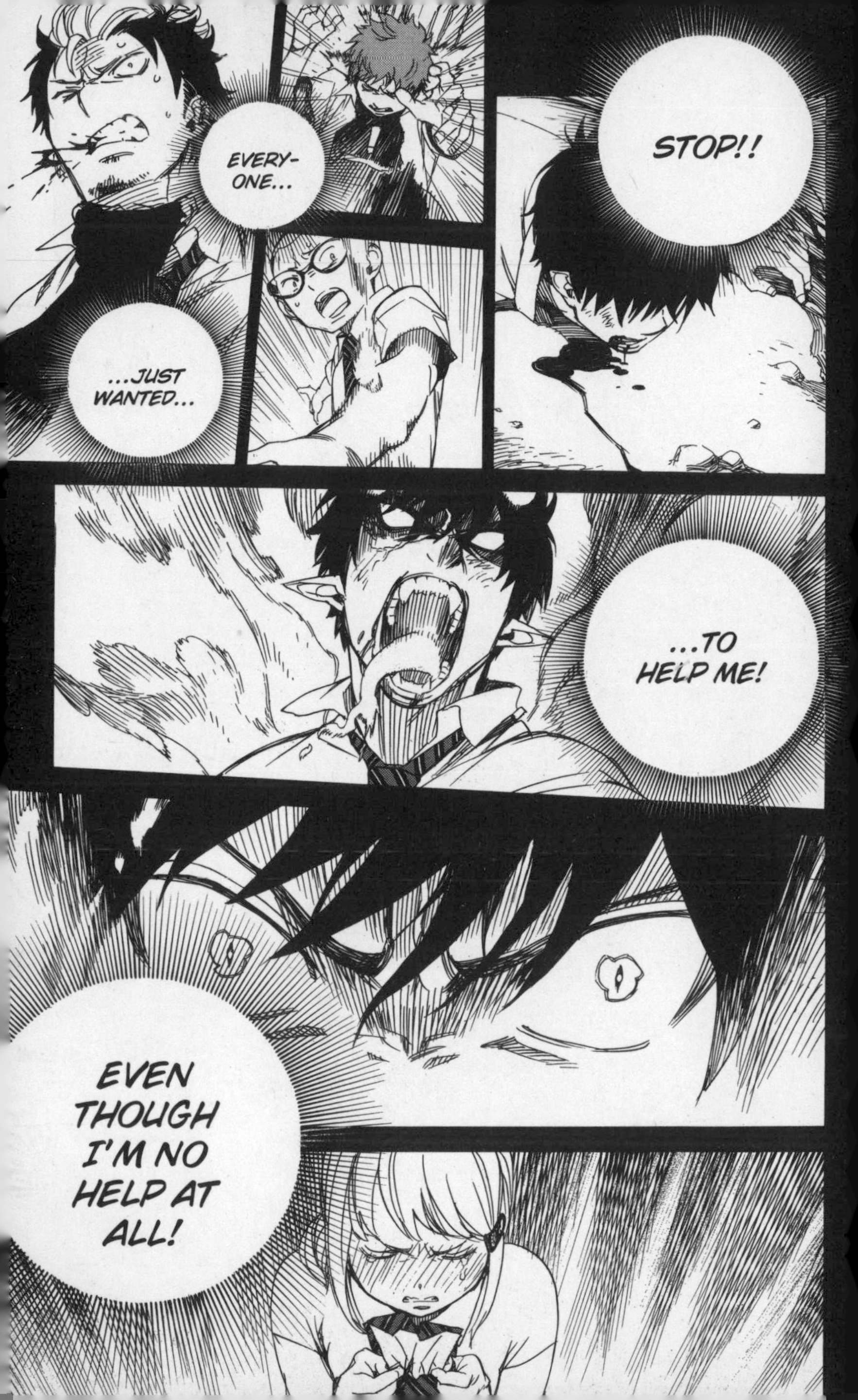
STOP!!
EVERY-ONE...
...JUST WANTED...
...TO HELP ME!
EVEN THOUGH I'M NO HELP AT ALL!

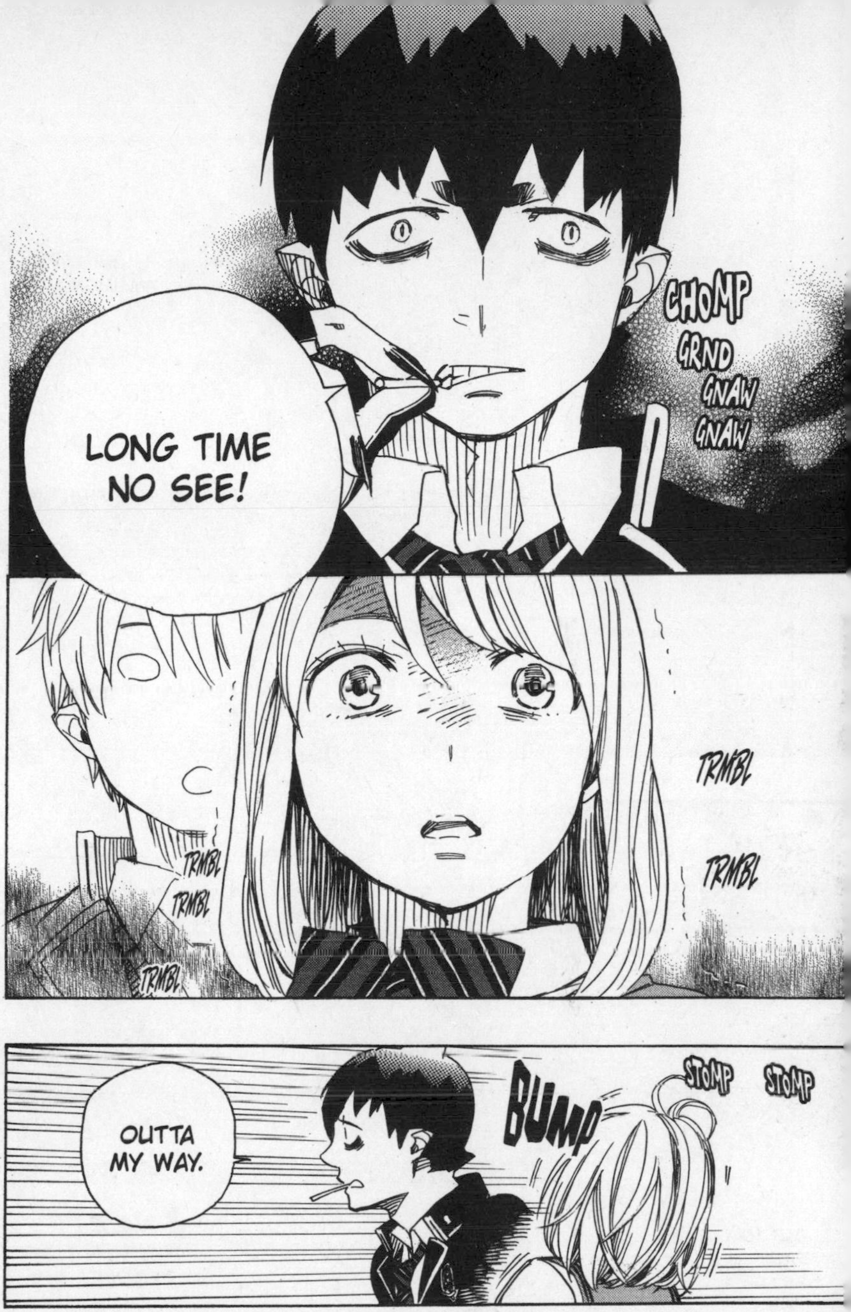
CHOMP
GRND
GNAW
GNAW
LONG TIME NO SEE!
TRMBL
TRMBL
TRMBL
TRMBL
TRMBL
STOMP
STOMP
BUMP
OUTTA MY WAY.

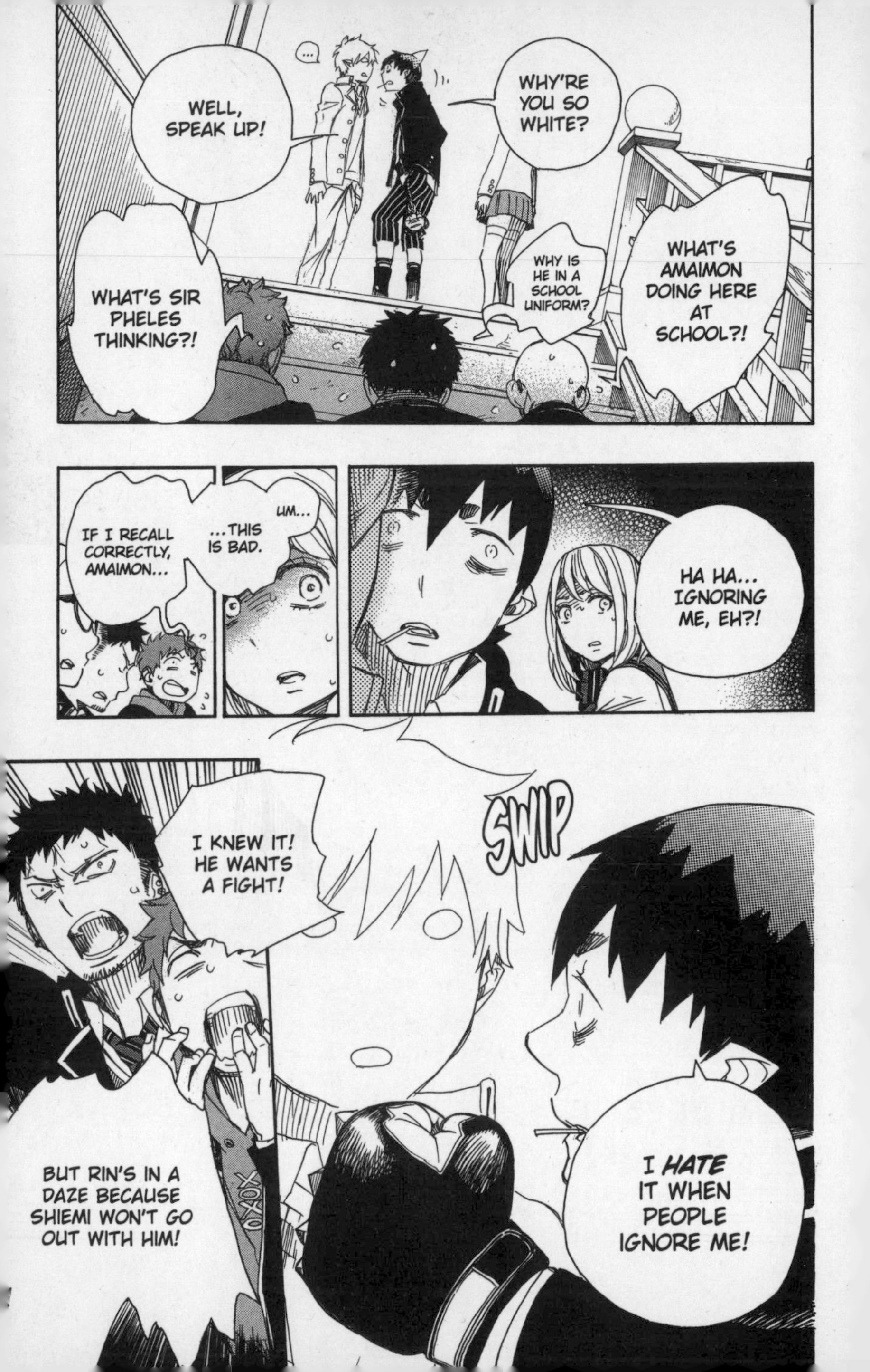
WHY'RE YOU SO WHITE?
...
WELL, SPEAK UP!
WHAT'S AMAIMON DOING HERE AT SCHOOL?!
WHY IS HE IN A SCHOOL UNIFORM?
WHAT'S SIR PHELES THINKING?!
HA HA... IGNORING ME, EH?!
UM...
...THIS IS BAD.
IF I RECALL CORRECTLY, AMAIMON...
SWIP
I HATE IT WHEN PEOPLE IGNORE ME!
I KNEW IT! HE WANTS A FIGHT!
BUT RIN'S IN A DAZE BECAUSE SHIEMI WON'T GO OUT WITH HIM!

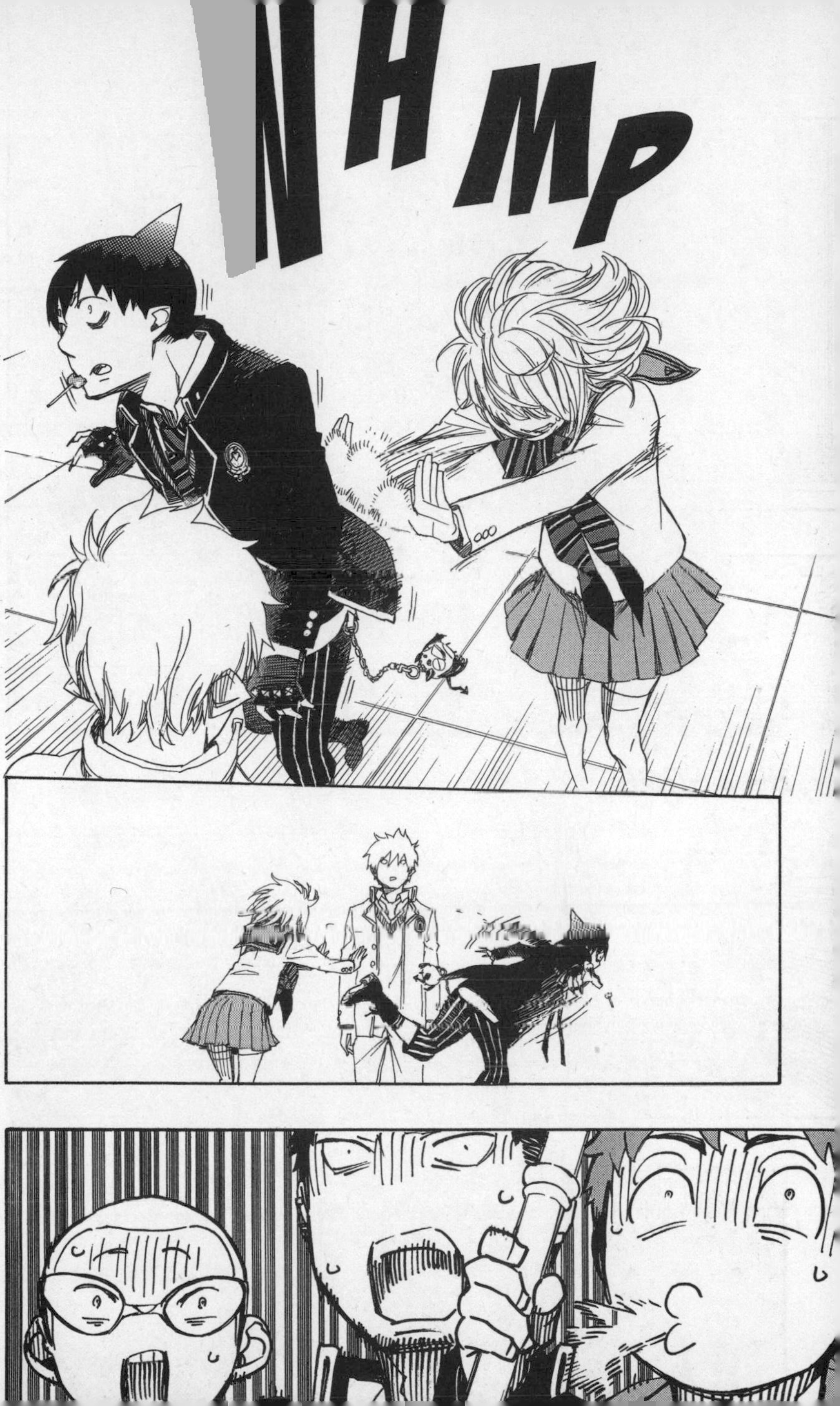
NHMP

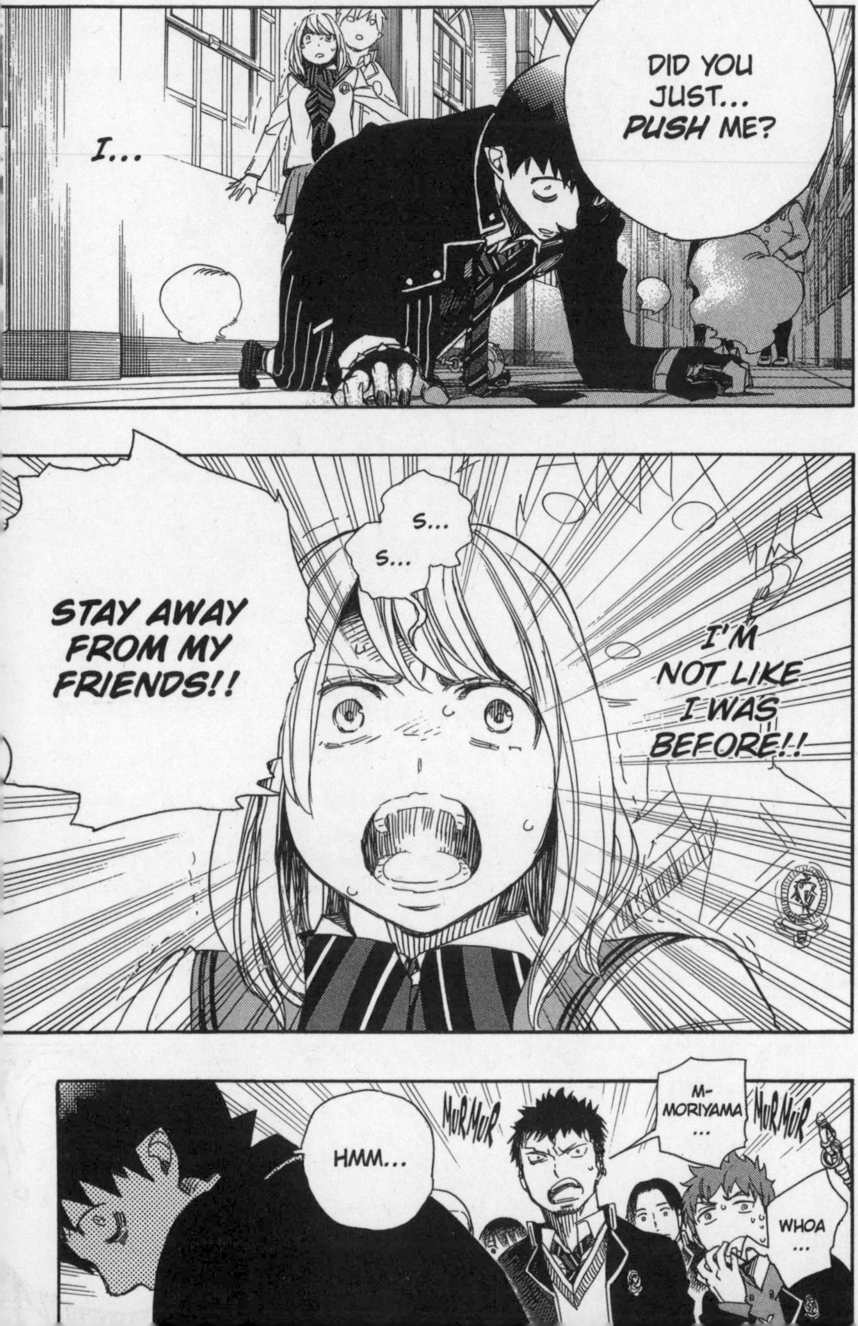
DID YOU JUST... PUSH ME?
I...
S...
S...
STAY AWAY FROM MY FRIENDS!!
I'M NOT LIKE I WAS BEFORE!!
MURMUR
M-MORIYAMA ...
MURMUR
WHOA ...
HMM...

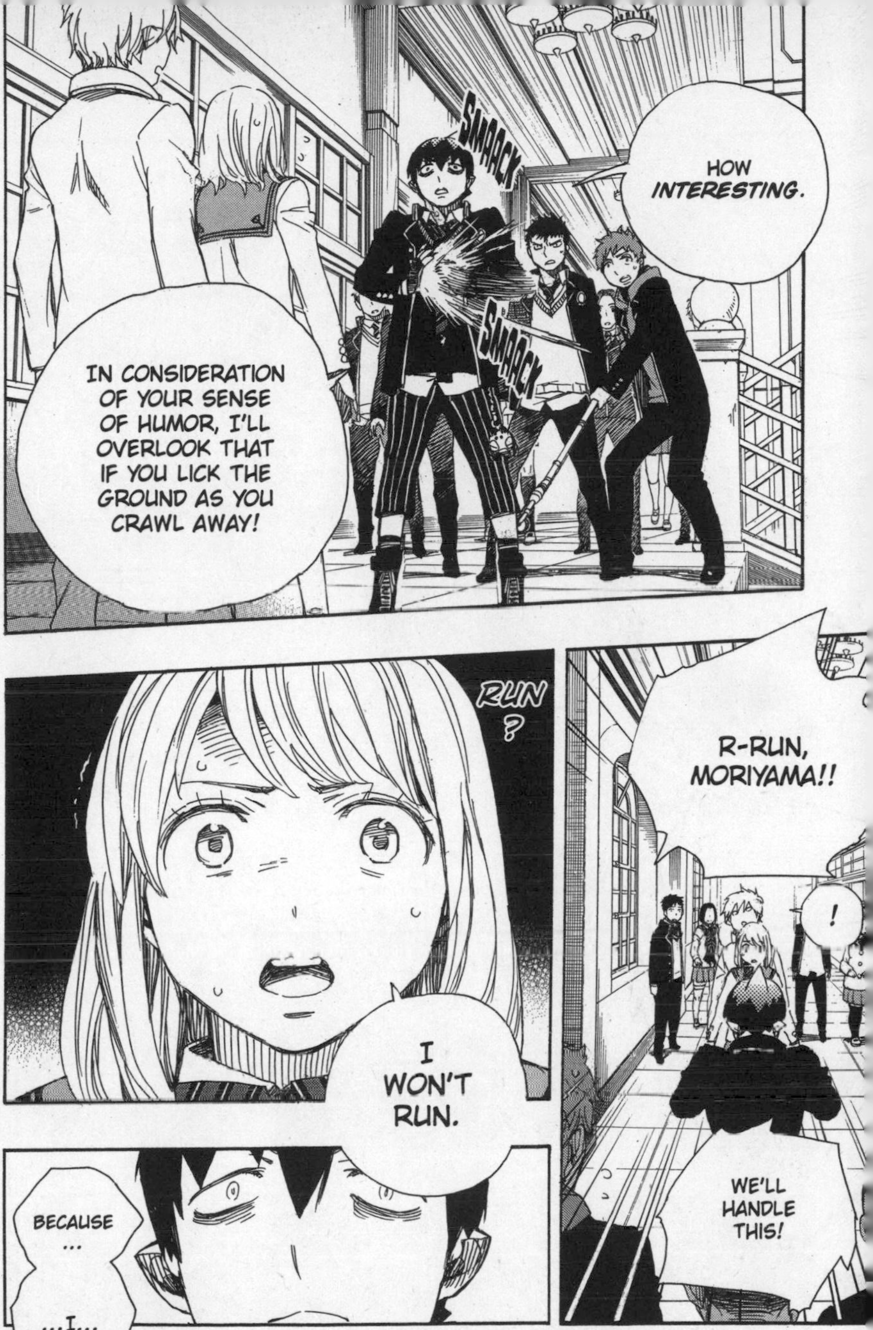
HOW INTERESTING.
SMAACK
SMAACK
IN CONSIDERATION OF YOUR SENSE OF HUMOR, I'LL OVERLOOK THAT IF YOU LICK THE GROUND AS YOU CRAWL AWAY!
R-RUN, MORIYAMA!!
!
WE'LL HANDLE THIS!
RUN?
I WON'T RUN.
BECAUSE...
...I...

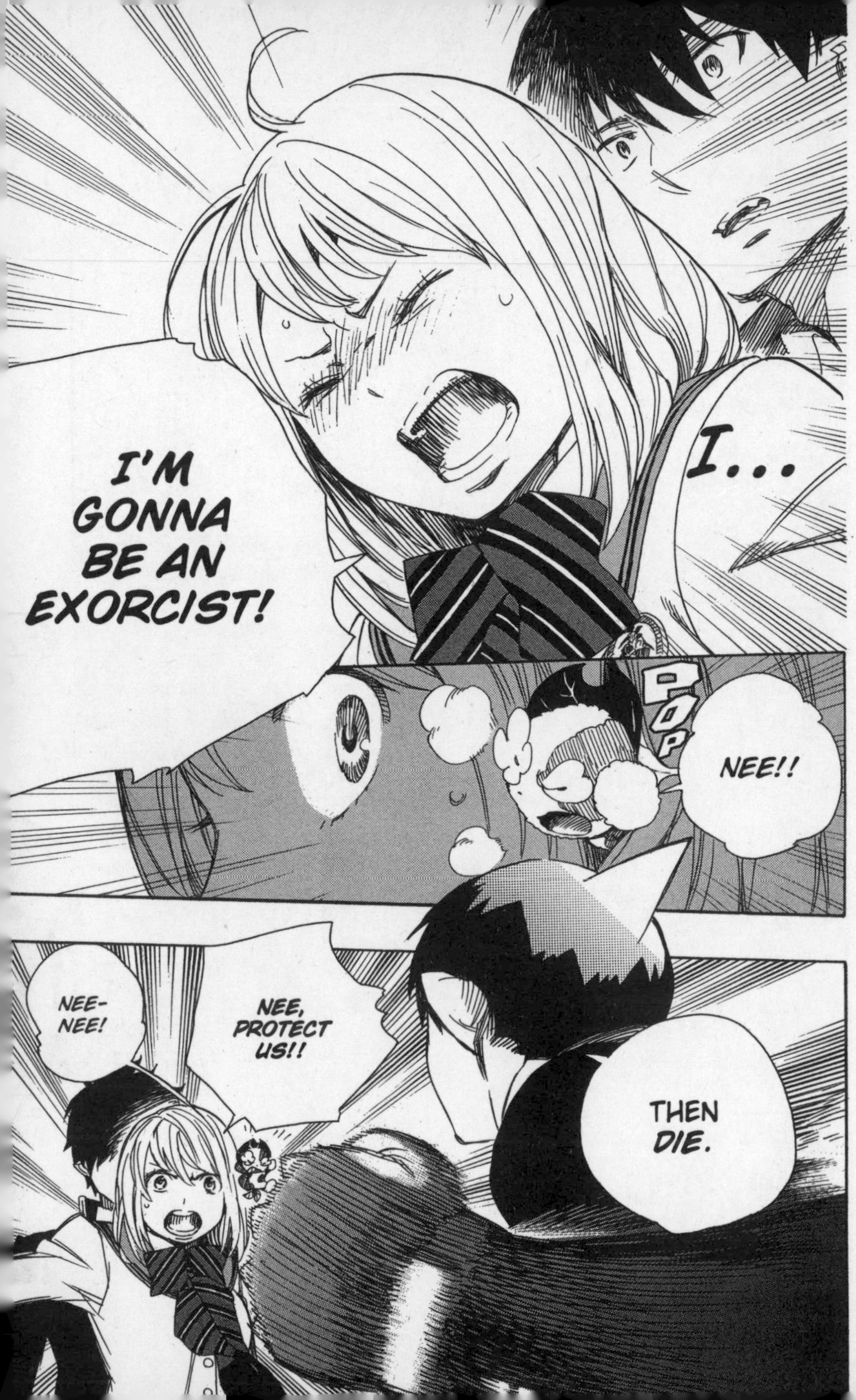
I...
I'M GONNA BE AN EXORCIST!
POP
NEE!!
NEE, PROTECT US!!
NEE-NEE!
THEN DIE.

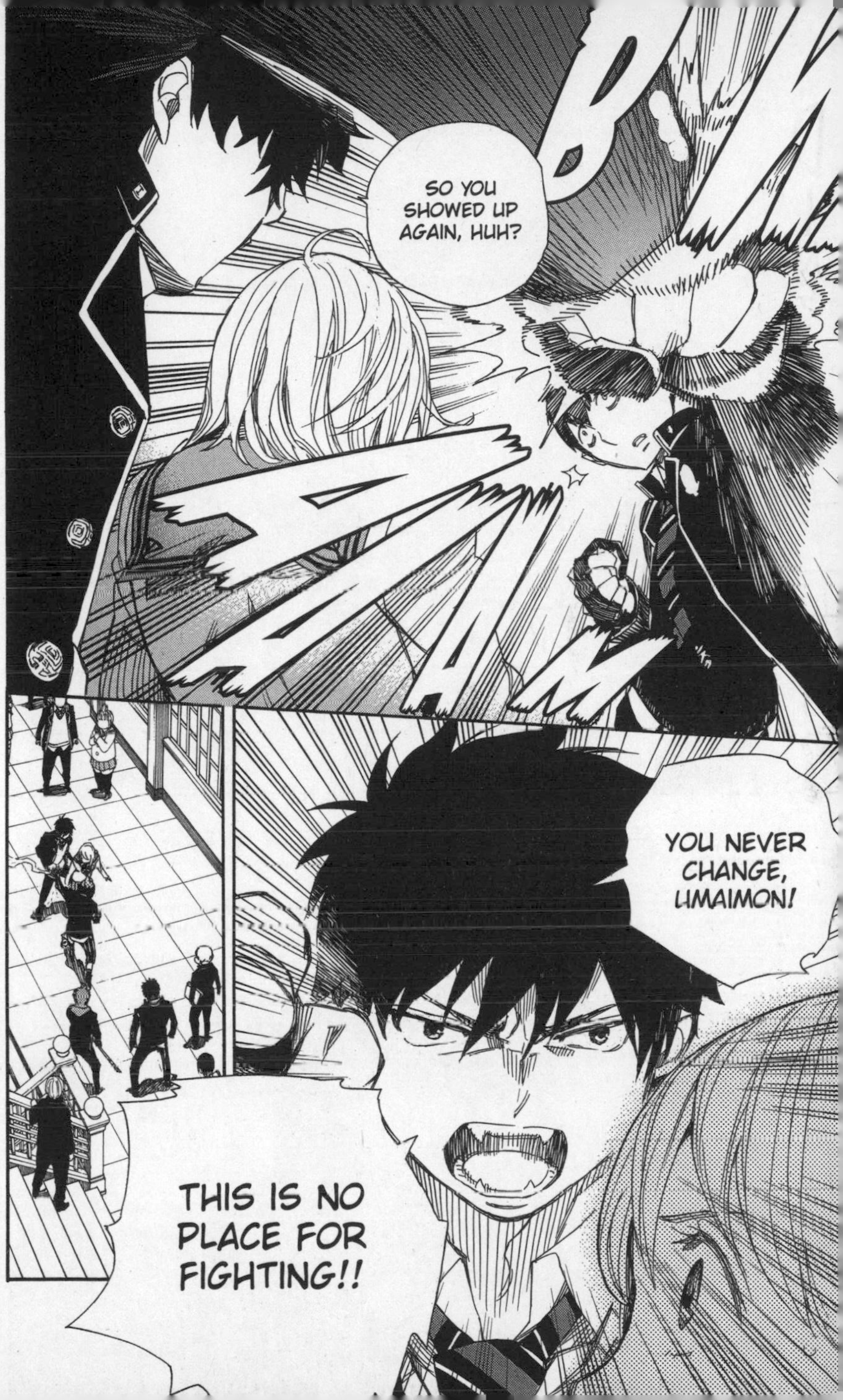
SO YOU SHOWED UP AGAIN, HUH?
YOU NEVER CHANGE, UMAIMON!
THIS IS NO PLACE FOR FIGHTING!!

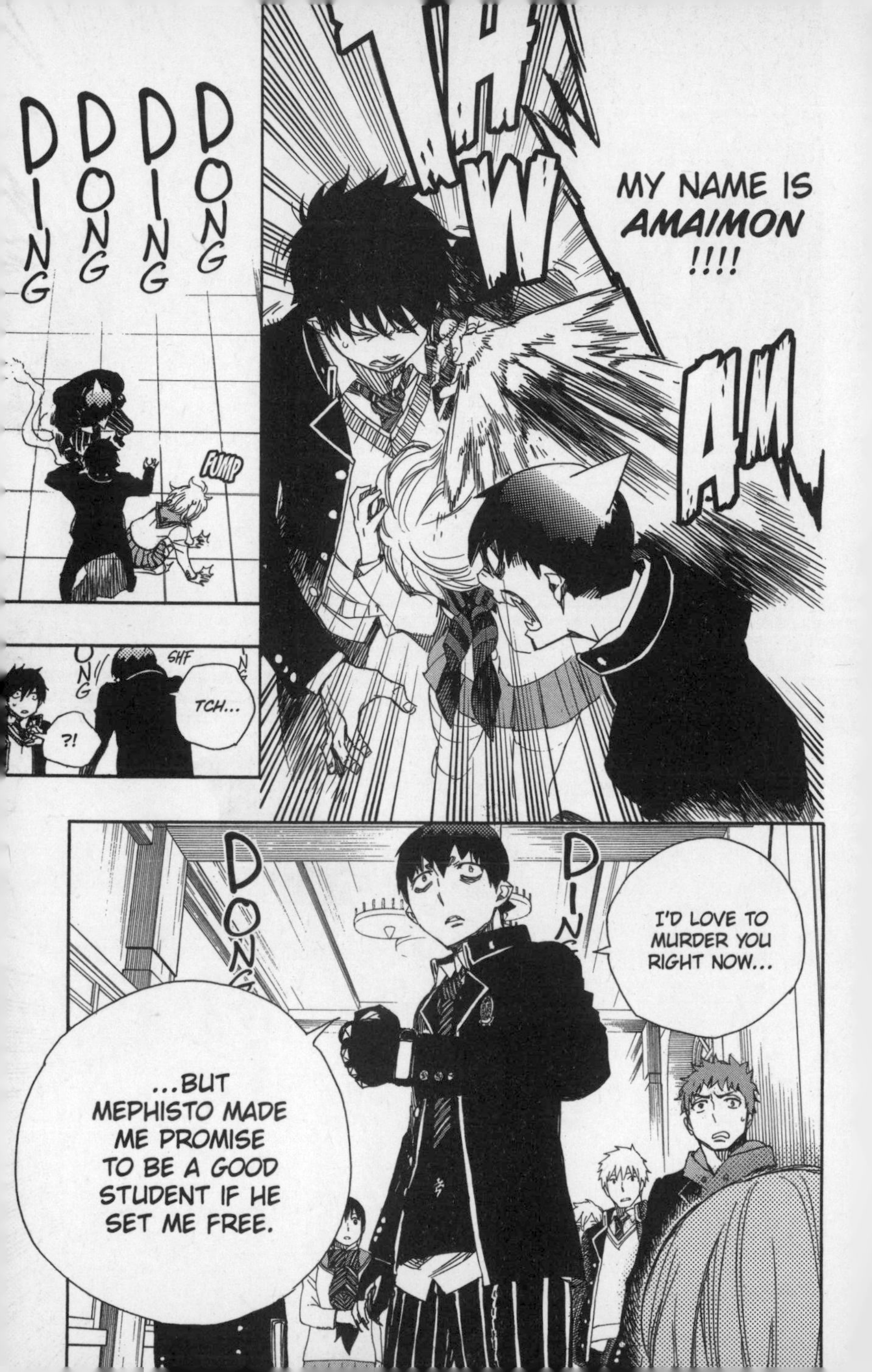
MY NAME IS AMAIMON !!!!
DONG
DING
DONG
DING
FUMP
SHF
TCH...
?!
I'D LOVE TO MURDER YOU RIGHT NOW...
...BUT MEPHISTO MADE ME PROMISE TO BE A GOOD STUDENT IF HE SET ME FREE.

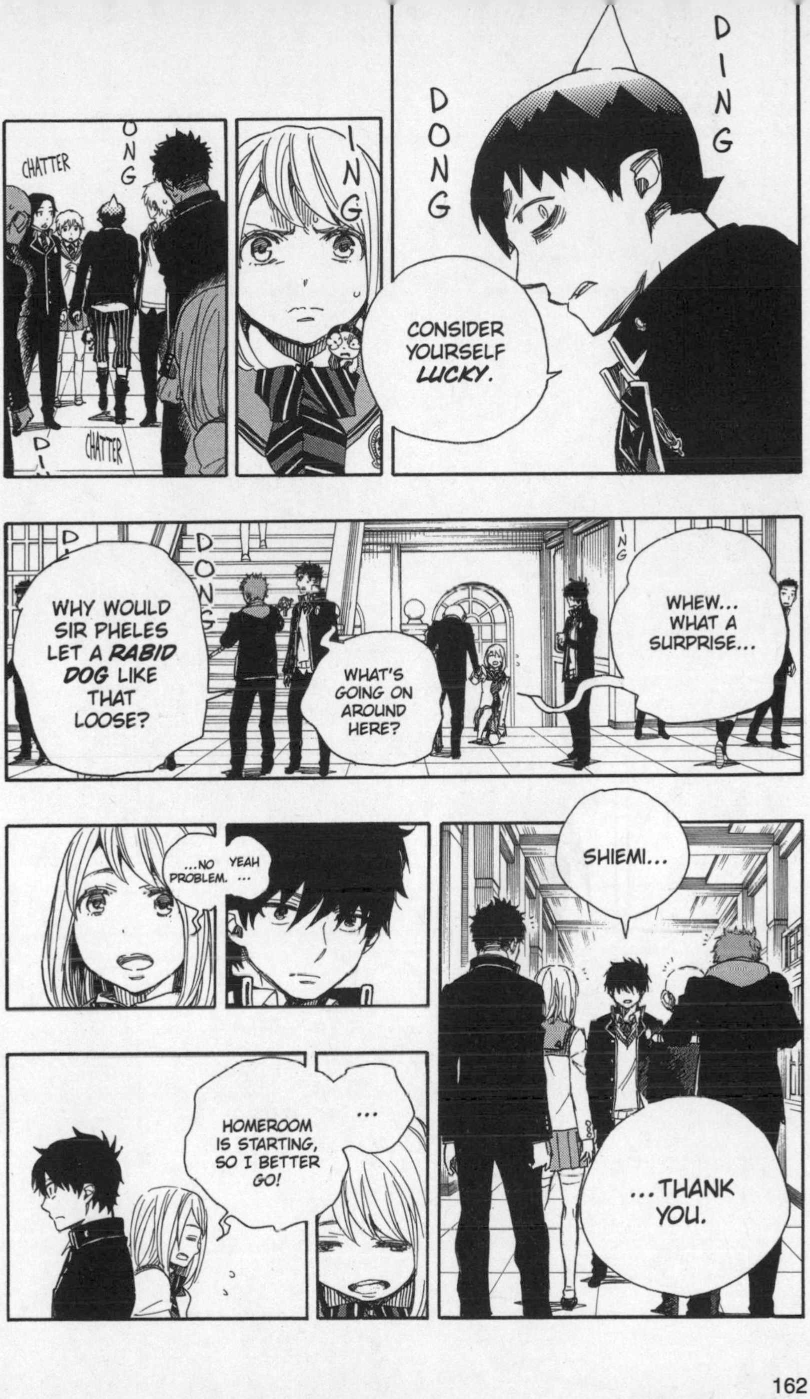
DING
DONG
CONSIDER YOURSELF LUCKY.
ING
ONG
CHATTER
CHATTER
WHEW... WHAT A SURPRISE...
ING
DONG
WHAT'S GOING ON AROUND HERE?
WHY WOULD SIR PHELES LET A RABID DOG LIKE THAT LOOSE?
SHIEMI...
...THANK YOU.
YEAH ...
...NO PROBLEM.
...
HOMEROOM IS STARTING, SO I BETTER GO!

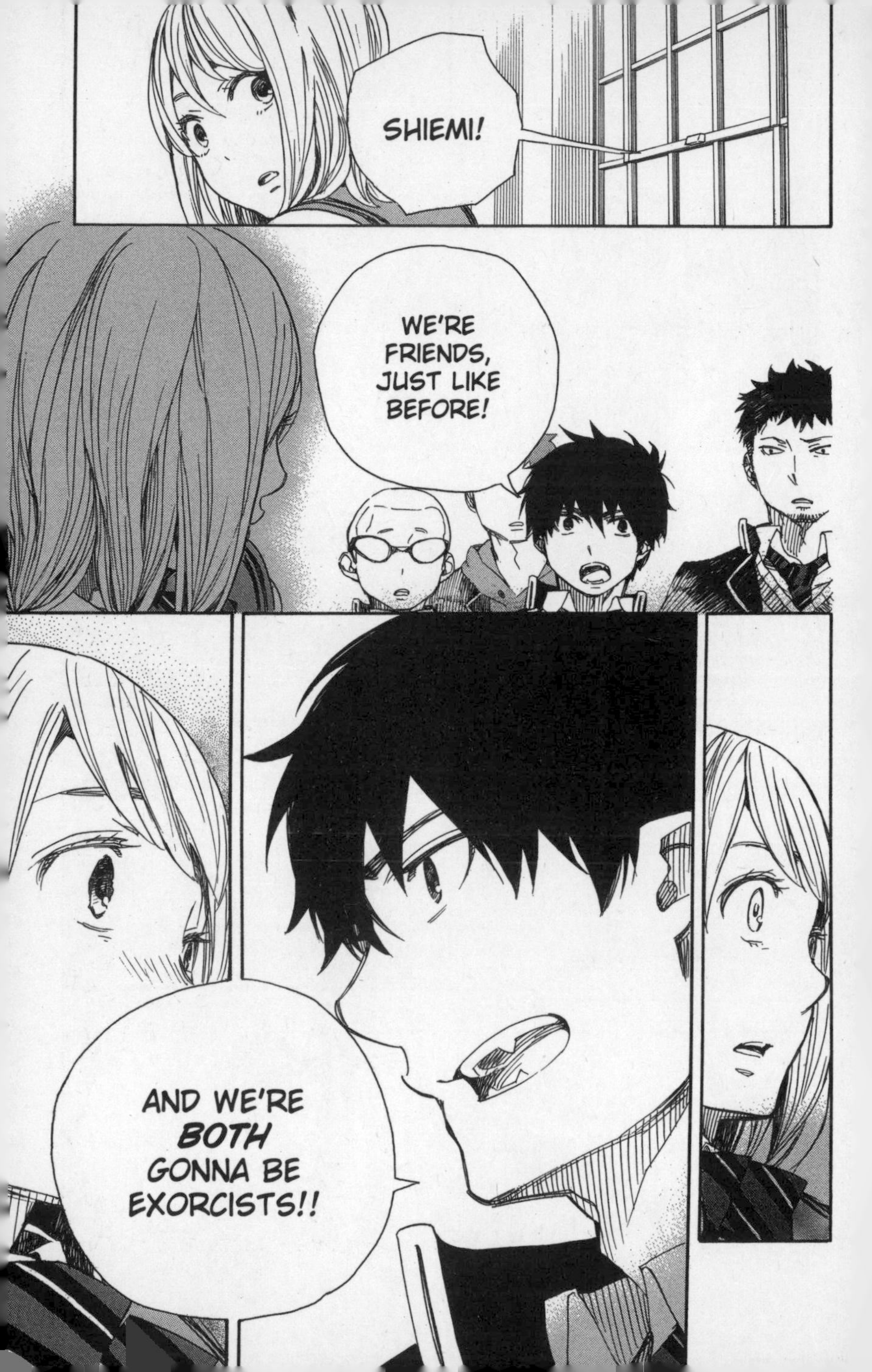
SHIEMI!
WE'RE FRIENDS, JUST LIKE BEFORE!
AND WE'RE *BOTH* GONNA BE EXORCISTS!!

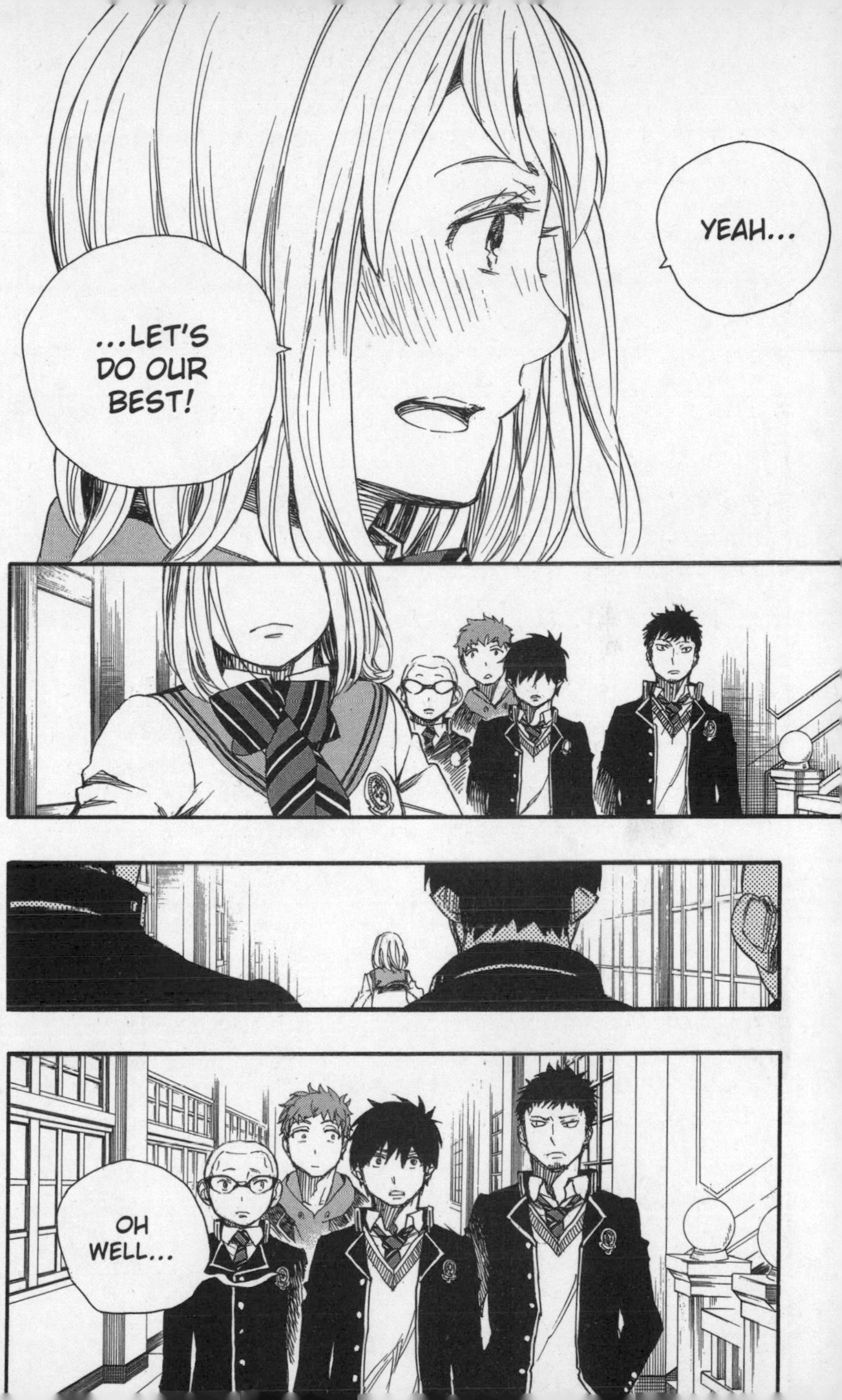
YEAH...
...LET'S DO OUR BEST!
OH WELL...

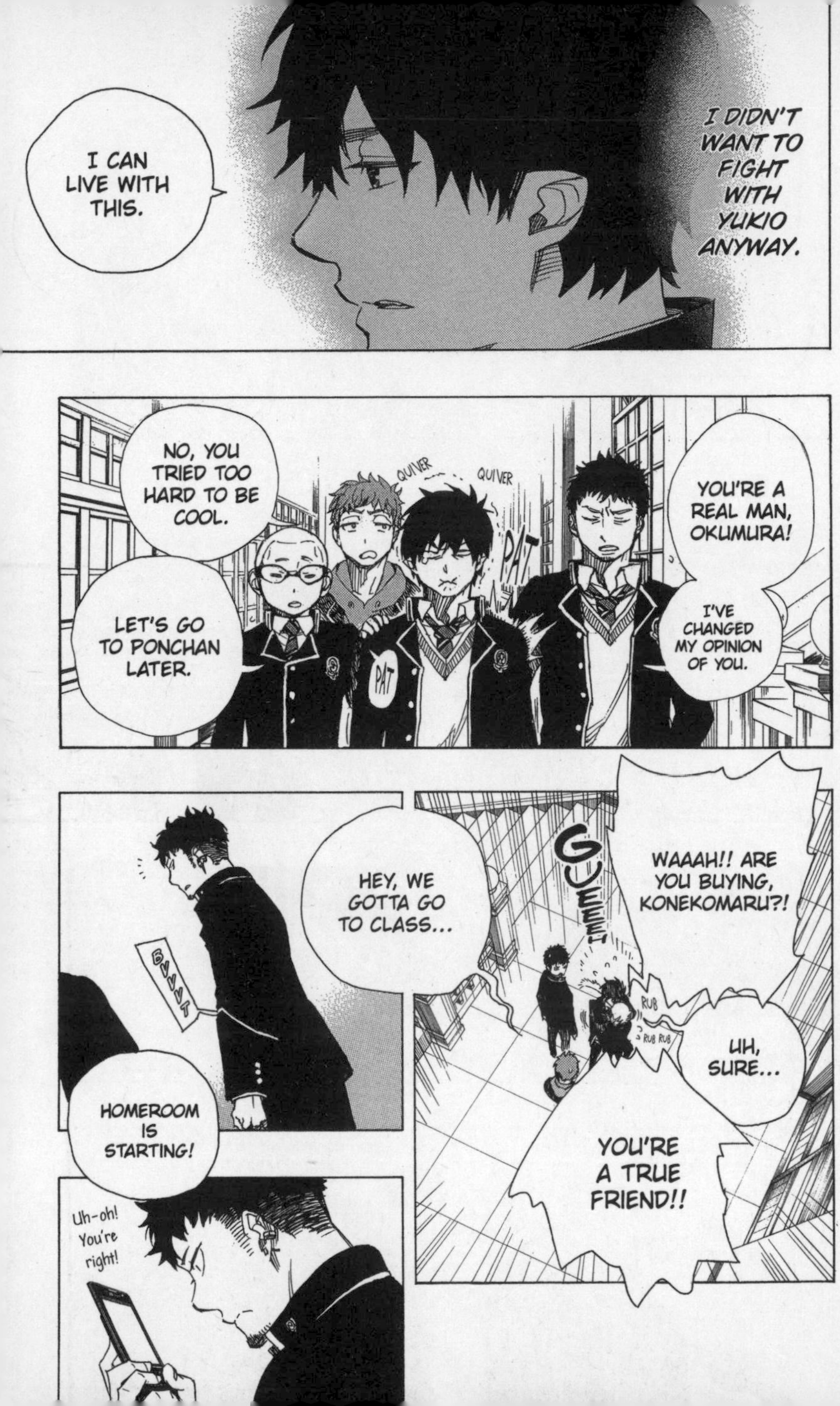
I DIDN'T WANT TO FIGHT WITH YUKIO ANYWAY.
I CAN LIVE WITH THIS.
YOU'RE A REAL MAN, OKUMURA!
I'VE CHANGED MY OPINION OF YOU.
QUIVER
QUIVER
PAT
PAT
NO, YOU TRIED TOO HARD TO BE COOL.
LET'S GO TO PONCHAN LATER.
WAAAH!! ARE YOU BUYING, KONEKOMARU?!
GUEEEH
RUB
RUB RUB
UH, SURE...
YOU'RE A TRUE FRIEND!!
HEY, WE GOTTA GO TO CLASS...
BVVVT
HOMEROOM IS STARTING!
Uh-oh! You're right!

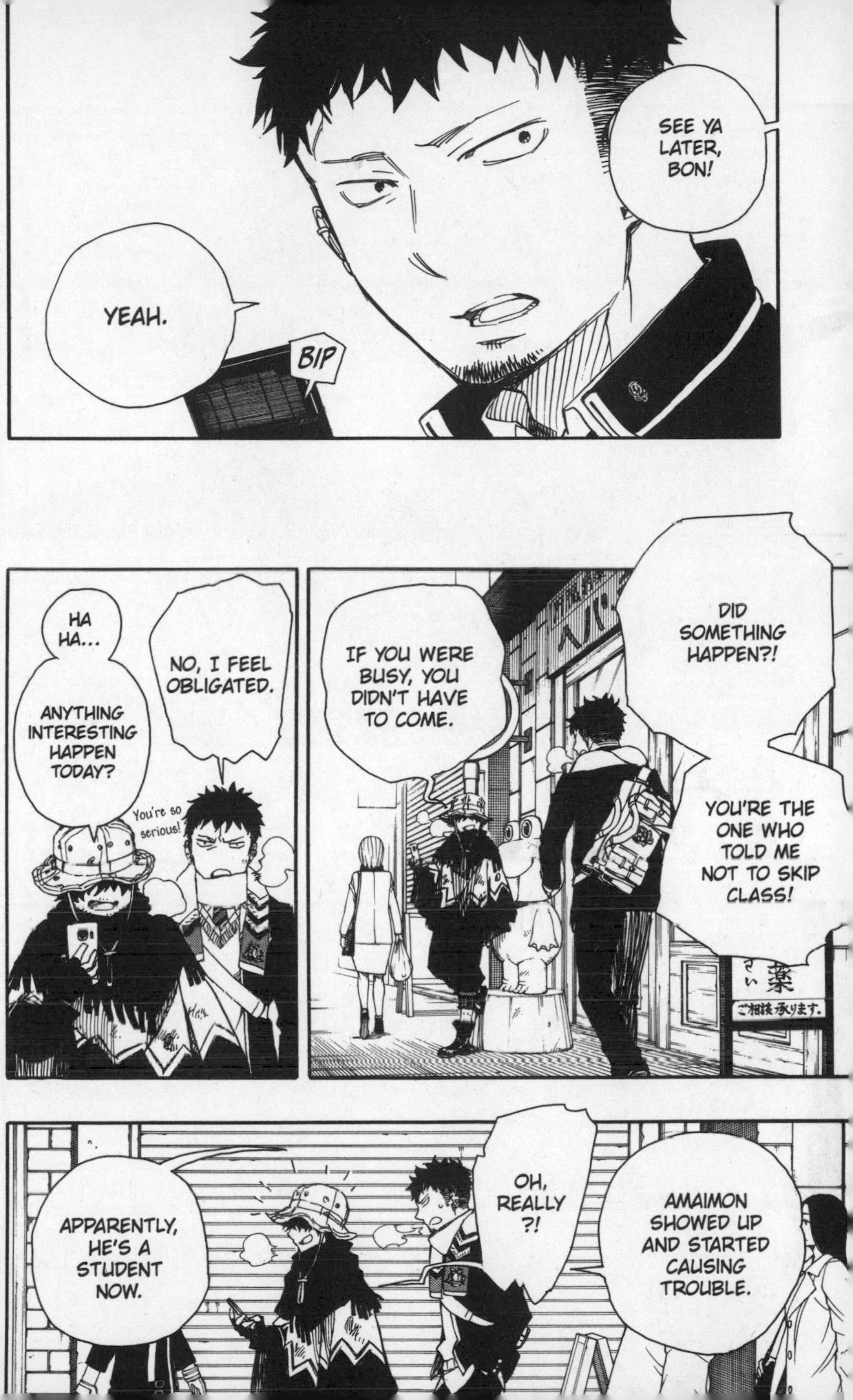
SEE YA LATER, BON!
YEAH.
BIP
DID SOMETHING HAPPEN?!
YOU'RE THE ONE WHO TOLD ME NOT TO SKIP CLASS!
IF YOU WERE BUSY, YOU DIDN'T HAVE TO COME.
薬
ご相談承ります。
NO, I FEEL OBLIGATED.
HA HA...
ANYTHING INTERESTING HAPPEN TODAY?
You're so serious!
AMAIMON SHOWED UP AND STARTED CAUSING TROUBLE.
OH, REALLY?!
APPARENTLY, HE'S A STUDENT NOW.

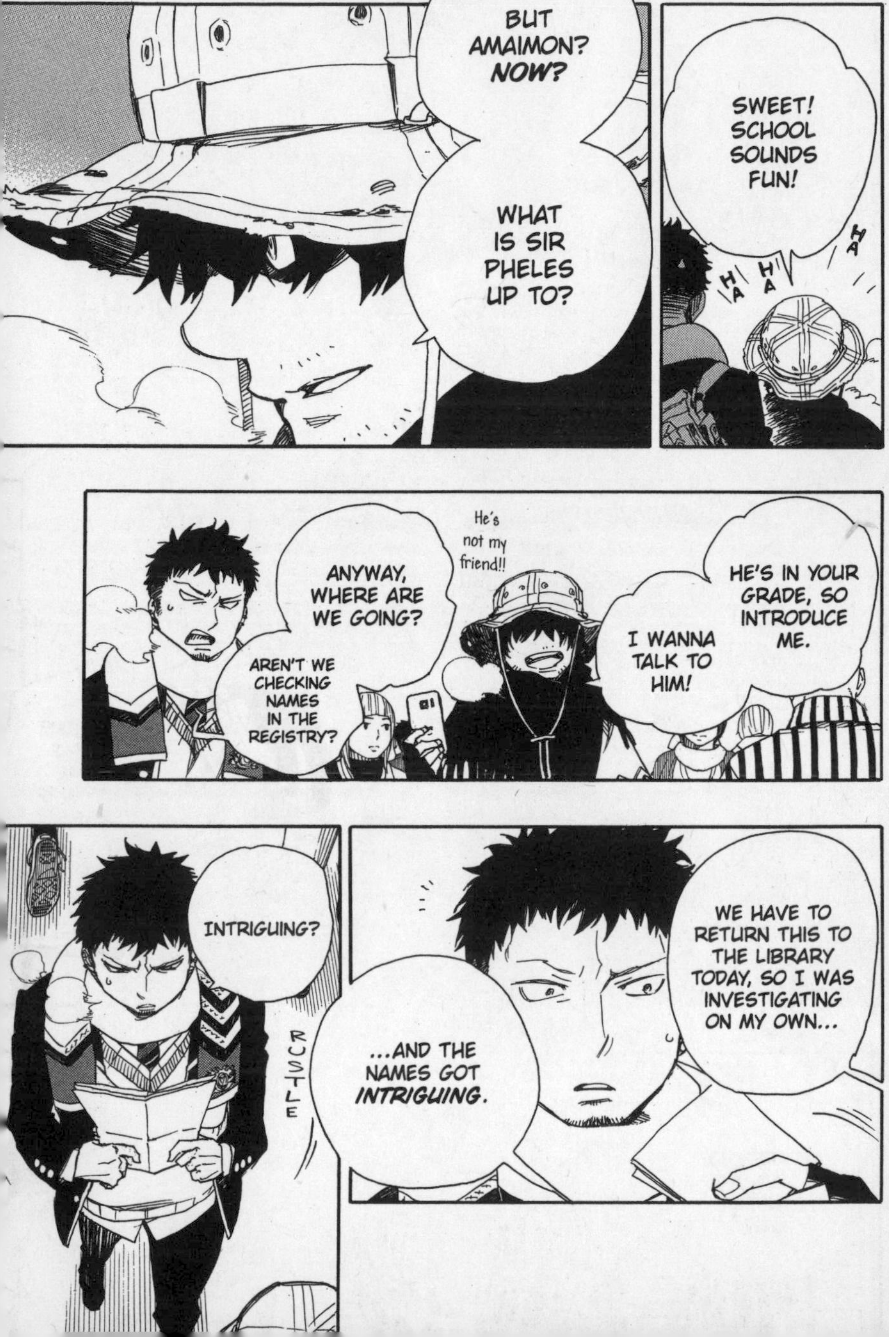
SWEET! SCHOOL SOUNDS FUN!
HA HA HA
BUT AMAIMON? NOW?
WHAT IS SIR PHELES UP TO?
HE'S IN YOUR GRADE, SO INTRODUCE ME.
I WANNA TALK TO HIM!
He's not my friend!!
ANYWAY, WHERE ARE WE GOING?
AREN'T WE CHECKING NAMES IN THE REGISTRY?
WE HAVE TO RETURN THIS TO THE LIBRARY TODAY, SO I WAS INVESTIGATING ON MY OWN...
...AND THE NAMES GOT INTRIGUING.
RUSTLE
INTRIGUING?

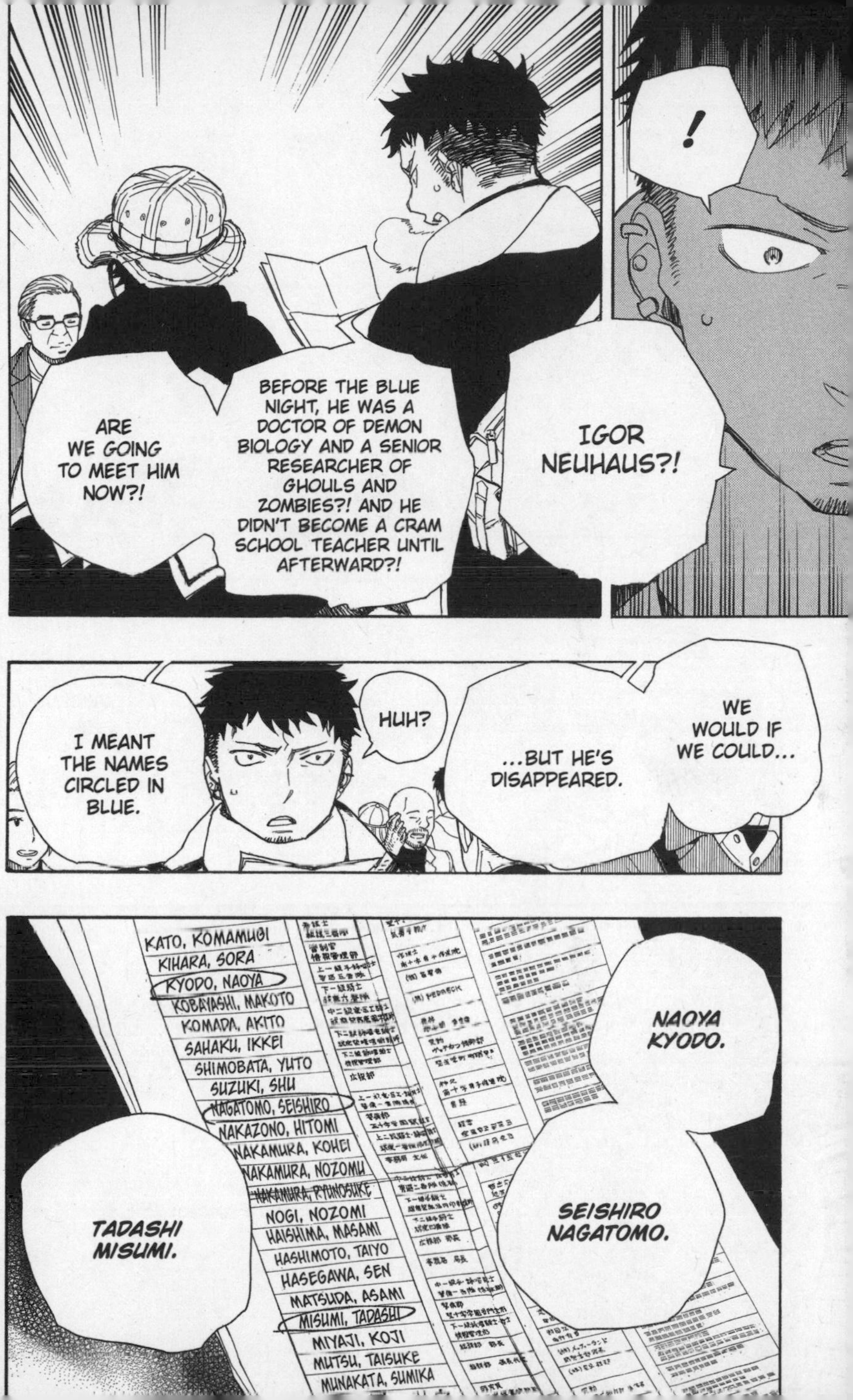
!
IGOR NEUHAUS?!
BEFORE THE BLUE NIGHT, HE WAS A DOCTOR OF DEMON BIOLOGY AND A SENIOR RESEARCHER OF GHOULS AND ZOMBIES?! AND HE DIDN'T BECOME A CRAM SCHOOL TEACHER UNTIL AFTERWARD?!
ARE WE GOING TO MEET HIM NOW?!
WE WOULD IF WE COULD...
...BUT HE'S DISAPPEARED.
HUH?
I MEANT THE NAMES CIRCLED IN BLUE.
NAOYA KYODO.
SEISHIRO NAGATOMO.
TADASHI MISUMI.
KATO, KOMAMUGI
KIHARA, SORA
KYODO, NAOYA
KOBAYASHI, MAKOTO
KOMADA, AKITO
SAHAKU, IKKEI
SHIMOBATA, YUTO
SUZUKI, SHU
NAGATOMO, SEISHIRO
NAKAZONO, HITOMI
NAKAMURA, KOHEI
NAKAMURA, NOZOMU
NAKAMURA, RYUNOSUKE
NOGI, NOZOMI
HAISHIMA, MASAMI
HASHIMOTO, TAIYO
HASEGAWA, SEN
MATSUDA, ASAMI
MISUMI, TADASHI
MIYAJI, KOJI
MUTSU, TAISUKE
MUNAKATA, SUMIKA

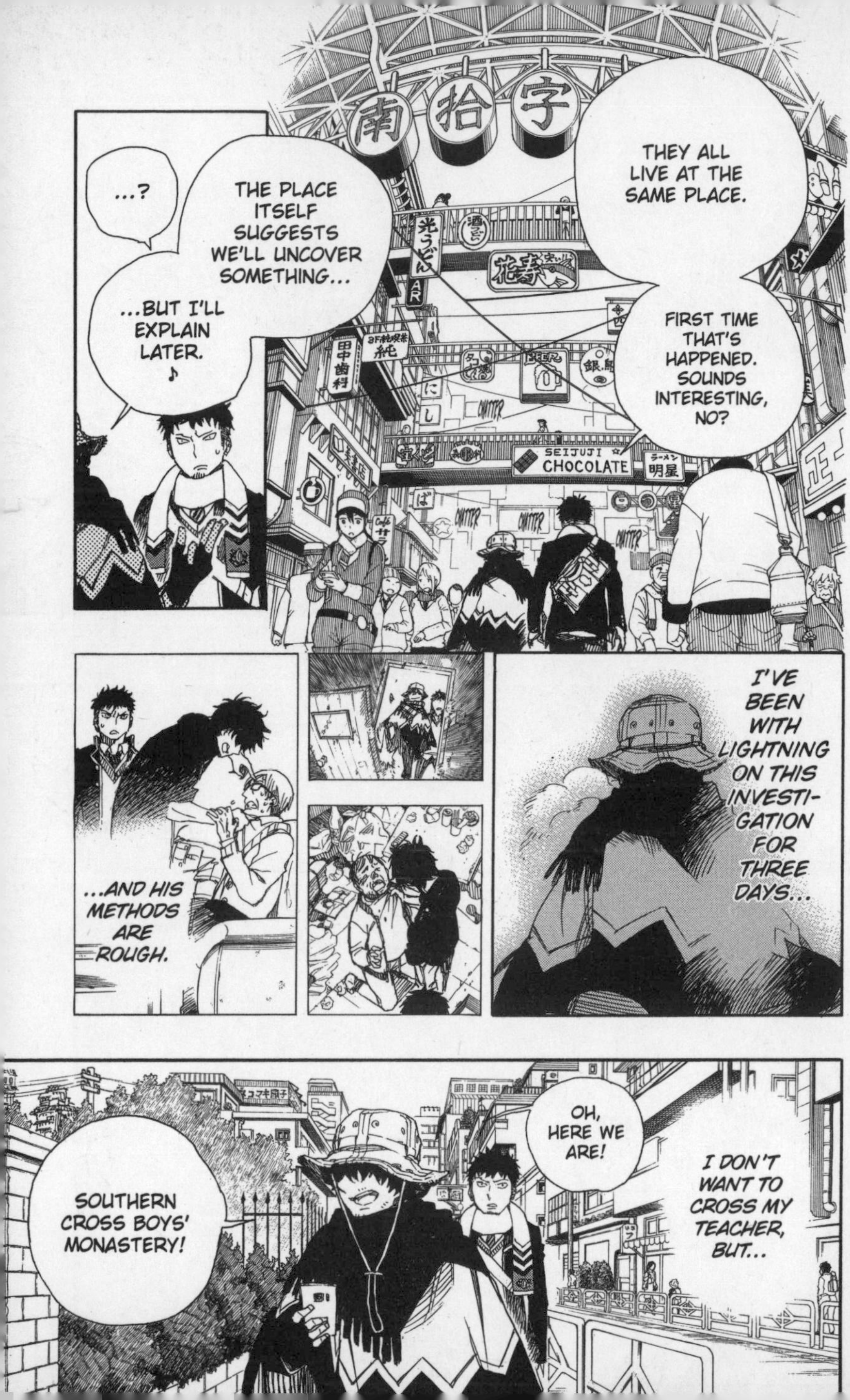
南拾字
THEY ALL LIVE AT THE SAME PLACE.
FIRST TIME THAT'S HAPPENED. SOUNDS INTERESTING, NO?
SEIJUJI CHOCOLATE
THE PLACE ITSELF SUGGESTS WE'LL UNCOVER SOMETHING...
...BUT I'LL EXPLAIN LATER. ♪
...?
I'VE BEEN WITH LIGHTNING ON THIS INVESTIGATION FOR THREE DAYS...
...AND HIS METHODS ARE ROUGH.
I DON'T WANT TO CROSS MY TEACHER, BUT...
OH, HERE WE ARE!
SOUTHERN CROSS BOYS' MONASTERY!

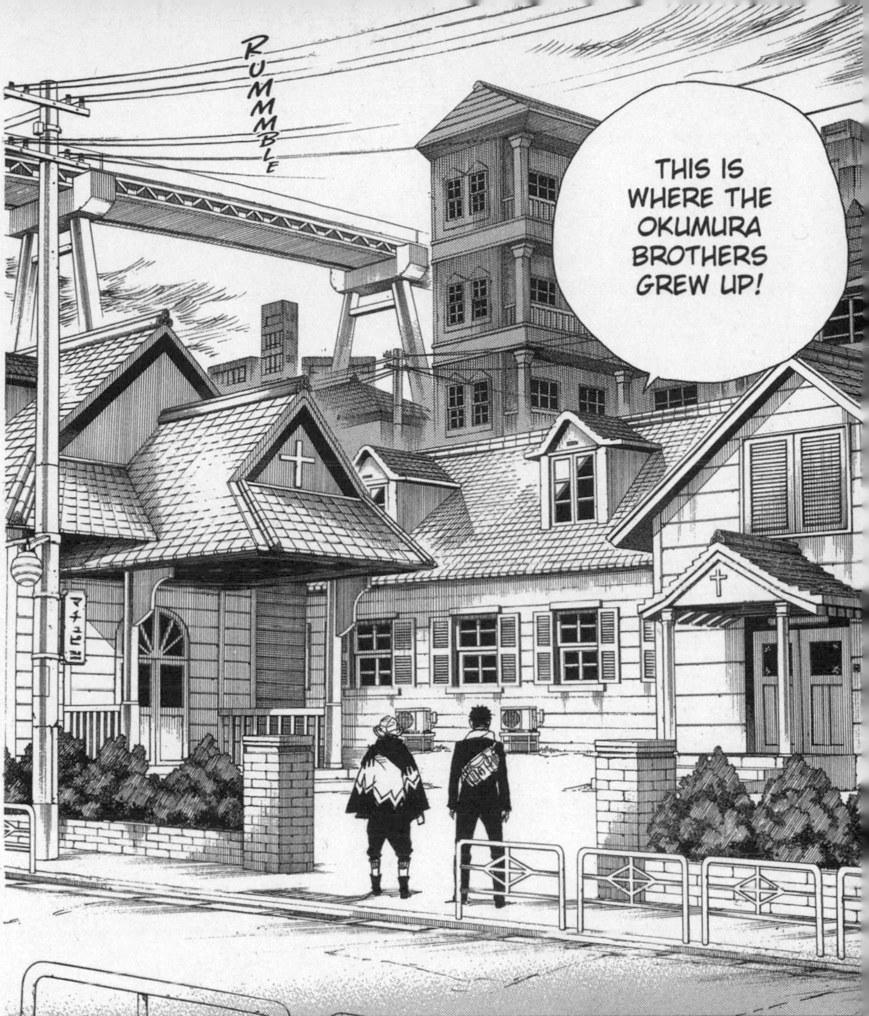
RUMMMMBLE
THIS IS WHERE THE OKUMURA BROTHERS GREW UP!

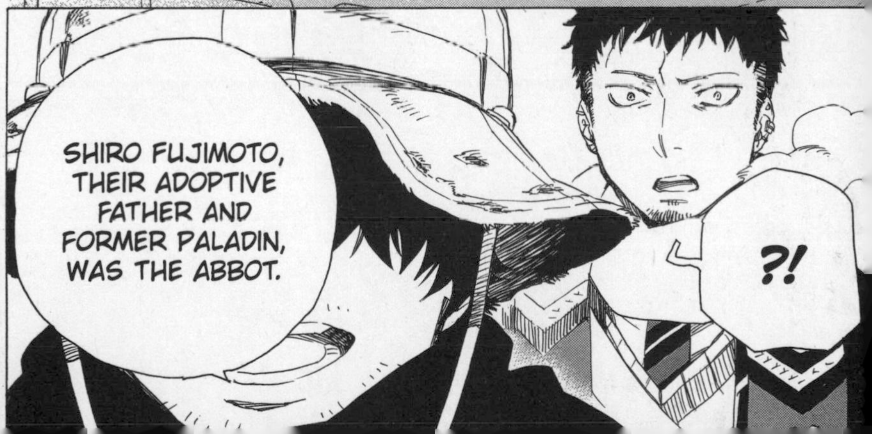
SHIRO FUJIMOTO, THEIR ADOPTIVE FATHER AND FORMER PALADIN, WAS THE ABBOT.
?!

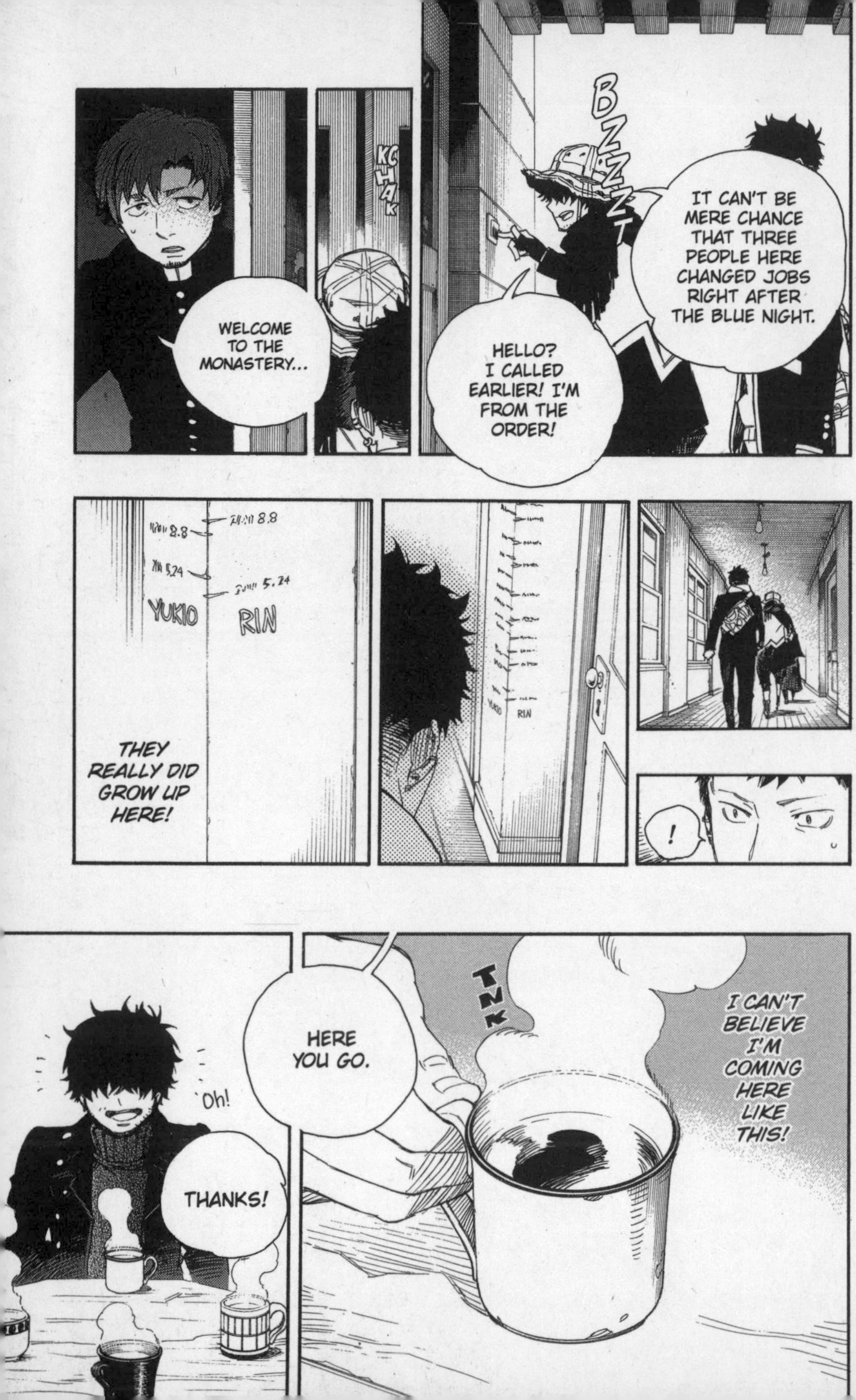
BZZZZT
IT CAN'T BE MERE CHANCE THAT THREE PEOPLE HERE CHANGED JOBS RIGHT AFTER THE BLUE NIGHT.
HELLO? I CALLED EARLIER! I'M FROM THE ORDER!
KCHAK
WELCOME TO THE MONASTERY...
!
YUKIO
RIN
YUKIO
RIN
THEY REALLY DID GROW UP HERE!
I CAN'T BELIEVE I'M COMING HERE LIKE THIS!
TNK
HERE YOU GO.
Oh!
THANKS!

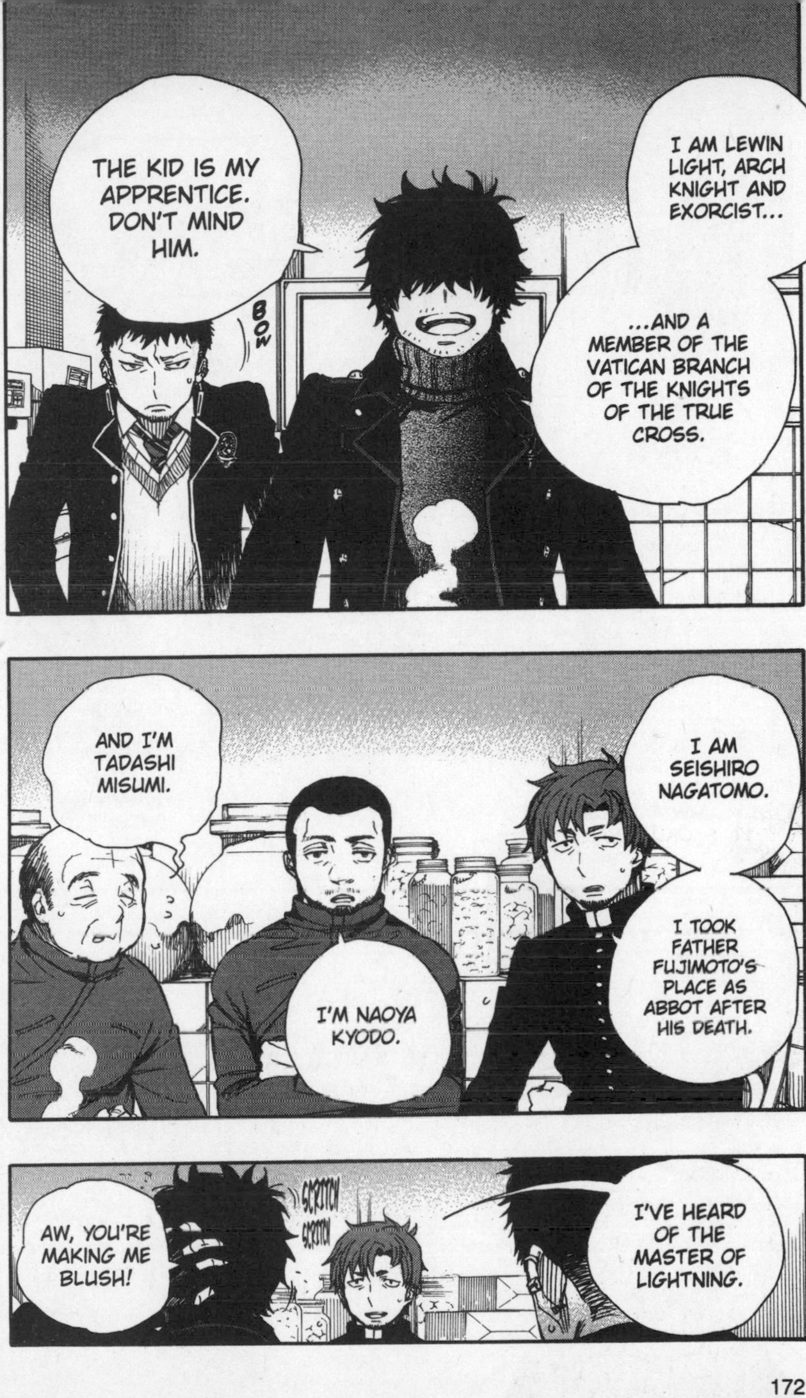
I AM LEWIN LIGHT, ARCH KNIGHT AND EXORCIST...
...AND A MEMBER OF THE VATICAN BRANCH OF THE KNIGHTS OF THE TRUE CROSS.
THE KID IS MY APPRENTICE. DON'T MIND HIM.
BOW
I AM SEISHIRO NAGATOMO.
I TOOK FATHER FUJIMOTO'S PLACE AS ABBOT AFTER HIS DEATH.
I'M NAOYA KYODO.
AND I'M TADASHI MISUMI.
I'VE HEARD OF THE MASTER OF LIGHTNING.
SCRITCH SCRITCH
AW, YOU'RE MAKING ME BLUSH!

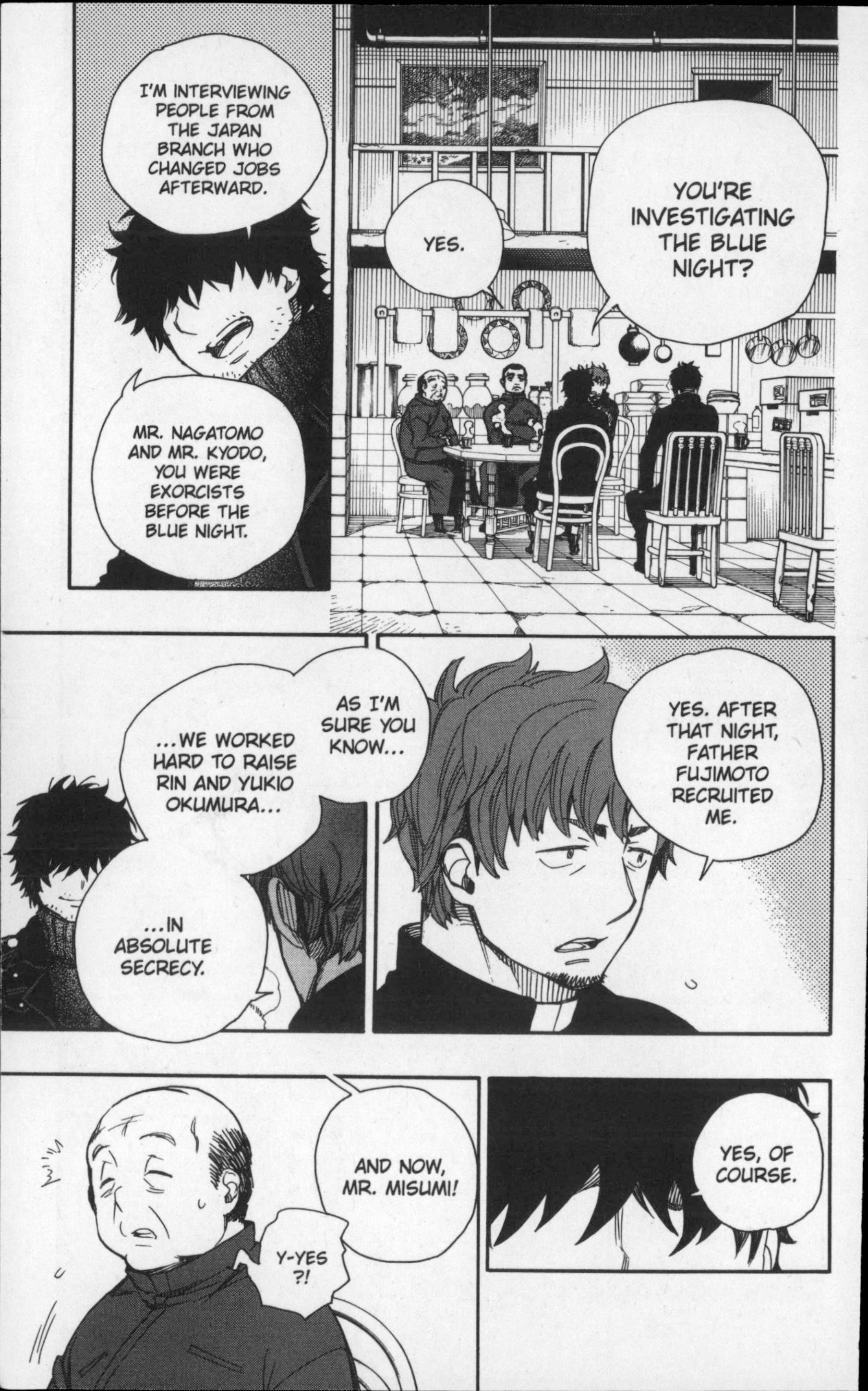
YOU'RE INVESTIGATING THE BLUE NIGHT?
YES.
I'M INTERVIEWING PEOPLE FROM THE JAPAN BRANCH WHO CHANGED JOBS AFTERWARD.
MR. NAGATOMO AND MR. KYODO, YOU WERE EXORCISTS BEFORE THE BLUE NIGHT.
YES. AFTER THAT NIGHT, FATHER FUJIMOTO RECRUITED ME.
AS I'M SURE YOU KNOW...
...WE WORKED HARD TO RAISE RIN AND YUKIO OKUMURA...
...IN ABSOLUTE SECRECY.
YES, OF COURSE.
AND NOW, MR. MISUMI!
Y-YES ?!

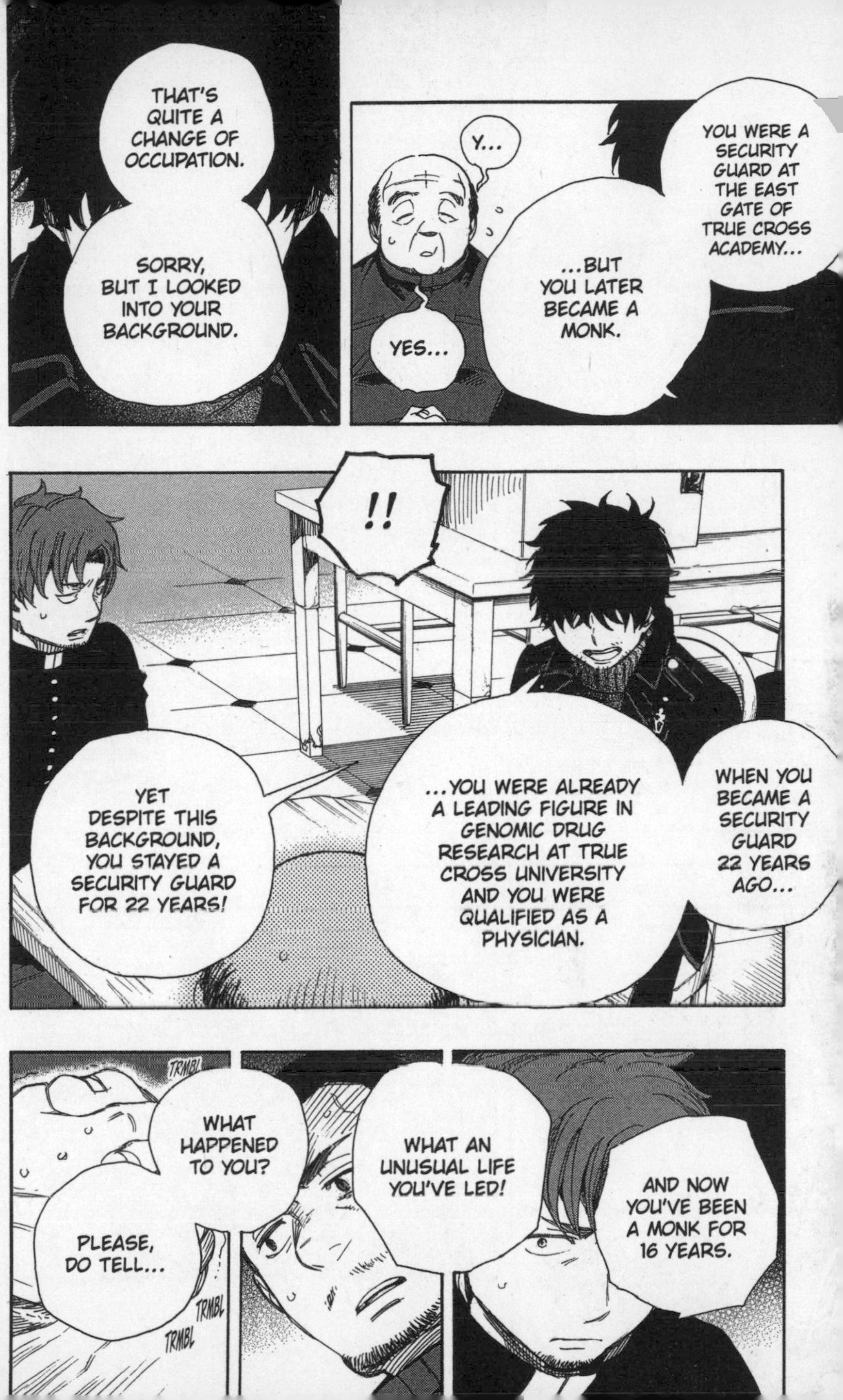
YOU WERE A SECURITY GUARD AT THE EAST GATE OF TRUE CROSS ACADEMY...
Y...
...BUT YOU LATER BECAME A MONK.
YES...
THAT'S QUITE A CHANGE OF OCCUPATION.
SORRY, BUT I LOOKED INTO YOUR BACKGROUND.
!!
WHEN YOU BECAME A SECURITY GUARD 22 YEARS AGO...
...YOU WERE ALREADY A LEADING FIGURE IN GENOMIC DRUG RESEARCH AT TRUE CROSS UNIVERSITY AND YOU WERE QUALIFIED AS A PHYSICIAN.
YET DESPITE THIS BACKGROUND, YOU STAYED A SECURITY GUARD FOR 22 YEARS!
AND NOW YOU'VE BEEN A MONK FOR 16 YEARS.
WHAT AN UNUSUAL LIFE YOU'VE LED!
TRMBL
WHAT HAPPENED TO YOU?
PLEASE, DO TELL...
TRMBL
TRMBL

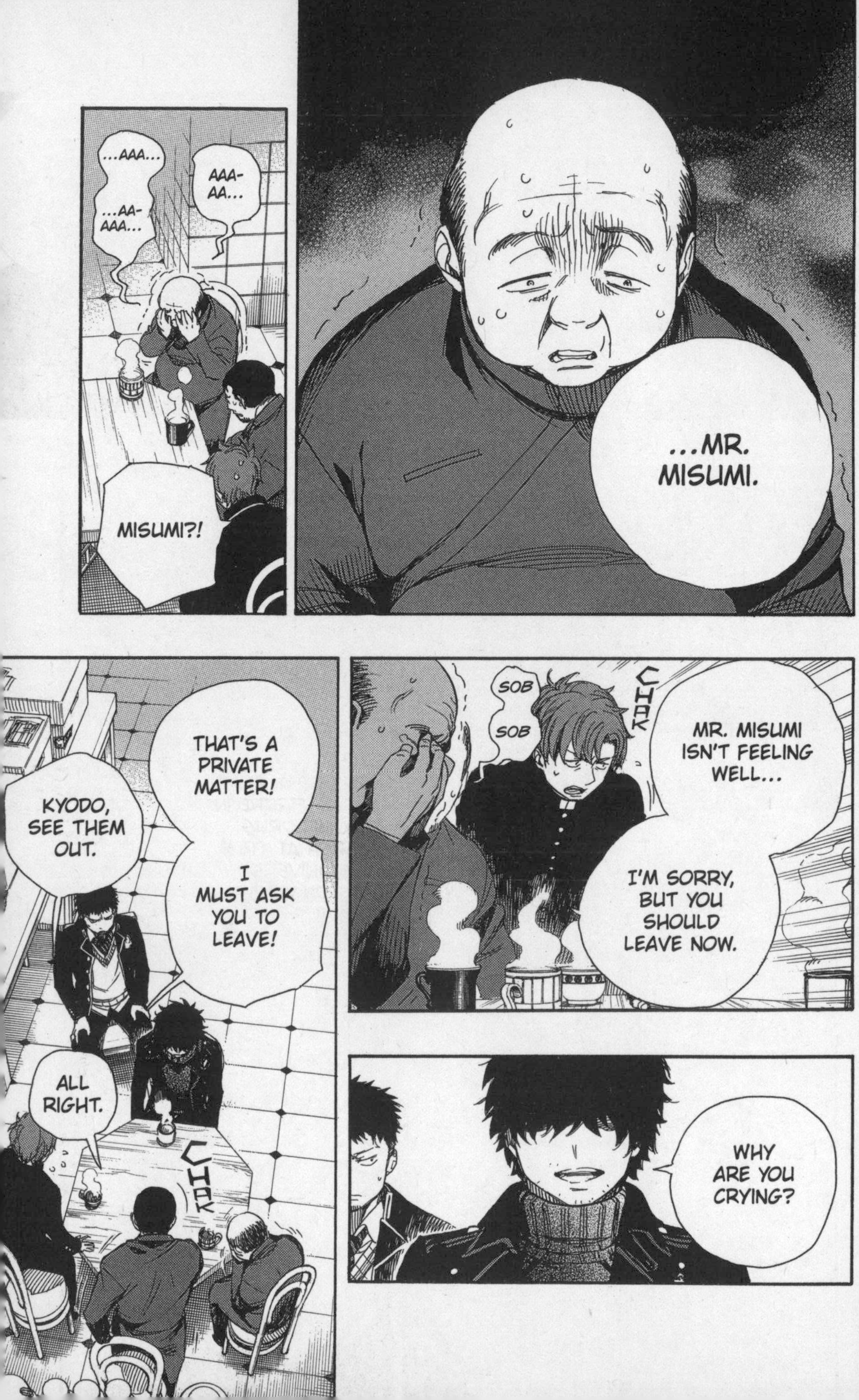
...MR. MISUMI.
AAA-AA...
...AAA...
...AA-AAA...
MISUMI?!
CHAK
MR. MISUMI ISN'T FEELING WELL...
SOB
SOB
I'M SORRY, BUT YOU SHOULD LEAVE NOW.
WHY ARE YOU CRYING?
THAT'S A PRIVATE MATTER!
I MUST ASK YOU TO LEAVE!
KYODO, SEE THEM OUT.
ALL RIGHT.
CHAK

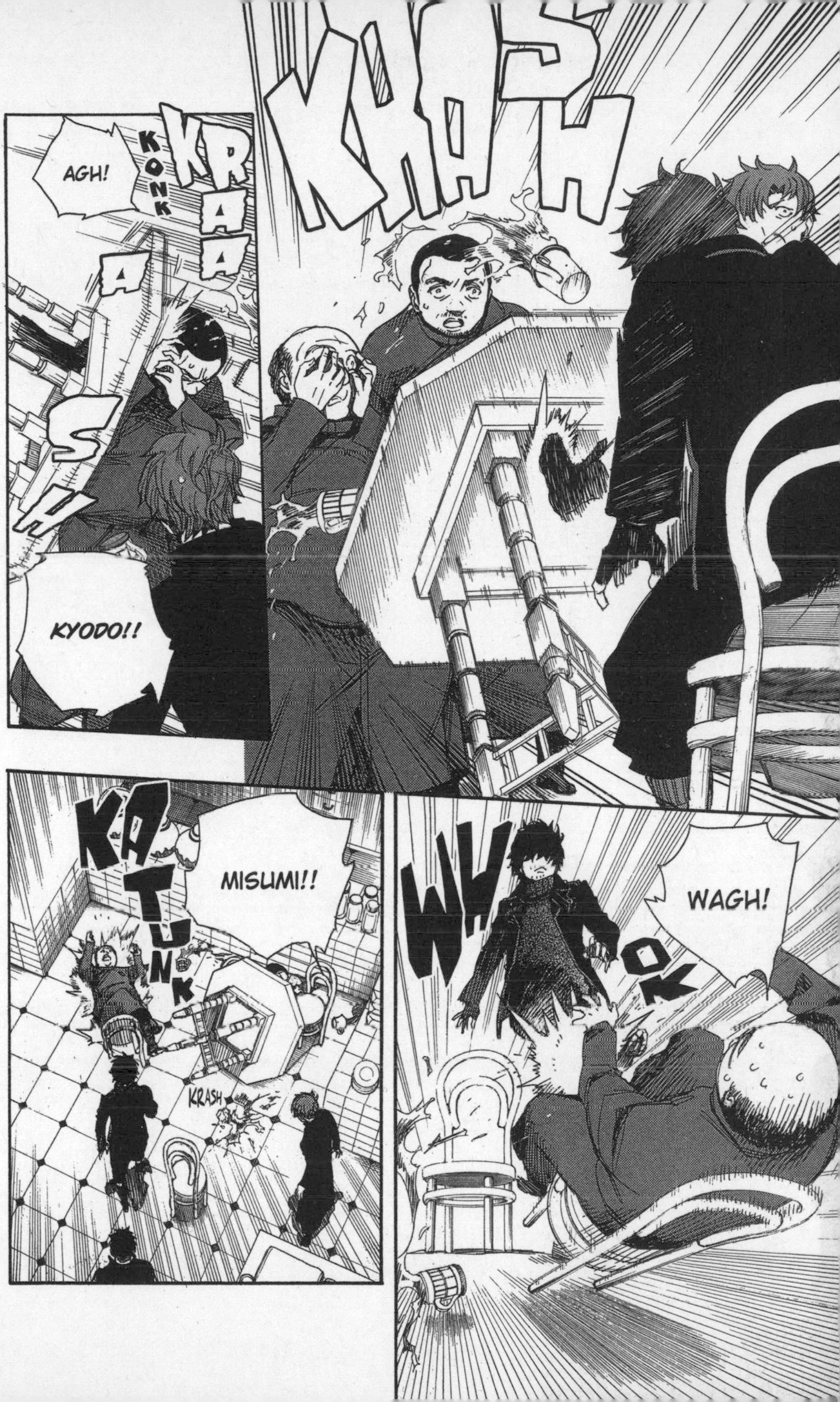
KRASH
AGH!
KONK
KRAAA
SH
KYODO!!
WAGH!
WHOK
MISUMI!!
KATUNK
KRASH

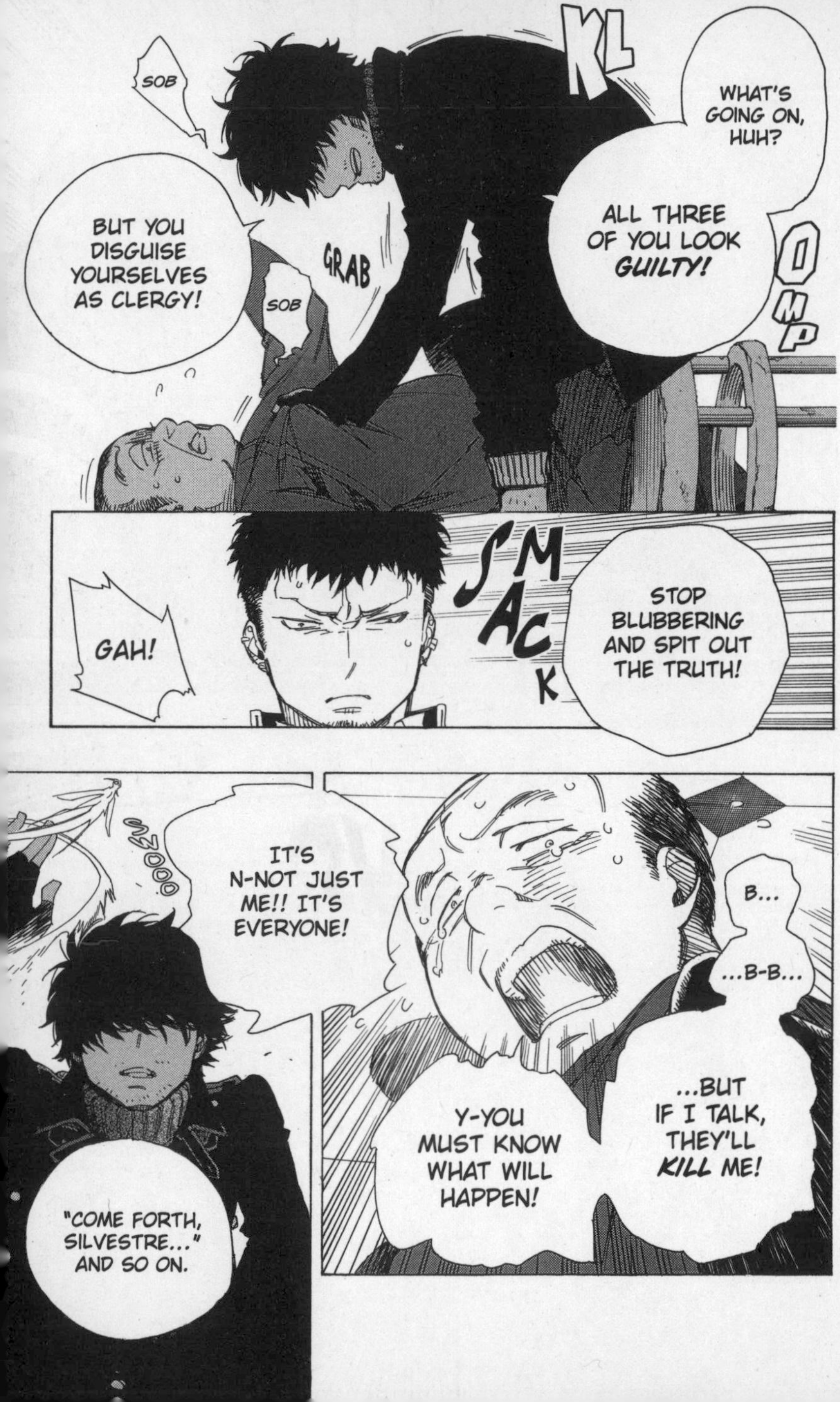
KL
WHAT'S GOING ON, HUH?
ALL THREE OF YOU LOOK GUILTY!
OMP
SOB
BUT YOU DISGUISE YOURSELVES AS CLERGY!
GRAB
SOB
SMACK
STOP BLUBBERING AND SPIT OUT THE TRUTH!
GAH!
B...
...B-B...
...BUT IF I TALK, THEY'LL KILL ME!
Y-YOU MUST KNOW WHAT WILL HAPPEN!
IT'S N-NOT JUST ME!! IT'S EVERYONE!
"COME FORTH, SILVESTRE..." AND SO ON.

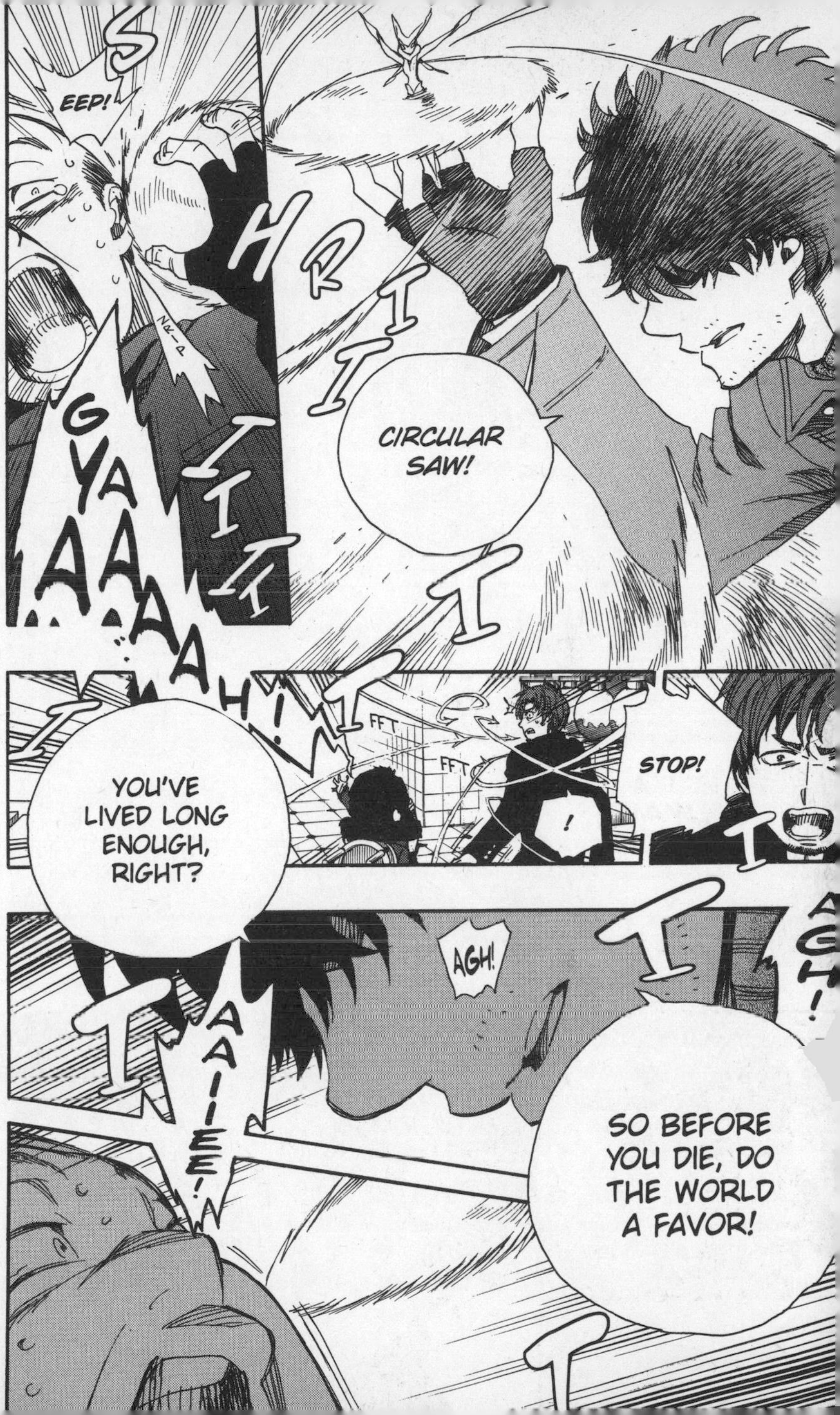
CIRCULAR SAW!
HRIIIIII
S
EEP!
NRIP
GYAAAAAAH!
STOP!
!
FFT
FFT
YOU'VE LIVED LONG ENOUGH, RIGHT?
AGH!
AGH!
SO BEFORE YOU DIE, DO THE WORLD A FAVOR!
AAIIEE!

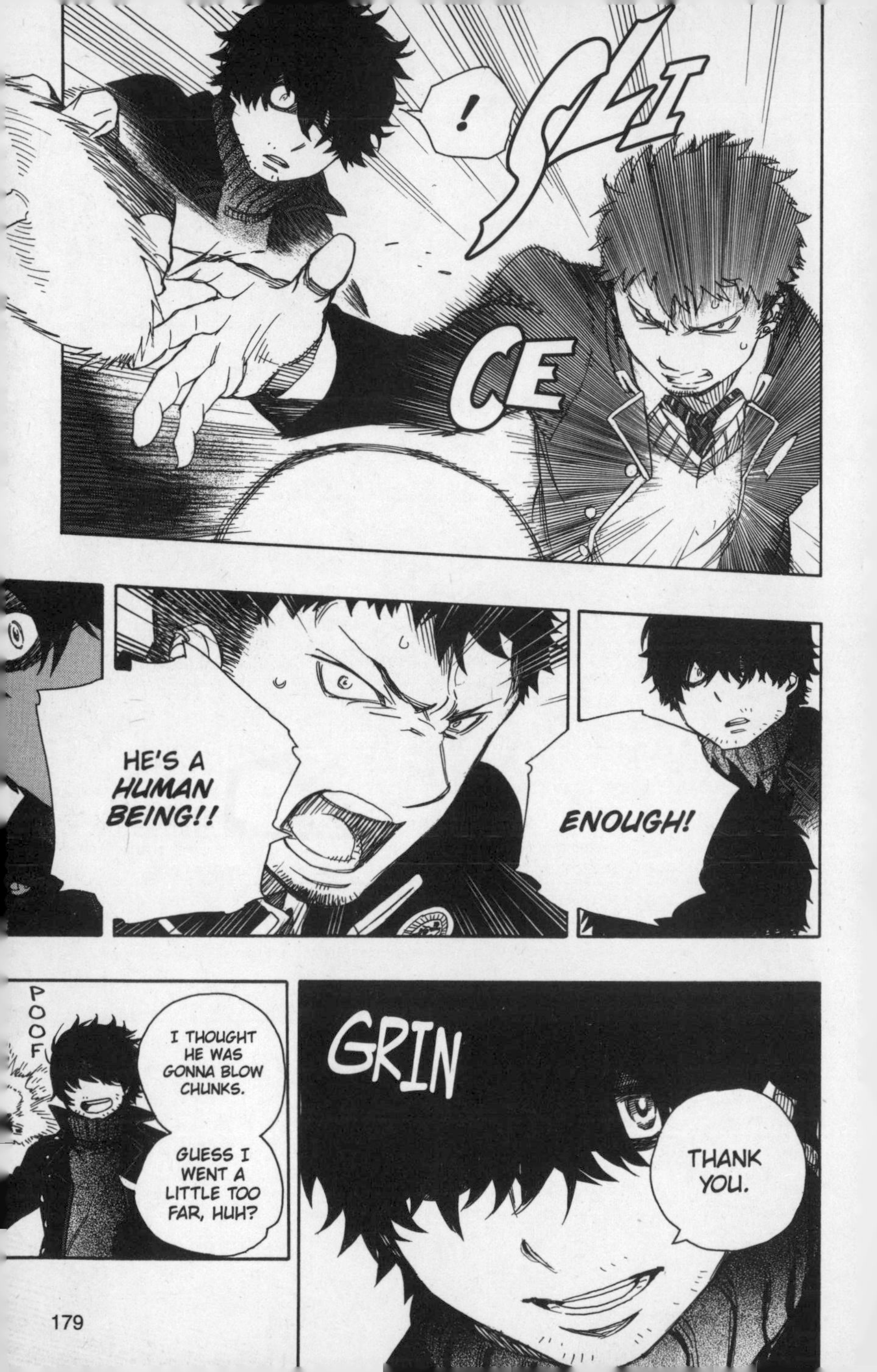
!
SLI
CE
ENOUGH!
HE'S A HUMAN BEING!!
GRIN
THANK YOU.
POOF
I THOUGHT HE WAS GONNA BLOW CHUNKS.
GUESS I WENT A LITTLE TOO FAR, HUH?

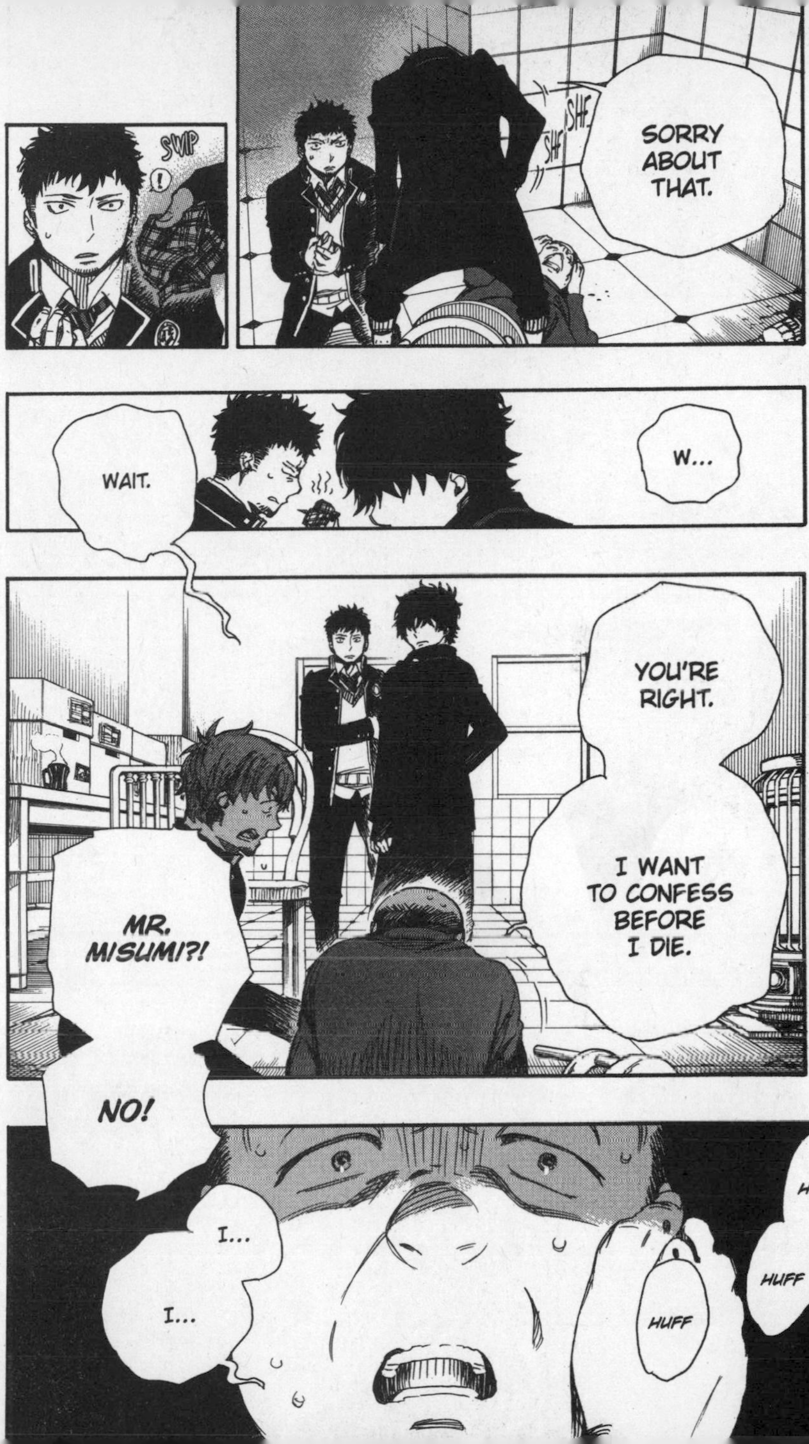
SHF
SHF
SORRY ABOUT THAT.
SWIP
!
W...
WAIT.
YOU'RE RIGHT.
I WANT TO CONFESS BEFORE I DIE.
MR. MISUMI?!
NO!
HUFF
HUFF
HUFF
I...
I...

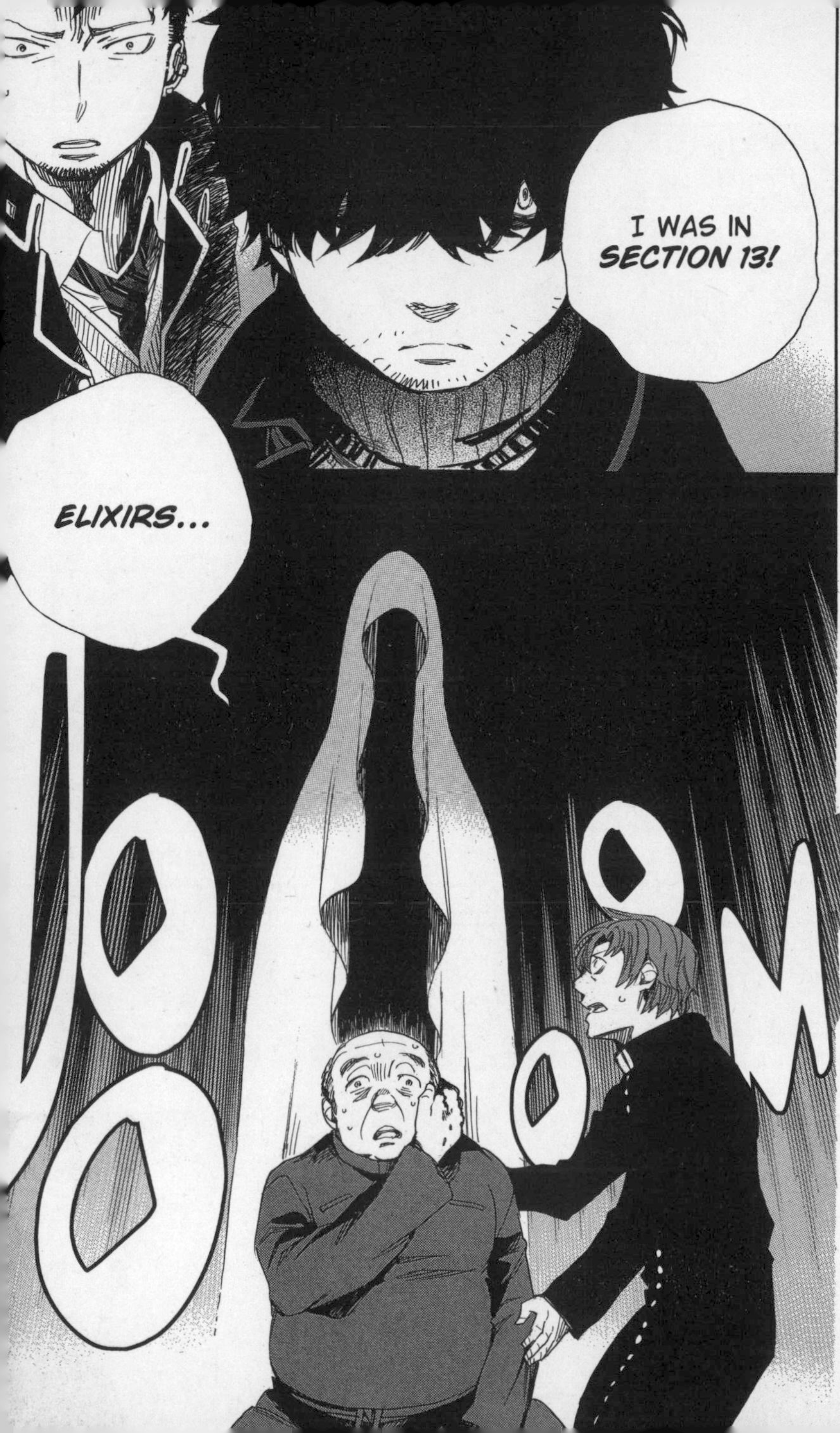
I WAS IN SECTION 13!
ELIXIRS...

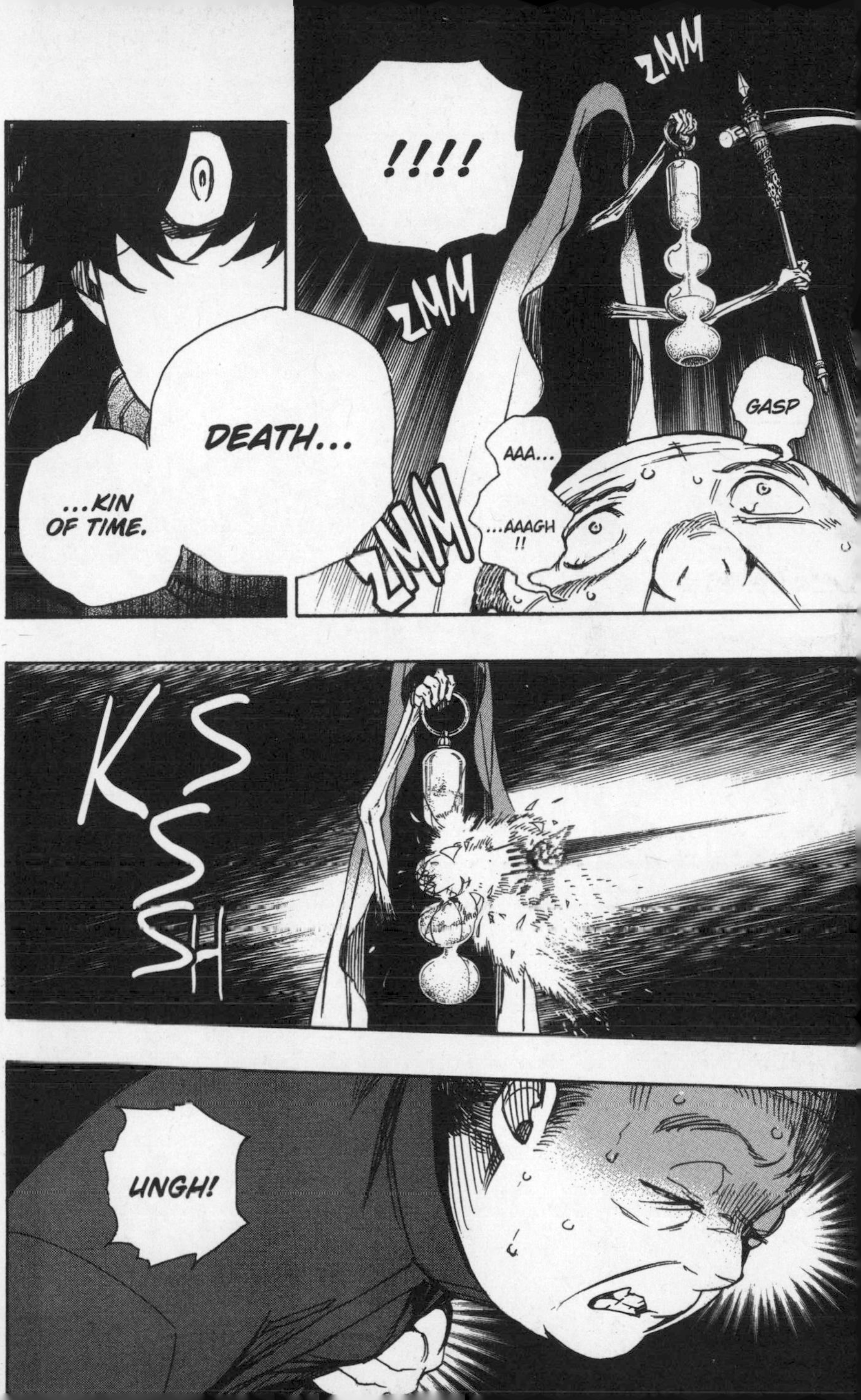
ZMM
!!!!
ZMM
GASP
AAA...
...AAAGH !!
ZMM
DEATH...
...KIN OF TIME.
KSSSH
UNGH!

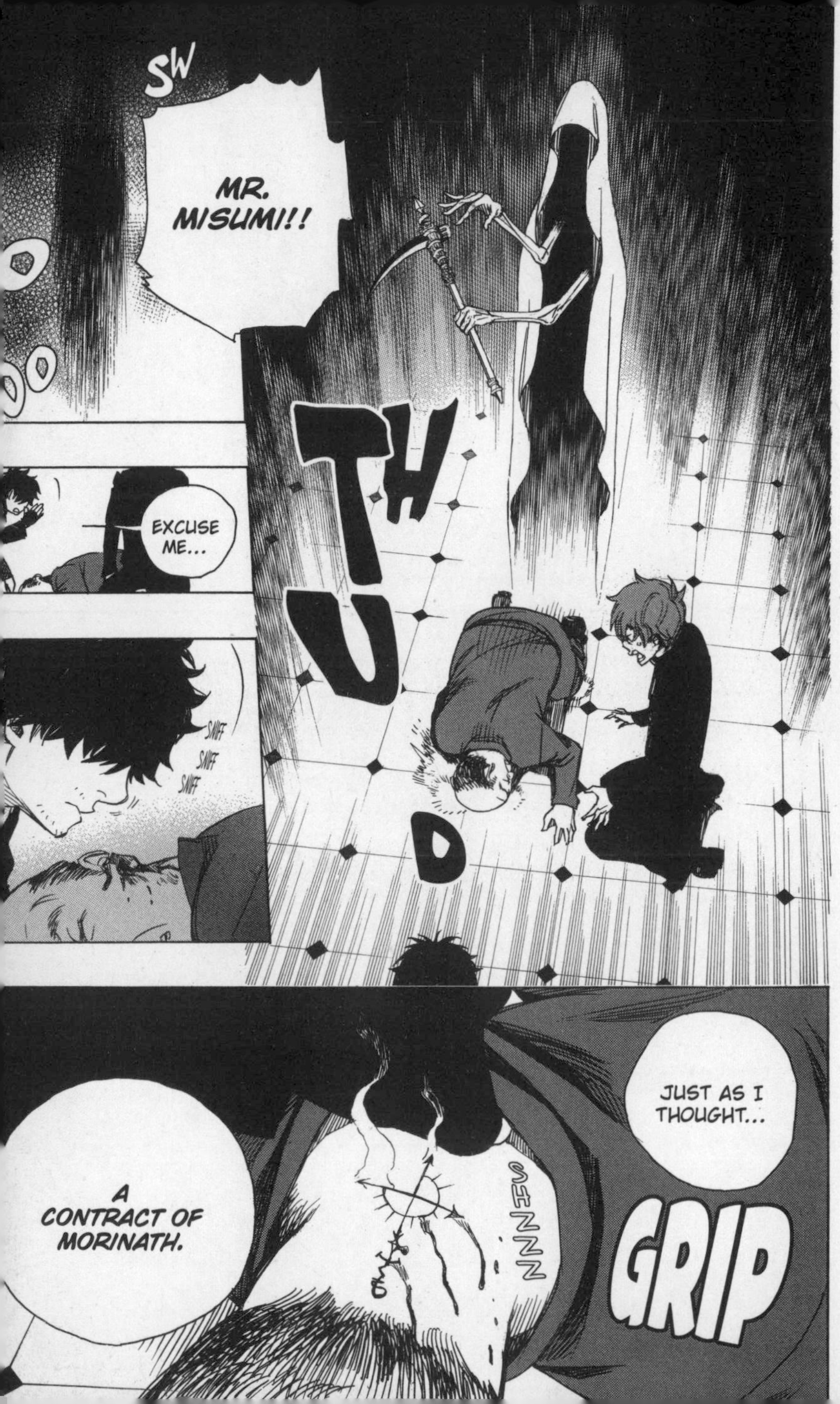
THUD
SW
MR. MISUMI!!
EXCUSE ME...
SNIFF
SNIFF
SNIFF
JUST AS I THOUGHT...
GRIP
SHZZZ
A CONTRACT OF MORINATH.

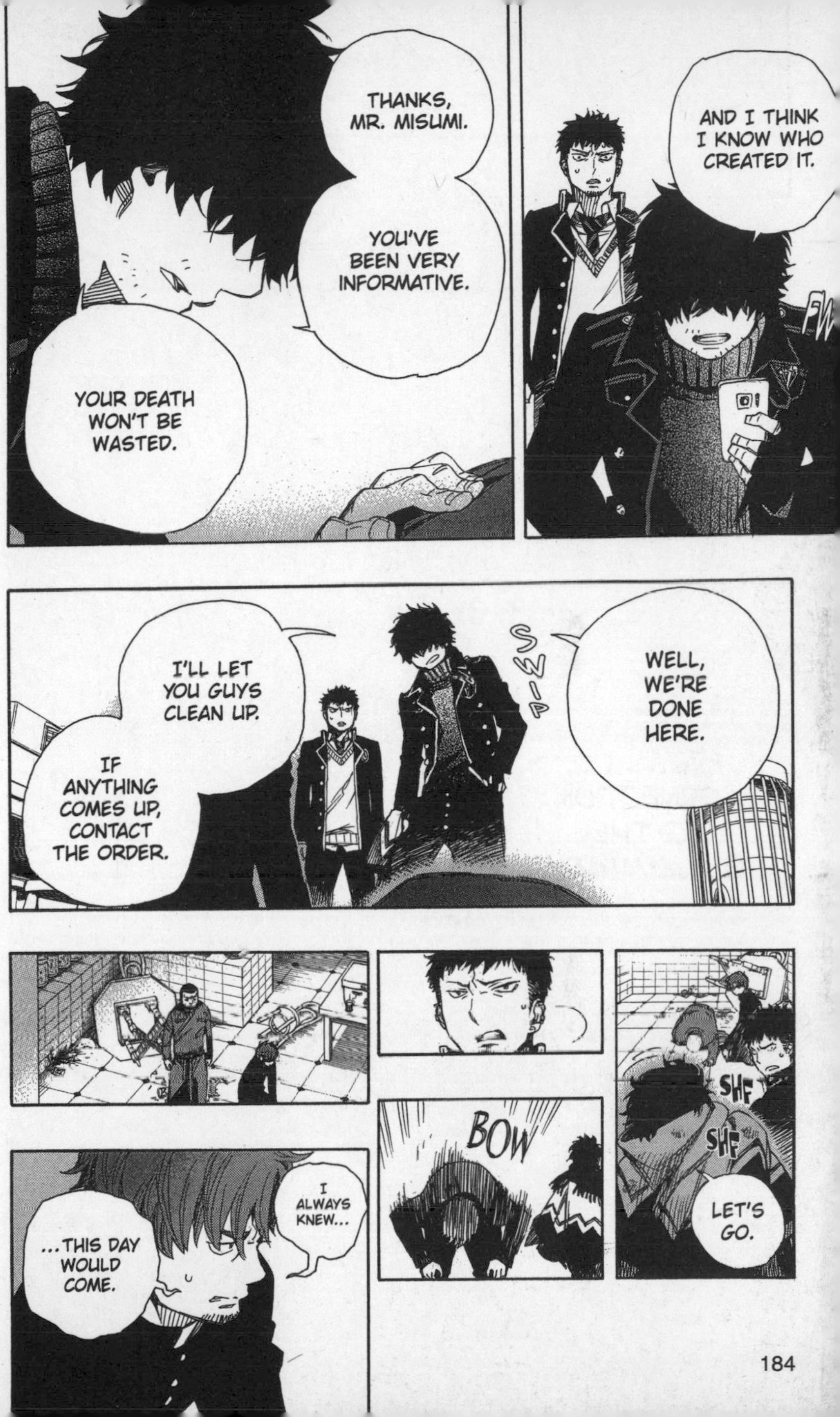
AND I THINK I KNOW WHO CREATED IT.
FW
THANKS, MR. MISUMI.
YOU'VE BEEN VERY INFORMATIVE.
YOUR DEATH WON'T BE WASTED.
WELL, WE'RE DONE HERE.
SWIP
I'LL LET YOU GUYS CLEAN UP.
IF ANYTHING COMES UP, CONTACT THE ORDER.
SHF
SHF
LET'S GO.
BOW
I ALWAYS KNEW...
...THIS DAY WOULD COME.

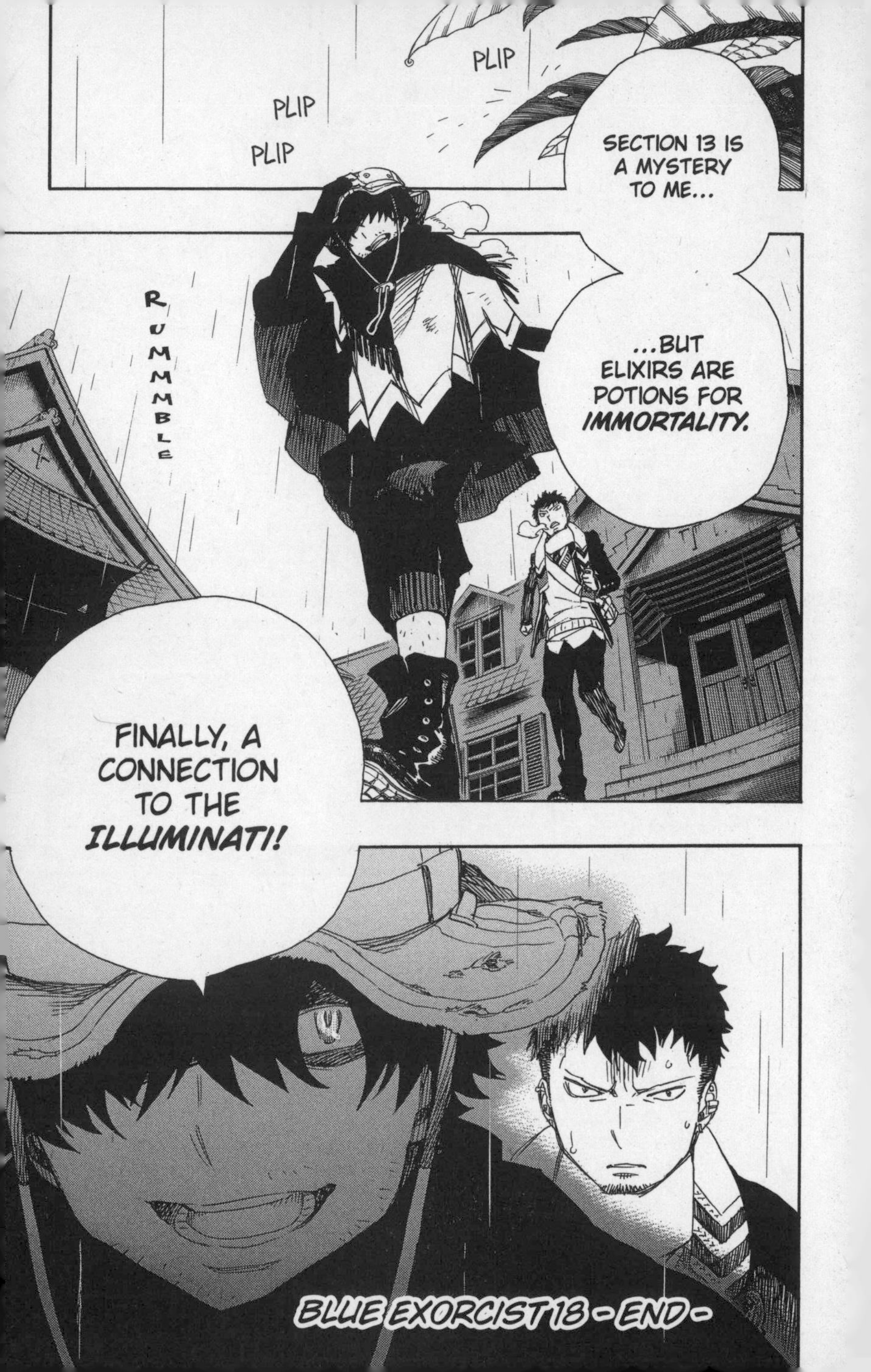
SECTION 13 IS A MYSTERY TO ME...
PLIP
PLIP
PLIP
...BUT ELIXIRS ARE POTIONS FOR IMMORTALITY.
RUMMMBLE
FINALLY, A CONNECTION TO THE ILLUMINATI!
BLUE EXORCIST 18 - END -

Blue Exorcist Chapter 83: Sprout

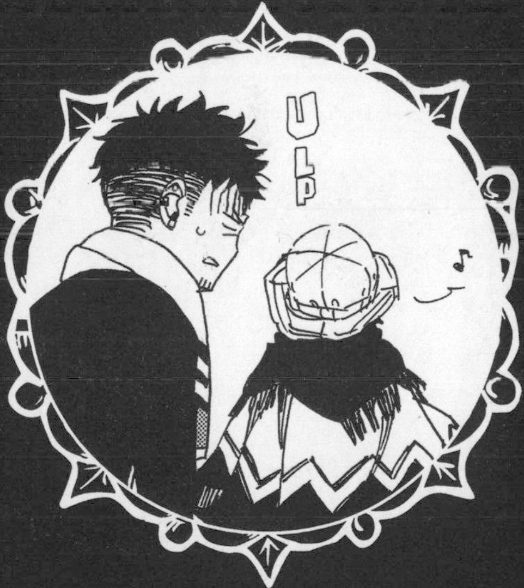
Ulp

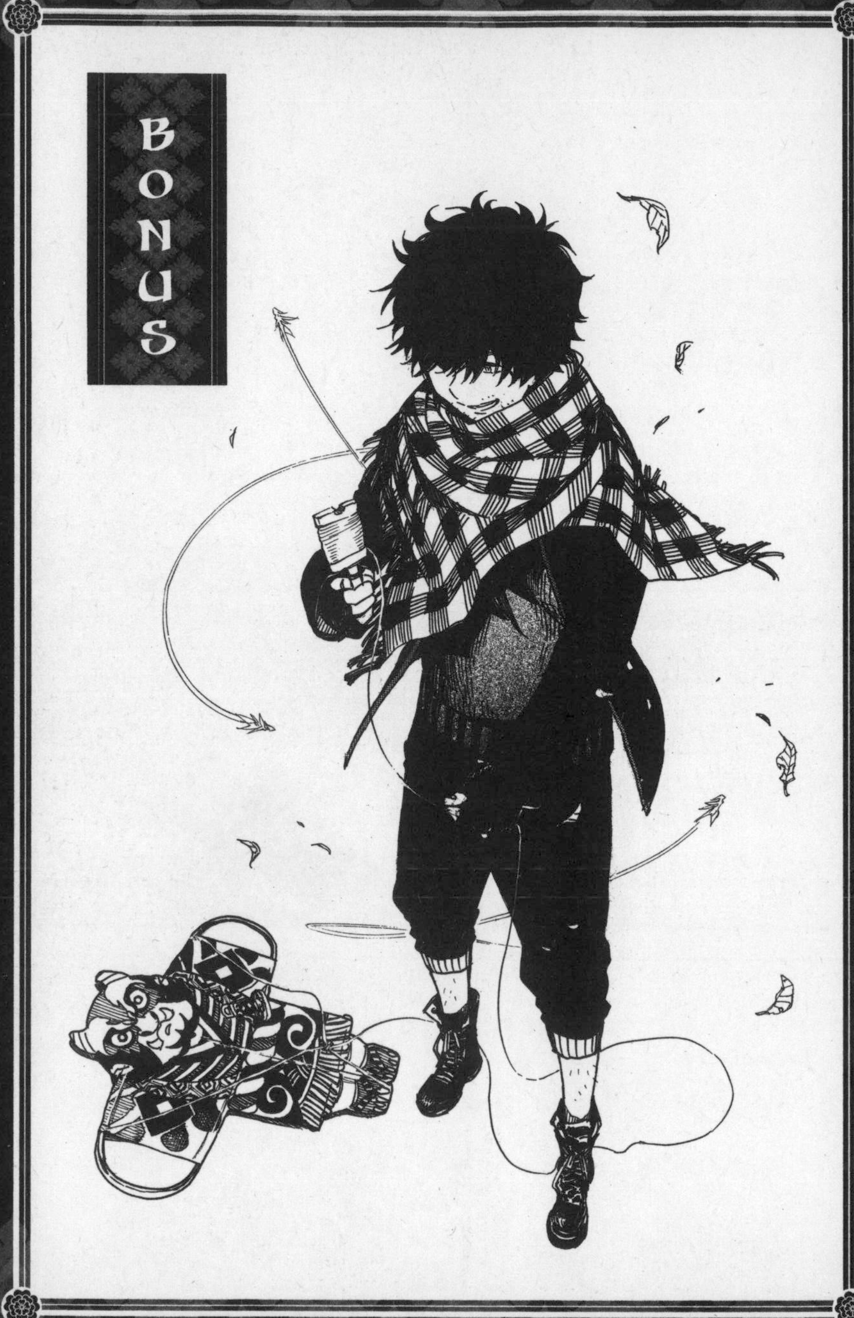
BONUS

BLUE EXORCIST BONUS

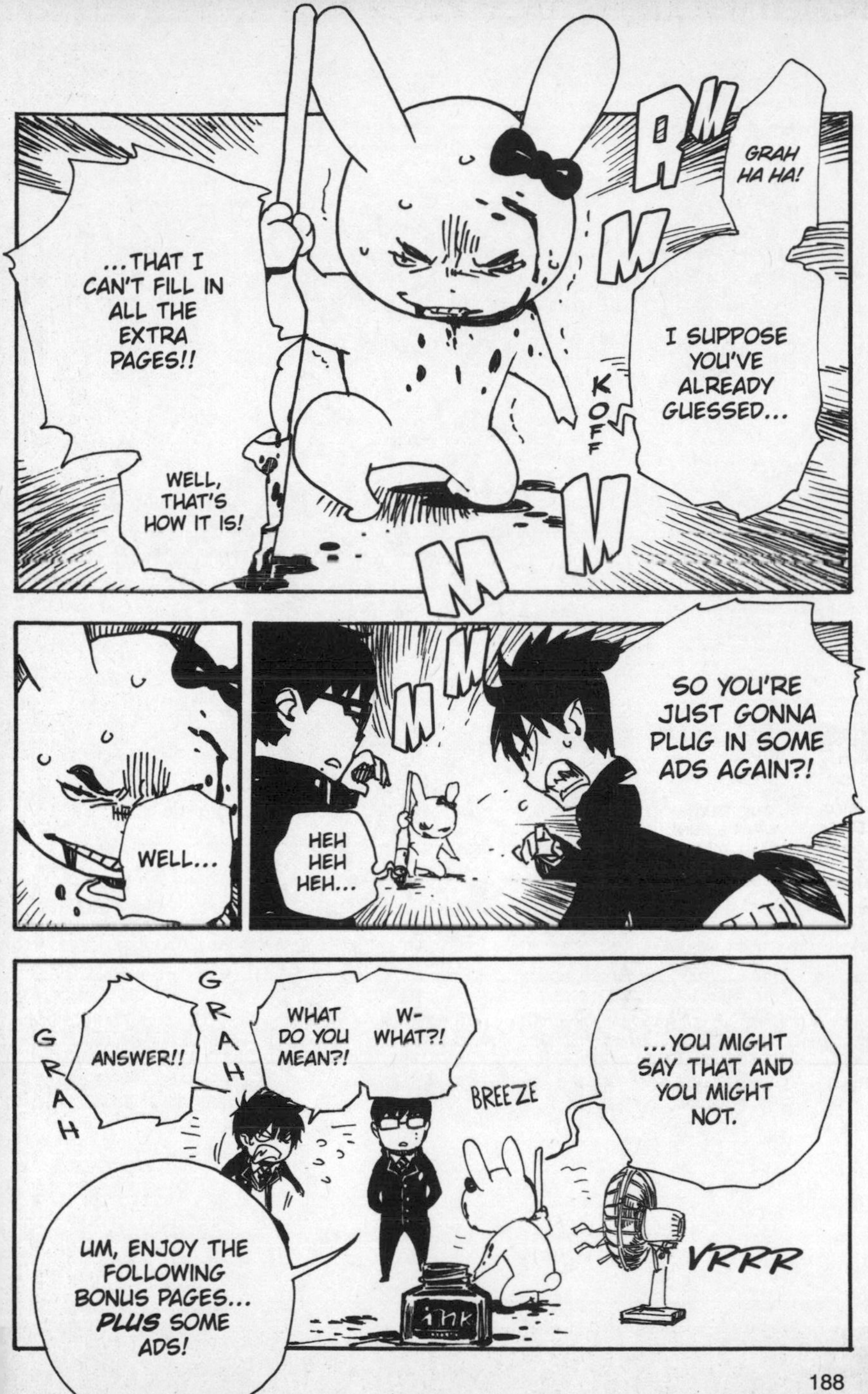
GRAH HA HA!
RMMM
I SUPPOSE YOU'VE ALREADY GUESSED...
KOFF
...THAT I CAN'T FILL IN ALL THE EXTRA PAGES!!
WELL, THAT'S HOW IT IS!
MMM
SO YOU'RE JUST GONNA PLUG IN SOME ADS AGAIN?!
HEH HEH HEH...
WELL...
...YOU MIGHT SAY THAT AND YOU MIGHT NOT.
VRRR
BREEZE
W- WHAT?!
WHAT DO YOU MEAN?!
GRAH
ANSWER!!
GRAH
UM, ENJOY THE FOLLOWING BONUS PAGES... **PLUS** SOME ADS!

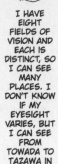

BLUE QUESTORCIST

LET'S GET VOLUME 18'S *QUESTORCIST* ROLLING!

HOW GOOD IS HACHIRO'S EYESIGHT? HUMANS HAVE DIFFERENT DEGREES OF EYESIGHT IN EACH EYE, SO IS EACH ONE OF HACHIRO'S EYES DIFFERENT?

KOUSEI (24), IWATE PREFECTURE

HMM... LET'S ASK HIM!

I HAVE EIGHT FIELDS OF VISION AND EACH IS DISTINCT, SO I CAN SEE MANY PLACES. I DON'T KNOW IF MY EYESIGHT VARIES, BUT I CAN SEE FROM TOWADA TO TAZAWA IN AKITA PREFECTURE.

W-WOW!!

HACHIRO WAS A GOD, SO I WORRY ABOUT WHAT HE'S UP TO NOW...

HOW DOES EVERYONE AT THE CRAM SCHOOL AND THE INSTRUCTORS FEEL WHEN THEY WATCH TELEVISION PROGRAMS ABOUT DEMONS AND OTHER SPOOKY STUFF?

PRESIDENT!!!! (?), OSAKA PREFECTURE

I'VE BEEN GETTING THIS QUESTION FOR A WHILE, SO LET'S HAVE EVERYONE ANSWER!

I DON'T WATCH SUCH PROGRAMS. THEY REMIND ME OF WORK, SO THEY'RE NOT ENJOYABLE.

I WATCH THEM SOMETIMES. FAKE MEDIUMS AND COMPUTER GRAPHICS SUPPOSEDLY SHOWING GHOSTS MAKE ME LAUGH.

YOU CAN LAUGH AT THAT? WHEN I WATCH THAT STUFF, I'M LIKE, "THERE'S NOTHING THERE!" AND "THAT WON'T EXORCISE DIDDLY SQUAT, YOU MORONS!" AND "IT'S RIGHT BEHIND YOU!!" THERE'S SO MUCH TO MAKE FUN OF THAT IT WEARS ME OUT, SO I DON'T WATCH THOSE SHOWS VERY OFTEN.

BUT THAT'S WHAT'S FUN! THEY CRACK ME UP, SO I WATCH 'EM ALL THE TIME! I ESPECIALLY LOVE HOW CUTE THE IDOLS AND ACTRESSES ARE WHEN THEY SQUEAL IN FEAR! ♡

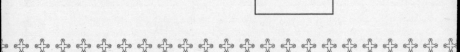

WHAT INTERESTING HOBBIES YOU HAVE, SHIMA...

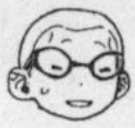

I'VE NEVER REALLY LIKED SCARY THINGS, SO I DON'T WATCH THOSE PROGRAMS. WHEN I'M NOT ON A MISSION, I DON'T WANT TO BE SCARED.

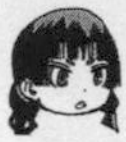

I THINK SCARY VARIETY SHOWS ON TV ARE RIDICULOUS, SO I DON'T WATCH THEM, BUT I DO ENJOY HORROR FICTION LIKE TV DRAMAS, MOVIES AND MANGA.

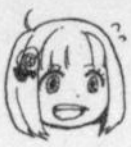

I DO TOO! WE DON'T HAVE A TV AT HOME, SO I DON'T KNOW ABOUT TV PROGRAMS, BUT I READ A LOT OF HORROR AND MYSTERY NOVELS. I CAN'T STOP MYSELF FROM READING ON SUMMER NIGHTS BECAUSE OF THE CHILL IT GIVES ME!

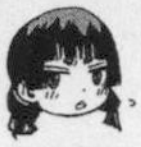

WE'RE SURPRISINGLY THE SAME THAT WAY.

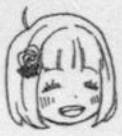

YEP! I'M SO GLAD!

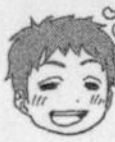

YEAH, IT'S PRETTY CUTE! ♡

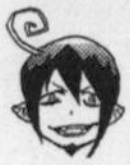

I ABSOLUTELY LOVE HORROR—BOTH FICTION AND VARIETY SHOWS! THE HUMAN IMAGINATION FAR SURPASSES WHAT DEMONS WOULD COME UP WITH.

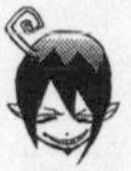

LIKE HORROR ABOUT ZOMBIES AND SHARKS! I RECENTLY SAW A SHOW ABOUT A DEMON-POSSESSED SHARK DOING BATTLE AGAINST AN EXORCIST. IT WAS HILARIOUS! (SNORT)

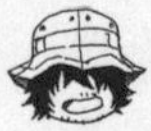

I ENJOY THAT STUFF TOO, BUT NOT JUST ON HORROR PROGRAMS. YOU CAN SEE PARANORMAL BEINGS BEHIND NEWSCASTERS AND HANGING OUT ON THE SETS OF VARIETY SHOWS.

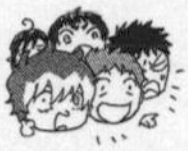

YEAH, THAT HAPPENS!!

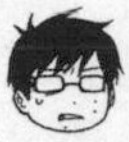

THAT'S WHY I DON'T WATCH TV. EVEN IF I WATCH A VARIETY SHOW FOR LAUGHS, WHEN A GHOST STARTS CUTTING INTO THE CONVERSATION, IT'S JUST NO FUN.

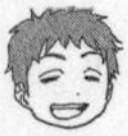

THAT TOTALLY CRACKS ME UP!

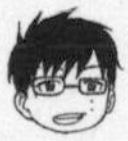

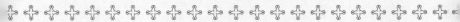

WHAT ABOUT YOU, RIN? YOU'RE UNUSUALLY SILENT.

WELL, I HAVEN'T HAD THE CHANCE TO WATCH MUCH TV EVER SINCE I LEARNED I'M SATAN'S CHILD. HEY, WE DON'T EVEN HAVE A TV... I WANNA WATCH TV!!

NO.

HUH?! BUT I'VE BARELY SAID ANYTHING!!

WHAT KIND OF AUTHORITY DO EXORCISTS HAVE IN SOCIETY?

PRESIDENT!!!! (?), OSAKA PREFECTURE

GOOD QUESTION!

HM? THIS IS THE SECOND QUESTION FROM PRESIDENT!!!!

YEAH... THEY'RE IRRESISTIBLE QUESTIONS, SO THIS PERSON MUST HAVE AN ADVANCED QUESTION SENSE!

IS THERE SUCH A THING AS QUESTION SENSE?

ANYWAY, LET'S HAVE THE PRESIDENT HIMSELF ANSWER THE QUESTION.

I'M OVERJOYED TO SHOW UP SO MUCH THIS TIME! EXORCISTS' AUTHORITY IN SOCIETY? THEIR SOCIAL STANDING? WELL, IN TERMS OF YOUR SOCIETY, EXORCISTS ARE LIKE THE CLERGY AND POLICE IN ONE. THE KNIGHTS OF THE TRUE CROSS HANDLE THREATS TO SOCIETY THAT INVOLVE DEMONS. THE ORDER IS A CORPORATION. WE'RE NOT CIVIL SERVANTS, BUT WE DO HAVE A LICENSE TO EXORCISE. IN SCALE AND NUMBER OF MEMBERS, THE ORDER IS CLOSER TO A FIRE DEPARTMENT THAN A POLICE FORCE. THE GENERAL PUBLIC VIEWS THE ORDER AS AKIN TO THE PRIESTHOOD, BUT MOST HUMANS CAN'T SEE DEMONS, SO THEY OFTEN RIDICULE EXORCISTS AS CHARLATANS AND WITCH DOCTORS. IS THAT ENOUGH TO ANSWER YOUR QUESTION?

THIS QUESTION IS FOR TODO. IN VOLUME 8, HE SAID HIS EYESIGHT HAD IMPROVED, BUT LATER HE WAS STILL WEARING GLASSES. IS THAT BECAUSE HE FEELS A SENSE OF AFFINITY WITH YUKIO?

MIKUROKURO (12), FUKUSHIMA PREFECTURE

...!!

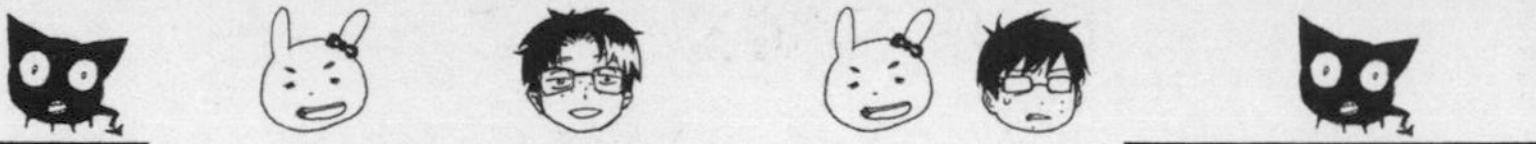

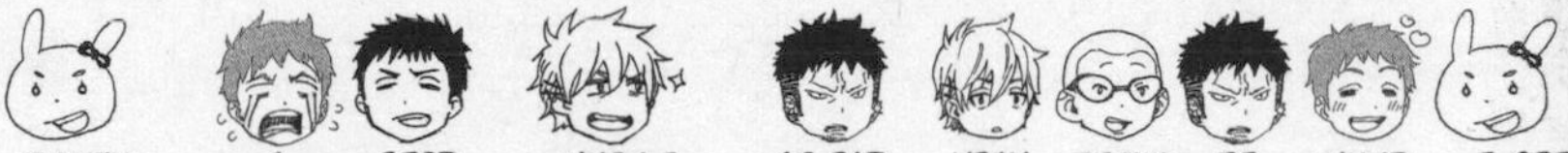

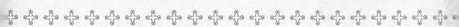

YES, WELL, UM, THAT IS ODD. LET'S ASK!

I'VE WORN GLASSES EVER SINCE I WAS LITTLE. WITHOUT THEM, I FELT LIKE SOMETHING WAS MISSING, SO I CAN'T HELP BUT PUT THEM ON. BASICALLY, THEY'RE JUST AN ACCESSORY. THANK YOU FOR THE QUESTION.

OH! LIKE PEOPLE WHO ALWAYS NEED SOMETHING IN THEIR MOUTHS!

WHO IS THE MOST POPULAR BOY IN THE SHIMA FAMILY?

KIIKO (18), KANAGAWA PREFECTURE

I GET THIS QUESTION A LOT TOO!

HUH? WELL, THE ANSWER IS OBVIOUS!

IT MUST BE JUZO.

DEFINITELY JUZO.

YEAH, IT'S BIG BRO JUZO.

AS FAR BACK AS I CAN REMEMBER, HE'S NEVER BEEN WITHOUT A GIRLFRIEND.

WHEN I WAS A KID AND HE CAME HOME ON VALENTINE'S DAY CARRYING A MASSIVE LOAD OF CHOCOLATE, HE LOOKED LIKE A GREAT HUNTER MAKING A TRIUMPHANT RETURN WITH HIS TROPHIES.

STOP. THAT WAS A LONG TIME AGO...

ARRRRRGGGGGHHHHH!!!!

THAT'S ALL FOR NOW!

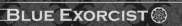

BLUE EXORCIST 18

◉ Art Staff

 EVADE! GRAAAH!!! Miyuki Shibuya

 AAGH! DARYL!! GLENN!! (THE WALKING DEAD CHARACTERS) Erika Uemura

 IT'S SO GROSS! Ryoji Hayashi

 NICE TO MEET YOU! Mari Oda

◉ Art Assistants

 I'M WORRIED BECAUSE MY HOUSE IS RUN-DOWN... Yamanaka-san

 FOLLOW ME!
*SPLATOON Yanagimoto-san

 I BOUGHT IT IN NY! Yamagishi-san

 I WANT TO MOVE... Yoshiyama-kun

 YES! BING Obata-san

◉ Composition Assistant

 KYOTO'S GREAT! Minoru Sasaki

◉ Editor

 I WANT THEM TO BE HAPPY! Shihei Lin

◉ Graphic Novel Editor

 I WAS SURPRISED THIS TIME! Ryusuke Kuroki

◉ Graphic Novel Design

I'M ALSO HAVING THEM DESIGN FOR A PROJECT STILL IN THE WORKS! Shimada Hideaki

Daiju Asami (L.S.D.)

◉ Manga

GLENN... ABRAHAM... (THE WALKING DEAD CHARACTERS) Kazue Kato

(In no particular order)
(Note: The caricatures and statements are from memory!)

 Look forward to volume 19 and check out the anime!!

About Arias

Exorcists must chant Arias correctly through to the end. They are nowhere near discovering all the Death Verses and Summoning Verses for demons.

Requirements for a Good Aria

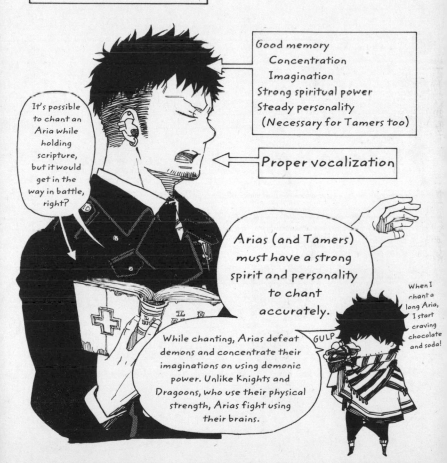

Good memory
Concentration
Imagination
Strong spiritual power
Steady personality
(Necessary for Tamers too)

It's possible to chant an Aria while holding scripture, but it would get in the way in battle, right?

Proper vocalization

Arias (and Tamers) must have a strong spirit and personality to chant accurately.

While chanting, Arias defeat demons and concentrate their imaginations on using demonic power. Unlike Knights and Dragoons, who use their physical strength, Arias fight using their brains.

GULP

When I chant a long Aria, I start craving chocolate and soda!

Types of Arias

There are two main types.

❶ Summoning Verse

[In combination with magic seals and circles, the Exorcist summons a demon and, on the basis of a contract, wields demonic power.]

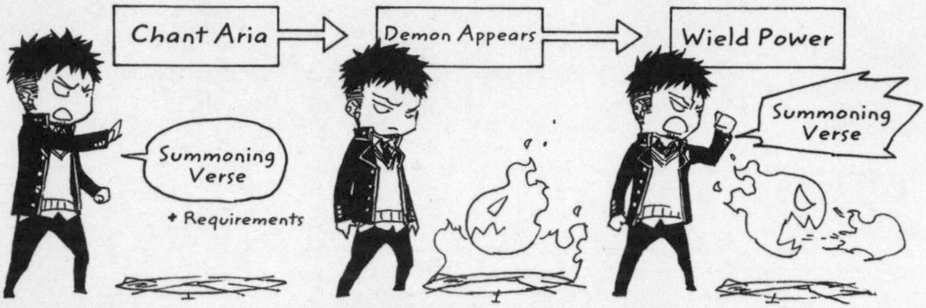

Chant Aria
Demon Appears
Wield Power
Summoning Verse
+ Requirements
Summoning Verse

❷ Death Verse

[For this deadly method of exorcism, the Exorcist correctly completes a chant in order to destroy a demon.]

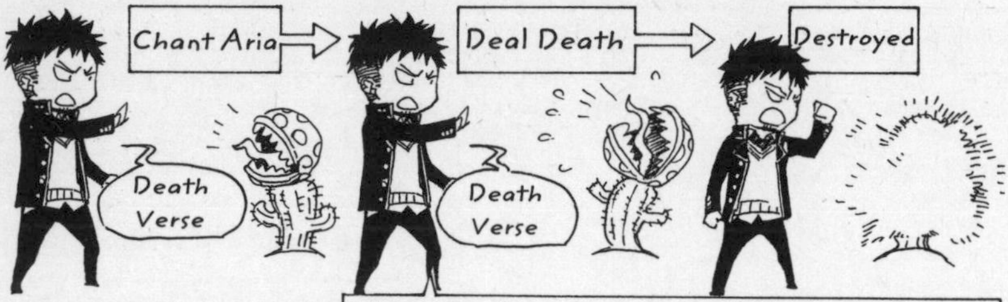

Chant Aria
Deal Death
Destroyed
Death Verse
Death Verse

※A strong Aria will weaken a demon at the first step.

Abbreviating Summoning and Death Verses

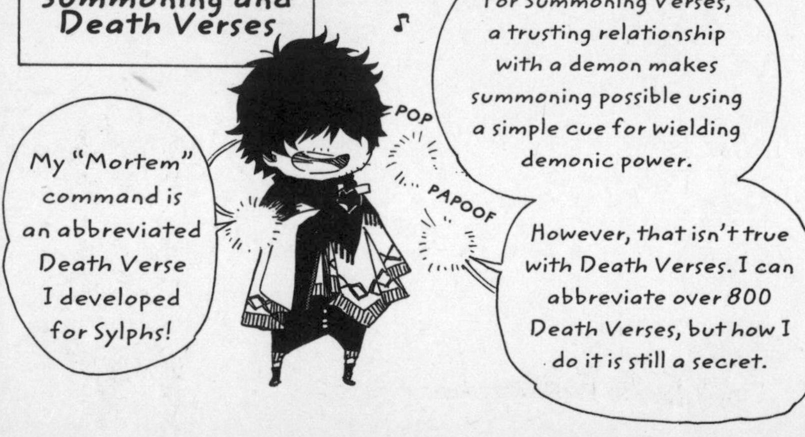

For Summoning Verses, a trusting relationship with a demon makes summoning possible using a simple cue for wielding demonic power.
However, that isn't true with Death Verses. I can abbreviate over 800 Death Verses, but how I do it is still a secret.
POP
PAPOOF
My "Mortem" command is an abbreviated Death Verse I developed for Sylphs!

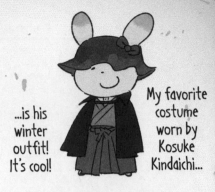

My favorite costume worn by Kosuke Kindaichi...
...is his winter outfit! It's cool!

Kazue Kato

Another school interlude is beginning,
but this time it's full of tension!
And mystery!
And suspense!
I put so much work into it
I could explode!

Enjoy volume 18!

BLUE EXORCIST

BLUE EXORCIST VOL. 18
SHONEN JUMP ADVANCED Manga Edition

STORY & ART BY KAZUE KATO

Translation & English Adaptation/John Werry
Touch-up Art & Lettering/John Hunt, Primary Graphix
Cover & Interior Design/Sam Elzway
Editor/Mike Montesa

AO NO EXORCIST © 2009 by Kazue Kato
All rights reserved.
First published in Japan in 2009 by SHUEISHA Inc., Tokyo.
English translation rights arranged by SHUEISHA Inc.

The stories, characters and incidents mentioned in
this publication are entirely fictional.

Printed in the U.S.A.

Published by VIZ Media, LLC
P.O. Box 77010
San Francisco, CA 94107

10 9 8 7 6 5 4 3 2 1
First printing, January 2018

www.viz.com

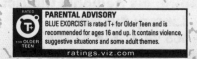

THE WORLD'S MOST
CUTTING-EDGE MANGA
SHONEN JUMP
ADVANCED
www.shonenjump.com

In the next volume...

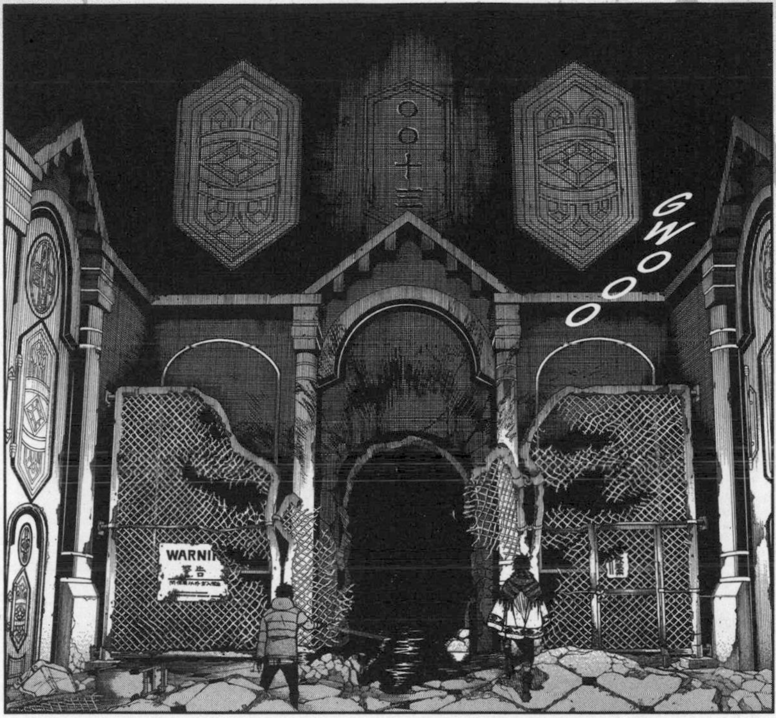
GWOOOO
WARNI
警告

Mephisto Pheles has freed his brother Amaimon from imprisonment and set him loose on True Cross Academy to serve his own agenda. While the Exwires deal with Amaimon's surprise reappearance, Lewin Light, a.k.a. "Lightning," continues to investigate the mysterious Section 13 and its connection to the Blue Night event that seems to be the source of all the current troubles. Together they delve deep beneath True Cross Academy, shedding light on long-lost chambers shrouded in darkness and the terrible secrets that were buried there for a reason...

Coming January 2018!

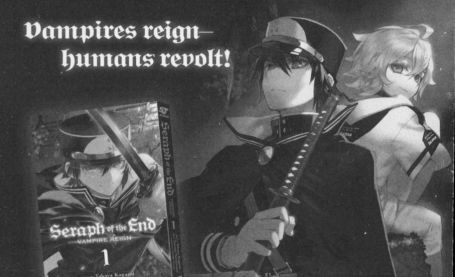

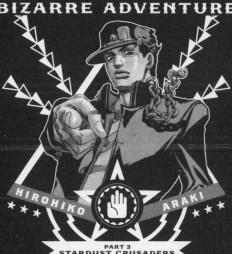
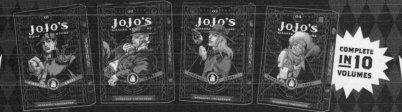
  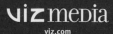

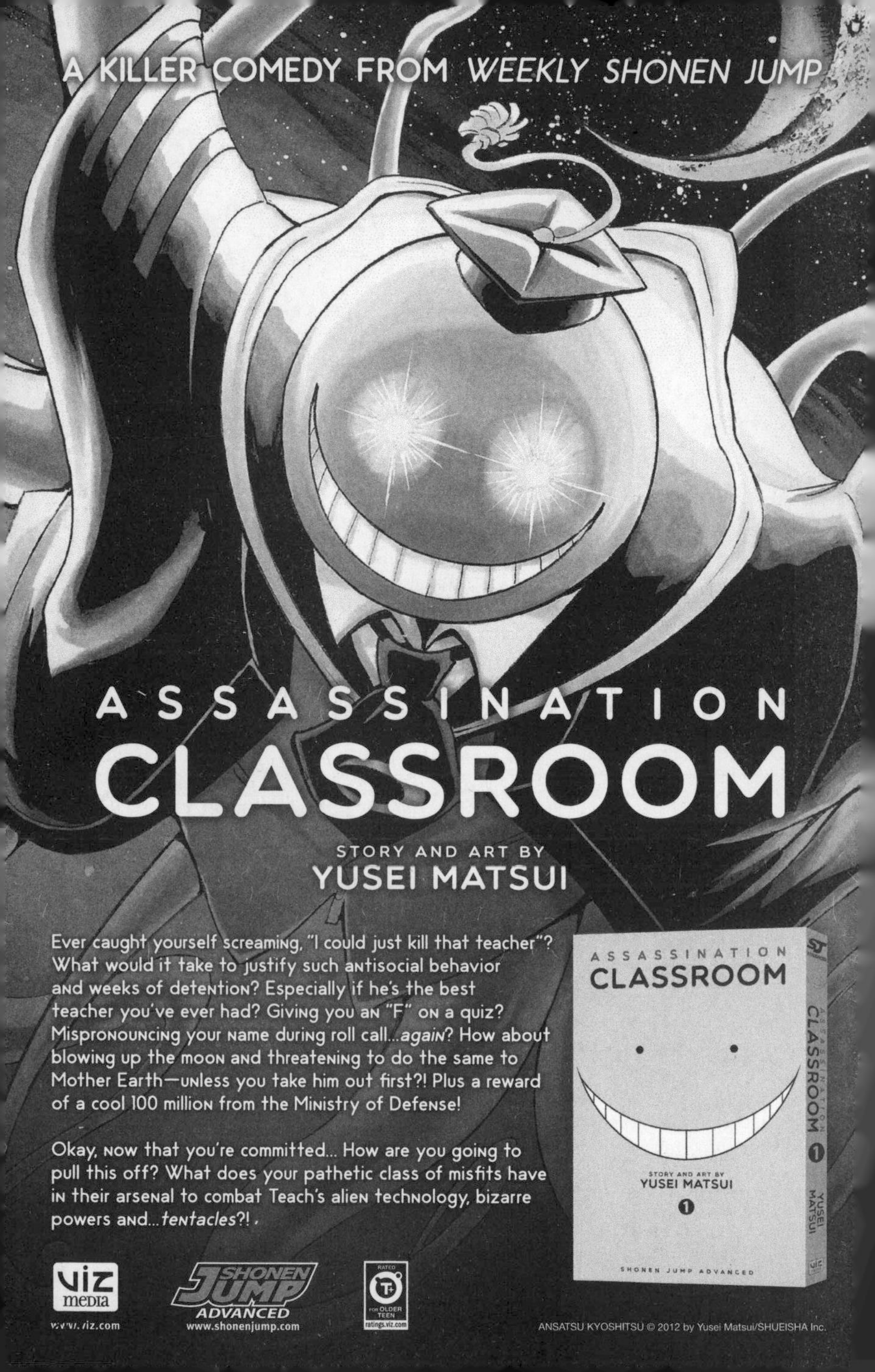
A KILLER COMEDY FROM *WEEKLY SHONEN JUMP*
ASSASSINATION CLASSROOM
STORY AND ART BY
YUSEI MATSUI
Ever caught yourself screaming, "I could just kill that teacher"? What would it take to justify such antisocial behavior and weeks of detention? Especially if he's the best teacher you've ever had? Giving you an "F" on a quiz? Mispronouncing your name during roll call...*again*? How about blowing up the moon and threatening to do the same to Mother Earth—unless you take him out first?! Plus a reward of a cool 100 million from the Ministry of Defense!
Okay, now that you're committed... How are you going to pull this off? What does your pathetic class of misfits have in their arsenal to combat Teach's alien technology, bizarre powers and...*tentacles*?!
ASSASSINATION CLASSROOM
STORY AND ART BY
YUSEI MATSUI
1
SHONEN JUMP ADVANCED
viz media
www.viz.com
SHONEN JUMP ADVANCED
www.shonenjump.com
RATED T+ FOR OLDER TEEN
ratings.viz.com
ANSATSU KYOSHITSU © 2012 by Yusei Matsui/SHUEISHA Inc.

You're the Wrong

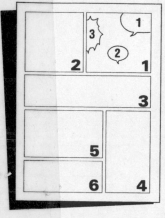

Whoops! Guess what? You're starting at the wrong end of the comic!

…It's true! In keeping with the original Japanese format, **Blue Exorcist** is meant to be read from right to left, starting in the upper-right corner.

Unlike English, which is read from left to right, Japanese is read from right to left, meaning that action, sound effects and word-balloon order are completely reversed… something which can make readers unfamiliar with Japanese feel pretty backwards themselves. For this reason, manga or Japanese comics published in the U.S. in English have sometimes been published "flopped"—that is, printed in exact reverse order, as though seen from the other side of a mirror.

By flopping pages, U.S. publishers can avoid confusing readers, but the compromise is not without its downside. For one thing, a character in a flopped manga series who once wore in the original Japanese version a T-shirt emblazoned with "M A Y" (as in "the merry month of") now wears one which reads "Y A M"! Additionally, many manga creators in Japan are themselves unhappy with the process, as some feel the mirror-imaging of their art skews their original intentions.

We are proud to bring you Kazue Kato's **Blue Exorcist** in the original unflopped format. For now, though, turn to the other side of the book and let the adventure begin…!

—Editor

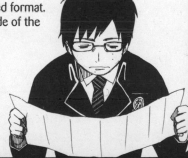